John Ellor Taylor

Our Common British Fossils and Where to Find them

A Handbook for Students

John Ellor Taylor

Our Common British Fossils and Where to Find them
A Handbook for Students

ISBN/EAN: 9783337415556

Printed in Europe, USA, Canada, Australia, Japan

Cover: Foto ©Paul-Georg Meister /pixelio.de

More available books at **www.hansebooks.com**

OUR

COMMON BRITISH FOSSILS

AND

WHERE TO FIND THEM

A Handbook for Students

BY

J. E. TAYLOR, PH.D., F.G.S., ETC.

EDITOR OF "SCIENCE-GOSSIP,"
AUTHOR OF "THE SAGACITY AND MORALITY OF PLANTS," ETC.

WITH 331 ILLUSTRATIONS

London

CHATTO AND WINDUS, PICCADILLY

1885

[*The right of translation is reserved*]

PREFACE.

THE following pages are intended as a help to the young student of geology, who is usually bewildered by the abundance of invertebrate fossils when he first commences collecting them himself. There are books of a much higher and more extensive character, such as the treatises on Palæontology by Owen and Nicholson, to which I am hopeful this present volume will prove introductory.

I have not attempted to introduce the student to other than invertebrate fossil animals, not only because these are by far the most numerous, but also because such an attempt would have expanded the volume beyond due limits.

I have recollected the nature of the difficulties which beginners in fossil-collecting feel, and have tried to meet them. My hope has been rather to whet the appetite than to satisfy it.

IPSWICH, *March* 3, 1885.

CONTENTS.

CHAPTER		PAGE
I.	FOSSIL SPONGES, ETC.	1
II.	FOSSIL CORALLINES	35
III.	FOSSIL CORALS	55
IV.	ENCRINITES	98
V.	FOSSIL STAR-FISHES AND SEA-URCHINS	130
VI.	FOSSIL WORMS (ANNELIDÆ)	158
VII.	TRILOBITES AND OTHER FOSSIL CRUSTACEA	174
VIII.	FOSSIL SEA-MATS (POLYZOA)	209
IX.	FOSSIL LAMP-SHELLS (BRACHIOPODA)	222
X.	FOSSIL MOLLUSCA (PALÆOZOIC, OR PRIMARY)—BIVALVES AND UNIVALVES	239
XI.	FOSSIL MOLLUSCA (MESOZOIC, OR SECONDARY)	253
XII.	FOSSIL MOLLUSCA (CAINOZOIC, OR TERTIARY)	271
XIII.	FOSSIL CEPHALOPODS	296
	INDEX	325

LIST OF ILLUSTRATIONS.

A

Acroculia haliotes, 124
Actinocrinus triacontadactylus, 101, 118
—— cuspidatus, 119
Agnostus pisiformis, 186
Ammonite, foliated chambers of, 306
Ammonites amaltheus, 313
—— bifrons, 311
—— communis, 311
—— Cooperi, 314
—— falcatus, 316
—— lautus, 316
—— Mantellii, 315
—— obtusus, 312
—— varicosus, 314
Amplexus coralloides, 63, 64, 65
Ananchytes ovata, 150
—— interior cast of, 150
Annelida, jaws of, 162
Anthracosia robusta, 249
Apiocrinites rotundus, 111
Apus productus, 195
Arenicolites sparsus, tracks of, 165
—— burrows of, 165
Asaphus caudatus, 177
Astarte Omallii, 287
Asterias tessellata, 132
Astræa rotulosa, 67
—— favosa, 68

Astræa ananas, 69
Australian feather-star, 102
Astrocœnia gibbosa, 91
Atrypa reticularis, 225
Aviculo-pecten papyraceus, 250

B

Baculites vertebralis, 323
Balanophyllia regia, 75
Beaked ammonite, 310
Belemnites hastata, 297
—— puzosianus, 297
—— (restored), 297
—— abbreviatus, 298
—— mucronata, 298
Bellerophon hiulcus, 248
Belinurus trilobitioides, 180
Bopyrus crangorum, 182
Botryllus on sea-weed, 214
Brachiopod, larval development of, 235
Buccinum undulatum, 282

C

Calymene Blumenbachii, 177
Cardiola interrupta, 244
Cardita imbricata, 274
Cardium Lillanum, 270
Caryophyllia, 56, 74

Ceratites nodosus, 306
Chain-coral, 61, 62
Chama squamosa, 269
Choanite, 22
Cidaris coronata, 146, 149
Clisiophyllum, 72, 73
Clymenia, 305
Comatula, 102
Crania, 226
Crioceras, 317
Crotalocrinus rugosus, 124
Ctenodonta contracta, 245
Cupressocrinus, 120
Cyathaxinias, 65
Cyprina islandica, 286
Cypræa Europæa, 284
Cyrena antiqua, 272
Cyrtoceras Murchisoni, 300

D

Dendrophyllia, 56
Dianchora striata, 269
Diastopora Oolitica, 217, 220
―― cells of, 218
―― ventricosa, 219, 220
Dibunophyllum, 86
Didymograptus, calycles of, 44

E

Echinus esculenta, 145
―― granulosus, 152
Emarginala fissura, 279
―― reticulata, 284
Encrinus moniliformis, 101
Entomostracan, 201
Eucalyptocrinus, 117
Euomphalus pentangulatus, 250
Euryale costosa, 105, 107
―― palmifera, 106
Exogyra conica, 270
Eyes of trilobite, 180

F

Fascicularia aurantium, 220
Favosites cervicornis, 76
―― fibrosa, 77
―― Gothlandica, 57, 58
Feather-star, development of, 99
Fenestella membranacea, 216
―― nodulosa, 216
―― plebeia, 215
Fissurella Græca, 280
Flustra, 213
―― cells of, 214
Foraminifera in Chalk, 32, 33

G

Galerites albogalerus, 151
Gervillea, 258
―― anceps, 269
Glauconome elegans, 216
―― flexicarinata, 215
Glyptocrinus, 119
Graptolite, twin, 43, 45
Gryphæa incurva, 257

H

Hamites attenuatus, 319
Heliolites interstinctus, 79, 80
Heliopora cærulea, 59
Hippopodium ponderosum, 260
Histioderma Hibernicum, 166
―― tubular case of, 167
―― extremity of tube of, 168
Homalonotus, 189

I

Ichthyocrinus, head of, 117
Inoceramus sulcatus, 263
―― Cuvieri, 264
―― concentricus, 270
Isastræa insignis, 92
―― oblonga, 93

K

Koninckphyllum, 87

L

Larva of king-crab, 178
—— trilobite, 178
Larval development of crab, 205
Leptæna transversalis, 224
Limulus, 179
Lingula, 224
—— anatina, 223
—— Lewisii, 224
Litharæa, 95
Lithostrotion junceum, 63
—— basaltiforme, 70
—— Phillipsii, 64, 71
Lituites articulatus, 300
Lonsdalia rugosa, 88

M

Mactra, 281
Marsupiocrinites cœlatus, 124
Marsupites Milleri, 131
Membranipora membranacea, 210
—— polyps of, 211
—— cells of, 212
Micraster, 151
Millepora alcicornis, 60
Montilivaltia trochoides, 93
Murchisonia gracilis, 240
Mya arenaria, 286

N

Nassa, 284
Natica monilifera, 284
Nereis, 169
Notopocorystes, 205
Nucula Cobboldiæ, 291

O

Obolus, 225
Oculina axillaris, 66
Ogygia Buchii, 190
Omphyma subturbinata, 75
Ophiocoma, 137
Ophiolepis Damesii, 142, 143
Ophiura granulata, 108
Orthis elegantula, 225
—— striatula, 227
—— resupinata, 230
Orthoceras, 299, 300
—— laterale, 299
Orthonota parallela, 240
Ostrea vescicularis, 270

P

Palæocoma Marstoni, 136, 139
—— Colvini, 139
Palasterina primæva, 135
Paradoxides Tessini, 188
—— Davidis, 189
Pearly nautilus, 301, 302
Pecten asper, 268
—— Beaveri, 265
—— inequivalvis, 268
—— interstriatus, 267
—— orbicularis, 266
—— quadricostatus, 270
—— varius, 280
Pectunculus glycimeris, 283
Pentacrinus Caput-Medusæ, 100
—— briareus, 110
Pentamerus Knightii, 225
Pentremites florealis, 132, 139
Phacops caudatus, 191
Phillipsia, 191
Pholas, in burrow, 284
Phragmacone, 298
Phragmoceras ventricosum, 321
Pileopsis ungarica, 283

Plagiostoma giganteum, 259
Platycrinus trigintidactylus, 119
Pleurtomaria carinata, 249
Polypora, 216
—— tuberculata, 217
Posidonomya, 248
Poteriocrinus, head of, 122; stem of, 123
Prestwichia, 178
Productus giganteus, 229
—— horridus, 230
—— punctata, 229
—— scabriculus, 230
Protaster Miltoni, 134
Pterinea subfalcata, 244
Purpura lapillus, 282
Purpura tetragona, 290

Siphonia pyriformis, 20
Smilotrochus granulatus, 94
Spicules of recent sponges, 7; fossil, 8, 9
Spirifer, coils of, 227
—— cuspidatus, 228
—— speciosus, 227
—— striata, 228
—— trigonalis, 227
Spondylus spinosa, 269
Sponge imbedded in flint nodule, 21
Stalked barnacle, 203
Stenopora fibrosa, 77
Stromatopora concentrica, 15
Strophomena depressa, 226
—— rugosa, 226
Syringopora ramulosa, 59

R

Radiolarian, 33
Retepora, 216
Rhodocrinus, 120
Rhynchonella pleurodon, 228, 229
—— pugnus, 226
Roots of encrinites, 120
Rostellaria Parkinsonii, 270

S

Sabella unispira, 163
Salenia, 152
Scaphites aqualis, 318
Scrolis Fabricii, 193
Sertularia abietina, 41, 42
—— fusca, 36
Sessile barnacle, 203
Shell of ammonite (section of), 307, 309
Shells of recent cuttle-fish, 304
Shrimp parasite, 182

T

Taxocrinus, 118
Tellina crassa, 283
Tentaculites annulatus, 164
Terebratula biplicata, 234
—— caput-serpentis, 237
—— deformis, 236
—— dorsata, 236, 237
—— hastata, 228
—— recent species of, 237
—— showing loop, 237
Teredo tubes, 273
Thecosmilia annularis, 93
Trigonia costata, 255; recent, 256
Trinucleus fimbriatus, 180
—— Lloydi, 191
Trochus, 281
Trophon contrarius, 281
Turritella, 275
—— granulata, 269
Turrilites, 303, 318
—— Bergerii, 319

Turrilites costatus, 320
—— tuberculatus, 320
—— undulatus, 319

U

Uraster rubens, 133

V

Ventriculites, 22, 23, 24
Vincularia, 217

Voluta athleta, 276
—— Lamberti, 291

W

Woodocrinus macrodactylus, 121
Worm-tracks, 161

Z

Zaphrentis, 65

OUR COMMON BRITISH FOSSILS.

CHAPTER I.

FOSSIL SPONGES, ETC.

THERE are few sciences more dependent on others than Geology. Certainly there is none which sends the young student so eagerly to other sciences for assistance. The fossils he meets with in the rocks are far more abundant than he imagined before he began to study geology. Indeed, the young geologist, when his eyes are first opened, is astonished at the abundance of fossil remains within the immediate neighbourhood of his home, unless the latter happen to be on the granite or metamorphic rocks. He wonders how it is he never noticed them before. Fragments, or whole specimens of fossils, animal and vegetable, are constantly turning up before his eager and enthusiastic eyes, either in their parent rocks, or in the boulder clays which have been formed out of them. The very rocks of the hills and mountains seem to be almost wholly composed of them—nay, the solid dry land of the globe appears to have been mainly put together by the agency or through the instrumentality of life!

No sooner has the young beginner appreciated the wealth of objects by which he is surrounded, or to which he may obtain easy access, than the first fit of *collecting* takes possession of him. His holidays are spent in fossiliferous localities; and his leisure time in reading about them, or in arranging his cabinet. At length he feels the need for more knowledge than he possesses about the many strange forms he comes across. He has at first an idea that they are altogether different from anything now existing, and perhaps a feeling of something like *disappointment* comes over him when he learns they are constructed on the same plan as living animals and plants; and that in many instances the same generic and even specific forms are still in existence. This state of mind, however, soon gives way to thorough admiration, when he catches a glimpse of the life-plan of the globe. He sees that, beginning with the lowly and humble organisms, it has developed into the present Fauna and Flora; that the stream of life, issuing like a rill from such obscure springs as are hardly discernible in the distant Laurentian period, has been gaining in volume and depth as it has passed onward, in unbroken continuity, through all the succeeding ages, until it has opened out in the grand ocean of existing life! Every fossil he picks up is a letter in the great stone book; and many such letters, properly put together, have spelled out some of the most wonderful generalizations of the human mind. For geology as a science is peculiar in this respect, that in proportion to the degree of intellectual labour bestowed upon it, the resulting knowledge is wider and broader than that afforded by any other science—except, perhaps, astronomy. Not only does the new knowledge tell the student of other life-periods beside the present, not only does it extend the duration of the globe infinitely beyond the brief six thousand years uneducated people still imagine mark its existence, but it convinces the young student beyond a doubt, that if the present living animals and plants are evidences of the Creator's wisdom and power, the same may be said of the extinct faunas and floras of preceding epochs. Nay, when he learns properly to connect their nature and distribution with the present, he sees that all are links in the great chain of vitality, of which existing animals and plants are only the continued living forms!

The next step in the process of geological reasoning which fossils suggest, is no less interesting or instructive. From seeing how many of our rocks, especially limestones, are formed wholly by vital agencies, the student perceives that the physical geography of every past age is related to the present.

The rocks forming the dry land are for the most part of *marine* origin—were formed along the floors of ancient seas, when dry land doubtless occupied some parts at least of the areas of existing oceans; although it should be remembered that modern science is actively developing the theory of the relative permanency of ocean-beds and continental areas. No fact is more readily or surely known than that sea and land have frequently changed places. Upheavals and depressions of the earth's crust, producing marvellous physical results, and affecting the distribution of life-forms in every period of our planet's history, are of insignificant importance when we regard the bulk of our earth as a planet. It is the sum total of these depressions and upheavals, as well as of the atmospherical and marine wear-and-tear of the solid rocks, which has eventually given the surface of the globe its present physical geography.

Of all these things the geological student has to take heed. He discovers that geology, after all, is but the complete record of the physical geography of the past; and that, as Lyell and others have demonstrated, the physical changes everywhere going on at the present day do not differ in their nature, and *probably* not very greatly in their *intensity*, from those which took place in former geological periods. But, undoubtedly, the nature of geological study obliges the young beginner first to pick up an elementary knowledge of natural history. How can he understand anything of the fossil plants, shells, bones, teeth, etc., he meets with in every geological formation, unless he knows something about similar objects now in existence? Fossils only differ from their modern representatives in that they belong to *extinct* zoology and botany, instead of to the still existing divisions of these kingdoms of life. Thus the geological student is forced continually to widen his sphere of research, and he finds that every additional bit of knowledge of any other science helps him all the more to understand that which he has selected as his special hobby.

Geology is essentially an open-air study. It leads one into the most beautiful of landscapes, to the most charming bits of scenery. The tame flatness of the plains reveals to the geologist comparatively little, unless coal or salt-mining has partly turned the earth's crust inside out; or railway cuttings have laid open sections instructive both as regards the strata and the fossils they contain. Boulder clay pits or natural tarns will occasionally prove interesting. But to study the stony science in its fulness we must "gang to the hills!" There, where the heather is purplest, and the atmosphere exhilarates like old wine, we are most likely to read off the "record of the rocks!" Healthful activity is required, and the memory is stored with remembrances of sunny days and clear skies, never to be forgotten!

In the course of the following chapters I purpose

doing my best to introduce the young student to the "happy hunting-grounds" of our various geological formations. I intend to limit myself to the *common* fossils, unless occasionally tempted to mention a few for the purpose of further whetting the appetite. And, whilst I describe the spots where the young geologist is most likely to "make a bag," I shall give a brief description of the natural history relationships of the numerous extinct organisms.

For a long time it was the practice to regard the most doubtful fossil marine organisms, which had no particular shape or external structure by which they could be at once recognized, as "a kind of sponge." Thanks, however, to the labours of such men as Hinde, Sollas, and Carter, it is no longer possible to avail ourselves of such a fossil lumber-room, where our ignorance and mistakes can be screened. For, although there is some doubt and disputation as to the exact zoological rank of sponges—whether they belong to the *Protozoa* or *Cœlenterata*—there is little concerning their habits and structure. The extended use of the microscope in geology, and the practice of cutting transparent sections of any doubtful fossil, so as to enable the student to identify it by its organization, at once enables him to detect "sponge structure," or rather the mineral part of that structure. For in fossils the sponge-flesh, or *sarcode* as it is called, has of course disappeared, and left no trace behind it.

As the reader may see by referring to Mr. Saville Kent's splendid work on "Infusoria," this sponge-flesh is frequently almost made up of collared in-

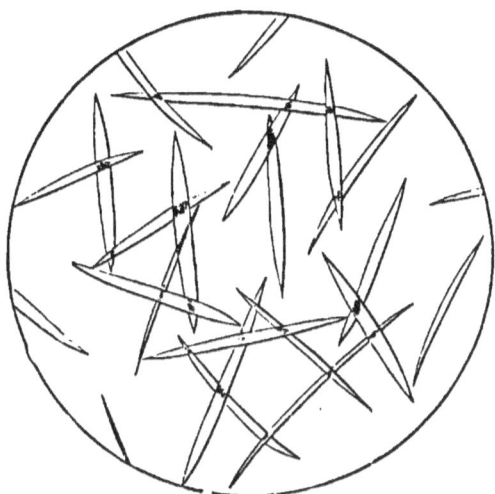

Fig. 1.—Spicules of Recent Sponge (*Chalina*).

fusorians, in company with myriads of still more simple organisms resembling *Amœba*. A living sponge, therefore, may be regarded as a colony of lowly organized animals, just as a mass of living reef-coral is a colony of sea-anemone-like animals.

Let us carry this illustration a little further. The coral-anemones differ from our well-known sea-anemones by the hard limy substances in their interiors, due to the calcification of the tissues. These remain behind after death, and when the flesh has

8 OUR COMMON BRITISH FOSSILS.

decomposed, such durable limy substances are popularly denominated "coral." Similarly with sponges.

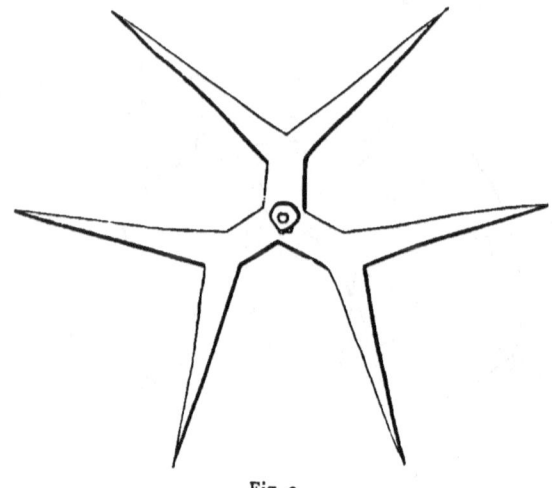

Fig. 2.

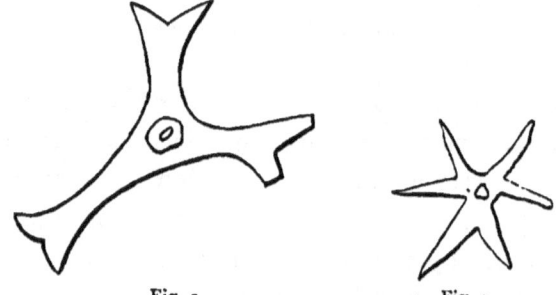

Fig. 3. Fig. 4.

Figs. 2-4.—Fossil Sponge Spicules, from Blackdown and Haldon, all drawn on the scale of $\frac{1}{24}$th to $\frac{1}{1800}$th of an inch. (After H. J. Carter.)

When alive the outer layer of "sponge-flesh" is usually permeated with myriads of exceedingly small solid bodies, called fibres and *spicules*. The latter are of a variety of shapes, from the most simple to

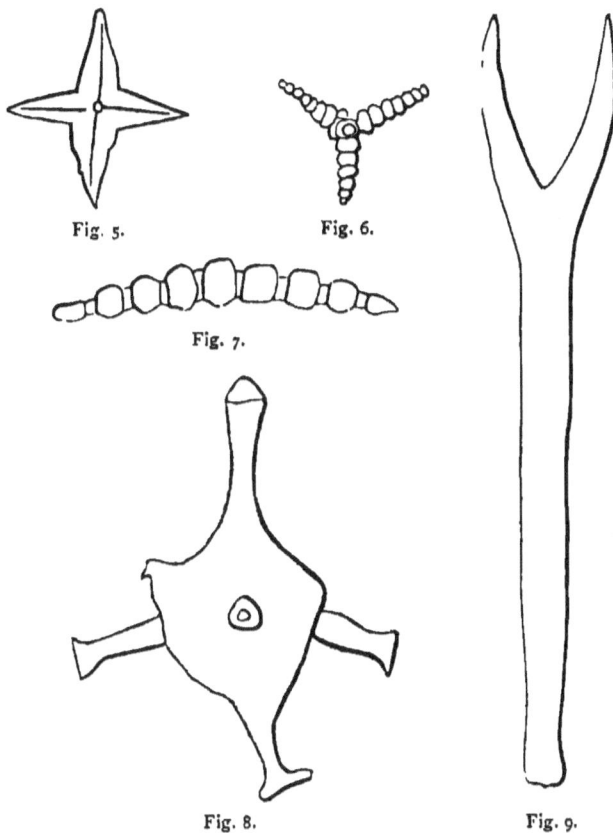

Figs. 5–9.—Fossil Sponge Spicules, from Blackdown and Haldon, all drawn on the scale of $\frac{1}{4}$th to $\frac{1}{100}$th of an inch. (After H. J. Carter.)

the most complex, but they are interwoven so closely together that when the sponge is dead and its "flesh" has decomposed, there is left behind the skeleton, formed by the interlacing of the above-mentioned *spicules*.

We may practically regard these "spicules" as having been crystallized within the soft, white-of-egg-like sponge-flesh. They are not always of the same chemical composition—indeed they rarely are, even in the same species or individual. But there is generally an exclusive majority of spicules of the same chemical or mineral composition. The fibres are formed of a substance chemically resembling that which enters into the composition of horn, hair, wool, or feathers, and which is characteristically an animal production, called *chitine*. Our washing-sponge is the skeleton of the *Chitinous* group. Their skeletons, being usually fibrous, could hardly be expected to be found in the fossil state, unless they underwent a change. Two other classes of sponges are recognized by naturalists, and by some are named according to the substance of which the spicules of the skeleton are composed. Thus, in one group the spicules are formed of *lime*, and so the term *calcareous* is applied to them. Ten species of this sort of fossil sponge are found in the Ludlow rocks. In the other kind, the spicules are formed of silica or flint, and accordingly this group of sponges is termed *siliceous*. The last group possesses the most complex and beautifully shaped spicules, and the dead skeleton formed by them is one of the most lovely of zoological objects, as everybody acquainted with the recent species *Euplectella aspergillum* ("Venus' flower-basket") will readily allow. The accompanying wood-cuts show the appearances of recent and fossil sponge-spicules under the microscope.

The siliceous sponges are again sub-divided into several groups, named respectively *Monactinellidæ*, *Tetractinellidæ*, *Hexactinellidæ* (that is, "one, four, and six-radiated spicules"), and *Lithistidæ*. We know nothing of fossil sponges except the mineralized spicules they have left behind, and these have been frequently much changed since the sponges were alive. *Limy* spicules are often dissolved away, and perhaps left no trace behind them, unless the hollows they had left have been filled with flint. But there are numerous cases where even flint spicules have been dissolved, and where lime has replaced silica. Until a few years ago, it would have been much questioned whether the siliceous spicules of sponges could be replaced by any other mineral matter; but there is now little doubt that organic silica can be removed, although geologists can only record the observed fact without explaining it. Some siliceous spicules have been replaced by iron pyrites, in the Lower Cambrian rocks of North Wales.

Nevertheless, fossil sponges possessing a siliceous or flinty skeleton, are likely to be much more numerously preserved than those sponges whose skeletons were composed of a less endurable mineral. Hence the former appear to be more numerous and widespread. Dr. Hinde refers to instances where the spicules of Tetractinellid, or *four-rayed* sponges, are numerous enough to form thin strata.

The *Hexactinellid* sponges are distinguished by having *six-rayed* spicules, so arranged that the rays are usually at right angles to each other. These spicules are sometimes united, sometimes free, and they frequently form a trelliswork after the appearance of "Venus' flower-basket." These are all inhabitants of the deepest parts of the sea, and as our white chalk is one of the geological formations deposited perhaps in deeper water than any other, the number of species of fossil *hexactinellid* sponges found fossilized in its strata is very great. The *Ventriculidæ* (formerly thought to be zoophytes allied to the *Alcyonia*, or "dead men's fingers") are perhaps the most numerous of all the chalk sponges, and even the external shapes of many of them approach very near to that of "Venus' flower-basket," and still more to the recent sponge called *Holtenia*.

The *Lithistidæ* are sponges whose spicules are also composed of silica, but they are arranged in *fours*, and the rays are *not* arranged at right angles. The extremities of the spicules are usually so divided or notched that those of each other can interlock. This interlocking builds up a loose but continuous framework. One of the commonest of the fossil sponges in the Lower Chalk is *Siphonia*, which may be regarded as a characteristic lithistid sponge. Fossil sponges are always commonest in limy and arenaceous rocks.

As regards the *habits* of recent sponges, it is as well to be acquainted with them, for they throw light upon the conditions of ancient sea-beds, inasmuch as we find that modern sponges are characterized by the same habits as the oldest kinds. In this way a knowledge of recent and fossil forms is reciprocal in its illustrative effect. Thus the genus *Cliona*—a remarkable sponge which has the habit of *boring* into the denser structure of bivalve shells, as may be seen in a thick-shelled, deep-sea oyster on the nearest fish-stall—has indulged in this habit ever since the Silurian period. Shells of fossil *Pterinea*, in the Malvern beds, are frequently found perforated by ancient burrowing sponges; and in the chalk near Norwich we find the solid cones of *Belemnites* (internal bones of ancient cuttle-fishes) riddled through and through by boring sponges, which have thus left a very delicate but graceful pattern of the walls of the burrows. Again, in our British seas particularly, we have a large number of existing sponges encrusting or growing on other natural objects; and we find *fossil* sponges such as *Sparsispongia* which adopted this habit as far back as the Silurian times.

It is probable that in the earlier seas of the globe the divisions of the lower marine animals were not so distinctly marked off from each other as they are now. This accounts for the difficulty some of our best naturalists find in assigning certain fossils to their true classification. Thus, Mr. Carter thinks that *Parkeria* (a not uncommon fossil in the Upper Greensand of Cambridgeshire, and which was originally described by Dr. Carpenter as a gigantic foraminifer an inch in diameter, whose walls are composed of cemented grains of sand instead of "shell") is in reality a hydrozoon allied to the pretty *Hydractina* found coating the outsides of many living whelk shells. The same naturalist believes that *Stromatopora* is of similar character. The latter is a very abundant fossil in the Devonian limestone. In the quarries at Newton Abbot one can hardly pick up a piece of stone which does not contain some species of *Stromatopora*. It is found in the Silurian, Devonian, and even Carboniferous limestones. The beautiful flesh-tinted marbles obtained from the Devonian limestones near Torquay, when polished, show excellent sections of *Stromatopora*. How this fossil has been bandied about from scientific pillar to scientific post! For a long time it was regarded as a species of coral. Then it was supposed to be a calcareous sponge. Next it was imagined it might be somehow intermediate between the *hexactinellid* sponges and such hydrozoan corals as the recent and abundant *Millepora*. Professor Nicholson threw out the hint that this fossil might be related both to sponges and foraminiferæ; whilst Professor Sollas holds to its being a *hexactinellid* sponge.

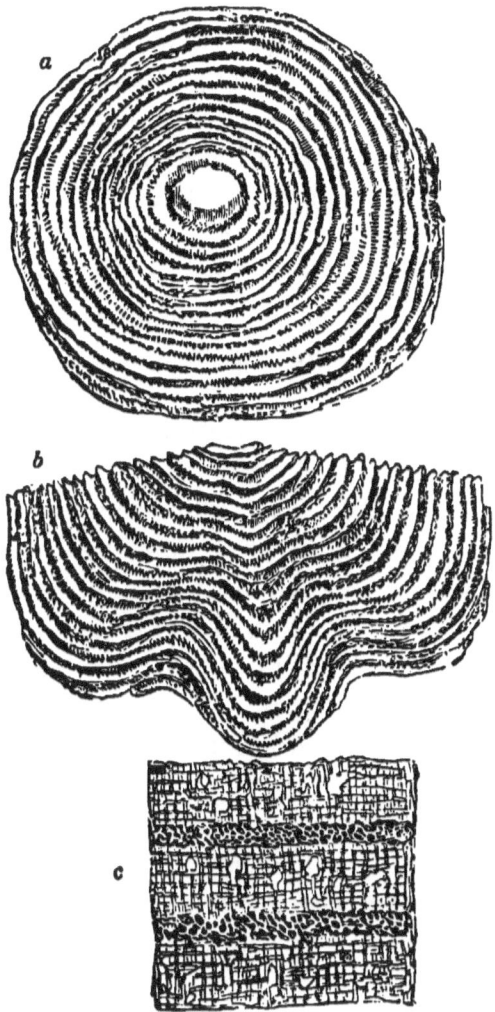

Fig. 10.—Sections of *Stromatopora concentrica* (Upper Silurian and Devonian formation): *a*, surface of fossil; *b*, vertical section; *c*, portion of *Stromatopora concentrica* (magnified).

The discovery that many sponges which originally possessed flinty or siliceous spicules have had them converted into lime—a most unexpected metamorphosis, but one which cannot be gainsaid—has greatly perplexed naturalists as to which were formerly *calcareous* and which *siliceous* sponges. Thus Zittel, the great authority on fossil sponges, regards those which are so abundant in the Coral Rag beds at Farringdon, as *calcareous;* whereas Carter thinks they were originally siliceous sponges whose spicules have been chemically changed.

This only shows how involved are the problems dealing with the most simple and rudimentary of marine animals. But the fact remains, that sponge-life has not materially altered from the very earliest period of our planet's history until now. There is a much greater variety of species in recent seas than perhaps was ever the case before, although it is doubtful whether sponges are as abundant in any of our great seas or oceans as when the European Chalk was deposited.

Fossil sponge-hunting becomes most interesting when we come to the Cretaceous or chalk formation. True, we find fossil sponges in all marine calcareous and arenaceous formations, from the Silurian upwards. Even fresh-water sponges, closely allied to that now abundant in rivers and streams (*Spongilla fluviatilis*), are known to have been in existence during the Purbeck limestone stage of the Secondary epoch.

Apart from fossilizing for *Stromatopora*—certain to be found in most quarries where the Upper Silurian or Devonian limestone is worked—until we come to the Carboniferous limestone we should hardly reckon our sponge "finds." *Calcispongia, Protospongia, Ischadites, Astylospongia,* and *Amphispongia* are not uncommon Silurian genera found near the Malverns, at Ludlow, and in the Longmynds. Fifteen species of sponges are described from the Carboniferous limestone, *Palæacis* being the commonest. The young hunter for this kind of geological spoil should first make himself acquainted with the various appearances of sponge structure under the microscope—with the fibrous as well as the spicular details. Then he will be prepared, when out on his rambles, to examine any suggestive materials. One of the most profitable geological rambles, in this respect, I ever experienced was on the Carboniferous limestone of Black Head in County Clare—a spot not likely to be soon forgotten by those who love natural scenery. The limestone is traversed by numerous joint-fissures, in which grow the loveliest of ferns, the maidenhair (*Adiantum capillus-veneris*) being especially luxuriant and abundant. Before us break the rollers of the wide Atlantic; behind us the hills rise in gentle slopes—for they are formed of black, fossiliferous Yoredale shales.

The walls by the roadside, which take the place of hawthorn hedges, are crowded with fossils. Some of the limestone appears friable and "rotten." This is just the material to look for *microzoa*, for *Radiolarians*, sponge-spicules, etc. Those of a fossil "glass-rope" sponge (*Hyalonema*) are met with in abundance.

Mr. James Thomson, F.G.S., discovered a bed of "rotten limestone" at Cunningham Baidland, Dalry, Ayrshire, and the spot is now well known to all Glasgow geologists. Sponge spicules, notably those of *Hyalonema*, are abundant, and they are found converted from their original siliceous to a calcareous composition. Several other places where microzoa occur have been made known in Scotland; and Mr. John Young, F.G.S., has carefully examined their materials and published details of his discoveries in the "Transactions of the Glasgow Geological Society."

Whenever the rock appears "rotten," or the thin beds of limestone shale which are frequently "sandwiched" between the limestones seem more than usually crumbly, the student should box some of the material, and carefully note where he obtained it. At home, with the aid of the microscope, he can occupy his winter evenings in its examination, and perhaps he may thus add to our scanty knowledge of Palæozoic sponges.

Until we come to the Cretaceous rocks, we know almost less of the *structure* of the Secondary sponges than of those just mentioned. There must be remains of them somewhere, and by looking out keenly for rocks having a peculiar structure, which the student will soon recognize, he may fill up some of these numerous blanks in our information. The Portland stone is in places crowded with tri-radiate sponge-spicules; the Kentish Rag is frequently so full of the same objects that it hurts the hands of the men who work in it. In the rocks of the Great Oolite Mr. Etheridge says sponges abound, nine species being known.

At Haldon Hill, near Exeter, we have an outlier of Greensand, where a thin layer contains *lithistid* sponge-spicules very abundantly. Mr. Carter thinks this bed of sponge-spicules may have been formed along the sea-floor, after the manner in which a similar layer of sponge detritus is now forming at sea, about one hundred miles to the north of the Butt of Lewis.

The *powder* to be found in most hollow flints is the best kind of material microscopically to examine for spicules. Dr. Hinde, who has published an interesting essay on "Fossil Sponge-Spicules from the Upper Chalk," therein shows how much can be seen and discovered by carefully examining only a few ounces of this material. Those who have geologized on the flints found in chalk strata are well aware that the chalky material filling the hollow flints is of a different appearance, both to the eye and the touch, than the chalk itself. Dr. Hinde calls this powder "flint-meal"—a term which conveys a capital idea of what it is like. Wherever there are chalk flints the student may be sure to find abundance of fossil sponges. The hollow ones should have their interior contents carefully boxed for subsequent examination. I have frequently carried as much "flint-meal" away in a small pill-box as afforded a week's work with the microscope.

Many flints are called "rotten" by the quarrymen because they are permeated by irregular canals, branching off from each other like the twigs of a tree. Sometimes these canals are filled with "flint-meal," which should be carefully collected. The surfaces of the walls of these branching canals or passages are always rough. It does not require much acumen to see that these are due to fossil-branching sponges, resembling in shape the *Chalinas* and *Halichondrias* of our British seas. All geologists are now agreed that the flints of the chalk formation somehow assumed their present shapes, appearance, and distribution through the agency of crops of sponges which flourished on the ancient Cretaceous sea-bed. Con-

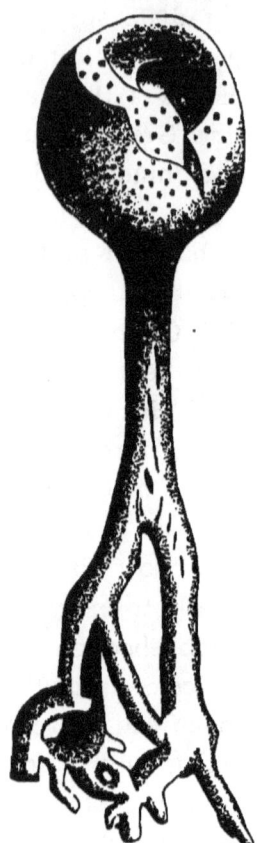

Fig. 11.—Common Fossil Sponge from Greensand (*Siphonia pyriformis*).

sequently the study of the chalk-sponges is intimately connected with the origin of chalk-flints, and perhaps also with that of "chert."

No one can work at these flints long without seeing that the external shapes of the flint-nodules are very often determined by the shapes of the fossil-

Fig. 12.—Common Branching Sponge, imbedded in flint-nodule.

sponges they enclose. In many instances the surfaces of the flints are marked by indications of the enclosed fossils cropping out. This is particularly the case with the *Ventriculites* and the *Spongites* (as Mantell called them). The latter are the branching sponges which cause the flints to be "rotten." In the pits near Lewes, *Spongites ramosus* may be gathered, twelve to fifteen inches long. In many places, as in

Fig. 13.—Horizontal section of Flint, containing Choanite, or lower part of Ventriculite, showing sponge foldings.

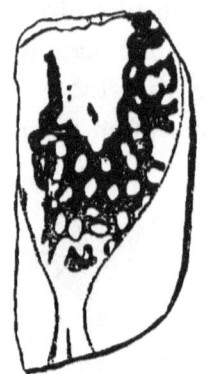

Fig. 14.—Longitudinal section of Ventriculite imbedded in flint.

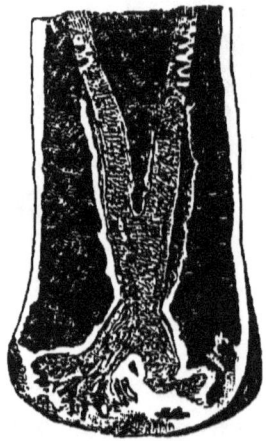

Fig. 15.—Longitudinal section of Ventriculite in flint-nodule, showing roots.

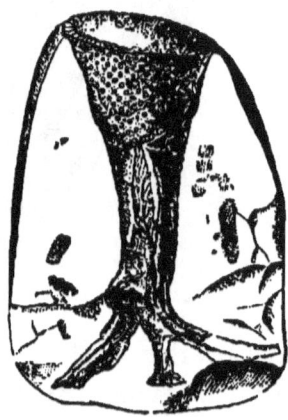

Fig. 16.—Ventriculite in Flint, showing external markings in upper part.

any chalk pit on Salisbury Plain, the collector finds that nearly every flint is "rotten;" the branching canals within represent the entombment of sponges which have decayed, all but their spicules, now forming the "flint-meal." The most "rotten," or *sponge-bearing* chalk-flints I ever worked upon are those of

Fig. 17.—Ventriculite.

Flamborough Head, in Yorkshire, and Trimingham, in Norfolk. In both cases the fossil sponges are of the kind called *Lithistid*, the *hexactinellid* sponges being rare. The external shapes of *lithistid* sponges vary to an enormous extent, even in the same genus.

Generally, however, they are of a *stony* character and solid everywhere, except in the pure white chalk.

The *Ventriculite* family of sponges are *hexactinellid*, and their shapes and structures are often very beau-

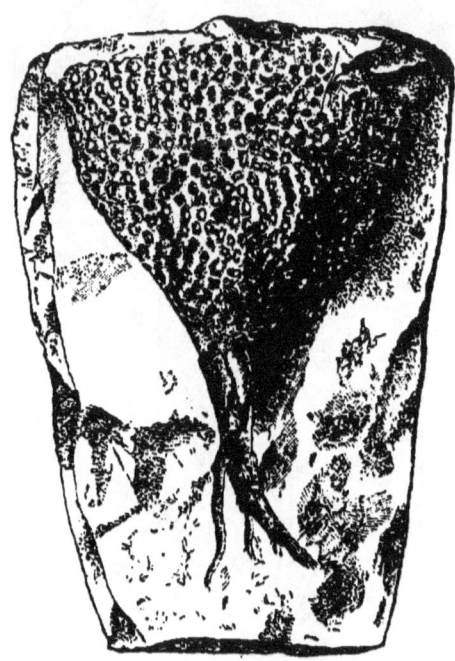

Fig. 18.—Ventriculite.

tiful, a slight magnifying power showing a similar latticed appearance to that we admire so much in the modern "Venus' flower-basket" (*Euplectella*). In the white chalk of Sussex, Wiltshire, and Norfolk, Ventriculites occur in great numbers, *Ventriculites radiatus* being perhaps the commonest. This species frequently forms the nucleus of flints, the flinty matter just covering it, and thus assuming its shape. The general shape of these Ventriculites is that of an old-fashioned wine-glass. The stems and bases of such an imaginary wine-glass (when thoroughly silicified) are the well-known *Choanites* of the "Brighton pebbles." A nearly allied and very elegantly marked genus of sponges is *Coscinipora*. If we try to imagine a Ventriculite flattened down into the similitude of a finger-basin rather than a wine-glass, we shall form a good idea of a much larger, nearly related, and not uncommon *hexactinellid* sponge, called *Cephalites*. Other pretty fossil sponges belonging to this division are *Camerospongia*, *Cœolptychium*, and *Callodictyon*.

The *lithistid* sponges are very abundant in some parts of the Lower Cretaceous rocks. The principal genera are *Siphonia*, *Polypothecia*, *Scyphia*, etc. The former genus is perhaps the commonest, and there are several species classified as belonging to it. Most young geologists are acquainted with the pear-shaped, stony heads of a species called *Siphonia pyriformis*. Very frequently they break off the stalks, and we find head, stalk, and roots separately. In the "firestone" of St. Catherine's Hill, above the road from Niton, Isle of Wight, we may obtain any quantity of *Siphonia Websteri*; near Ventnor, *S. pyriforme* is abundant. In the Upper Greensand at Farnham, in

Surrey, these sponges are very abundant; but they have undergone a chemical metamorphosis, and have been converted into phosphate of lime to more than fifty per cent. On this account they are worked, and ground up into artificial manure, or super-phosphates. At Farringdon, in Berkshire, and at Warminster, we have the geologically famous "sponge-gravels," an ancient sea-bed, with whole and broken shells, fragments of Echinoderms, etc., through which is dispersed an abundance of fossil sponges. That called *Manon* is common, and the quarrymen term it "petrified salt-cellar." I have often noticed that when fossils obtain popular names, it is a sign of their abundance. In the Upper Greensand at Folkestone, the fossil sponge termed *Scyphia meandrina* is especially abundant.

Polypothecia is one of the commonest of the fossil sponges met with in the Greensand at Warminster. It is a branched sponge, allied to those known as *Spongites*, and it puts one in mind of our common British *Chalina*, so abundant along our coasts. When found it is usually of a stony texture, but sections of it show it to belong to the *lithistids*.

One of the most gigantic of probable sponges is that called *Paramoudra*, abundant in the chalk near Norwich. There is now little doubt this singular object was a sponge. It is frequently found in the chalk, always extending upwards in a perpendicular fashion to the height of five or six feet, and having a basal diameter of two feet. Its appearance is like that of a series of cups one inside another, the largest ones at the bottom, and the smallest at the top. The topmost segment is usually crowned with an extinguisher-like cap, at the side of which we observe a perforation, which is connected with the traces of a pipe running down the centre of the chalky core occupying the segments of this peculiar fossil. Each segment is therefore hollow, or rather occupied with a dense core of chalk. The country people use the segments for flower-pots in their gardens, after they have removed the chalky core.

Fossil sponges are also obtained by hammering the most likely and "rotten" of the flint pebbles forming the gravel of the eastern and southern counties of England. It is only when we are familiar with the extent and thickness of these sheets of gravel that we can form an idea of the extent to which the chalk has been denuded; for every one of these flint pebbles is a broken-up, rounded, or liberated portion of a flint nodule, which was originally formed by chemical segregation in the ooze of the Cretaceous sea-bed.

The comparatively recent application of the microscope to rock structures has supplied us with abundant materials for generalization. This instrument enables us to detect plentiful traces of fossils where, to the naked eye, the rocks appear quite destitute of them. This is particularly the case in limestone beds. Among the most numerous of the organic remains thus identified are those small and beautiful objects, the *foraminifera*. Microscopically small though they are, it is questionable whether the bulk of our limestones is not more due to them than even to ancient coral-reefs!

The fossil foraminifera are usually represented by small limy shells, or casts of them. The creatures to which these belonged were of very low organization, rising scarcely above the zoological rank of the little *amœbas* of our ponds and ditches. These minute shells are abundantly perforated, in one division, for the passage of spider's-web-like threads of protoplasm which proceed from the animal's body; in another division the shells are imperforate. Sometimes the soft bodies were protected by walls of minute sand-grains. The oldest so-called, but much debated organism yet recognized, is *Eozoon Canadense*, and this is regarded as a foraminifer. We pass over the *Eozoon*, however, because its organic nature is still held to be doubtful. "Eozoonal structure," as it is now termed, is not confined to the oldest Laurentian rocks. Professor King has discovered it in the *Ophite*, or metamorphosed Liassic rocks of the island of Lewis. It is also abundant in the green crystalline marbles, of Lower Silurian age, in Connemara, in Ireland; and something approaching it has been found in Sutherlandshire. Now, the distribution of *lowly* organized forms can never be safely accepted as indicating the age of a rock. Naturalists are well aware that the most lowly organized animals and plants are those which have had the widest distribution, both in time and space. It is the most highly organized species of animals and plants which best mark the geological ages of formations. So that the fact of finding "Eozoonal structure" in limestones other than the Laurentian, is of itself no evidence against the animal nature of the *Eozoon.*

In many places such limestones as the Carboniferous do not show visible traces of fossils. I have frequently found, in such cases, that a prepared section of such a rock shows it to be unusually rich in foraminifera. In some parts of the world limestones have been almost wholly composed of the shells of these lowly organized animalcules, such as the *Fusulina* Carboniferous limestones of Russia and North America, the *Nummulite* limestones, of which the Egyptian Pyramids are built, etc. In England, our white chalk is very largely composed of foraminiferal remains, chiefly *Globigerina*, represented by species which are still living in the Atlantic and Pacific, where the recent dead shells are accumulating and decomposing and forming a similar bed of chalky ooze on the ocean-floors. Some species of foraminifera, such as the recent *Webbina rugosa*, have been found in the fossil state in the Lias rocks, so that they have been in continuous existence ever since. One species, *Saccamina Carteri*, forms almost entire beds of limestone in the north of England and the south of

Scotland. This is a tolerably large kind, being nearly one-eighth of an inch in length.

The Carboniferous limestone in many places is very rich in foraminifera. According to Mr. Etheridge, these are represented by fourteen genera and forty-eight species. The most important genera are—*Saccamina, Stacheia, Nodosinella, Dentalina, Textularia, Fusulina, Calculina*, etc.

The White Chalk, however, is the great storehouse of well-preserved and easily extracted fossil foraminifera. These minute shells are especially abundant in some kinds of "flint-meal," obtainable from hollow flints, as already described. The chief genera of Cretaceous foraminifera are—*Globigerina, Dentalina, Marginulina, Frondicularia, Textularia, Gaudryina, Verneuilina, Bulimina, Truncatulina, Rosalina, Rotalina, Cristellaria, Lituola*, etc.

These minute but exceedingly beautiful fossils may be extracted from any piece of white chalk as follows:—

First, get together an apparatus consisting of two ordinary medicine bottles, and about eighteen inches of small indiarubber tubing, such as can be purchased at any chemist's. Procure a piece of soft chalk, the softer the better, and that which has been partially broken up by the action of the weather better still. Scrape this with a knife to a fine powder, and put it in one of the bottles, which should not be more than about one-tenth full; then fill up the bottle three-parts full of water and shake vigorously and repeatedly; allow this to stand for some time, and then draw off the milky fluid with the siphon. Do this again and again, until when shaken up the bottle appears as if it were no longer full of a milky fluid, but, when placed close to the eye against a bright light, of small separate grains diffused in the water. These are the treasures we are in search of, but they have next to be separated from the larger fragments of chalk which have not been disintegrated by the scraping and shaking. To do this shake up the bottle, and with the siphon immediately draw over water and foraminifera into the second bottle; thus a certain portion of shells together with nearly all the water is drawn over. Allow these to settle; then draw off the clear water and repeat the process until all or nearly all the shells are in the second bottle, leaving the lumps, etc., in the first; then filter with blotting-paper, and dry in an oven, when they will be ready for mounting. I reckon about one pill-box full of foraminifera to a washing, and store the preparation dry. Boil them in a test-tube with turpentine, and mount in balsam.

The more solid limestones of the Silurian or Carboniferous age, in which we suspect the presence of foraminifera, must of course be treated in another way. The student may frequently detect the presence of foraminifera by means of a good Coddington lens. Thin chips of the limestone should be carried away, ground on one side, mounted on glass, and then ground on the other side until they are thin and transparent enough to be properly mounted for microscopic examination. In this way some exquisite geological slides may be prepared.

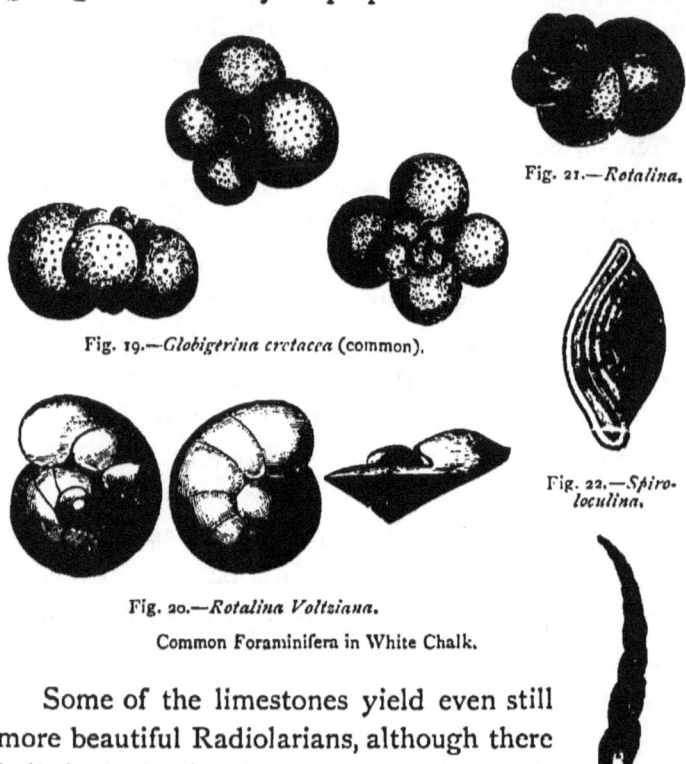

Fig. 21.—*Rotalina.*

Fig. 19.—*Globigerina cretacea* (common).

Fig. 22.—*Spiroloculina.*

Fig. 20.—*Rotalina Voltziana.*
Common Foraminifera in White Chalk.

Fig. 23.—Recent species of *Dentalina.*

Some of the limestones yield even still more beautiful Radiolarians, although there is little doubt that, in some way, the bands of chert which run through our Carboniferous and other limestones, have been formed partly through the agency of these siliceous-shelled animalcules, for we usually find them absent where chert-bands occur, and present where they do not; as if, in the former case, their silicated shells had been dissolved, and the silica drained off to

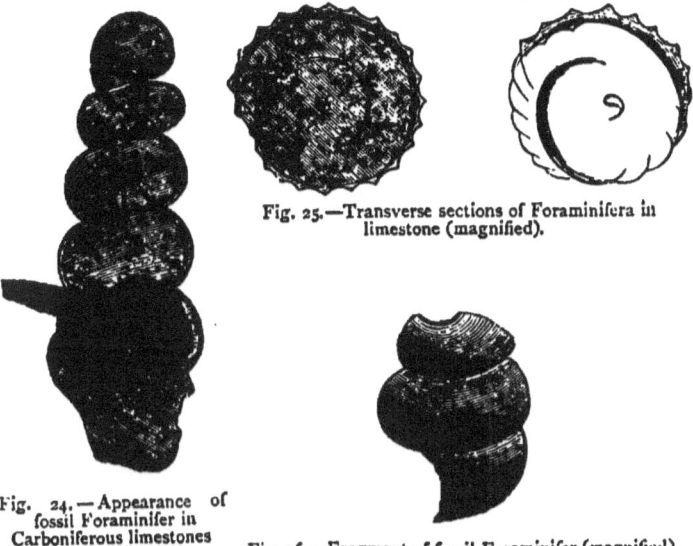

Fig. 25.—Transverse sections of Foraminifera in limestone (magnified).

Fig. 24.—Appearance of fossil Foraminifer in Carboniferous limestones (magnified).

Fig. 26.—Fragment of fossil Foraminifer (magnified).

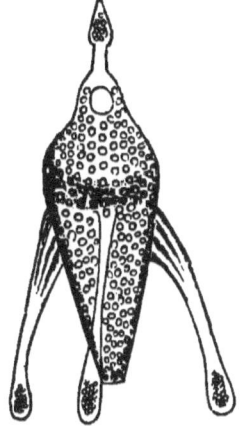

Fig. 27.—Radiolarian (recent).

form the chert. This is frequently the case in the chalk. Radiolarians and other minute siliceous organisms are present in great abundance, diffused through the chalk where there are no flint-bands or nodules; whereas the chalk is always freest from them where such nodules regularly occur.

In this manner the student perceives that the presence or absence of some of the most minute of animal remains may determine the petrological character of the great rock masses which build up the continents of the globe.

CHAPTER II.

FOSSIL CORALLINES.

REGARDING another group of fossils (named after Professor Oldham), geologists have long been in doubt as to whether they were animal or vegetable. *Oldhamia* is called a *zoophyte*, an unfortunate designation, which often conveys to many people the idea that such objects are partly animal and partly vegetable. The name was originally intended to express only their *external* resemblances to plants; but it is constantly twisted to signify a hybrid combination of animal and vegetable characters. The *Oldhamia*—the fossil about which I am now speaking—has been alternately regarded as a seaweed and a zoophyte. Mr. Salter thought that possibly it was a *calcareous* or limy seaweed, like the common *Corallina officinalis*, which may be found abundantly in every rock-pool at low water. The latter is undoubtedly a seaweed; but its limy structure and jointed stem caused it to be regarded by the earlier naturalists as a *Coralline;* whence its name. Professor Edward Forbes believed that the *Oldhamia* showed, at the articulations of the stems, the positions of the minute cells of zoophytes. The most likely idea is that this very pretty and interesting fossil—the *oldest* British organic form with which we are certainly acquainted—was related to the little "sea-firs" so abundant nowadays along our coasts. Indeed, not a few of these Sertularians (as

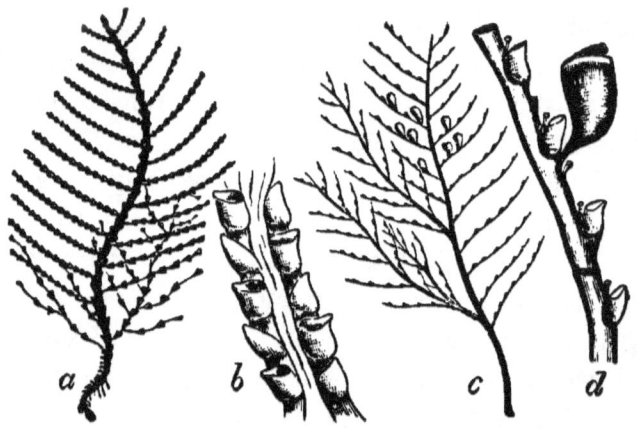

Fig. 28.—*a*, *Sertularia fusca*; *b*, Pinna, with calycles (magnified); *c*, *Plumularia frutescens*; *d*, Pinna, with calycles, nematophores, and capsule (magnified).

they are called) resemble in external shape the *Oldhamia*. The dry portion that remains when the zoophytes are dead, is of a *horny* nature, and formed of *chitine*. This is one of the most indestructible of animal substances, and is likely to be preserved when others would be decomposed. If the *Oldhamia* had been calcareous, the limy matter would have been dissolved away, and few or no traces of them would have been left. The most probable zoological position of the *Oldhamia* is among the *Hydrozoa*, of which the " sea-firs " (commonly mistaken for seaweeds) which may be seen abundantly clustering on the backs of oyster-shells in any fishmonger's shop, are the most familiar examples. The *Graptolites*, which are so numerous in the Lower Silurian rocks, as we shall presently see, probably belonged to another division of the same class of lowly organized marine animals.

Two species of *Oldhamia* are known to geologists, each distinctly marked from the other. Both are found in the same locality—viz. the Cambrian rocks of Bray Head, about four or five miles from Dublin. The place is easily reached, and will not soon be forgotten by the geological student. The rocks where the *Oldhamia* occur are beyond the village, and form the southern horn of the bay. They are very smooth and fissile, and almost of a claret-colour. The fossils, which sometimes occur along with the borings and traces of marine worms, lie in zones, for certain strata yield them more abundantly than others. In the neighbourhood of the bathing-place, where the sea-water appears unusually pure and green in comparison with the claret hue of the rocks, the *Oldhamia* may be gathered in abundance. The species *antiqua* also occurs in yellowish shales of the same geological age, in Carrick mountain, county Wexford. Hitherto, both species have been limited to the Cambrian rocks of Ireland, where, however, they do not seem to have a very wide distribution. The other species (*Oldhamia radiata*) differs from the former in having the setæ circularly radiated instead of being fan-shaped. It is also found at Bray Point, county Wicklow, and the student will there readily meet with it in the strata known to all in the neighbourhood as the "Periwinkle Rocks."

Apart from the pleasure of collecting these neat little fossils, the visit to Bray Head will amply repay the tourist. It is one of the pleasantest seaside watering-places in Ireland. The zoology of the rock-pools about the Head is very rich, and the visitor interested in this study and geology might profitably spend a few days there. Nor would his pleasure be marred by the demonstrative gaiety of the humble wedding-parties which make Bray their place of festivity. The village is easily reached by rail from Dublin; and is especially interesting to the geologist as the locality where the "oldest British fossil" is found.

Of the many thousands of species of fossils found in the rocks of Great Britain, from the most ancient to the most recent, perhaps no group so markedly distinguishes a formation as that popularly termed *Graptolites*. They are peculiar to the Cambrian and Silurian systems, and have not hitherto been found elsewhere; being most abundant, however, in the Lower Silurian rocks. Wherever the Lower Silurian rocks have been explored, if they have been unmetamorphosed so that the fossil remains have not been obliterated, Graptolites have been generally found in large numbers. Not unfrequently they are so abundant as to form a kind of carbonaceous matter in the rocks where they are enclosed. Their geographical distribution is exceedingly great, and, as they mark definite geological horizons, no other group of fossils is more valuable in enabling us to arrive at the age of the rock-zones where they are found.

To the palæontologist and zoologist the Graptolites are unusually interesting, on account of their resemblance to, and yet marked deviation in structure from, a well-known and widely distributed living group of marine objects. Moreover, even among the Graptolites themselves there is a striking differentiation; a "differencing," however, which has a foundation of resemblance to start from. Perhaps more papers have been written about the Graptolites than any other fossils, not even excepting Trilobites and Ammonites; and not a few workers have come to wordy blows about them! This difference of opinion has arisen from the endeavour to stretch or expand palæontological facts so as to fit them into the natural history scheme formed for the purpose of classifying and arranging *recent* animals. Now that the theory of evolution has gained ground among our best naturalists, let us hope its Christian effect will be to remove all accessory causes of "bad blood," by pointing out that, however perfect our existing scheme of classification may be for living forms, it is unphilosophical to expect it will fit with equal accuracy those of long bygone periods, when animals frequently possessed characters which have since been divided among different genera. Indeed, it would appear as if the Graptolites were, in some respects, a class of those "missing links" which connected two great divisions of animal life now distinct from each other.

The young geological student finds himself in no small degree perplexed when he first endeavours to find out the zoological relations of the Graptolites. Page refers some of them to the true "sea-pens" (*Pennatula* and *Virgularia*), with which, however, they have nothing in common, except the mere external resemblance the double Graptolites bear to them. The *Pennatulidæ* are nearly related to those familiar objects of our coasts, popularly called "dead men's fingers" (*Alcyonium digitatum*). Other writers place the Graptolites among the *Polyzoa*, or "sea-mats." They are now, however, regarded by Lapworth, Hopkinson, and others as undoubtedly *Hydrozoa*, and very nearly related to the "sea-firs" (*Sertularidæ*). They differ from the Sertularians in some marked particulars, especially in the possession of a *solid* axis—whence their general name of "Rod-bearers" (*Rhabdophora*); among others, in the possession of characters which caused Professor Allman, the great authority on the *Hydrozoa*, to regard them as intermediate between the *Hydrozoa* and *Rhizopoda*

Mr. Hopkinson does not think there is any absolute structural difference between Graptolites and Sertularians, and his recent discovery of *gonothecæ* (or egg-bearing capsules) in Graptolites, similar to those seen in Sertularians, has confirmed his opinion.

In the "sea-firs" (Figs. 28 and 29), we have a horny stem, hollow throughout, giving off branches, like a miniature tree. These branches are also hollow, and

Fig. 29.—Common Sea-fir (*Sertularia abietina*).

communicate with small cups called *Hydrothecæ*. In each of the latter a distinct zoophyte lives, capable of slowly putting forth its fringe of tentacles beyond the rim, and of withdrawing them again. Each individual is connected, by means of the simple fleshy tissue (*cœnosarc*) which fills the hollow stems and branches, with every other on the same colony or polypary. At the base of each of the small cups is a partition, just separating the individual zoophytes. The horny matter, it must be remembered, is secreted by the soft, simple flesh (*cœnosarc*). At certain times there will be borne on the branches, horny capsules, much larger than usual. These are the *gonothecæ*, for the special purpose of reproduction. The young ova issue hence as little free-swimming animals; some of them to assume, during their wandering life—and before they settle down to bud and produce a "sea-fir" colony

Fig. 30.—Magnified calycles (*a*) and capsule (*b*) of common sea-fir (*Sertularia abietina*).

—the appearance, and partly also the structure, of jelly-fish.

Now in many respects the Graptolites resembled recent Sertularians. First, they were composed of a similar horny or *chitinous* external substance, which, indeed, is all that is left of them in the fossil state, just as the entangled masses of the "sea-firs" so often picked up along the coast and mistaken for seaweeds, are all that is left of the living colony of which they formed the more solid and endurable parts. The Graptolites also were like the Sertularians in being compound animals, or rather, a colony of simple, *hydra*-like creatures; whence the name of *Hydrozoa*. In the Graptolites, however, the horny cups are crowded closely together, so that they are all in con-

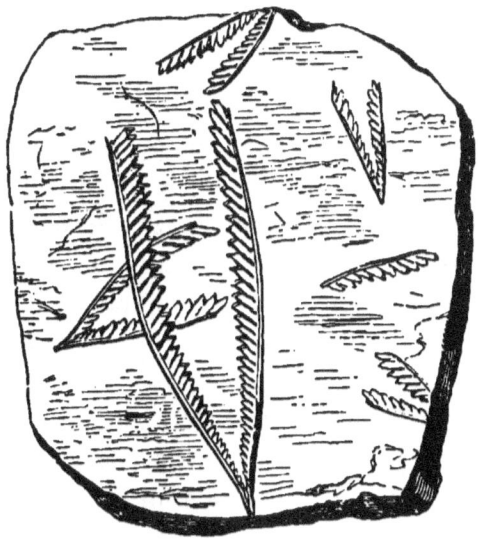

Fig. 31.—Twin Graptolite (*Didymograptus Murchisoni*).

tact (Fig. 32), whereas in the modern Sertularians they are distinct. In one genus of Graptolites, however, the cups are separate, and from the resemblance they have to the teeth of a rake (Latin *raster*, a rake), these forms go by the name of *Rastrites*. They are usually coiled up like toothed watch-springs, and are among the prettiest of all the Graptolites. Their resemblance to the brass-toothed wheels of watches is often still further borne out by the Rastrites having had their substance converted into iron pyrites, the gilt outlines standing forth in very bright relief from the surfaces of the black shales in which they are imbedded.

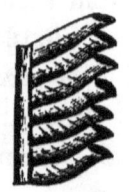

Fig. 32.—Calycles of *Didymograptus Murchisoni* (magnified).

These toothed projections, seen on the outer margins of both single and double Graptolites alike, are regarded by most naturalists as identical with the cups of recent "sea-firs," or Sertularians, and therefore as having contained zoophytes when the Graptolites were alive. Professor Allman, however, doubts whether the Graptolites had cups at all, and thinks that these projections were like those seen on the embryonic stem of the Lobster's horn Coralline (*Antennularia*), which bear *nematophores*. Dr. Nicholson figures the egg-bearing capsules of Graptolites in his "Manual of Palæontology," and his "Monograph of the *Graptolitidæ*," where he sets forth their resemblance to the *gonothecæ* of the Sertularians. He states he found them both attached to the branches of the Graptolites, and separate, and has no doubt as to their being the egg-bearing cases of the ancient Graptolites. Neither Allman nor Carruthers, however, assents to this conclusion. The former believes that the Graptolites did not bear egg-cases at all, but developed themselves by budding, just as the banks of that oceanic sea-weed called *Sargassum* are formed. In the possession of the cups, perhaps filled with protoplasmic matter, called *nematophores*, Professor Allman thinks the Graptolites were nearly related to rhizopod animals, and thus included characters now belonging to two well-marked groups of marine animals.

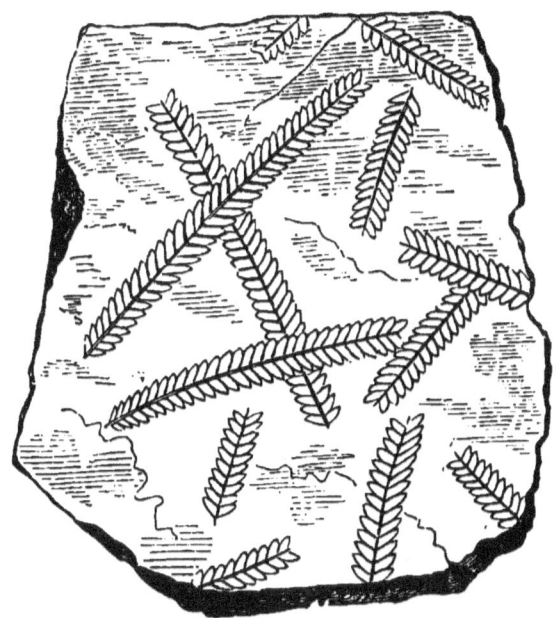

Fig. 33.—Double Graptolite (*Diplograptus pristis*).

All naturalists are agreed that the rod-bearing Graptolites differed from the "sea-firs" in not being fixed or rooted, as the latter always are. They were therefore free, and no doubt gathered in great banks, as appears from the usual way in which they are found fossilized. So far, their development by budding, after the manner of the *Sargassum,* or "gulf-weed," would appear to be probable. Mr. John Hopkinson, F.G.S., has shown that Graptolites may be grouped into two great divisions, in one of which a fibrous rod strengthened the outside of the single Graptolites, or was in the centre in the double species. This rod, Nicholson thinks, was originally hollow, and filled in with living material. It must not be confounded, however, with the hollow space (*cœnosarc*) communicating with each cup, which was undoubtedly filled with the "common flesh." The Graptolites which possessed these rods are called *Rhabdophores:* all of them were free and unrooted. But there is another distinct group of Graptolites of simpler structure, always branched, and "dendroid," or "tree-shaped," like the Sertularians. These are termed *Cladophora*, by Mr. Hopkinson, who has shown that they were fixed or rooted, like the "sea-firs," and probably were very similar to them.

The reader who perceives the nature of the discussion which has contributed so many opinions to the natural-history relations of these interesting fossils, will arrive at the conclusion that their nearest living allies are the "corallines," or "sea-firs" (*Sertularidæ*), although they probably had strong affinities with a group of animals even lower in organization than the latter, namely, the *Rhizopoda*, of which Sponges and Foraminifera are examples.

Mr. Carruthers published a "Revision" (now obsolete, however), in which the leading types of Graptolites are grouped as follows, beginning with *Rastrites* :—In this genus the polypary consists of a simple, slender, hair-like tube, from which project a series of detached cups (*hydrothecæ*). (2) The old genus, which was named by Linnæus *Graptolithus*. This has given the popular name to the entire group. In it the polypary is simple, and the cups are so thickly grouped along one side that they are all in contact with one another (Fig. 31). (3) The genus named *Crytograptus* by Mr. Carruthers, in which the polypary grows in one direction, and gives off simple or compound branches at intervals. (4) The genus *Didymograptus*. In this we have, as it were, a twin Graptolite, of a forked shape, with the cups arranged within the fork (Fig. 31). The symmetrical forms assumed by the coupled branches, or polyparies, are various in different species. (5) *Dichograptus;* a bilaterally branched, and rebranched genus of Graptolites. (6) *Cladograptus;* another compound or bilaterally branched genus. In this the branches often give rise to other irregular branches, the first part of the name signifying a branch. (7) *Dendrograptus* is a much-branched, "tree-shaped," and rooted Sertularian-like Graptolite, with a thick main stem. It belongs to the *Cladophora*. (8) *Diplograptus* (Fig. 33). In this the cups are arranged on each side the axis, so as to present the appearance of two single Graptolites being placed back to back. (9) *Climacograptus;* a genus so named by Professor Hall, of America, in which the polypary has a double series of cells hollowed out of the outer covering. (10) Lastly, we have *Dicranograptus;* having double rows of cells in the lower part, with branches possessed of only single rows of cups or cells.

In the Arenig rocks of Ramsey Island, the dendroid forms seem to be tolerably abundant, and Mr. Hopkinson has shown that these have a nearer relation to the species of Graptolites in the Quebec group of Canada than any other found in Great Britain. The bilaterally branched or double form of Graptolite seem to be peculiar to the Lower Silurian rocks; whilst the fewer species met with in the upper strata are usually of a simpler character. Some compound forms seem to have attained great length; thus, a species of *Pleurograptus* has been traced over three feet long, although even this does not seem to have been the full size. The Skiddaw Slates were formerly believed to form the lowest horizon where the Graptolites were met with, but Mr. Hopkinson's discovery of them, lower down in the Arenig rocks, not only extends their antiquity, but, owing to the similarity of type between the Arenig species and those from Quebec, suggests that their geographical distribution into colonies occurred later on through the subsequent geological changes which took place. Still older species of Graptolites have been discovered by Dr. Callaway, in the Upper Lingula Flags, and one is named *Bryograptus Callavei*. Another genus is *Clonograptus*, found in the Shineton shales of Shropshire.

One of the very best hunting-grounds for British Graptolites is Dumfriesshire. That county is largely underlaid by Lower Silurian rocks, originally deposited along the floors of ancient seas as so much marine mud. Little did the numerous Graptolites know that they were forming no insignificant part in laying down the foundations of the "Land of brown heath and shaggy wood;" a land to be uplifted for ages above sea-levels, on which the storms and atmospherical action of thousands of centuries would be expended, until its surface had become carved into hill and dale, lake and valley, gorge and glen, over all of which genius should throw the halo of ever-enduring romance! This wild land teems with as many relics of the semi-barbarous mediæval human period as it does with primeval fossils. The heroes not only of Scott, but of many an unchronicled feud and deed of daring, have sought shelter in glens and linns where the black shales through which these had been cut were crowded with pyritized Graptolites. At Moffat, for instance, the black shales of the Silurian rocks abound with these interesting fossils. Owing to the softish nature of the shales, and the way in which they allow water to ooze through their joints, many of the glens in them are well wooded, and rich in flowering plants. In the shales there *Diplograptus pristis* and *Climacograptus rectangularis* are abundant, the latter species particularly so.

The neighbourhood of Moffat, also, is good ground for Graptolites. Many new species have been recently described from this district. At Hart Fell such forms as *Diplograptus pristis*, *D. foliaceus*, *D. mucronatus*, *Dicellograptus*, *Dicranograptus sextans*, and many other commoner forms occur. In this remarkable region, rendered classic by Burns and Hogg, the geological student cannot cast his eyes in any direction without recognizing some kind of geological agency or another. All the hills hereabout show traces of glacial action, in rounding, striæ, or otherwise. Burns' "Craigieburn Wood" lies itself in the heart of the graptolitic shales; whilst the student of Scott's "Red Gauntlet" will hardly fail to recognize the graphic scenery delineated in that novel, in his additional wanderings after fossils. Birk Hill is one of the best places in Dumfriesshire for Graptolites of all kinds. Glenkiln Burn is another equally good hunting-ground, where, perhaps, the largest specimens of *Pleurograptus* are to be unearthed. Garple Linn, Duff-Kinnel Burn, and Dob's Linn are other rich storehouses of Graptolites. The latter spot is a waterfall sacred to the memory of two Covenanters, who are said to have been much annoyed by Satan. If these two worthy Scots had been looking for Graptolites, they would not have been troubled by such a personage.

These Moffat Graptolite-bearing shales are the oldest fossiliferous strata in Scotland, and they attain a total thickness of six hundred feet. They have been grouped by Professor Lapworth into three divisions, called Birkhill shales, Hartfell shales, and Glenkiln shales; and each division is split up into "zones," marked by the presence of certain characteristic species of Graptolites. These divisions of the Graptolite shales have been recognized by geologists elsewhere, as in North and South Wales, etc.

The shales in which Graptolites occur are nearly always of a black colour, and these beds are usually distributed in long lenticular areas through otherwise unfossiliferous rocks.

Burns' own county of Ayrshire is not without various geological attractions, although the scenic features are not on so grand a scale as elsewhere. In the metamorphosed Lower Silurian slates of Cairn Ryan we meet with abundance of *Diplograptus pristis*. The Girvan district has long been famous for its Silurian fossils, and recently Messrs. Etheridge and Nicholson have published a splendid monograph upon them. Nearer home, Graptolites are very abundant in the black shales which crop out in the basement of the little gorge on the top of the hill just above Lowwood, on the eastern shores of Windermere, and not more than a couple of miles from Ambleside. They are found on almost every piece of shale, *Diplograptus, Rastrites, Graptolithus*, etc., all of them beautifully pyritized. From the base of the gorge, where these fossils may be hammered out in abundance, we gain a magnificent view of Windermere, set in its rich framework of green woods, greener than arboreal vegetation anywhere else in Great Britain! The geological eye takes in the rounded rocks which lie outside the woody belt, and does not pass by the heaps of morainic matter which frequently form the eastern coast-line. Ice-action speaks forth plainly from every part of this district.

Of course, the Lower Silurian rocks, so well developed in North Wales, are not in many places bad Graptolite stores. In the easily identified black, slaty shales which crop out in the railway cutting near Conway station, and banks of the Seiont, near Carnarvon, the young collector may find sufficient to satisfy all his cravings. In various places around Welshpool, as at Fflyrnwy, near Llanfair, the flag-stones abound in Graptolites. The slate-quarries of Llansantfraid, Denbighshire, are famous for them, and the geological tourist may find *Diplograptus pristis* in great numbers, associated with other familiar species. In the black shales which crop out in many places near Builth, and in the bed of the Wye, *Dicellograptus* and *Climacograptus* are in profusion. It will be seen, therefore, that in South Wales, as well as the north of the Principality, wherever the Lower Silurian rocks are well developed, and especially where the shales have a black, finely laminated appearance,

Graptolites may be looked for with every prospect of their discovery.

The black shales at Garth, near Portmadoc, which belong to the Upper Arenig rocks, are in places crowded with Graptolites. The richest locality in South Wales is perhaps Ramsey Island, where, in the dark shales forming the cliffs, there are plenty of *Phyllograptus*, *Callograptus*, *Ptilograptus*, and *Tetragraptus*. The promontory of St. David's is now known to contain them, especially at Llanvirn and Whitesand Bay. Abereiddy Bay is a good locality for finding *Didymograptus* and *Dicellograptus*. At Tarannon, in North Wales (a lovely neighbourhood to select for a walking-tour), no fewer than twenty-three species of Graptolites have been met with, distributed through five genera.

The Skiddaw and Keswick district is usually rather poor in fossils, although to the geologist this is atoned for by the physical geology being among the most interesting examples in Great Britain; whilst for beauty and diversity of scenery, it would be difficult to find its equal in our land. In the black slates, the geological student should look closely for Graptolites. No fewer than twenty-seven species have been obtained thereabouts. At Coniston, in the easily recognized " mud-stones," we find another colony of Graptolites, of which twenty-five species have been described.

The Ludlow shales, in the Upper Silurian rocks, saw the last of this ancient and easily identified group of fossils. Only one genus of the *Rhabdophora*

(*Monograptus*) is there represented, but eight species have been recognized as belonging to it. Of the *Cladophora* there are several species of *Dendrograptus* and *Ptilograptus*. The Wenlock shales are the home of *Cyrtograptus*, which may be found at Builth, and in the Pentland Hills.

At Key's End Hill, Malvern, and also near Portmadoc, we find an abundance of another pretty fossil coralline called *Dictyonema sociale*. In the Carboniferous rocks we find *Palæocoryne*, and other probable corallines.

Graptolites must be sought for where the black shales crop out, and these are usually amid the grandest or the prettiest and loveliest bits of river, hill, and mountain scenery. Nature holds forth charms of her own to tempt the geological student from the busy haunts of men to the quietest parts of her sanctuary, where she deigns to unfold the mysteries that were originally hidden for him when "the foundations of the earth were laid."

CHAPTER III.

FOSSIL CORALS.

PERHAPS no fossils have such a geological value as corals. If extinct species were marked by the same habits as their modern representatives (and in many cases the families of living corals are so ancient, and the extinct forms glide so imperceptibly into existing kinds, that there is no absolutely strongly marked line of division), then their value to the physical geologist who endeavours to restore the conditions of primeval seas is immense. For coral-animals can only flourish where the sea-water is clear, and therefore where no muddy sediments are forming. Coral-animals are easily separable into two groups — the single or simply compound corals, which are usually inhabitants of deeper water; and the reef-building corals, which cannot live and flourish beyond the depth of twenty-five fathoms. Moreover, according to Darwin, coral reefs indicate to the physical geographer slowly subsiding areas of the sea-floor. They are also indicative of a certain degree of ocean temperature, for we do not meet with them where the sea-water is cooler than 62°, and therefore the sub-tropical belts of our globe now roughly comprehend their distribution. But we find fossil corals of all kinds—simple, compound, and reef-building. They are characteristic of many thick limestone formations, from the Silurian upwards. We have in the British Islands abundance of fossil reef-building corals, where their modern representatives could not now live. What climatal changes these

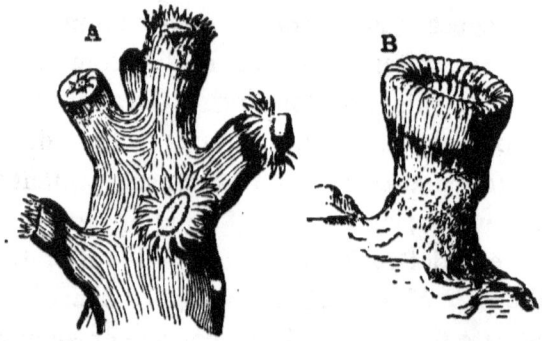

Fig. 34.—A, *Dendrophyllia*, a compound Coral; B, *Caryophyllia*, a recent Coral.

valuable fossils indicate! Not less important are the conditions of the ancient seas they lay before us. We carry our minds back to a period when there were coral islands, fringing-reefs, and barrier-reefs in British seas. These reefs also tell the geologist of the adjacency of land, and inform him of the fact that the sea-floor was in a state of subsidence.

Moreover, few fossils are prettier, more easily procurable, or look better in the cabinet, than corals.

FOSSIL CORALS.

They are found in nearly every marine limestone formation. No other fossils can be so well studied,

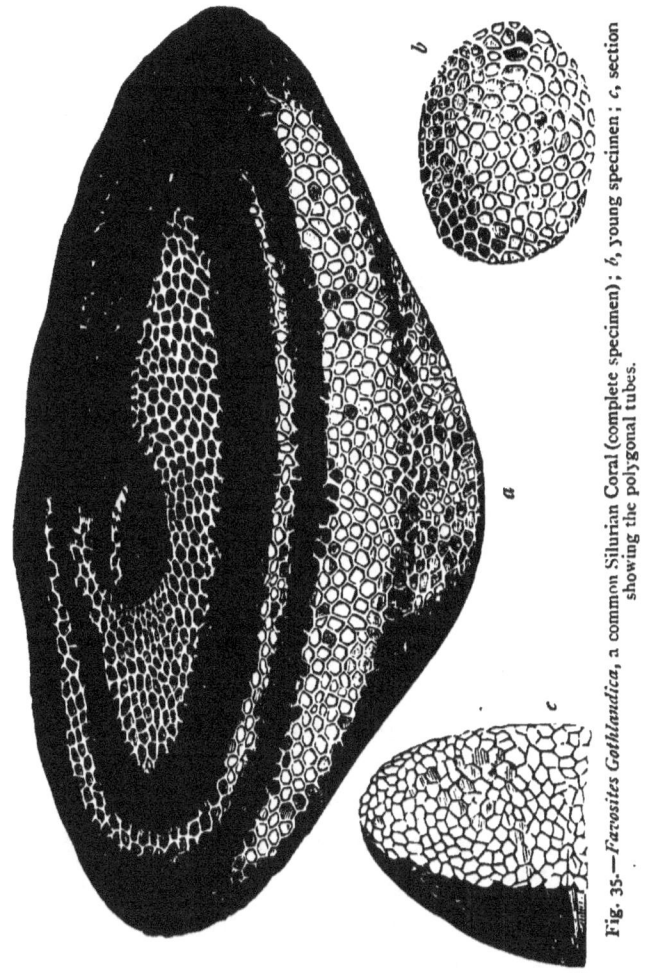

Fig. 35.—*Favosites Gothlandica*, a common Silurian Coral (complete specimen); *b*, young specimen; *c*, section showing the polygonal tubes.

cut into sections, and examined under the microscope. And they are so very abundant that the limestone walls in the hilly districts where Silurian, Devonian, Carboniferous, or Oolitic limestone crops up, are often composed of little else than blocks of fossil coral.

We are beginning to understand the true relationship of living and extinct corals better than we did, thanks to the labours of Dr. Sorby, Professor M. Duncan, and Professor H. N. Mosely. Formerly these animals (classified chiefly by the stony or limy parts they leave behind) were all grouped among that order of the *Actinozoa* called *Zoantharia*, of which the common

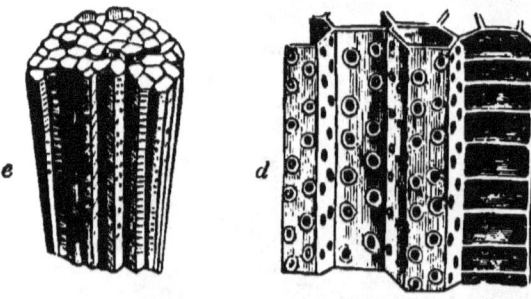

Fig. 36.—*Favosites Gothlandica*: *e*, cluster of tubes of Favosites; *d*, tubes (magnified), showing tabulæ and perforations connecting the tubes.

sea-anemone is a type. The order *Zoantharia* was split up into three divisions, called *Tabulata, Rugosa*, and *Aporosa*. It was thought the two former were Palæozoic types of corals, and the third of Neozoic and Recent corals. Let us examine the fundamental difference of these three groups. The tabulate corals are remarkable, and, indeed, obtain the name which distinguishes them, for the partitions which seem horizontally to split them up into chambers.

They are compound corals, whose shapes are modified by the manner in which they grew, so that some are polygonal, or many-sided, and others oval or round.

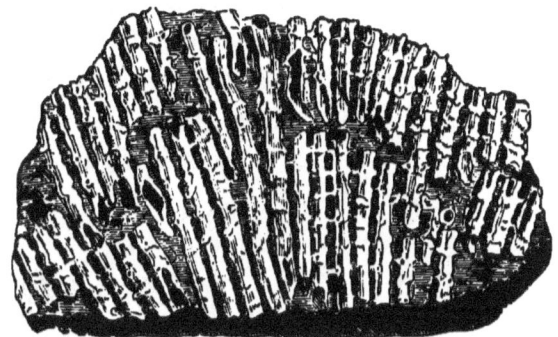

Fig. 37.—*Syringipora ramulosa*, a common Carboniferous limestone Coral.

The most remarkable of these tabulate fossil corals are *Heliolites*, *Favosites*, the pretty "chain-coral"

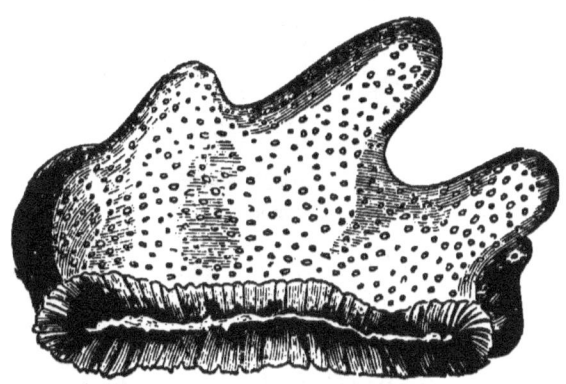

Fig. 38.—*Heliopora cærulea*, a recent Alcyonarian Coral.

(*Halysites*), *Syringipora*, etc. It will be seen from Fig. 36, which shows a magnified section of a very abundant Silurian coral (*Favosites Gothlandica*), that the coral-pipes—as we may call them—are separated into horizontal chambers. The walls are perforated, as they are in some of the *Alcyonaria*, possibly for transverse canals. It will also be seen that the interiors of the corals are *not radiated*—that is, have not those vertical plates springing from the walls which are called *septa*; or, if they are present in Tabulate corals

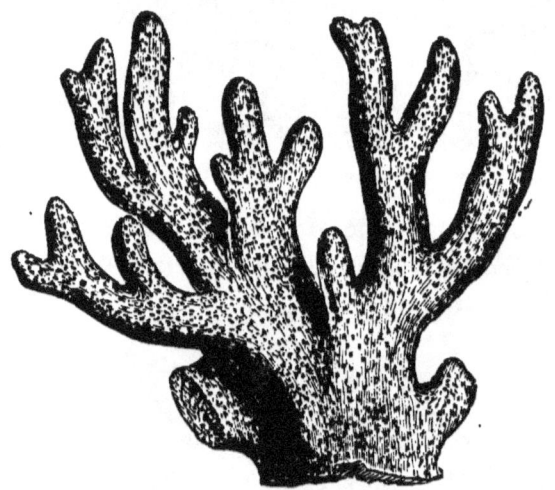

Fig. 39.—*Millepora alcicornis*, a recent Hydrozoan Coral (Bermudas).

they are very feebly marked. This general absence of septa is the leading distinction of Tabulate corals. Professor Mosely thinks that most, if not all, of this group are in reality not Zoantharians, or *true* corals, but Alcyonarians, of which the recent common Organ-pipe coral (*Tubipora musica*) is the best example. Some of the so-called corals, as the Millepores, he proved not to be corals at all, but demonstrated they actually belong to another class, the *Hydrozoa*. In other words, they are the remains of colonies of animals allied to Sertularians, but possessing *limy* structures, instead of the *chitinous* or horn-like material which composes the solid parts of our "sea-firs." Professor Mosely shows there is a peculiar division of labour in the polyps of

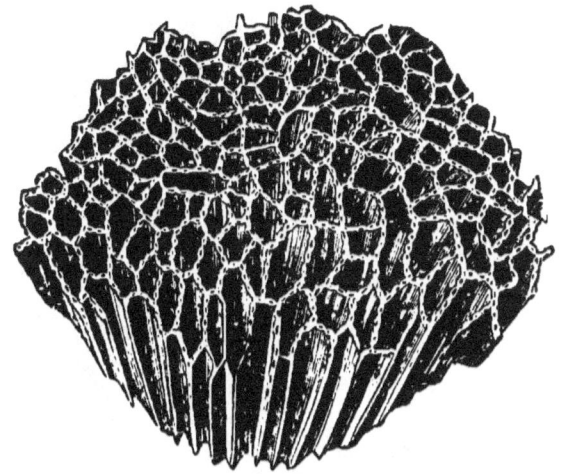

Fig. 40.—Section of "Chain-Coral" (*Halysites catenulatus*), showing tubes (Upper Silurian formation).

modern Millepores, some of the zoophytes catching the food and others digesting it, after they have received it from the catchers. This is the case in Stylaster, where the food-catching zoophytes much resemble the tentacles arranged round the mouth of the common sea-anemone.

The abundant recent coral *Heliopora cærulea*

(whose specific name comes from the bright blue colour of the stony structure, which in other modern corals is usually white) is an Alcyonarian, more nearly related to some sea-fans than to true corals. It is plentiful in equatorial seas, and especially off the Bermudas. It has not indistinct traces of septa. The genus of fossil corals called *Heliolites*, abundant in

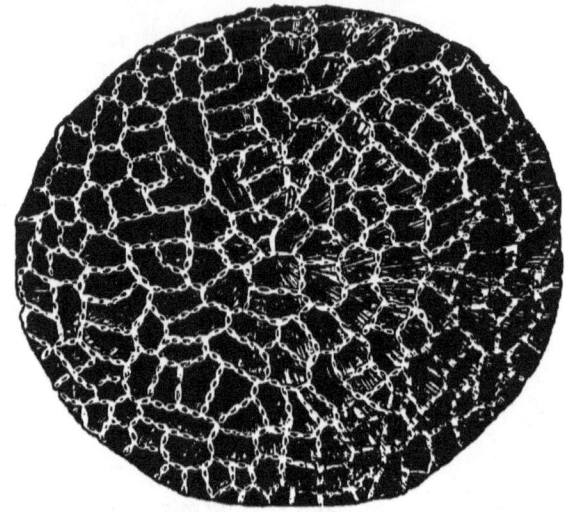

Fig. 41.—" Chain-Coral " (*Halysites catenulatus*), as usually found intact in round masses.

the Silurian and Devonian limestones, does not differ in any important particular from the living *Heliopora*, and, like it, no doubt belonged to the *Alcyonaria*.

The division of fossil corals called *Rugosa*, on the other hand, is distinguished by well-marked septa, radiating from the coral walls towards the centre, in the pretty star-shaped fashion which caused Cuvier to

FOSSIL CORALS. 63

group these objects, along with others similarly star-rayed in their shapes, into the sub-kingdom *Radiata*, now no longer accepted by naturalists. In this radiated structure, therefore, the rugose corals re-

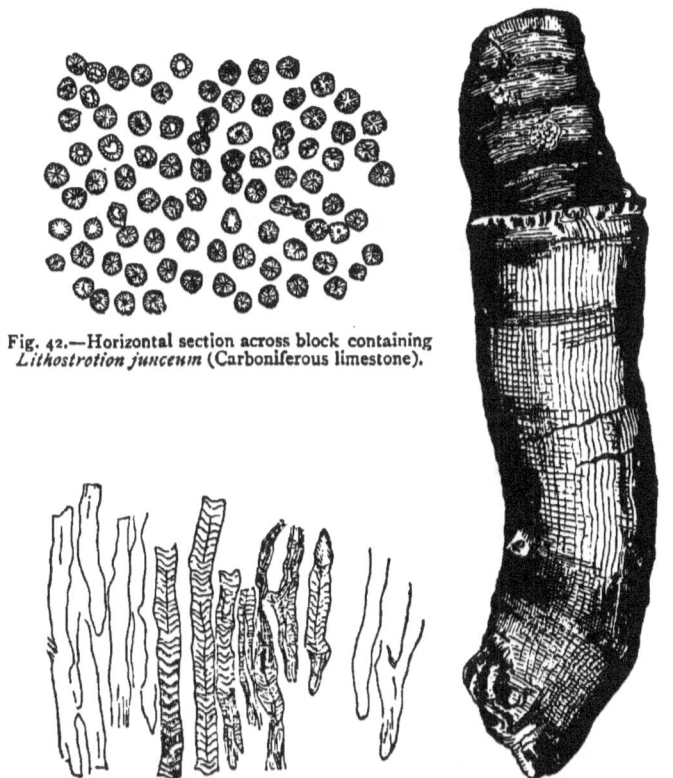

Fig. 42.—Horizontal section across block containing *Lithostrotion junceum* (Carboniferous limestone).

Fig. 43.—Vertical section of *Lithostrotion junceum*,

Fig. 44.—*Amplexus coralloides* (Carboniferous limestone).

semble the aporose corals. But whereas the tabulate and rugose corals (with few exceptions) are limited to Palæozoic rocks, the aporose corals are peculiar to those formed since then. Again, the septa, or radiating plates, of the rugose corals are in multiples of *four*, whilst those of aporose corals are in multiples of *six*. Besides this means of distinguishing the aporose corals from any of the others, the fact that they never have *tabulæ*—that is, are not divided into horizontal layers—is another important distinction. When

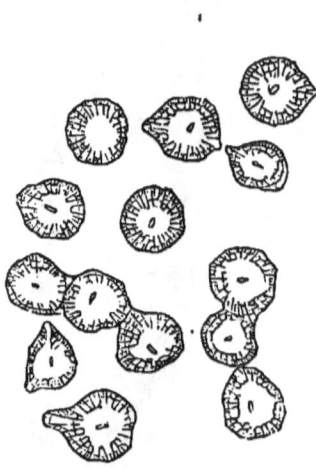
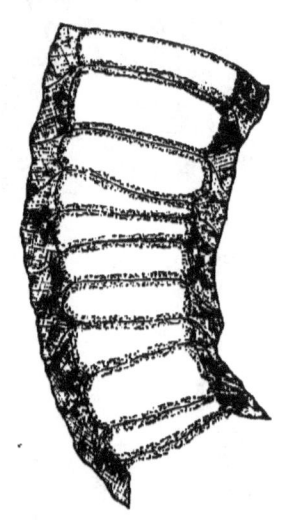

Fig. 45.—Horizontal section of *Lithostrotion Phillipsii* (Carboniferous limestone).

Fig. 46.—Vertical section of *Amplexus coralloides*, showing the *tabulæ*.

the tabulate corals have only faint traces of septa, we can still see they are in multiples of four, and they thus show their structural relationship to the *Rugosa*. Dr. Sorby has shown that the tabulate corals are built up of calcite, whilst the Neozoic and modern corals are formed of that limy structure known as arragonite. It may be that the *Rugosa* are descended from the

Tabulata, which would at once make it clear why the tabulate corals appear in such numbers of species and individuals in the Silurian and Devonian seas. In the Carboniferous rocks the most numerous corals are the rugose kind, in which the radiated structure is very plainly visible, as in *Lithostrotion junceum*, etc., of which we give illustrations of the transverse appearance they present when cut and polished. For some of my illustrations I am indebted to Mr. James Thomson, F.G.S., of Glasgow—one of the most

Fig. 47.—Horizontal section of *Amplexus coralloides*, showing feebly developed septa.

Fig. 48.—*Cyathaxinia* (Carboniferous limestone). A, horizontal section.

enthusiastic and diligent students of Palæozoic fossil corals in Europe. I have already said that the numerously represented fossils called *Stromatopora*—abundant in our Silurian and Devonian limestones—are now believed to be calcareous sponges, or sponges whose abundant limy spicules amalgamated into the concentric rings characteristic of their structure. This structure may be studied in any polished mantelpiece formed of Devonian marble from the quarries of Newton Abbot and the neighbourhood. By far the prettiest of the Palæozoic fossil corals are those

F

belonging to the *Rugosa*, such as *Strombodes*, *Cyathophyllum* (perhaps the most plentiful of them all), *Cyathaxinia* (a simple coral), *Lithostrotion*, *Lithodendron*, etc. Perhaps the single coral which may be regarded as the simplest in structure is Am-

Fig. 49.—Recent Arborescent Perforate Coral (*Oculina axillaris*).

plexus, and there is reason for believing that many more elaborate fossil corals pass through a kind of Amplexus stage.

A fourth division of corals is termed *Perforata* (Fig. 49.) These are the familiar twig-like, branched corals, whose surface breaks out here and there into flower-like calyces, and whose tips usually terminate in the same sort of objects. The entire structure is distinguished by its light and porous character—whence the name of the group. In spite of their apparent fragility, we find them living amid the most violent of seas, for their rapid growth enables them to withstand the destructive effects which would otherwise break them up. The division *Aporosa* did not

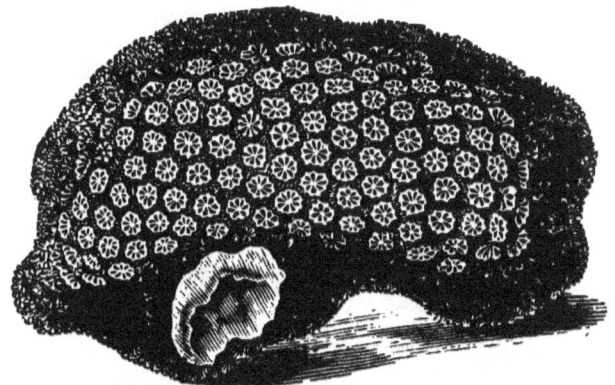

Fig. 50.—*Astræa rotulosa*, a recent West Indian compound Coral.

make its appearance in Primeval seas, but is first observed in strata of the Secondary period, although its species are most abundant in the present epoch. The *Perforata* are feebly represented among primary fossils by Silurian and Devonian genera, such as *Protarca* and *Pleurodictyum*. Perhaps the modern *Perforata* are better known by their common name of Madrepores.

The intervening spaces in the branched or arborescent corals, between where one flower-like calyx is seen and another, is called the cœnenchyma. They are the equivalents of the "inter-nodal spaces," or distances which separate leaves from one another, in the branches of a tree. It is the rapid porous growth of these parts which enable such compound corals to

Fig. 51.—*Astræa favosa*, a recent East Indian Coral.

stand against a good deal of marine wear-and-tear. It is these parts, also, which bind the various corallites together into one colony. In deep-sea corals this cœnenchyma rarely exists as a means of rendering them compound, but a different method of "compounding" takes place. *Oculina* is said to be the only large coral now found in northern seas; but our

British rocks, especially the Carboniferous limestone, are in places almost entirely composed of corals, reef-building, deep-sea, and shore-loving species.

There is often a difficulty in recognizing which of the fossil corals were "reef-builders," and which were not. For it does not follow that because the fossil corals are of a compound character they were therefore engaged in the work of reef-building. Perhaps the safest plan is to trace the existing genera of reef-builders as far back in geological time as we can, or at any rate to compare the fossil kinds with their nearest living representatives.

Fig. 52.—*Astræa ananas*, a fossil Coral, common in the Silurian limestones.

Few genera are more distinctively "reef-builders" than the *Astræa*, whose characteristic star-like arrangement of polypes or corallites (the latter often so close together that they press each other into oval or polygonal shapes), has given to this genus its distinctive name. The widespread geographical distribution of the genus *Astræa*, and the fact that it is engaged, in areas separated by enormous geographical distances, in reef-building, would be an incidental proof to a geologist of its geological antiquity, even if this genus were not found in our Upper Silurian and Devonian limestones. Thus *Astræa rotulosa* (Fig. 50) is a living species of this interesting genus of corals found abundantly in West

Indian seas, where it is met with in coral-reefs, and masking and adhering to natural rocks. *Astræa favosa* (Fig. 51), on the other hand, is peculiar to the East Indian seas, where it is hardly less abundant. *Astræa ananas* (Fig. 52) is a common fossil in the Silurian limestone at the Wren's Nest, Dudley, in the formation of which we can hardly doubt that it and

Fig. 53.—*Lithostrotion basaltiforme*, an abundant compound Rugose Coral in the Carboniferous limestone. The *lighter* parts show the transverse structure, as seen when the coral is cut for sections.

its compeers took a considerable part. For Professor Owen tells us that the Wenlock Edge, in Shropshire, belonging to the same formation, is nothing more or less than an ancient coral-reef thirty miles in length! The Plymouth limestone belongs to the Devonian period, and in it we find this and other genera of reef-building corals; and many of our best palæontologists are of the opinion that this limestone is nothing more than a Devonian coral-reef skirting the old land-regions composed of Cambrian and Silurian rocks.

Hunting for fossil corals in the older rocks implies visits to some of the most picturesquely romantic spots in Great Britain, with here and there a little variation in some localities whose ancient loveliness

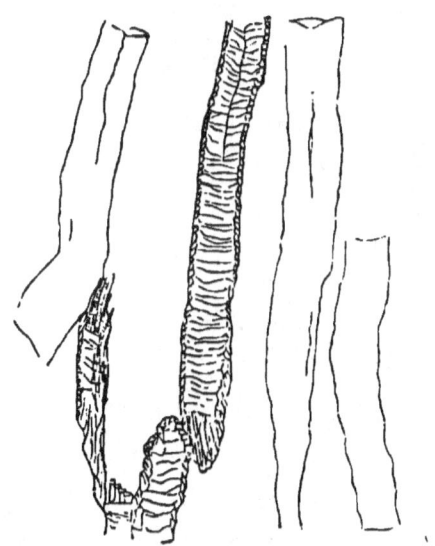

Fig. 54.—Vertical section of *Lithostrotion Phillipsii*, showing tabulæ.

has had to give way to the deforming ugliness of extensive mining or manufacturing operations. This is the case with the Wren's Nest, near Dudley, formed of a romantic cluster of highly inclined Upper Silurian limestones rising from beneath the Coal formation which extends up to their very base. These limestone slabs are hard, as if the soft organic matter of the molluscs and corals, whose hard parts almost wholly make up the rocky mass, had thoroughly permeated

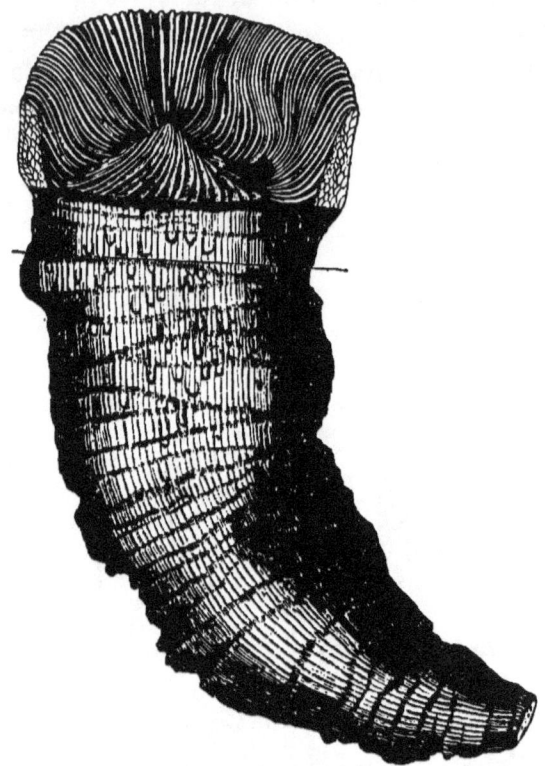

Fig. 55.—Clisiophyllum, a single fossil Coral, characteristic of the Carboniferous limestone formation.

it, and thus produced a similar induration to that effected by sculptors, when they boil their porous plaster casts in oil to render them tougher and more durable. But hard as the Dudley limestone is, the fossil corals are harder, and as the faces of the slabs are weathered, the fossils stand out in high relief. To a young geologist who is fleshing his maiden hammer, such a sight as is here presented produces an effect not likely to be forgotten during life. Myriads upon myriads, here lie entombed the exuviæ of primeval seas! No museum in the world could attempt to vie with these almost bare or lichen-covered slabs for variety and abundance of organic remains. Hours can easily be spent in climbing from crag to crag, in and out of the brushwood which is irregularly growing where the layers of soft slate are intercalated between the limestone slabs; and one forgets that the wide-stretching plain at the foot of the "Nest" is superficially crowded with ironworks, manufactories of all kinds, forests of chimneys (many of them out of the perpendicular), colliery works in various stages of mining development as to the modern character of their pit gear, and densely packed regular or irregular rows of unpicturesque-looking houses. The walls of the old castle look over this modern scene of energy and mechanics; and the old and the new, even in human history, are thus brought into strange juxtaposition.

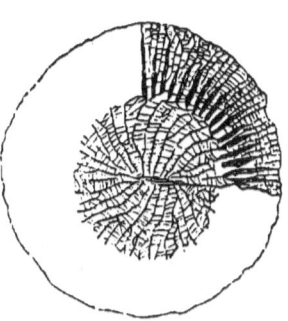

Fig. 56.—Transverse section of Clisiophyllum, showing (in part) details of structure.

Leaving out other fossils, the student may find at the Wren's Nest, or in the quarries opened in the limestone, abundance of such corals as *Favosites Gothlandica*, *F. polymorpha*, etc., and various species of such characteristic Silurian corals as *Omphyma* (in great abundance), *Cystiphyllum*, *Porites*, *Heliolites*, *Palæocyclus*, *Columnaria*, *Halysites* (the well-known and very plentiful "chain-coral"), *Strombodes*, *Cyathophyllum*,

Fig. 57.—*Caryophyllia*, a recent British Coral (natural size).

etc. Not only is there an abundance of species of fossil corals, simple and compound, but of genera and species as well. Compared with this wealth of Zoantharian life, our modern seas are quite poverty-stricken. All that even the warmer waters of our Devonshire and Cornish coasts can now support are a few pretty but insignificant corals, the largest of which is *Caryophyllia*, a genus which first appeared in the seas of the globe during the formation of the Wenlock limestone, and has been in existence ever since. Another recent British coral is the little *Balanophyllia regia*. Both these British corals may be seen in the living state in the small table tanks at the Crystal Palace and Brighton Aquaria, and a brief examination of them will enable the student to form a good idea of how the hard calcareous substance which remains as "coral" is secreted by the investing flesh. He will also be able to restore, in imagination, the vivid and many-coloured appearance presented by the sea-floors of the Palæozoic epoch, when corals were so abundant, from the tints and colours which characterize the flesh of living coral-animals.

Fig. 58.—*Balanophyllia regia*, a recent British Coral (natural size).

A quieter place for fossil coral-hunting than Dudley is the neighbourhood of Wenlock, in Shropshire, where that division of the Upper Silurian formation called "Wenlock limestone" crops up, and whence it has derived its name. No better place would be

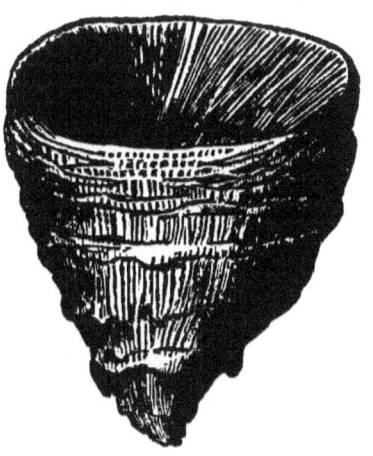

Fig. 59.—*Omphyma subturbinata*, a common Silurian fossil Coral.

found for a short tour, and fossil-collecting might be agreeably diversified by a little archæology, which the old Norman abbey, etc., of the town would afford. All the fossil corals mentioned as abundant at Dudley are also to be found in the neighbourhood of Wenlock, with the addition of the beautiful *Lonsdalia Wenlockensis*. Benthall Edge, about two miles distant from Wenlock, is a famous place for fossils, and

Fig. 60.—Section of *Favosites cervicornis*, an abundant Devonian Coral.

corals are there especially abundant, and in excellent preservation. It overlooks the Severn, and the busy but still picturesque Coalbrook Dale. Wenlock Edge is interesting to the physical geologist, for it stands up from amid the softer Wenlock shale. As might be expected, the greater ease with which the latter has yielded to weather action has caused it to be denuded into the plain which it now underlies. How abundant the fossil corals are in the limestone here may be gathered from Professor Owen's statement just referred to, that "Wenlock Edge is itself a coral-reef thirty miles in length." Nearly all the fossil Upper Silurian corals figured and described by Edwards and Haine in the publication of the Palæontographical Society are found in the neighbourhood of Wenlock. There are plenty of quarries about, and the student finds abundance of materials of all kinds.

From Wenlock, the geological wanderer makes

Fig. 61.—*Stenopora* (or *Favosites*) *fibrosus*, an abundant Silurian Coral.

his way to other classic grounds, whose names are famous to the reader of "Siluria." The various subdivisions of the upper beds crop out over a large extent of Salopian country. Among localities to be specialized is Aymestry (a place which has given its name to one of the uppermost Silurian beds). Craven Arms station, near Church Stretton, is a capital place for the student to make for, if he wishes to be placed at once on Silurian ground. The Aymestry limestone is seen forming the bold hills of View Edge and Stokesay camp, and the limestone in places literally abounds with the well-known and characteristic fossil brachiopod *Pentamerus Knightii*. The Garden House quarries at Aymestry are capital collecting grounds. Indeed, a good many of the fossils figured by Sir Roderick Murchison in his "Silurian System" were obtained at these quarries. Nearly every village in the neighbourhood has several outcrops of or quarries into the rocks, where fossils may be abundantly hammered out. The commonest of the fossil corals are *Cyathophyllum* (often well known among the quarrymen and others by the name of "petrified ram's horns," in allusion to the irregular way in which the stony corallum usually twists), *Heliolites interstinctus*, *Halysites*, and *Omphyma* (one species of which, *O. subturbinata*, is a very widely and plentifully distributed Silurian coral).

The Malvern Hills also afford several noticeable localities where the Silurian strata yield fossil corals. In Eastnor Park, just beneath the picturesque Herefordshire Beacon—one of the loveliest spots in that picturesque district—we have hammered out some splendid corals. Should the geologist pedestrinate this park towards the end of March, he will see such a wealth of wild Daffodils as even Wordsworth's poem does not give the faintest idea of! The Woolhope Valley should also be mentioned, and here the commonest corals to be exhumed are

FOSSIL CORALS.

Omphyma (several species), *Cyathophyllum, Halysites, Zaphrentis, Astræa,* etc. The best localities thereabouts are Checkley Common, Dennington, Warslaw, and Dormington (the limestone at the latter place appears to be simply an ancient local coral-reef, crowded with "chain-coral" and *Favosites Gothlandica;* it is wonderfully full of fossils of various kinds). At May Hill there are several quarries, in which the fossil "chain-coral" (*Halysites catenulatus*) and *Favo-*

Fig. 62.—*Heliolites interstinctus,* a common Silurian Coral.

sites gothlandica are abundant. The Silurian rocks of the Malvern Hills are nearly everywhere plentiful in fossils, although evidences of the reef-building corals only occur here and there. The following are all capital collecting grounds:—Netherton Valley, Stonesway, about Nenning's Farm, Colwall Copse, the quarries along the Marthon road, Martley, and Blaisdon Edge (where extensive quarrying of the Wenlock limestone is carried on). Nor should the picturesque town of Ledbury be neglected—with quietest of old English suburbs, the whole town set in a framework of woods and wooded hills. The latter are frequently pierced by quarries, from which numbers of fossil corals, characteristic of the Upper Silurian formation, may be obtained. To feel how delicious is the quiet seclusion of a town like this, the pedestrian should enter it about two o'clock some summer's afternoon!

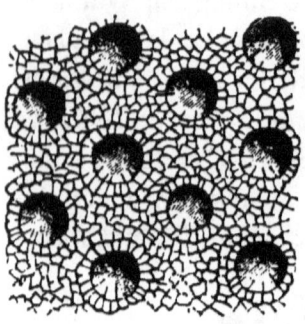

Fig. 63.—Portion of *Heliolites interstinctus* magnified, to show corallites.

The lateral foldings of the Upper Silurian strata of North Wales have frequently obliterated the organic remains, or left them represented by only feeble impressions. Of course, except a few single and solitary corals, we should not expect to find—nor do we find —fossil corals abundant in any other than limestone deposits, all other strata being formed in more or less muddy water, as the nature of the sediments shows; whilst coral animals are noted for their love of clear water, and their dislike to turbid. Hence in such beds as the Bala limestone we frequently find abundance of fossil corals. One of the best localities I know of in North Wales is Mynydd Fronfrys, a few miles from Llangollen. In an old quarry along the Oswestry road there is a perfect feast of fat things in the shape of abundant and beautifully preserved Silurian fossils; and the spot is so quiet, and in the midst of such delightful and little-visited Welsh scenery, that my readers would be thankful for directing them to the place, if it were for that alone.

The Coniston limestone, which runs an irregular course through the Lake District, is in places full of fossil corals, as at Sunny Brow and Long Steddale. In the neighbourhood of the little town which gives to this stratum its name, may be obtained *Monticulipora, Stenopora* (or *Favosites*) *fibrosus, Petraia*, the latter now known to be only natural casts of *Cyathophyllum*, etc. The fossil coral *Heliolites megastoma* found in this bed is remarkable for its well-developed septæ. Some lovely spots may be found where there is good geologizing on these beds. One of the best I know is on the road to Troutbeck, near Windermere. This road crosses the hill where the limestone crops up, and the walls by the roadside are formed of the local rock. They are perfect museums, but, numerous though they are, all the fossils occur as *casts* or impressions; and the rock is often quite "rotten" from the abundance of these casts. This is due to the lime (which formerly entered into the composition of the fossils) having been gradually dissolved away by the rain-water which has been percolating these fossiliferous rocks ever since they were converted into dry land. Among the most abundant of the fossils is *Favosites fibrosus*, perhaps the oldest known British species, and one of the widest distributed of all Silurian corals. Many varieties of it are known, and among others one which is seen encrusting univalve shells as if it had destroyed them, after the fashion which is still practised by some mechanically parasitic zoophytes in modern seas. The stone walls on and about breezy Applethwaite Common are often full of small kinds of fossil corals, as impressions of *Cyathophyllum, Favosites, Heliolites*, etc.

The Caradoc rocks contain by far the largest number of species of fossil corals of any of the *older* Palæozoic rocks, about forty-two different kinds having been described. One remarkable fact concerning these ancient corals is that we often find one genus represented by only one species. This is particularly the case in the Upper Llandovery rocks, where, out of sixteen genera of fossil corals, no fewer than eleven have only one species each.

A very rich development of corals seems to have taken place during the period when the Upper Silurian and Middle Devonian limestones were deposited. No fewer than seventy-six species have been obtained from the Wenlock rocks of Great Britain alone; whilst from the Devonian strata fifty-two species have been catalogued. The Carboniferous limestone, however, appears to have been deposited when the ancient coral fauna had reached its greatest development, for one hundred and forty-one species have been enumerated from this formation alone!

These numbers, however, do not convey to the mind of the student such a clear idea of the relative abundance of fossil corals in the older rocks, as he can get for himself by geologizing in two or three localities where corals are abundant.

Mr. Etheridge thinks that during no period in the physical history of the British Isles has there been such a remarkable assemblage of corals as when the Middle Devonian rocks of North and South Devon were formed. Out of fifty-two species not one passes to the Carboniferous formation, and none are common to the Silurian rocks of any area. The limestones of Torquay and Newton Abbot are simply Devonian coral-reefs of great magnitude.

Some splendid geologizing may be obtained in the neighbourhood of Girvan, in Ayrshire—a rather complicated tract of Upper Silurian rocks. The district is a pleasant one to work in, with the Atlantic on one side, and the hilly sheep-pastures on the other. Numerous quarries may be found, and pleasant little adventures made along miniature gorges cut by the "burns," where we hammer at the rocks which crop out. Within six or seven miles of Girvan there are at least forty good fossilizing spots. The best of them is Woodland Point—an exceedingly rich treasure-house of Silurian fossils. Here many corals may be collected, such as *Heliolites*, *Plasmopora*,

Halysites, Favosites, etc. One common fossil coral is evidently peculiar to this neighbourhood, and has been named by Messrs. Nicholson and Etheridge (who have published a valuable work on the Girvan fossils) *Favosites Mullochensis.* This fossil coral is also common at Mulloch Hill, near Girvan—whence its specific name. Many other fossil corals are obtainable at Mulloch Hill.

The Wenlock limestone at Marloes Bay, Pembrokeshire, contains some good fossil corals. In Ireland, Silurian corals are to be met with in greater or less abundance at Dingle, Bull's Head, Cahercouree, Ardaun, Kilbride, Cong, and Ferriter's Cove.

The neighbourhood of Tortworth, in Somersetshire, has long enjoyed a geological reputation for its fossil corals; Cuttimore's Quarry, perhaps, being the best. The country about Old Radnor abounds with them. The quarries at Mocktree, not far from Ludlow, abound in Silurian fossils generally, and in corals especially; and the student will be delighted with the lovely scenery of the country round about.

I have alluded to the corals of the Devonian rocks. These do not weather out or knock out so readily as the corals from the Silurian and Carboniferous limestones. The interstices of the Devonian corals, as well as their matrices, are filled in with compact sediment, so that we are forced to cut and polish slices to discover their structures and relationships. Very beautiful is a collection of these polished sections, owing to the lovely and variable tints of the limestone, which range from grey to yellow, pink, and red. Thin slices mounted on glass for the microscope form exquisite objects. The student may obtain for himself any quantity of coralliferous rock in and about Torquay. By *moistening* the dried and perhaps worn surface of the rock, the included corals become plainly visible. Devonian corals are also obtained at Plymouth, Teignmouth, and Ilfracombe.

Speaking of British fossil corals, perhaps it would be impossible to direct the student to richer fossiliferous deposits than the lower Carboniferous strata of Scotland. Mr. James Thomson, F.G.S., is of opinion that their abundance in Scotland is due to the strata of the latter having been deposited in shallow water, whilst the English Carboniferous or "Mountain" limestone was laid down in deep water. But the great thickness of the limestone in Derbyshire (about four thousand feet) indicates a depression of the sea-floor all the time the beds were forming; for its mineral characters would have been altered if it had simply filled up an ocean basin to that depth. As we have already seen, a gradually lowered sea-bed has been stated by Darwin to be necessary to continuous coral growth.

Of all the Carboniferous corals the genus *Zaphrentis* is one of the most widely distributed and generally abundant. It is usually found in a very perfect condition, and may often be seen in the walls in limestone countries, so weathered that it stands out in high relief. This coral is not only abundant whereever the Carboniferous limestone occurs in Great Britain, but it is also distributed through the strata

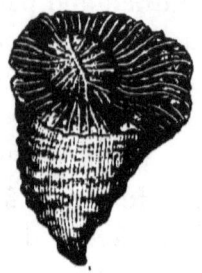

Fig. 64.—Fossil Coral (*Dibunophyllum*).

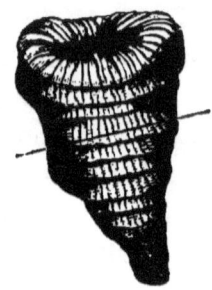

Fig. 65.—*Zaphrentis*.

from the bottom to the top, although the smallest specimens are usually found in the upper beds, and the largest in the lower. The fact that it is plentifully found where *shale* bands occur shows that it affected shallow water, for shale is a muddy deposit. At Swansea *Zaphrentis cylindacea* occurs more than one foot in length, and three and a half inches in diameter.

Fig. 66.—Transverse section of *Zaphrentis*, cut through upper figure at the point traversed by a line.

The genus *Dibunophyllum* (Thomson) differs from *Zaphrentis* in the structure of its calycle or cup. This coral, and other genera such as *Rhodophyllum, Koninckophyllum, Aspidophyllum, Clisiophyllum, Histiophyllum, Cyclophyllum*, are found most abundantly in the lower strata of the Scottish

Carboniferous limestone system. Beith, in Ayrshire, and Dunbar, Haddingtonshire, are capital collecting grounds for all the above-mentioned fossil corals; and I may add that they are in a better state of preservation at Beith than anywhere else in the United Kingdom. *Aspidophyllum* occurs in abundance in the limestone of county Down, Ireland; and in the picturesque, terrace-like outcrops of the Carboniferous limestone strata at Blackhead, county Clare, both this and several other genera of corals are plentiful.

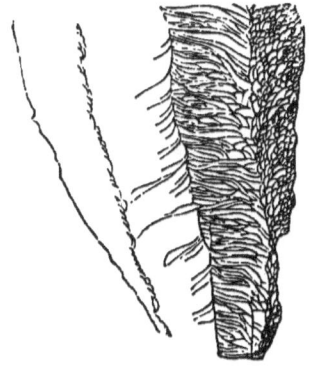
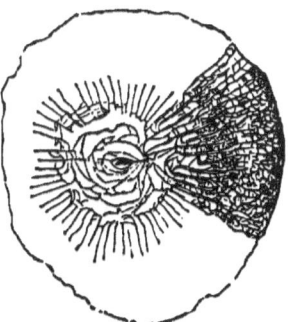

Fig. 67.—Vertical section of fossil Coral (*Koninckophyllum*).

Fig. 68. — Transverse section of fossil Coral (*Koninckophyllum*) in part showing cellular structure.

Lonsdalia (which obtained its name after the early geologist) is another abundant Carboniferous coral. It is very common in the neighbourhood of Mold, and may be extracted from the walls by the roadside in wonderful perfection. The uppermost beds of the fine escarpment of limestone called Eglwyseg at Llangollen, in North Wales, also contain it in large quantities. Indeed, we may regard that stratum as one of the finest Carboniferous coral reefs in Great Britain. There are many species of *Lonsdalia*, of which *rugosa* and *floriformis* are perhaps the most beautiful as well as the most abundant. Both show structure in the clearest manner, and thin sections of them, either transverse or horizontal, form exquisite low-power objects for the microscope. The follow-

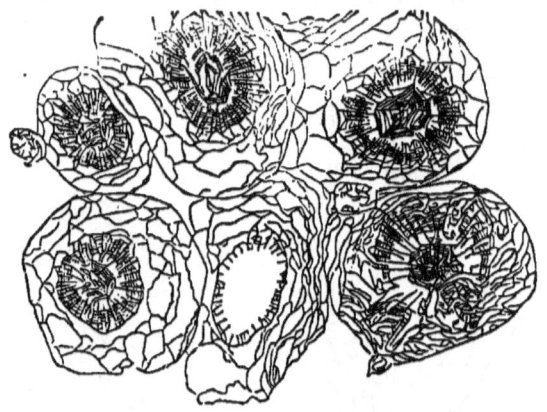

Fig. 63.— Transverse section of *Lonsdalia rugosa*.

ing are among the British localities where different species of *Lonsdalia* may be obtained :—Ecclefechan, (Dumfriesshire), Boghead, Lesmahago, Clifton (near Bristol), almost every part of Derbyshire where the Carboniferous limestone crops up (but particularly near Castleton), and in the Welsh localities above mentioned. At Hafod and Boghead this fossil coral is found in very large masses, in a capital state of preservation.

Lithostrotion (Figs. 42, etc.) is a widely diffused

genus. Carboniferous limestone rock is frequently composed of its dense clusters of corallites, in masses, looking like so many bunches of twigs. *Lithostrotion junceum* is perhaps the commonest species. In Derbyshire *Lithostrotion arachnoideum* forms large masses of the limestone. When these corals weather out, they stand in relief on the stones, as if the latter were covered with dead ivy twigs.

The Carboniferous limestone rising behind the pleasantly situated town of Kendal, in Westmoreland, is rich in corals, *Cyathaxinia* being more abundant there than in any other English locality I know of. For immense variety of corals, however (associated with other fossils), and for the chance of picking up some good, rare, and, it may be, *new* things, commend me to the little quarry which has long been worked in the outlier of Carboniferous limestone at Hafod, about two miles from Corwen, in North Wales. The tourist will easily find it by taking the pretty footpath by the River Dee—just here almost at its best as regards lovely scenery. Having found the quarry, he will be safe for a few hours at the least. There is an abundance of the elegant coral *Phillipsastrea*. If the student's eyes are open, he may read off the story of that ancient coral-reef and its fauna without much fear of drawing false inferences.

Clitheroe is good for all the fossils of the formation I am speaking of; and at Bolland—about four or five miles off, in a very lovely and richly wooded part of the country—there is a classic ground for fossil corals.

The Permian has yielded very few fossil corals. *Chætetes* is said to be found at Humbleton Hill, Durham.

When we geologize on the limestone beds of the Secondary formations we lose sight of the old-fashioned types of coral, whose generic names by this time have become almost as familiar in our mouths as household words, and we are suddenly introduced to new forms. Many of them are very persistent through the Lias and Oolitic rocks, although other kinds are peculiar to the Chalk. Coral-reefs were abundant in British areas during both the Liassic and Oolitic periods, but not when our White Chalk was formed. The latter appears to have been deposited in deeper water than coral-reefs are built in, and we find the Cretaceous corals are therefore usually of single, non-reef-building kinds.

Chief among the genera of the earlier Secondary corals are *Thamnastræa, Latimæandra, Isastræa, Thecosmilia, Montlivaltia, Septastrea, Leptophyllia*, etc. The latter is plentiful in the Lias rocks in the Isle of Skye, associated with *Isastræa*. The number of localities where Lias corals may be obtained is very great. Cowbridge, in Glamorganshire, is one of the best. The visitor to Shakspeare's birthplace at Stratford may hammer them out of the beds at Watford Hill, or find them loosely lying on the surface. Frequently the latter is the best way of getting them, as the shale weathers, and the corals imbedded in it get liberated. At Cherrington, near Shipston-on-Stour, very numerous and fine specimens are picked up off the fields ; *Montlivaltia Victoriæ* (perhaps the largest of our simple fossil corals) is not uncommon. Brocastle, Ewenny, Marton near Gainsborough, Larne near Belfast, Fenny Compton in Oxfordshire, Harbury, Aston-Magna, Down-Hatherley, the neighbourhood of Lyme Regis, Ilminster, etc., are places where Lias corals can be obtained more or less abundantly.

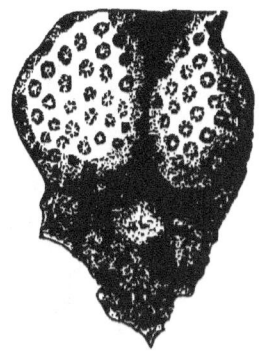

Fig. 70.—*Astrocœnia gibbosa* (Lias, Brocastle).

In the Inferior Oolite at Crickley, East Coker, Painswick, Dundry Hill near Bristol (a splendid fossil hunting-ground for fossils of various sorts), Leckhampton, *Isastræa, Latimæandra, Thamnastræa*, etc., may be found. At Cloughton Wykneare, Scarborough, there is a "Millepore bed"—a stratum of fossil *Polyzoa*, but also containing corals, which extends over a good distance. The quarries in the neighbourhood of Scarborough are famous for Oolitic corals; nowhere else is the characteristic *Thamnastræa concinna* more plentiful, for it sometimes occurs in bands two feet thick, and in lines of nodules which extend over a large area, so that they may be worked by the geologist at Hackness, Ayton (where the best specimens are obtainable), Seamer, Toton, Wykeham, and Brompton—localities which are close together. The *Thamnastræa* is broken up to mend the roads with; and the student will find capital geologizing in the heaps of stone by the roadside, which await parochial relief to break them up and prepare them.

Higher up in Oolitic strata, localities where fossil

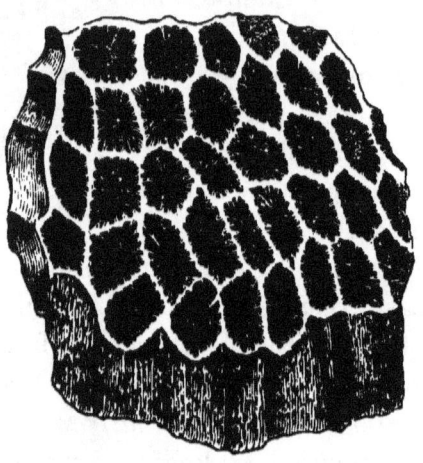

Fig. 71.—*Isastræa insignis* (Lower Lias).

corals can be collected are in the neighbourhood of Cirencester and Bath; at the latter place the rock is frequently full of *Calamophyllia*, resembling petrified straws. The very name of one division of this interesting formation—"the Coral Rag"—indicates how plentiful these kinds of fossils are in it. About fourteen different species, chiefly *Astræidæ*, have been obtained from this bed. Steeple Ashton (in Wiltshire) and Malton (in Yorkshire) are well-known coral collecting grounds. At the former place we

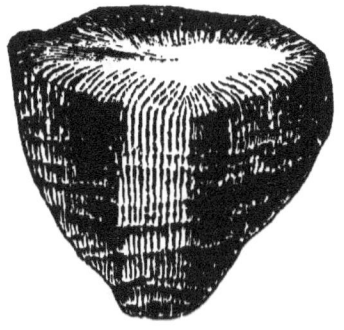

Fig. 72.—*Montlivaltia trochoides* (Inferior Oolite).

Fig. 73.—*Isastræa oblonga* (Portland stone).

get *Thecosmilia annularis*—a fine, branching, shrub-like coral, about two feet high. The Portland stone at Tisbury contains a bed of *Isastræa oblonga*—a lovely coral, completely silicified. When splinters of this are rubbed down to a thin shaving, and then mounted on glass for the microscope, they form exquisite objects,

Fig. 74.—*Thecosmilia annularis* (Coral Rag).

showing every line and trace of the coral structure.

The charming neighbourhood of Stroud is one of the best Oolitic coral-grounds in England; certainly it is so as regards varieties, and perhaps also for numbers of specimens. The student who visits the neighbourhood for the first time will be delighted with the peculiar scenery of the "bottoms," as the deep, narrow valleys are locally called. At Frith Quarry, about two miles from Stroud, we have an ancient "barrier-reef," full of *Thamnastræa, Isastræa, Thecosmilia, Latimæandra*, etc., the species most plentiful being *Thecosmilia gregaria*. On the opposite side of the valley, the hill is crowned with another coral-reef. In places, these beds of corals are nearly twenty feet thick.

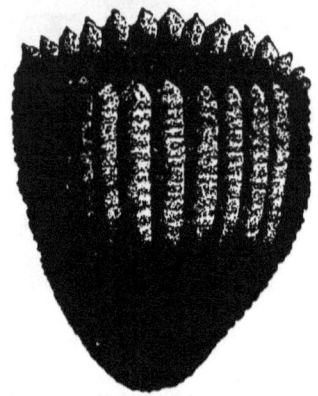

Fig. 75.—*Smilotrochus granulatus* (Gault).

The Cretaceous strata, from the bottom to the top, are distinguished for the numbers of *single* corals. *Smilotrochus, Brachycyathus, Trochocyathus, Leptocyathus*, etc., are characteristic of the Lower Cretaceous, Gault, and Upper Greensand, and are found at Folkestone, East Shalford, Surrey, in the "Bargate stone" near Guildford, Farringdon (where the fossils are very abundant, and in good preservation), Haldon Hill near Exeter, and in the peculiar phosphatized fossils of the Cambridgeshire Greensand. The singular bed of red chalk at Hunstanton, on the Norfolk coast (one of the most charming of quiet seaside resorts, and possessing a neighbourhood full of geological and botanical interest), takes the place of the Gault, but has a few characteristic fossil corals of its own, such as *Micrabacia, Cyclolites, Podoseries,* etc., which are allied to the Madrepores, and are therefore indicative of warm water conditions. *Cyclolites Fittoni* is common in the Gault beds at Folkestone.

Parasmilia, Cælosmilia, Trochosmilia, Caryophyllia, etc., are characteristic of the Upper White Chalk of Britain. The latter coral is plentiful at Dunstable; in the chalk pits near Charlton railway station; and also

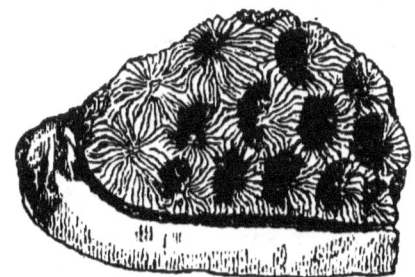

Fig. 76.—*Litharæa*, an Eocene Coral.

near Lewes. *Trochosmilia* is most abundant in the Norwich Chalk, which perhaps occupies the highest strati-geographical position in the Cretaceous system of Great Britain, its fossil corals having an appearance which reminds the geologist of those found in the still later formation of Faxoe, in Denmark. The chalk cliffs at Trimingham, on the Norfolk coast, about fifteen miles from Norwich, contain the same peculiar coral fauna. The corals are frequently found imbedded in flints, and I have specimens in which the silica has retained the impression, if not the structure, of the coral flesh. Many of the Norwich fossil corals have the exteriors coated over with fossil Polyozoa. The best pits for these fossils about Norwich are Mousehold Hill, Thorpe, Postwick, Trowse, and Eaton ; but everywhere in the chalk there is an absence of reef-building species of corals.

The Tertiary rocks of this county are rather poor in corals. We have no positive evidence of coral-reefs, unless the slight appearances seen at Brackleham warrant us in thinking some traces are found there. The railway cutting yields several species, chief among which are three belonging to the genus *Solenastræa*. A large fossil Madrepore favours the reef idea. Other corals met with are *Oculina, Solenastræa, Stylocænia, Astrocænia, Trochocyathus, Dendrophyllia, Litharæa Websteri*. The latter is very common. Other localities are Brook (in the New Forest), Bramsham, and High Cliff (in the Isle of Wight). At Haverstock Hill we get *Leptocyathus, Turbinolia*, etc., from the London Clay ; in the Isle of Sheppey, *Paracyathus* is a not uncommon fossil coral.

We now "take a leap" to the Pliocene beds of Suffolk, where, in the Coralline Crag of Orford, Gedgrave, Sudbourne, and Ramsholt (close to the tidal river Deben), we get *Cryptangia Woodi*, a fine branching coral ; *Flabellum Woodi*, a pretty, wedge-shaped, *single* coral, about an inch in length ; *Spheno-trochus*, etc. The latter is a small single coral, related to a living British species. It is found in great abundance at times, and occurs also in the Red Crag, in the pits at Foxhall and Bentley, near Ipswich; as well as at Felixstowe, Kirton, Bucklesham, Waldringfield, and other places in the neighbourhood of the same town, where it may be found in company with another common coral, *Balanophyllia calyculus*. All of the above places are highly fossiliferous, and most of them are very quaint and quietly picturesque. Students in and near London could not select better localities for geological rambles, and it will only remain for them to stow away the abundance of fossils they meet with; for Eastern Suffolk is little more than a Pliocene sea-bed!

CHAPTER IV.

ENCRINITES.

THERE are no fossils with which the delighted young geologist sooner becomes acquainted than those called *Encrinites.* Especially is this the case if he has worked among the rocks of the Palæozoic period. The limestones of the Silurian, Devonian, and Carboniferous epochs are often crowded with the varied remains of the fossils which half-popularly and half-scientifically come under the denominational name of Encrinites. True, the student frequently has hazy, and even erroneous, notions as to what they really are. But perhaps the most important thing to him is that they are fossils—remains of creatures which actually lived millions of years ago, in seas other than any now existing, and that he has collected them with his own hands. The first flush of geological investigation surrounds these common palæontological objects with a halo of interest which is not eclipsed even by fuller and more accurate knowledge of them. They are the treasured objects of sunny holiday rambles—

rambles which, even after the lapse of years, cannot be remembered without recalling the perfume of the heather, the hum of insects, the glint of sunshine on distant streams, and the shadows cast by cumulous clouds on the brown slopes of sunlit hills!

These Encrinites are often spoken of as *Zoophytes* —a term which, although still in use among naturalists, is a bad one. Encrinites have been loosely grouped among Zoophytes, and so have been regarded

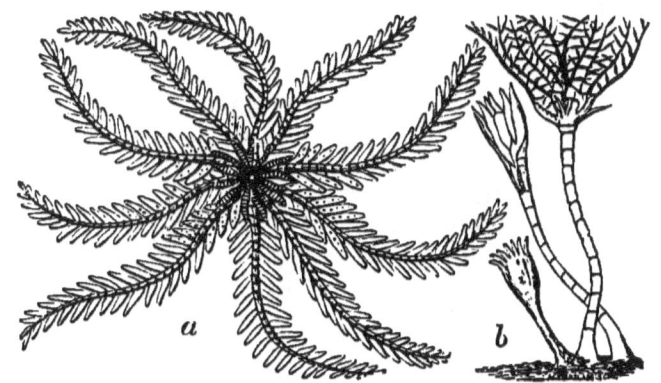

Fig. 77.—Development of the recent Rosy Feather-star (*Antedon rosaceus*): *a*, adult Feather-star; *b*, different stages in growth of the young stalked forms.

with the same degree of haziness. It is a duty, first of all, to *disabuse* the mind of errors, previously to placing before it legitimately deduced facts; therefore I may say that none of the Encrinite family have any or the slightest relationship with plants of any kind. They are most nearly related to such common marine animals—belonging to a group having a world-wide distribution—as the star-fishes and sea-urchins. In short, a living Encrinite is practically *a stalked star-fish.*

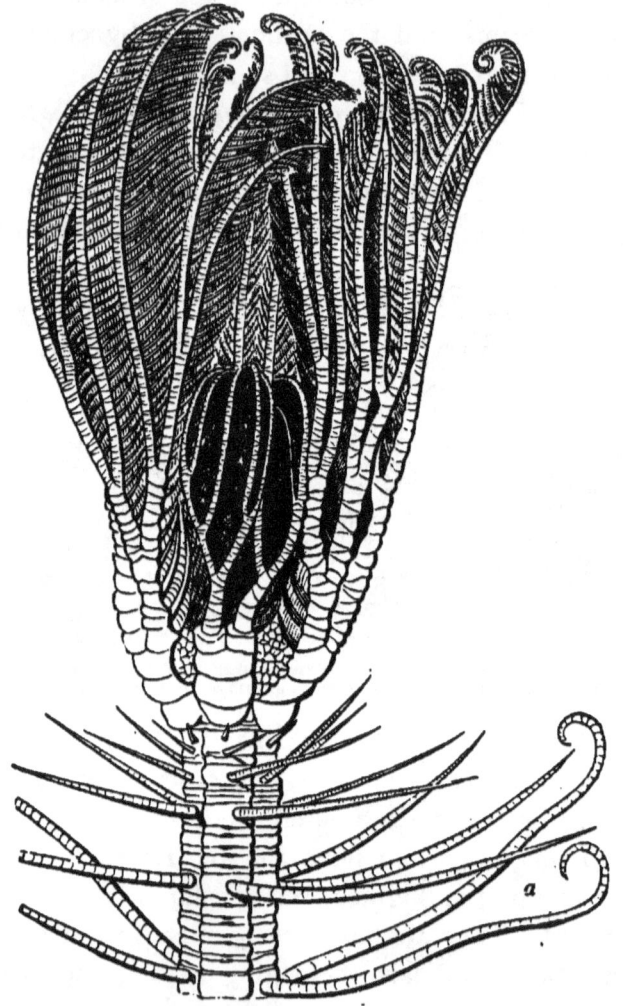

Fig. 78.—Living West Indian Encrinite (*Pentacrinus Caput-Medusæ*) (magnified).

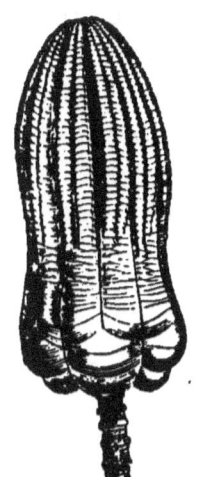
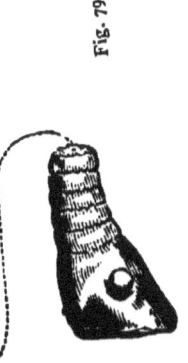

Fig. 79.—Triassic Encrinite (*Encrinus moniliformis*), found in the Muschelkalk of Germany.

Fig. 80.—Nave Encrinite (*Actinocrinus triacontadactylus*) (Carboniferous limestone formation).

At first sight it seems strange to associate the stemmed and jointed Encrinites with animals having the power of locomotion. Perhaps the fact that Encrinites were all fastened to one spot by means of a jointed stem (just as a flower is by its stalk), makes it difficult for the young geological student to under-

Fig. 81.—Recent Australian Feather-star (*Comatula adonæ*) (three-quarters natural size).

stand they are not Zoophytes, or "plant-animals." Then, again, the manner in which the feathered arms fold up against the body, just like the petals of a tulip when at rest; and the flower-like aspect resulting from this habit; the names attached to *parts* of

Encrinites, such as "stem," "calyx," etc. ;—all are apt to still further magnify the error with which the beginner starts, of imagining that the Encrinites

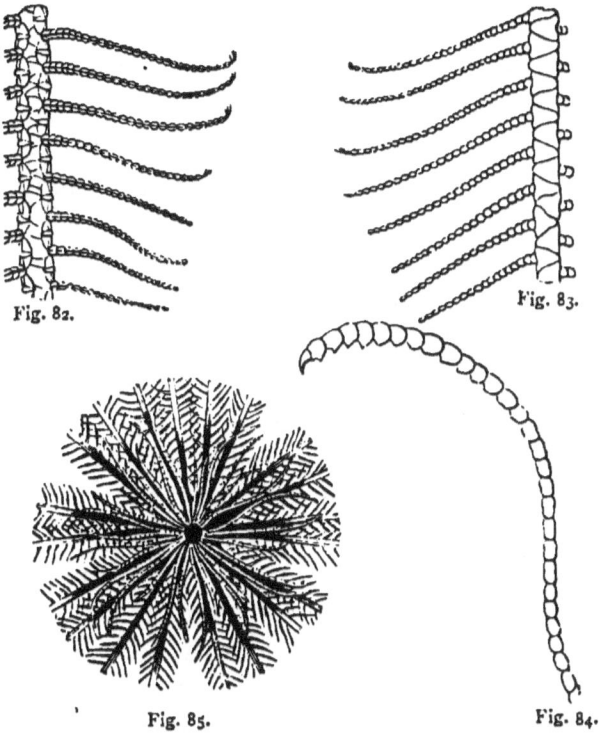

Fig. 82.
Fig. 83.
Fig. 85.
Fig. 84.

Figs. 82 and 83.—Portions of arms of *Comatula*, showing joints or ossicles (magnified).
Fig. 84.—One of the rays of arms of the *Comatula*, showing terminal hook (magnified).
Fig. 85.—*Comatula* (reduced).

have certain actual relation to plants which other marine animals do not possess.

This is entirely wrong : an elephant or a lion is

not more distinctively an animal than any species of Encrinite is, no matter what shape the latter may assume. But the history of Encrinites has been involved in a good deal of obscurity, from which it is now emerging. This was partly due to the fact that, a few years ago, few or no *real* Encrinites were known to be in existence, and none had been thoroughly dissected. The dredging expeditions of Carpenter, Wyville Thomson, and others brought to light several species. One called *Rhizocrinus lofotenesis*, found living in the deeper parts of the sea, between the extreme north of Scotland and Iceland, belongs perhaps to the same genus as that found fossil in our chalk strata. This recently discovered genus of living Crinoids has been well examined, and much light has consequently been thrown upon the structures of fossil Encrinites of all ages.

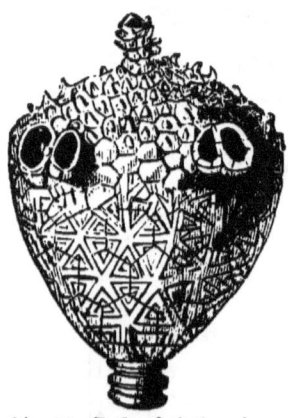

Fig. 86.—Body of *Actinocrinus*, showing proboscidal anus on summit, and articulating places of the arms.

Cuvier, and many naturalists after him, including even Agassiz, grouped the Encrinites among that hodge-podge of marine objects called *Radiata*. This term was about as expressive of any real facts, or mutual relationships, as the names of the orders and classes of plants under the Linnæan system of botany were to the plants themselves. The order *Radiata* was a kind of zoological "lumber-room," into which all kinds of little-understood creatures were thrust if they had radiating organs around the mouth; or even if the body itself was of a stellate or radiated shape, as in the case of the star-fishes. The *Radiata* is no longer used by modern naturalists, and most of the animals, living and extinct, formerly grouped under

Fig. 87.—American Feather-star (*Euryale costosa*).

that name, have been assigned to distinctive and clearly understood groups.

Thus all the spiny-skinned animals (*Echinodermata*) are now included in the sub-kingdom *Echinozoa*, formerly known as *Annuloida*, or "ring-like" animals. All are internally related (although their external

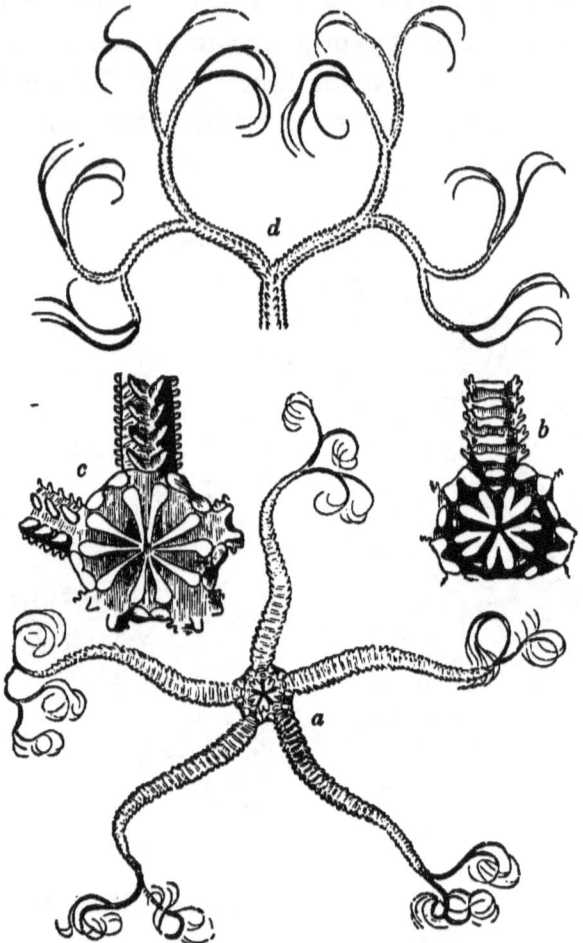

Fig. 88.—*Euryale palmifera*, showing at *b*, disk and part of arm (front view); *c*, ditto (back view); *d*, extremities of arms.

shapes may be different) by the possession of a peculiar

apparatus called the "water-vascular system." In the sea-urchins and common star-fishes this highly developed hydraulic machinery is immediately applied to locomotive purposes, and these creatures are thereby enabled to move about over the sea-floor. In the crinoids, the water-vascular system is also employed for respiratory purposes. But, even in the *shapes* of the *Echinodermata*, varied though they be, we pass very naturally from one type to another. Thus, we might begin with *living* Encrinites, such as the

Fig. 89.—Body, or centre, of *Euryale costosa* (back view).

Rhizocrinus of northern seas; the rare and beautiful *Pentacrinus Caput-Medusæ* of West Indian seas, nearly related to the abundant species (*P. briareus*) found in the Lias; and the little *Pentacrinus Europæus*, occasionally dredged up in quiet spots off the southern coasts of Ireland. The latter has a jointed stem, and is usually attached to Sertularians. It is now known to be only the *larval* stage of the common Feather-star (*Antedon* or *Comatula rosea*). The latter may be dredged up in immense quantities in the quieter parts

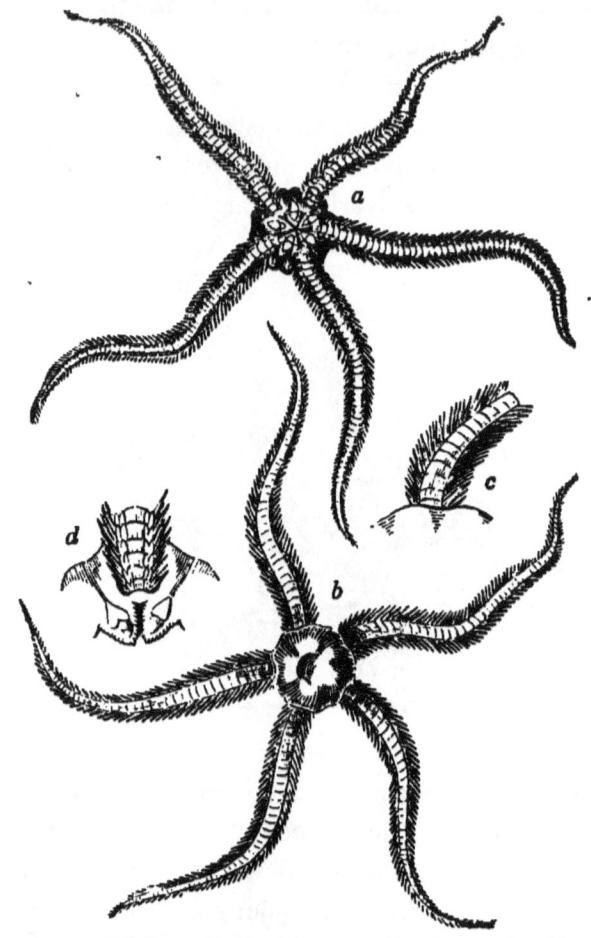

Fig. 90.—Common Brittle-star (*Ophiura granulata*), showing affinities with *Euryale palmifera*: *a*, front view; *b*, back view; *c* and *d*, magnified portions of arms.

of our sea-beds, but particularly in the Irish Sea, and

the bottoms of the salt-water lochs which indent the western coasts of Scotland. The *Comatula* is nearly related to another free-moving Echinoderm, the *Euryale*, a genus which has a very large geographical distribution. One living species of *Euryale*, called *palmifera* (Fig. 88), is evidently nearly related to the common brittle-stars (*Ophiuridæ*), which do not possess the ordinary water-vascular system, and are covered with rows of limy plates. The commonest of our British species is *Ophiura granulata* (Fig. 90). Thus we may pass, as regards their external forms, from true living crinoids, stalked and jointed, to others which are Crinoids only during the earlier part of their lives; thence to free-crawling *Comatulas* and *Euryales*, and through the latter to the brittle-stars. This remarkable relationship is still further indicated by the external limy plates which cover or otherwise enter into the structure of Crinoid, Feather-star, Euryale, and Brittle-star alike. A similar blending of the external shapes of allied forms may be seen in another large group of *Echinodermata*—the starfishes and sea-urchins. Thus, beginning with *Asterias* (noted for the body and arms being covered with limy plates), we pass on to the Cushion-stars, where the arms appear to have been stretched along their sides till they have grown together. Thence we pass by such forms as *Scutella* and *Spatangus*, until we come to the true and abundant sea-urchins (*Echinus*), so that the wide space between the Encri-

110 *OUR COMMON BRITISH FOSSILS.*

nites and the sea-urchins is bridged over by a large number of intermediate generic forms. Still more

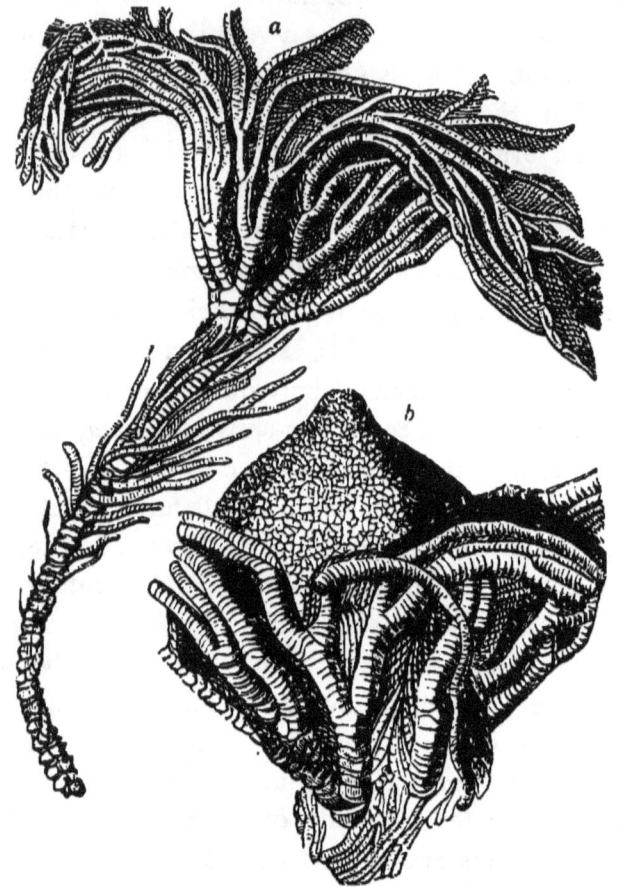

Fig. 91.—*Pentacrinus briareus:* a, common Liassic Encrinite; b, upper surface of body.

remarkable is the fact illustrated by Haeckel and others, that the young of all the Echinoderms, like

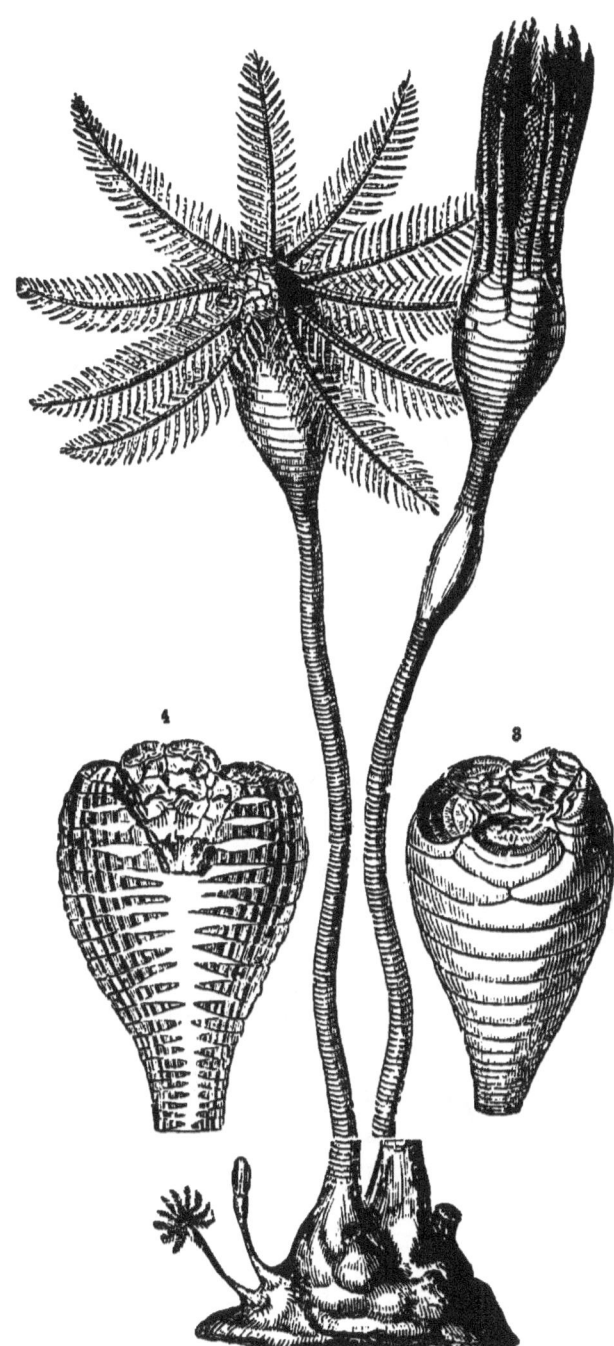

Fig. 92.—Pear Encrinite (*Apiocrinites rotundus*), from the Oolite formation, Bradford, near Bath: 3, body, or pelvis; 4, vertical section of ditto, showing stomach.

those of Crustaceas, are so alike that it is difficult to tell one from another. All commence life as free-swimming, worm-like larvæ.

The relationship between the Crinoids (or Encrinites) and the other leading members of *Echinodermata* is undoubtedly bound still more nearly together by the intercalence of several extinct groups. Thus the two extinct orders, *Cystidea* and *Blastoidea*, were in some degree intermediate between Encrinites and sea-urchins, in a manner that we have now no living examples of. The Tortoise-Encrinites of the Chalk (*Marsupites*), and the *Saccosoma* of the Oolite (most probably allied to the Feather-stars), are deeply interesting, inasmuch as they are stalkless fossil Encrinites.

If we consider the body and arms of an Encrinite, of any species, as a kind of star-fish attached to a jointed stalk, then the base of the Encrinite's body is called the "pelvis;" the mouth is uppermost, surrounded by the feathered arms—a position just the *reverse* of that which would be assumed by a star-fish, for the latter, in crawling over the sea-floor, has the mouth downwards. Both mouth and anus are usually present on the upper surface of the body of a Crinoid, the anus often terminating in a nipple-shaped protuberance. In the most ancient crinoids there seems to have been a difference from the structure seen in their *living* representatives. If we carefully examine the arms of recent Crinoids, we see they are *furrowed* on the upper surface. Both the arms and the pinnæ which give to them such a feathered appearance are formed of an immense number of limy joints. (In the extinct *Pentacrinus briareus*, found so abundantly in the Lias near Whitby, it is estimated that no fewer than one hundred and fifty thousand joints are employed in the construction of the five pinnated arms of one individual!) All are alike grooved on their upper surface, and thus we have channels or gutters running over every part of the upper surface of each arm. All this was covered, when the Encrinite was alive, by membrane and muscles, which kept the ossicles together. The membrane was covered with thousands of minute cilia. The latter were movable, and formed a motive machinery much in use among all kinds of the lower forms of aquatic animal life. The consequence of the general action of these vibratile cilia over the entire upper surface of the arms of the Encrinites was, that currents of water bearing food were constantly being deflected down the bases of the five arms. The main grooves of these were continued over the *surface* of the body of the Encrinite, and all converged towards the mouth, which was thus supplied with fresh food and fresh water.

In the Palæozoic Crinoids the arms are grooved above, but the grooves terminate at their bases, and do not continue over the surface of the body as just described. Instead they open into tunnels or channels which are excavated, so to speak, in the under-surface of the limy plates, and thus reach the mouth of the Encrinite *beneath* the plates, instead of from above. The arms of Encrinites are not hollow, as is sometimes supposed, but formed of solid joints, or *ossicles* as they are scientifically called. The joints of the stem, on the contrary, have a cavity running down their middle, of various shapes, sometimes round, and frequently five-petal shaped. This continuous hollow was formerly believed to be the alimentary canal, but the notion is now considerably modified. The joints of the stems of all species of Encrinites are either grooved or toothed along their margins. In this way they were firmly interlocked, and yet were capable of such free movement that there is no doubt the whole encrinital structure was swayed about by the tides and currents as freely as any of our large-rooted seaweeds. From what I have said as to the pinnated arms of Crinoids, it will be seen that the old notion of their being so many nets in which to catch organic waifs and strays, is not correct. In comparison with the size of the entire structure the stomach is wonderfully small, and enclosed in the large and densely plated body. Some of the Carboniferous Encrinites must have had stems of enormous length, judging from the strength and diameter of the joints. In the Yoredale shales of the valleys running from Hebden Bridge to Halifax, in Yorkshire, I have obtained connected stems of

Encrinites six or eight feet in length, the ossicles of which were not a fourth part the diameter of those abundantly met with in the Carboniferous limestones of Derbyshire.

Having briefly considered the general zoological structures and natural history habits of the *Encrinites*, both recent and fossil, let us now turn to their distribution in the various geological formations. They are by far the most abundant in the Primary rocks, although they range upwards into the Secondary strata, and frequently occur there in very large numbers. But their distribution in the Primary rocks is more general and abundant, and the types, or generic forms, are more numerous than we find them in the Secondary strata. Indeed, many of the limestones of the Silurian, Devonian, and especially of the Carboniferous formations, are largely, if not chiefly, built up of encrinital remains. As limestones are always indicative of what sailors call " blue water "— that is, water free from any muddy sediment and perfectly clear—it follows that such conditions must have favoured the growth of Encrinites. In this respect they were nearly related to the habits of reef-building corals, to whom muddy water is an abomination and sure death. A sudden surcharge of sea-water with mud brought down by rivers will almost immediately kill off millions of living coral polypes. And from what we learn of the Stony Record, the same thing happened in geological times to the immense groves of

Encrinites which sometimes for scores, if not hundreds, of square miles together, covered the ancient sea-beds. In the clay bands often intercalated in the Silurian and other limestones, we have frequent geological evidence of how large numbers of young Encrinites were killed by the muddied water, and eventually buried in the muddy sediments which had first destroyed them. The same is often true of the fine clayey shales of the Yoredale beds of Lancashire and Yorkshire, where entire specimens, stems, heads, and fingers, of frail but lengthy-stalked Encrinites are to be disentombed in the most perfect condition. The best place I know of, where these encrinital remains are to be found in the Yoredale series, may easily be discovered by following the bed of the river from Hebden Bridge, in Yorkshire, towards High Green Wood. The Yoredale shales crop out in cleanly cut sections, owing to the river frequently denuding them along the lines of natural joints. The geological student will there find strewn about, huge cubical blocks of thin dark shale, crowded with fossils, such as *Goniatites, Orthoceratites, Nautili,* and encrinital remains. He can while away many a pleasant hour in these secluded but exceedingly picturesque places, with the murmur of the stream in his ears, and the most picturesque hilly scenery ready to greet his eyes, whenever he thinks proper to turn them away from the absorbing employment of laying open, layer after layer, like the pages of a book, the thin laminæ of the shale-blocks he is working upon. These are verily written "within and without;" and the iron sulphite into which nearly all the organic remains of these beds have been converted, makes them look as if they had been electrotyped on the surfaces of the black shales.

At Bradford, near Bath, we have numerous Encrinites occurring in clayey rocks instead of in limestone, their usual storehouse. This clay (sixty feet thick) is in the Oolitic formation, and proves

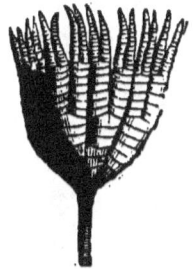
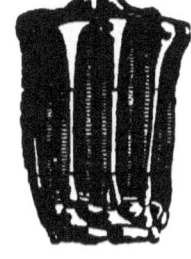

Fig. 93.—Head of *Ichthyocrinus*, an American Silurian genus of Crinoids.

Fig. 94.—Head of *Eucalyptocrinus*, a Devonian Encrinite.

exactly the same conclusion we have drawn from the Encrinites buried in the Primary rocks, namely, that muddy sediments always kill them off and bury them where they are. In the hard slates (formerly *shales*) of the Upper Silurian formation, about a couple of miles from Llangollen, in North Wales, the student may find some beautiful specimens of the characteristic Upper Silurian Encrinite known as *Actinocrinus pulcher*. Well does it deserve its specific name, for no Encrinite exceeds it in gracefulness of shape. At the slate quarries visible on the hillside, as we walk towards Val Crucis Abbey, there is an abundance of these fossil Encrinites; and although all the structure of the fossils has been completely altered since they were alive, and they are now really in the condition of natural casts, nobody will deny their beauty. I have seen slabs of six feet in length completely

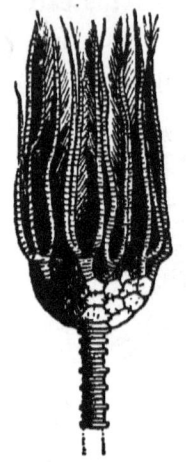
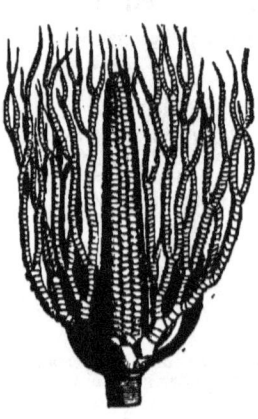

Fig. 95.—*Actinocrinus triacontadactylus*, a Carboniferous limestone genus.

Fig. 96.—Head of *Taxocrinus* (Devonian).

crowded with these Encrinites, roots, stems, and heads, just as they grew, looking for all the world like a fossil tulip-bed!

Again, what geological student who has made a pilgrimage through the Peak district of Derbyshire has not had his attention called to the "Encrinital limestone," as everybody calls the rock, which is so completely filled, or rather made up of Encrinite stems, that we sometimes find nothing else? "Screw-stones," the country folk call some of them—that name being given in reality to those siliceous casts of encrinital stems which occur abundantly in the

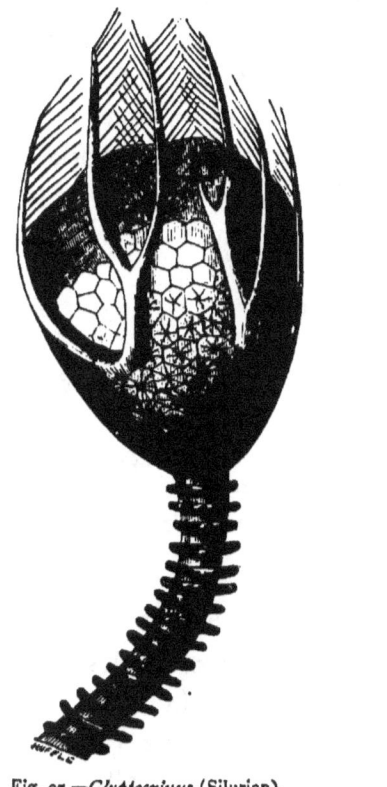

Fig. 97.—*Glyptocrinus* (Silurian).

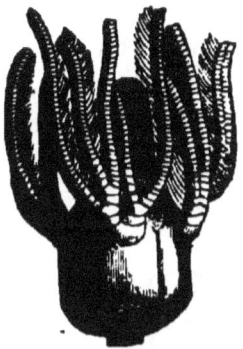

Fig. 98.—*Platycrinus trigintidactylus* (Carboniferous limestone).

Fig. 99.—Head of *Actinocrinus cuspidatus* (Carboniferous limestone).

chert-bands, where the original limy matter of the *ossicles* (or individual joints of the stems) has been dissolved away, leaving only thin plates of flinty material, such as was deposited between the joints, so arranged around the filled-up hollow of the so-called "alimentary" canal down the whole length of the stem, as to give it the appearance of the screwed end of a bolt. For mile after mile the geologist walks along the Derbyshire mountain roads and finds the stone walls on either hand composed of little else than encrinital remains. Sometimes the rock containing them is very hard, and then it will be worked as marble; which, when polished, is used for mantelpieces. Many of my readers must be acquainted

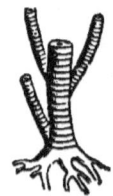

Fig. 100.—Head of *Rhodocrinus* (Carboniferous limestone).

Fig. 101.—Lower part of stem of Encrinite, showing mode of attachment to sea-bottom.

Fig. 102.—*Cupressocrinus*

with this polished grey marble, full of all sorts of objects, but especially of these Encrinite stems, cut across, lengthwise, or at all kinds of angles, so that the appearance varies with each individual fossil. When the limy matrix is quite black (as it is at Ashford, near Bakewell), the marble is all the more valuable for economic purposes, for the white fossils then stand out in splendid distinctness from the jet-black stone in which they are imbedded. The stones of the mountain roads are usually picked off the surface where the limestone rocks have been most weathered. And, as the structure of most fossils imbedded in limestones is such that they are harder

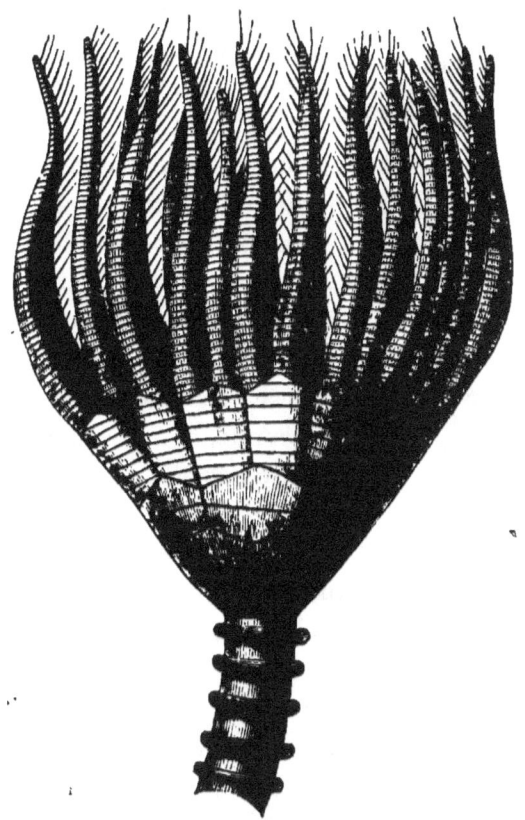

Fig. 103.—*Woodocrinus macrodactylus.*

than the limestone itself, it follows that when surface weathering has gone on for some time, the fossils stand out in relief. Millions of Encrinite stems may be found thus dispersed over the surfaces of the Carboniferous limestone whose fragments are used for wall-building. In Clitheroe, Lancashire, at a small elevation known as Salt Hill, the rock is built up of Encrinite stems. In this case, however, the fossils are loose and incoherent, stems and ossicles lying together almost uncemented by any matrix, or by one which speedily weathers and liberates the fossils. The consequence is that joints and short stems of Encrinites are so loose and abundant that they are procured as a kind of limy gravel to mend or make garden paths with!

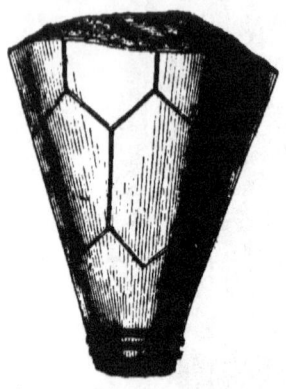

Fig. 104.—Head of *Poteriocrinus*.

Some of these abundant Encrinite stems in Derbyshire are often more than one inch in diameter. One species, known as *Poteriocrinus crassus*, was the most widespread and abundant of all the Carboniferous Crinoids. The head, or body of the Encrinite, was tapering, and in this respect it resembled the singular little *Rhizocrinus lofotensis* brought up from the bottom of the North Sea, in the living state, by Messrs. Carpenter and Wyville Thomson during one of their earlier dredging expeditions. This *Rhizocrinus* is one of the last survivors of a once cosmopolitan race of animals, now all but extinct, whose functions seem to be usurped by modern members of the sea-urchin family. Stems, and sometimes small heads, and the joints of the arms of an Encrinite

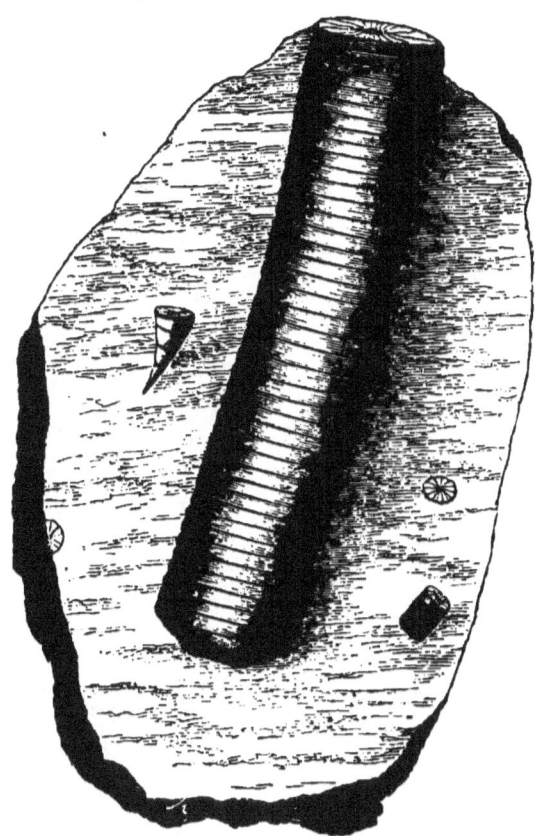

Fig. 105.—Stem of Encrinite most abundant in Carboniferous limestone (*Poteriocrinus crassus*).

nearly allied to the living *Rhizocrinus*, and almost as small as it, are frequently found in the Chalk, and especially on the *surfaces* of the flint nodules imbedded in the Chalk, in the neighbourhood of Norwich.

Glyptocrinus basalis is common almost everywhere in the Silurian rocks, but especially so in those of Wales. At Mynydd Fronfrys, about two or three

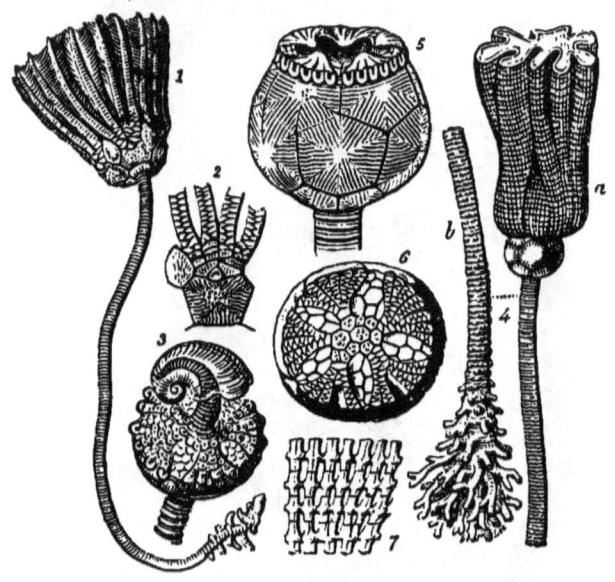

Fig. 106.—Fossil Encrinites found in the Wenlock limestone (Silurian). 1. *Marsupiocrinites cœlatus*; 2, base of arms of ditto (magnified); 3, proboscis of ditto inserted in fossil shell of *Acroculia haliotis*; 4, *Crotalocrinus rugosus* (reduced in size); 5, pelvis of ditto (natural size); 6, flat stomach surface of pelvis showing bases of the arms; 7, portion of the reticulated fingers of 4*a*, showing their anchylosation. (After Symonds.)

miles from Llangollen, large numbers of the remains of this fossil may be found associated with those of other common Silurian Crinoids. The generic name of *Glyptocrinus* (signifying " sculptured ") is in allusion to the highly ornamented basal plates of the body or pelvis. *Crotalocrinus* has the first part of its name derived from a Greek word signifying a "child's rattle," on account of its peculiar shape and appearance. The arms commence at the top of the body, and as the joints or *ossicles* are fastened to each other sidewise, as well as vertically, the arms have a subdivision resembling the meshes of a net, or the basketwork of a child's penny rattle. When portions of these arms are found, as they frequently are, on the surfaces of the Wenlock and Dudley limestones, they look like fossil *Polyzoa* or "sea-mats," and are frequently mistaken by young geological students for such. Another Silurian genus of Encrinites, called *Anthocrinus* from its flower-like appearance, has its arms subdivided, something after the fashion of those of the *Crotalocrinus*.

Periechocrinus, *Rhodocrinus*, *Taxocrinus*, and *Poteriocrinus* are other common Silurian genera, nearly always found in the various limestones of that formation. *Rhodocrinus*, or the "Rose Encrinite," ranges upwards in the Primary rocks to the Carboniferous limestone, in which it is found in and about Clitheroe, in Lancashire. The joints of its column may be known by the five-sided hole running through the middle. On examining the weathered surfaces of the Silurian limestones in the neighbourhood of Wenlock or Dudley, the student will often find splendid, sometimes perfect, specimens of one or another of the above-mentioned Crinoids. *Glypto-*

crinus appears to be most abundant in the Caradoc beds, and may usually be found where they are well exposed.

In the neighbourhood of Newton Abbot, Torquay, and elsewhere, where the Devonian limestones crop out, remains of Encrinites peculiar to this formation in their specific character, may be found, although not abundantly. It would seem as if corals, having pretty much the same marine habits as Encrinites, competed with them. Hence, as a rule, wherever fossil corals are very abundant, Encrinites are scarce; and contrariwise. This is markedly the case with the Devonian limestones of England, where fossil corals are very abundant, and Encrinites comparatively rare, except in certain localities. In the Eifel Mountains, the Crinoid family is better represented. One of the few characteristic genera is *Cupressocrinus*, or "Cypress" Encrinite; *Haplocrinus* is another. *Platycrinus*, a genus very abundant in the Carboniferous limestone, makes its first appearance in the Devonian strata. Its stem is a little flattered or lenticular, instead of being round, as is usually the case with Palæozoic Crinoids. The former part of its generic name signifies "breadth," on account of the basal and radial plates of the body being unusually broad in comparison with those of other Encrinites.

The Carboniferous limestone is undoubtedly the metropolis of the Crinoids. During its deposition in Europe, the number of genera and species reached its maximum. They were never so numerous before; they have gradually been dwindling away ever since, until our own epoch seems to be that when their final extinction will occur. Besides *Rhodocrinus, Platycrinus,* and *Poteriocrinus* (already referred to), we have the remains of such genera as *Actinocrinus, Cyathocrinus, Gilbertocrinus, Taxocrinus, Woodocrinus,* etc. Sometimes, as in the neighbourhood of Clitheroe, Lancashire, we get limestone seams composed of *heads* of Encrinites, just as elsewhere we get beds formed of their stems and arms. *Cyathocrinus, Actinocrinus, Platycrinus,* and *Poteriocrinus* are the commonest of Carboniferous genera, the latter being profusely abundant in Ireland and Scotland, as well as in every part of England where the Mountain or Carboniferous limestone appears. *Actinocrinus* is an abundant fossil in places; its name of " radiated " Encrinite being due to the thorn-like side-arms, which project, at irregular distances, from the main column. *Woodocrinus* was named after the late Mr. Edward Wood, of Richmond, in Yorkshire, its original discoverer. Although not a very widely distributed fossil, it occurs in large quantities and in great perfection in the Carboniferous limestone at Richmond, whence most of the finest specimens seen in private and public collections were obtained; thanks to the generosity of Mr. Wood, who worked a small quarry for the sole purpose of obtaining specimens to give away to his friends.

The Secondary Encrinites are mainly distinguished from those of the Primary rocks by the fact that the grooves in the arms are not arched over, but are continued over the central or upper surfaces. In England, the only member of the New Red Sandstone which yields fossil Encrinites—the Muschelkalk—is absent. In Germany, especially in the hilly country about Jena, where the Muschelkalk limestone crops out, the well-known "Lily Encrinite" (*Encrinus moniliformis*), (Fig. 79), abounds. In our Liassic and Oolitic rocks, Crinoids are sometimes very common. This is notably the case in the shales of the Lias about Whitby and at Lyme Regis, where several species of the beautiful *Pentacrinus* occur profusely. The heads and the wonderfully complex arms, which must have expanded like a living net when the animals were alive, are preserved in the greatest perfection, and are frequently converted into iron pyrites. The joints of the stems have long been known under the name of "St. Cuthbert's Beads," and, as such, Sir Walter Scott alludes to them in his "Marmion." In the Oolite we have such genera as *Millerocrinus* and *Apiocrinus*, the latter perhaps better known as the "Pear Encrinite." In the Bradford Clay, near Bath, the thick seam often swarms with joints and detached plates of the body, so that the student may here obtain material enough to exercise his ingenuity in reconstructing afresh the entire organism. The Apiocrinites were usually fixed to some hard body by means of the base of the column being spread out, something after the way in which such limy sea-weeds as the *Corallina officinalis* attach themselves to the sea-bed.

Species of Crinoids belonging to the genus *Bourgetocrinus* (allied to the living *Rhizocrinus*) occur rather scantily in the Chalk, although I have found them sometimes plentifully at Norwich, Guildford, and near Lewes. Both *Apiocrinites* and *Marsupites* are tolerably common in the Chalk at Margate, at the base of the cliffs. In some places in the London Clay, as at Witham, in Essex, joints of Encrinites allied to the *Pentacrinites*, now common in West Indian seas, are found. We have already seen the relationship which the Crinoids bear to the starfishes, through such forms as *Euryale* and *Comatula*. In like manner they are related to the sea-urchins through such fossil forms as the *Saccosoma* of the Oolite, and the *Marsupites* of the Chalk.

CHAPTER V.

FOSSIL STAR-FISHES AND SEA-URCHINS.

LET me next call attention to the commonest fossils belonging to the Star-fish and Sea-urchin family. Few fossils have a more attractive aspect than they, and none exceed them in the singular beauty of their structures, and their marvellous adaptation to their ancient habits of life.

Now that we have got rid of the useless term *Radiata* and are beginning to arrange animals in their natural relationship to each other, we have learned comparative zoology. To this most interesting study the whole science of palæontology—or that which deals with the extinct life of our globe—contributes equally with zoology. In surveying such a large natural group as that formed by the annuloid animals, we are frequently surprised by the singular way in which otherwise extreme types spring from almost common or neutral ground. Thus, the extinct groups of Cystideans and Pentremites, peculiar to the Palæozoic rocks, and which severally represent two different orders, in some measure come as near to the Encrinite family on one side, as the Pouch Encrinite (*Marsupites*) of the Chalk formation does both to them and the Echini on the other. The Cushion-stars (Goniasters) run very near to the Cake-urchins or Clypeasters, although the former are star-fishes and the latter sea-urchins, and perhaps both these touch as nearly as any of their class to the Cystideans, Pentremites, and Marsupites. In America, a genus of fossils called *Agelacrinus* connects Star-fishes with the Cystideans.

Fig. 107.—Extinct kind of Free Crinoid (*Marsupites Milleri*), from White Chalk.

Both star-fishes and sea-urchins are, geologically speaking, very ancient marine animals. With the exception of certain Brachiopoda, no other groups of animals have maintained their peculiar shapes for a longer time than the star-fishes. As far back as the Cambrian period we find two well-differentiated orders in existence, one represented by our modern "five-fingers" (*Uraster*) and the other by the brittle-stars (*Ophiura*). Evidently these two types have been in existence throughout all the silent revolutions, physical and biological, which have taken place on the surface of the globe; and our modern star-fishes are as lineal and directly uninterrupted descendants of these early Cambrian fossil forms, as mankind from their "first parents."

The upper part of the skin of such star-fishes as the "five-fingers" (*Uraster rubens*) is thickened and roughened by the presence of grains or irregular spicules of carbonate of lime. If these grains had gone on increasing in size by addition to their margins, they would have grown until they touched each

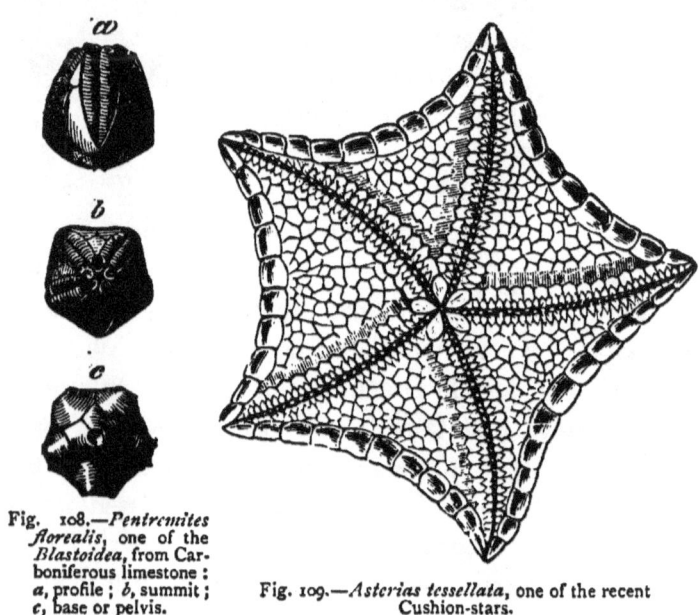

Fig. 108.—*Pentremites florealis*, one of the Blastoidea, from Carboniferous limestone: *a*, profile; *b*, summit; *c*, base or pelvis.

Fig. 109.—*Asterias tessellata*, one of the recent Cushion-stars.

other, but would not have fused, and then we should have had regular plates instead of grains, and the whole body would have been covered by a kind of tessellated pavement. This is how the arms of the brittle-stars (*Ophiuridea*) and the margins of the arms and body of the cushion-stars (Goniaster and Asterias) have been so regularly and beautifully jointed, the former even more effectually than a mediæval mail-clad knight. The two groups so anciently separated are easily recognized. Thus the "five-fingers" and "sun-stars" (Solasters) so abundant on our British coasts have the under surfaces of their arms grooved. In and out of these grooves we perceive rows of small, white, grub-like objects, which slowly wriggle

Fig. 110.—Recent "Five-finger" Star-fish (*Uraster rubens*).

to and fro if we turn a star-fish on its back, and finally end by bending over and attaching their tips to the ground by means of suckers. Then by a united exertion they pull over the star-fish to its proper position. A young observer has not long to experiment on living star-fishes before he finds that these grub-like objects serve all the purposes of feet—that the star-fishes can glide along even perpendicular surfaces by their means. They are hundreds in number, but all are fashioned alike, and the mechanism which renders them locomotive organs is of the most wonderful character. These feet are termed by naturalists ambulacral, but I defer a detailed description of them until we come to speak of the sea-urchins. The stomach of this kind of star-fish is continued up each arm, and this fact naturally groups

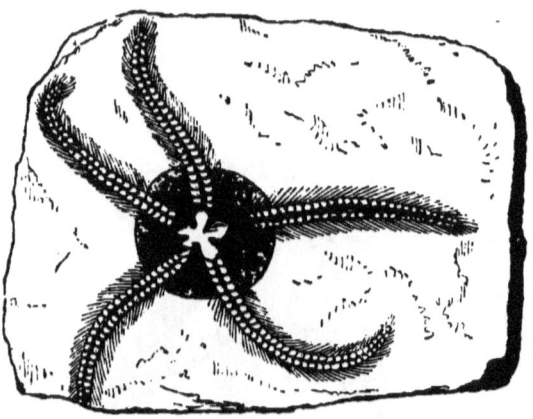

Fig. 111.—Fossil " Brittle Star-" fish (*Protaster Miltoni*) (Upper Ludlow rocks, Leintwardine).

together genera which may have a greater number of arms than five, and the "sun-stars" (Solaster), which have twelve.

In the "brittle-stars" (*Ophiuridea*), on the contrary, the stomach does not extend up the arms, although the nervous branches of the ganglion surrounding the mouth do. The "sun-stars" have only *two* rows of suckers, whilst the "five-fingers" possess *four.* In the "brittle-stars" we have the central disc covered with jointed calcareous plates, and the arms defended by four rows of the same. There are sucking feet, however, but the arms are chiefly employed as

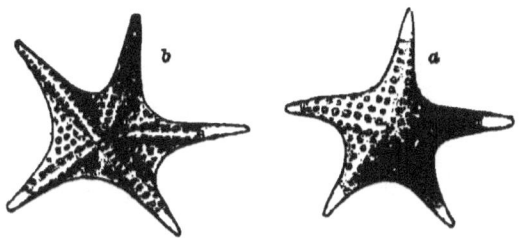

Fig. 112.—Fossil Star-fish allied to the modern (*Palæasterina primæva*): *a*, upper surface; *b*, lower surface (Ludlow rocks).

organs of locomotion, in which they are aided by short hooks. The latter take hold of the surface and thus obviate the necessity of sucking-feet. Nature has usually more than one way of meeting a difficulty, and this is a case in point with the progression of the star-fishes.

Many star-fishes are characteristically deep-sea animals, and perhaps the *Echinodermata*, to which both star-fishes and sea-urchins belong, range to and continue over deep parts of the ocean-bed, more than any other group of marine animals. Thus, during the deep-sea dredgings of the *Challenger*, such genera as *Ophiomusium*, *Archaster*, etc., were dredged up, the latter from more than a mile and a half depth of

Fig. 113.—*Asterias* (recent).

sea-water. A large star-fish, called Leptychaster, allied to our Luidia, was brought up off Cape Maclear, Kerguelen's Island, in very deep water. Another genus, *Hymenaster*, was found widely distributed over the sea-floor, and at depths ranging from about half a mile to more than three miles. Starfishes and their allies, the sea-urchins, are usually the commonest fossils of the Chalk formation, which was an oceanic deposit formed under similar circumstances to the "globigerina ooze" of the Atlantic. Dr. Wallich showed (when sounding in the *Bull Dog* for the first Atlantic cable) that the ocean floor was occupied by star-fishes, for these animals came up attached to the sounding-lead, and this incident first broke people's faith in the old-received notion that absence of light in the deep sea rendered it a desert for all animals except the Protozoa.

Fig. 114.—Fossil Star-fish (*Palæocoma Marstoni*) (Lower Ludlow rocks).

The *Asteroidea* (represented by our common "fivefingers"), and the *Ophiuridea* or "brittle-stars," as we have said, are found in Cambrian rocks. Specimens are often better preserved in the fossil state than dried recent specimens usually are in museums. Sea-urchins also lived in the Palæozoic epoch, but they do not appear to have thriven well. Only two genera are known, and these are represented by few species during periods long enough to form strata thicker than all the Secondary deposits taken together. But when we come to the Secondary period, we find the sea-urchins gaining ground. By-and-by, as in the Chalk formation, they are wonderfully common, and of multitudinous shapes and types. But by this time

Fig. 115.—Recent *Ophiocoma* (British seas).

the Encrinites, which we have seen were so plentiful on the floors of primæval seas, had begun to decline. Broadly, therefore, it may be stated that the sea-urchins began to flourish just when the Encrinites commenced to dwindle away.

Fossil star-fishes are not as a rule abundant, unless, perhaps, we except a particular stratum in the Middle Lias, where they are in places so plentiful that the seam is called the "star-fish bed." The oldest and chief forms are *Protaster, Palæaster, Urastella, Palæasterina*, and *Palæocoma*, the latter being related to our living "bird's-foot star-fish." At Leintwardine, where the Lower Ludlow rocks crop up and are quarried, we meet with both the kinds of fossil star-fishes of which we have been speaking. Speaking of *Protaster Miltoni* (one of the ancient "brittle-stars"), Mr. Salter says it is "abundant, and of all sizes," meaning, I suppose, in various stages of growth. Few localities are better worth a geological pilgrimage than this part of Shropshire. It is only nine miles from Ludlow, where the celebrated "Bone-bed" of the upper Silurian rocks may be advantageously studied. The Lower Ludlow rocks at Leintwardine are not much quarried, for they are a kind of "mud-stone," of little commercial value. Otherwise there is no doubt the number of fossil star-fishes which would be exhumed would be immense. Unfortunately, since Mr. Salter's time, the quarry on Church Hill, where the fossil star-fishes were once so abundantly found, has been either worked out, or excavation has been discontinued. In the larger quarry at Mocktree Hill, not far off, we again come upon tracts of this Silurian star-fish bed. Mr. Marston, of Ludlow, has a splendid series of these fossils, among them *Protaster Marstoni;* and in the Ludlow Museum the visitor may see slabs on which more than a score of fossil star-fish are crowded in picturesque confusion. Shepherd's Quarry, near Ludlow, is another good hunting-ground. In some respects, one species, perhaps the most beautiful of the entire group, named after Professor Sedgwick (*P. Sedgwickii*), is allied to the "feather-stars" (or rather to that division represented by Euryale), on account of the peculiar spines on the plates of its arms. This species is found only in the older rocks,

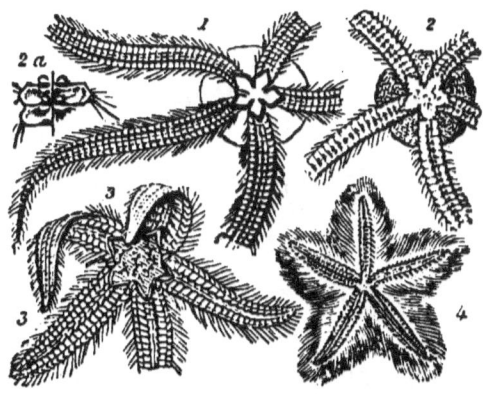

Fig. 116.—Upper Silurian Star-fishes (Ludlow rocks): 1 and 2. *Protaster Miltoni*; 2 a, small portion of arm magnified, showing plates; 3, *Palæocoma Marstoni*; 4, *Palæocoma Colvini*. (From Symond's "Records of the Rocks.")

such as the Caradoc beds at Bala, on the west side of the beautiful lake, and at Underbarrow, in Westmoreland. At Benson's Knot, Docker Park, and other places near Kendal, in Westmoreland, where the upper Ludlow rocks crop out and quarries are opened in them, a student may expect to find *Palæasterina primæva*, and *Uraster Ruthveni*, the latter named after one of the most diligent and devoted of amateur geologists that ever lived. Both the latter fossils belong to the same group as our modern "five-fingers," and they have been beautifully preserved (as any one may see, who pays a visit to the Kendal Museum), in spite of the skin being only thickened with calcareous spicules, and not plated. Two species of fossil star-fishes have been found rather plentifully in the Cambrian rocks at Welshpool, Meifod, and Corwen. The Silurian beds in a quarry at Rumney, about two miles from Cardiff, have yielded *Palæaster*. Dr. Ricketts has found *Protaster Salteri* on the east side of Bala lake; and the same species has also been met with near Llangower. Mr. W. J. Harrison believes there is a Rhætic stratum which deserves the name of a "star-fish bed." This bed occurs in the Spinney Hills, near Leicester, as a thin, sandy layer about half an inch in thickness, completely made up of the joints of star-fish. The Rhætic black shales at Garden Cliff, Westbury, Gloucestershire, have also yielded star-fish; and Mr. T. Stock has found remains of them in the same strata at Aust Cliff, on the Severn. Mr. Harrison further shows that remains of fossil star-fishes (probably *Ophiolepis Damesii*) occur in the famous richly fossiliferous Rhætic section which stretches along the coast from Penarth to Lavernock. Remains of star-fish from this place may be seen in Cardiff Museum. Next we come to the Lias strata for star-fishes, and we have already seen that one bed is especially rich in them. The

Liassic species usually belong to the "brittle-stars," and the commonest of these fossils is *Ophiolepis Egertoni*, found at Staithe, near Whitby; and also abundantly in various places in Dorsetshire, especially at Seaborne. Specimens of this star-fish may be seen in nearly every museum in England.

Pretty little specimens of *Ophiolepis* are found in the Lower Lias of Burton Passage, near Berkeley, in Gloucestershire. A well-known fossil Oolite starfish is *Ophioderma Egertoni*, abundant in the "starfish bed" at Down Cliffs, between Charmouth and Bridport Harbour, in Dorsetshire. *Astropecten* is, perhaps, the most beautiful of the fossil star-fishes found in the Oolite, and fine specimens may be seen in the museums at York and Scarborough. The neighbourhood of the latter place has yielded them in some numbers, and the young geologist may possibly be delighted by securing one for his own cabinet if he patiently goes on splitting the large nodules which fall out of the calcareous grit under Filey Cliff (near Filey Brig). *Astropecten* is also found in the Stonesfield Slate at Eyeford, Gloucestershire. *Ophiocoma* occurs in the calc grit beneath the Kimmeridge Clay, between Soundsfoot Castle, near Weymouth, and the Portland Ferry bridge. The Upper Greensand at Blackdown, Devonshire, yields several fossil star-fishes.

The marginal plates or ossicles of star-fishes allied to the cushion-stars (Goniaster) are not uncommon in the Chalk, and in the flints which come from that deposit. In the Chalk quarries at Gravesend, Charlton, many places in Kent and Sussex, as well as Norfolk (particularly about Norwich), remains of these Echinoderms may be found. I have seen perfect specimens imbedded in the flint nodules obtained from Ipswich and Norwich. All the Cretaceous star-fishes belong to

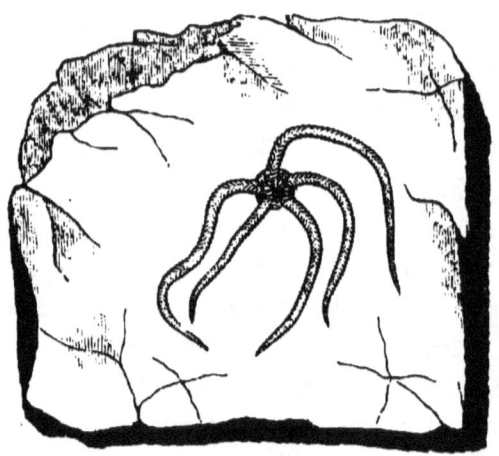

Fig. 117.—Fossil Star-fish from the Rhætic beds (*Ophiolepis Damesii*), lower side.

existing genera, such as *Stellaster, Goniaster, Orcaster,* etc. In the London Clay of the Isle of Sheppey we find similar remains of Goniasters; ossicles, plates, etc., in a more or less perfectly preserved condition.

We have already seen that, to a great extent, Encrinites occupy the place in the rocks of the Palæozoic epoch subsequently held by Sea-urchins and their allies in the Secondary strata, and in the seas of the present day. The Sea-urchins are more abundant now than at any previous period in the world's history. They inhabit every sea, and almost every depth in the seas. More than at any other time, one modern group of them (the *Echinoidea*) now merits the name of Echinodermata, or "Spiny-skinned," given to the entire order. The common Sea-urchins,

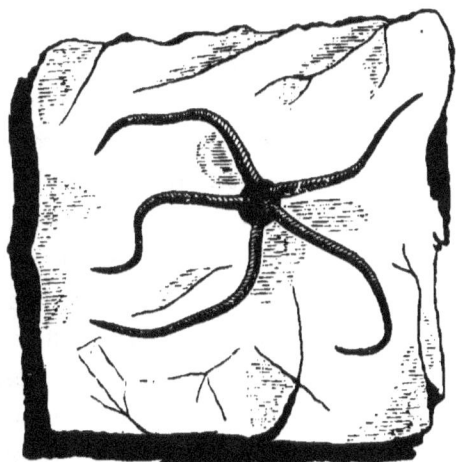

Fig. 118.—Upper side of ditto.

such as *Echinus esculenta* or *E. miliaris*, are covered with what are not inaptly called "spines."

The Echinoidea are doubly important, on account of their numerical abundance and wide distribution in the seas of the present day, and their great geological antiquity. Their general persistence in the rocks of every geological epoch from the Silurian up to our own is remarkable, and we find their species and types increasing in number in proportion as we approach the present epoch. The common sea-urchin (*Echinus miliaris*) is a familiar example. It well deserves its name, for, when alive, it is so thickly covered with spines as to greatly resemble the common hedgehog; when dead, these spines peel off, and the surface is then seen covered with minute knobs or tubercles, to each of which a movable spine was attached, on the principle of the ball-and-socket joint. The shell is composed of carbonate of lime, and is made up of an innumerable number of separate pieces, all of which are mosaicked together. No fewer than six hundred of these go to make up the entire "test," as the shell is technically called. And yet, although in the adult state it may be several inches in diameter, the shell has not been moulted since the animal was small. The membrane lining the exterior of the test or shell secretes the carbonate of lime diffused through the sea-water. As the membrane is inserted between every one of the six hundred and more plates, it is able to add lime along the edges of each, and thus the whole structure grows out uniformly and symmetrically, almost like the expanding of a bubble when blown out. A more beautiful architectural contrivance could not be imagined than is thus furnished by this insignificant creature!

Take one of the rounded tests we may pick up at the seaside, out of which the animal has been removed, and hold it up so that the light is seen through it. Besides the large apertures at the top and the bottom (anus and mouth), you perceive rows of minute punctures radiating, from the summit to the base. These punctures are called "ambulacral pores," and the plates (of which there are five rows) in which the pores occur are termed "ambulacral plates," for a reason that will shortly be seen. In addition to these, there is a plate specially perforated,

Fig. 119.—*Echinus esculenta*. On left-hand side is a fragment of test denuded of spines, and showing how the plates are mosaicked.

called the "madreporiform tubercle" (for it is porous and spongy, like the common Madrepore coral), and its office seems to be to admit the sea-water as through a filter. From this a sort of canal proceeds *internally* to a tube which surrounds the gullet at the base of the shell or test like a ring. From this circular canal there radiate, like the arms of a star-fish, certain other canals which pass in front of the rows of perforated plates, and meet together at the top. Each

L

of these five canals gives off in its course innumerable tubes, which protrude through the little punctures and lengthen at the will of the animal. At the base of each little water-tube is a little water-bag, and when this is compressed (as a boy squeezes a hollow indiarubber ball he has filled with water) the minute water-tubes, or "ambulacral feet," are lengthened even beyond the spines of the animal. Myriads of them can thus be protruded whenever the sea-urchin thinks fit, and they may then be seen wriggling and moving about like so many worms, as we saw was the case with a turned-over star-fish. At the tip of each is a sucker, and thus, when a few scores of the "ambulacra" are thrust forth, and have attached themselves to any object, they are enabled to warp the entire shell along. It is in this way, in fact, that most of the true Echinodermata crawl along the bottom of the sea. The reverent reader cannot fail to be struck with such a beautiful piece of construction, and a hint might here be furnished to our hydraulic engineers. That this principle has been in vogue for myriads of years is evident by the similar construction of the ancient Sea-

Fig. 120.—Test or shell of *Cidaris coronata*, showing the tubercles to which the bases of spines are attached (Oolitic formation).

urchins. Thus in the "fairy loaves," as they are called in the Eastern counties, where they literally abound (the chalk fossils known to geologists as *Ananchytes ovata*), we see five similar rows of perforations; and even the somewhat differently fashioned tests of the earliest genus of sea-urchins (*Palæechinus*), dating from Carboniferous if not from Silurian times, have perforated ambulacral plates, showing that these very ancient animals were then in possession of the hydraulic principle which has been of such inestimable value to their race. The Ananchytes of the Chalk, however, have very small tubercles, and the spines formerly attached to them must have been very small and bristle-like, as is now the case with those of the living Cake-urchin (*Bryssus lyrifer*), not uncommon in the muddy bottoms of the Kyles of Bute, the *Spatangus*, *Amphidotus*, and many others. This is not the case with the Cidarids found fossilized in the Chalk with them. The very large knobs or tubercles on the tests of the latter animals (which are especially abundant in tropical seas at the present time) give support to large spines, of a club-shape generally, and often ornamented by various devices. Their ball-and-socket principle of jointing, however, was in use in, and has been ever since, the geological epoch termed the Silurian, when the *Echini* were probably first introduced. In the Oolitic strata we meet with some of the handsomest specimens of Cidarids, and it is very peculiar that, like the fossil Oolitic corals, the fossil *Cidaridæ* resemble species now living in tropical and subtropical seas. The "cake-urchins," of which our recent British species of *Spatangus* is a well-known example, date from the Cretaceous, or Chalk period; and the fossils are so common as to have obtained the popular name of "hearts" in chalk districts. In number of species, however, and variety of external form, these *Echinoidea* are most abundant in Tertiary strata. It is a peculiar law in the history of a race of organic beings, that they have a period of introduction; one when they reach their maximum, both numerically and in variety of species; and another when these drop off one by one, and the race becomes extinct. We then find that the functions they performed are taken up by some other kindred group of animals, which, as a rule, is more highly endowed and specialized, and so its members have been able to thrust aside and extinguish their older comrades; just as British weeds are now supplanting the native plants of New Zealand and elsewhere.

The nervous system in a modern sea-urchin is arranged round the mouth, which is furnished with five hard calcareous teeth, to enable it to triturate its food. These teeth are worked by muscles, through loops, and the whole can be removed as easily as an artificial set of teeth. In this state the mechanism goes by the name of "Aristotle's lantern," and the seaside picker-up of "unconsidered trifles" frequently finds it lying by itself after the more fragile test has been broken to pieces. I have seen silicified specimens of Echini in Chalk flints near Norwich which have had these teeth fossilized, but such examples are exceedingly rare. Nevertheless, it affords another instance of the persistency of a plan. Generally speaking, the larger number of the Echinoidea of the Chalk seas had the mouth and anal aperture at the base; and such genera as Ananchytes, Holaster, Micraster, Galerites, etc., are grouped according to the position of these apertures, which is always constant in the same

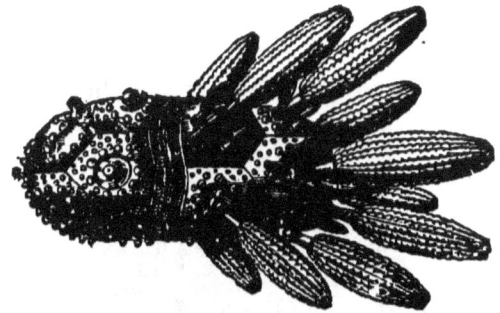

Fig. 121.—*Cidaris coronata*, showing mode of attachment of the club-shaped spines.

species. In the recent Echinus, as well as in the fossil Cidarids, the mouth is at the base and the anal orifice at the summit.

The modern Bryssus (as I have already noted) buries itself in very fine mud, on the organic matter of which it appears to feed, just as earthworms do on the black soils. The Micrasters and Spatangi of the Cretaceous period, which approach the Bryssus very nearly, both in shape and structure, may have buried themselves in the chalky mud of the ancient sea in a similar manner. Some of the modern Echini, on the other hand, have the power of hollowing for themselves holes in the rocks by the sea, especially in

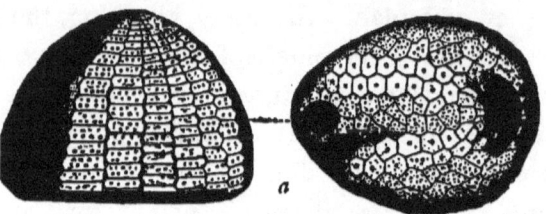

Fig. 122.—*Ananchytes ovata*, or "fairy loaf," a common Cretaceous Echinoderm: *a*, base, showing position of mouth and anus.

limestone rocks, which are not unfrequently found riddled by them, just as they are by Pholas and other

Fig. 123.—Natural flint cast of interior of *Ananchyte* (very common in Norfolk and Suffolk), showing the perforations (in relief) for ambulacral or sucking-feet.

boring molluscs. A pretty little sea-urchin, not quite so big as a threepenny piece, which we find not uncommonly fossilized in the Red Crag beds, is the

Echinocyamus. In some respects it is a connecting link between the Echini, or sea-urchins, and the "heart-urchins," or Spatangi. The common "sea-egg" (as fishermen call it), or *Echinus sphæra*, is as old as the Pliocene period, for I found it in the Coralline Crag beds. The common "sea-egg," however, is not the type with which we ought to compare the very abundant " fairy-loaves " (Ananchytes) found so plentifully in the chalk. The mouth and anus of Ananchytes are both at the base, whereas in the sea-

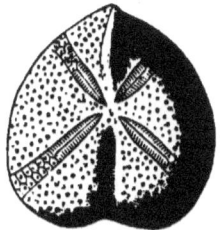

Fig. 124.—*Micraster*, a common Cretaceous Echinoderm, showing the "petaloid" arrangement of the ambulacral areas.

Fig. 125.—*Galerites albogalerus*, a common Cretaceous Echinoderm.

egg they are relatively at the base and the summit. In the *Ananchytidæ* must be included the extinct genera, more or less common in the Chalk, of Holaster, Galerites, etc., in which the basal position of mouth and anus is slightly different. Indeed, the genus Ananchytes appear to be entirely confined to the Cretaceous strata. The nearest *living* type of sea-urchin, allied to the Ananchytes, or "fairy-loaves," was dredged up in the North Atlantic during the *Challenger* expedition, from a depth of nearly three miles, and it is known by the name of *Calymne relicta*. The bottom of the Atlantic is remarkable for a number of creatures living there which are allied to those found in the fossil state in the Chalk formation. The family of sea-urchins called *Pourtalesia* is of this character, for it is allied to the extinct Ananchytes in many respects. But perhaps the most remarkable living Atlantic sea-urchin is *Salenia varispina*, dredged off Cape St. Vincent at a depth of nearly two miles. A few years ago this genus was believed to have been extinct for ages, for it was not found outside the

Fig. 126.—*Echinus granulosus.*

Fig. 127.—*Salenia personata.*

Chalk, unless we except the *Acrosalenia* of the London Clay, at Sheppey. Now it has turned up in the living state in the Atlantic. Salenia is common in the Chalk near Norwich, and internal flint casts are also found there so abundantly that they go by the name of "pick-cheeses"—"pick-cheese" being the name given to the ripened seed-vessels of the common mallow, which the flint casts of Salenia very closely resemble. Internal flint casts of Ananchytes, or "fairy-loaves," are abundant wherever the Upper Chalk crops out, and they are often remarkable for possessing the clearest and most distinct relics, in relief, of the ambulacral pores. Salenia are especially numerous and well preserved in the Greensand beds in the neighbourhood of Warminster, in Wiltshire— one of the pleasantest spots for geologizing that the student could desire.

Among the principal common fossil sea-urchins found in the Upper Greensand there, and at Chute Farm, are *Discoidea subulata, Epiaster* (a genus allied to *Micraster*), *Catopygus, Pyrina*, etc. The Lower Greensand beds are frequently rich in Echinoderms. Thus at Shanklin, in the Isle of Wight, we have a very rich "urchin" bed, containing many singular forms, such as *Clypeopygus, Enallaster*, and *Echinospatagus*. The last-mentioned fossil is very abundant in the Upper Greensand of Blackdown, Devonshire, where also many other species of the same kind of fossils are obtained. *Holaster suborbicularis* and *H. sub-globosus* are very abundant in a bed between the Chalk Marl and Upper Greensand at Abinger, in Surrey; also at Lewes, in a similar stratum. *Hemiaster* is a characteristic fossil in Grey chalk about Folkestone, at Hamsey, in Sussex, and Ventnor. The commonest Gault echinoderm found at Folkestone is *Hemiaster Bailyi*. The Red Chalk at Speeton contains *Discoidea, Holaster, Diadema*, and spines of Cidarids.

In the oldest known type of sea-urchin (*Palæechinus*) the test or shell was composed of more than twenty rows of plates, and the entire test was of a remarkable egg-like shape. *Archæocidaris* is the oldest known Cidaris, or knobbed sea-urchin, and it occurs in the Devonian rocks; but one species (*A. Urii*) is not uncommon in the Carboniferous limestone of the Derbyshire Peak district, and I have found its spines somewhat plentifully in the queer little limestone quarry at Hafod, near Corwen, in North Wales. *Palæechinus* seems to occur most plentifully in the Carboniferous limestone of Ireland. Some beds of the Inferior Oolite literally swarm with fossil Cidarids and Cake-urchins. The slabs of Oolitic limestone found in the quarries about Calne may be seen containing a dozen Cidarids, many of them with their spines still attached, just as when they were alive. Leckhampton Hill, near Cheltenham (from the summit of which the tourist can obtain a magnificent view of the Severn valley), is composed of rocks belonging to this formation in which *Hypoclypeus agariciforme* is abundant, as well as various species of Cidaris. Hartwell, in Buckinghamshire, is another good hunting-ground for fossil echinoderms. *Clypeus sinuata* is a fine, large, well-known fossil, well distributed in the Lower Oolitic rocks; it is, perhaps, most abundant in Wiltshire. The Cotswold Hills have numerous outcrops where quarries are opened in their Oolitic rocks, in which *Nucleolites*, *Cidaris*, and *Hemicidaris* are frequently very abundant.

Speaking of the fossil Echini of Calne, Dr. Wright says he has seen slabs from the beds of Coralline

Oolite at Calne in which were embedded as many as fifty specimens of *Echinobryssus scutatus*. *Clypeus Plotti* is so plentiful in the more central parts of the Cotswolds, especially near Naunton Inn, that cart-loads of it may be collected. One of the most beautiful of all the Oolitic Cidarids is *Acrosalenia hemicidaroides*, frequently found, with all its spines still attached to the body, at Chippenham—an excellent fossilizing locality—in company with another pretty species, *A. spinosa*. Rushden in Northamptonshire, Malton in Yorkshire, Charlcombe near Bath, Malmesbury, Minchinhampton, Sudely Hills, Gloucestershire (where *Pygaster semisulcatus* is found three and a half inches in diameter), Crickley, and Carnlong (Devon), are all good localities for fossil Oolitic Echinoderms. These fossil Cidarids are very beautiful objects when denuded of their thick, club-shaped spines (Fig. 120); the test is seen ornamented with and composed of a series of polygonal plates, each with a large round tubercle in its centre, and a pearl-like setting of a ring of smaller ones around it. Even the club-like spines are frequently beautifully sculptured, and the student can plainly see in their hollow bases how they were attached to the round tubercles, after the mechanical fashion known as a "ball-and socket joint." The quarries at Calne and Chippenham, in Wiltshire, are especially famous for their abundant yield of fossil Cidarids. *Echinobryssus* and *Clypeus* are fairly common in the rocks of Constitution

Hill, Banbury, unless the pits are now filled in. The Oolitic rocks which crop up from Grimston to Burdale, near Scarborough, contain beds full of *Echinobryssus scutatus*, besides spines of *Hemicidaris*. Various species of Cidardis are also found in the Kentish and Norfolk Chalk, either whole or as detached plates; and sometimes we find the impression of one of the latter on a flint, when it presents a very pretty appearance. Solitary club-shaped spines and impressions of the same in flint are very common in the Chalk formation generally. In the Greensand at Warminster, which crops out from under the escarpment of the Downs, the geological student may find a good assortment of fossil Echinoderms, such as Nucleolites, Caratomus, *Cidaris pusio, Goniophorus favosus* and *G. lunulatus, Holaster granulosus, Micraster lacunosus, Salenia clathrata, S. geometrica, S. ornata, S. umbrella*, etc. Faringdon, in Berkshire, is another rich Greensand formation abounding in fossil Cidarids, where *Salenia petalifera* is especially plentiful. Charlton, near Woolwich, is a good place for Chalk Cidarids; and the well-worked pit near the railway station will afford the student good specimens of many other Cretaceous fossils besides; whilst the Tertiary sands overlying the Chalk sections are in places rich in peculiar fossils. Very fine Cidarids may be obtained from the Chalk quarries at Grays, Essex. The Chalk near Caterham yields Holaster and others. The Chalk quarries near Hitchin station are very rich in *Holaster globosa*, etc.

The rambler can hardly go into the wrong quarry in the Upper Chalk for Ananchytes, Micraster, Galerites, etc. They are especially numerous in the large Chalk-pits which nearly surround the city of Norwich. The white-surfaced Chalk-flints, which lie in heaps in the quarries ready for breaking up into road metal, should be carefully examined—if possible one by one. I have found many "fairy-loaves" and their kind half-imbedded in these hard flints, plainly showing that the latter must have been soft when the fossils were thus buried. In the Chalk-pits about Guildford may be collected *Holaster planus*, *Micraster corbrevis*, *M. testudinarium*, etc. Cidarids are abundant in the Chalk at Gravesend and Dorking. The commonest of these in this formation is *Cidaris clavigera*. Another common fossil of this kind is *Cyphosoma corollare*, abundant at Brighton, Gravesend, and Woolwich. Cardiaster (allied to Holaster) is found at Maidstone. Many of these Chalk-pits are in lonely localities—just the very places a man would select for quiet walks, or for attractive scenery; and indeed, the tourist finds that the fossiliferous rocks usually crop out where Nature is apparelled in her most attractive garb.

CHAPTER VI.

FOSSIL WORMS (ANNELIDÆ).

DARWIN recently showed how geologically important is the common earth-worm. A biologist as intimately acquainted with the life-histories of other insignificant creatures would be able to prove that the most insignificant of them plays some part or other in geological operations. They may not be Founders of continents, like the Foraminifera and the Corals; but the world would have been different in some way or another if they had not existed.

A Worm is the lowest member of a sub-kingdom of animals on which perhaps more changes have been rung than any other. It is an annulose, or ringed animal. It forms the fundamental structure which may be modified according to circumstances, into a lobster, crab, scorpion, spider, butterfly, beetle, bee, dragon-fly, cockroach, or house-fly; besides other creatures which crawl, fly, and swim. Throughout life it may retain the primitive structure we are acquainted with in the common earth-worm or lob-worm; or this may be but the first stage in a series of subsequent improvements and modifications, as in the grub-like larvæ of the bee and beetle, or the caterpillars of the moth and butterfly.

Just as the worm or annelid type is largely a fundamental one, so is it one of the most ancient, geologically speaking. In rocks, where traces of neither mollusc nor zoophyte are visible, tracks of ancient sea-worms have long been known. No other creature can claim such a geological immortality. Not even the foraminifera are such eloquent or trustworthy witnesses of the slowness with which certain deposits were laid down than they. In all marine formations, from the Cambrian to the latest Tertiary, sea-worms have left abundant proofs of their existence.

Many of the so-called "worm or annelid tracks" in Silurian rocks, such as those denominated *Chondrites* or *Cruziana*, may have been left by creeping mollusca or crawling crustacea. But in the absence of the solid parts of these creatures in the fossil state, it is safer to assign such tracks to worms. In deposits where fossil univalves and crustaceans are actually met with, such tracks may have been left by them. Still, the careful student cannot but be aware, from his quiet study of any low-water mud or sand-flat at the present day, that for one track left of crustacea or mollusca, ten are left by sea-worms. In short, they are the great track-makers, as well as sand-diggers; and we may safely give them this position without minimizing the importance of the markings left by other animals.

If *subsidence* of certain parts of the sea-floor were not accepted as a geological and geographical fact, sea-worms would prove it more than any other animals. For when we find such rocks as the Longmynds, composed of strata all more or less of a similar physical character and composition, on whose upper surfaces are innumerable tracks of sea-worms for at least one mile in vertical thickness, no other theory could account for the conditions under which they had been formed than that which declares the sea-bed was slowly subsiding, at about the same rate that the sediments were accumulating. Moreover, the same worm-tracks more or less indicate the depth at which such deposits were formed, for we never find these markings in strata of deep-sea origin; and the supplementary evidence of the ripple-marks so frequently occurring in worm-tracked strata, is confirmatory on this point.

Geology has little or nothing to say concerning terrestrial worms, unless it refers to their physical action in modern times. I am not aware of a single species which can be safely referred to the same habitats as our common earth-worms, although I have little doubt this class has been in existence, perhaps during the entire Tertiary period, if not longer. I have therefore only to do with sea-worms. These, as we now know them, may be divided into two groups, those which crawl or swim

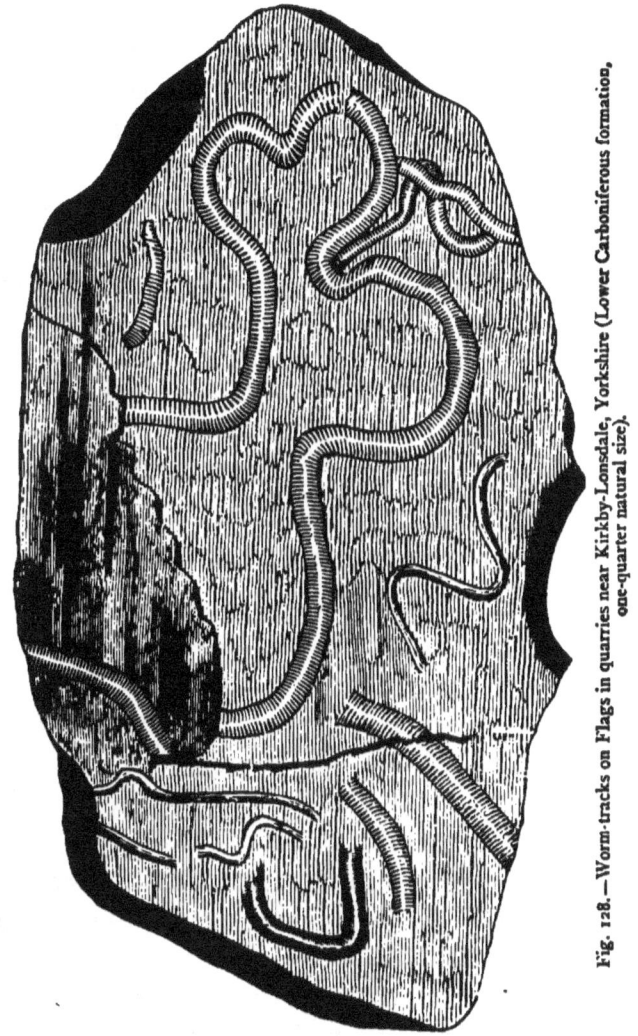

Fig. 128.—Worm-tracks on Flags in quarries near Kirkby-Lonsdale, Yorkshire (Lower Carboniferous formation, one-quarter natural size).

about (as the lob-worms and the *Errantia* generally),

M

and those which adopt a fixed existence. The former have no hard parts to leave behind them when they die, except their horny jaws, and these have been found by Dr. Hinde in considerable quantities in the Silurian and other rocks. Until a few years ago we were entirely indebted for proofs of the former existence of this class of sea-worms to the tracks they left behind them on primæval mud-flats, and the discovery of their jaws is additional evidence in favour

Fig. 129.—Horny Jaws of modern marine *Annelida*.

of these tracks being of annelid origin. The other class of sea-worms, adopting a settled marine life, live in tubes, which are formed of grains of sand, etc., cemented together, as in the instance of our modern *Terebella;* or they may be leathery, as in the recent *Sabella;* or their outer skin may secrete lime, and thus form a solid tube, as illustrated by the empty tubes we see attached to old oyster-shells, stones, and rocks. In both the latter cases the breathing organs are gathered into one place, and form a beautiful feathery tuft, sometimes brightly coloured, as in those of that little coiled worm which rejoices in such a high antiquity, the *Spirorbis*.

Let us take the wandering worms (*Errantia*) first in order, as they probably were first in point of appearance in the earlier seas of our globe. The names assigned to the commonest of the tracks and trails believed to have been left by them are borrowed in most instances from modern genera; thus we have *Phyllodocites, Myrianites, Crossopodia, Arenicolites,* etc. The markings we have to explain are of two kinds, burrows and trails. The sea-worms making the former were doubtless of similar habits to our common lob-worm (*Arenicola piscatorum*) and the generic name of *Arenicolites* at once indicates this.

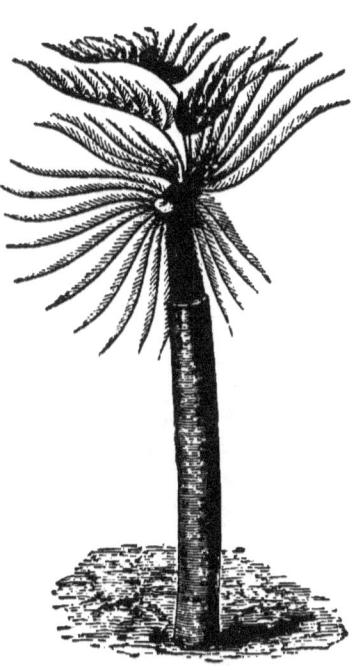

Fig. 130.—Coriaceous tube of *Sabella unispira* (recent).

The Cambrian rocks of Bray Head, near Dublin, have long been famous for the occurrence of markings left by an ancient burrowing worm, named by Dr. Kinahan *Histioderma Hibernicum,* associated with the zoophyte *Oldhamia.* The tubular casts of these worm-holes may be obtained. The upper part swells out into a trumpet-shaped mouth, frequently very prettily marked. The holes of *Arenicolites sparsus* and *Arenicolites didymus* are in pairs, and are found in the same beds as *Histioderma*.

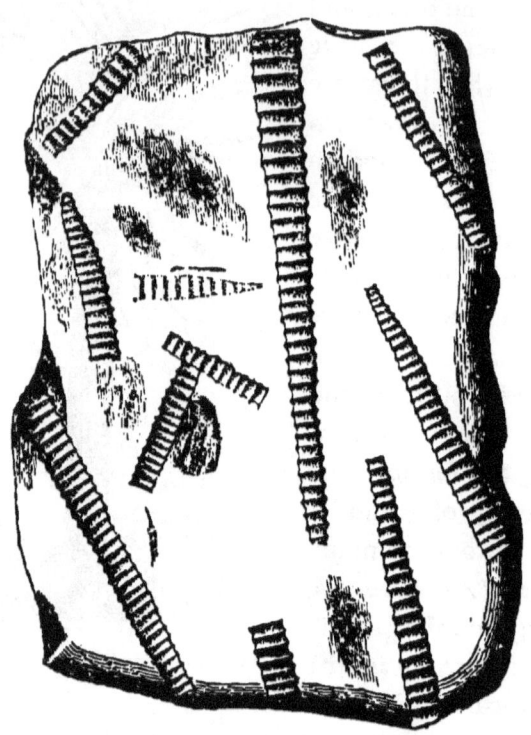

Fig. 131.—*Tentaculites annulatus* (a supposed Silurian Annelid with calcareous tube).

The flag-stones obtained from the Millstone grit formation in Lancashire and Yorkshire have their surfaces frequently knobbed irregularly with the casts of worm-furrows. Young geologists who often sigh

for opportunities to geologize abroad should keep
their eyes open to the periodical mending of the roads
and causeways of the towns in which they live. In
the neighbourhood of Manchester and Sheffield the

Fig. 132.—Tracks and Burrows of *Arenicolites sparsus*, with *Oldhamia*.

newly laid flags are often seen ripple-marked, and
worm-tracked or worm-burrowed. The Cambrian and
Silurian sandstones afford
similar evidence of shallow
water deposition. In the
Stiper Stones (Upper Cam-
brian) both casts and
burrows are abundant. In
the Bangor slate quarries
the markings are called
Chondrites, from the original belief that they were
impressions left by seaweeds, but I favour the
theory of their annelid origin. In the slate quarries

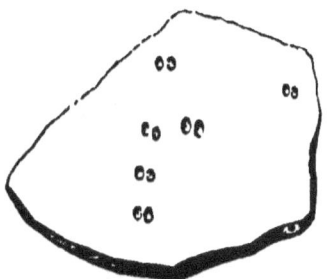

Fig. 133.—Burrows of *Arenicolites didymus*.

near Douglas, in the Isle of Man, there may be frequently found the tracks of two kinds of sea-worms, *Nereis* and *Nemertites*. As before remarked, however, the Longmynd rocks afford by far the largest number of evidences of ancient sea-worms. In the Wrekin the quartzite beds yield *Arenicolites Uriconiensis*, which may be considered the oldest known British fossil. The rocks of St. David's contain both *Arenicolites* and *Serpulites*. In the Skiddaw slates,

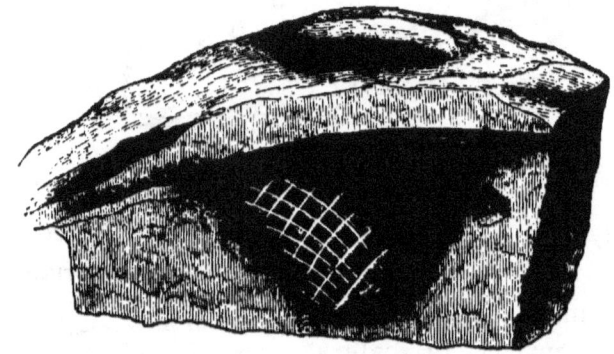

Fig. 134.—Burrow of *Histioderma Hibernicum*.

near Keswick, Cumberland, ten species of the remains of fossil-worms have been catalogued, among which *Scolithus* and *Helmintholithus* are the most abundant. One remarkable species has been named *Stellascolites*.

In many parts of Great Britain the lower Carboniferous rocks possess most abundant traces of worm-tracks. Any tourist who has visited the magnificent Cliffs of Mohr, in county Clare, Ireland, cannot fail to have noticed the dark slaty flags of the district,

FOSSIL WORMS.

marked all over, below and above, with sinuous worm-tracks. These cliffs rise sheer out of the green Atlantic to a height of three hundred feet, and appear to be of the same character throughout. Everywhere, where it is possible to examine them, the thin flags are crowded with these peculiar markings. People who have been to the celebrated quarries in the same geological formation near Kirkby-Lonsdale, will have observed the flags impressed in a similar way. I give a sketch of them as they appear in a hand specimen. As these Kirkby-Lonsdale flags are much in demand by house-builders in the north, and therefore get widely distributed, some of my readers may have seen them a long way from their parent quarry. The commonest of these worm-markings is *Crossopodia*. In Penwhapple Glen, Girvan, Ayrshire, many species of worm-tracks have been recognized, belonging to *Nereites*, *Myrianites*, *Crossopodia*, *Nemertites*, etc.; annelid markings are also found in the shales at Moffat. A peculiar kind of worm-track, called *Cymaderma*, is left on the surfaces of the

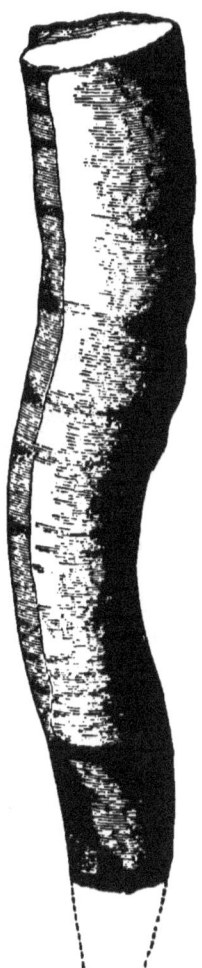

Fig. 135.—Large tubular Case of *Histioderma Hibernicum*.

Lower Carboniferous rocks near Settle, in the Valley of the Ribble.

No doubt most, if not all, of these tracks were made by worms like our common *Nereis*. This had long been suspected before Dr. Hinde, by dint of great patience, discovered annelid jaws in the Silurian shales at Ludlow, Much Wenlock, Iron Bridge, Stoke Edith, and elsewhere. These are figured in his paper on the subject read before the Geological Society. The largest of the annelid jaws he found so plentifully did not exceed one-fifth of an inch. Dr. Hinde has proved that these jaws differed as much among themselves so far back as the Silurian period as they do now—a plain indication of the antiquity of the tribe.

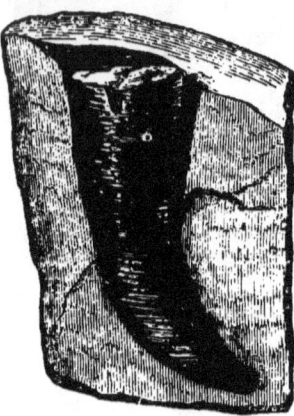

Fig. 136.—Extremity of Tube of *Histioderma Hibernicum*.

Worms which form tubes cannot of course make tracks, but they leave evidences of their existence behind them in the fossil tubes they once inhabited. These sometimes form strata of no inconsiderable thick-

Fig. 137.—*Serpula* with tentacles expanded (recent).

ness. Indeed, any geological student who has visited the seashore of St. Bee's, Cumberland, at low water, will have noticed extensive beds formed solely of the cemented sand-tubes of modern species of *Sabellaria*. *Sabellaria* and *Terebella* are very common tubed worms in British seas, both of them constructing sand-cemented tubes. The latter is always abundant where there is a hard, clayey sea-bottom. It is rarely

Fig. 138.—*Nereis* (recent).

that we get these worm-tubes fossilized, as they tend to fall into their component grains of sand when the worms die.

With the hard, calcareous tubes of such species of sea-worms as *Serpula* and its kind, we have no difficulty. This form of Annelid has had, perhaps, a more stereotyped or stable form of existence than any other creature in the world. There is no ostensible difference between many Silurian-tubed worms and those now in existence. The pretty little *Spirorbis* found in the Upper Silurian rocks has had a continuous and unchanged existence through every geological period until now. We find it attached to fossil shells and corals in the Silurian and Devonian limestones. Fourteen species occur in the Carboniferous rocks, some of them found adhering to the trunks of *Sigillaria* and almost encrusting them, just as we find them adhering to the larger seaweeds along our shores. Under the names of *Serpulites*, *Cornulites*, *Tentaculites*, *Conchiolites*, etc., the sea of every geological period has abounded in tubed worms. The Wenlock limestone literally swarms with these tapering elegant tubes, ringed like the tentacles of insects, and hence called *Tentaculites*. This is a type of what is called a *free* worm-tube, *i.e.* one that is not attached to shells or rocks, like the modern *Serpula*. By some geologists it is still regarded as a pteropod mollusc allied to *Hyale*. *Cornulites* is another genus nearly related to it, and both are characteristic of the Silurian formation. The chief species in the latter rocks is *Cornulites serpularius*. It is frequently found as much as three to four inches in length, ringed, and gradually tapering to a point. Casts of this species of worm-tube frequently occur, and the young student might be easily misled by them into thinking it was a different fossil to the *Cornulites* found with its external shape ; for this internal cast is in a series of sharply marked off segments, one within but less than another, like the fully drawn-out parts of an old-fashioned telescope. This species is very abundant in the Woolhope beds. *Ortonia* (named after Professor Orton) is a genus of abundant annelid tubes, also free, which is peculiar to the Upper Silurian rocks of North America. *Tentaculites annulatus* is the commonest of our British species; *T. ornatus* being perhaps the prettiest. The former is more abundant in the Lower Silurian rocks at May Hill and elsewhere, and the latter in the Upper. The Wenlock shales are very rich in fossil worms, Mr. Etheridge recording no fewer than thirty-five species of all kinds, Dr. Hinde having added twenty-four. Among the characteristic forms of these beds are *Trachyderma* and *Aranellites*.

No doubt there were ancient sea-worms resembling *Serpula*, and it is possible some may have been intermediate between it and the modern *Sabella*, which latter is possessed of a leathery tube, often strengthened by adhering sand-grains. Thus, in the Upper Silurian rocks above Ludlow, we meet with numerous traces of a thin calcareous worm-tube, transversely striated, and very ribbon-like, called *Serpulites longissimus*. *Trachyderma coriacea* is still more like a Sabella tube stiffened by a deposit of lime. *Scolioderma serpulites* is found in the rocks of the Wrekin and in the holly-bush sandstones near Malvern. *Serpulites dispar* is abundant about Ludlow, and also in the Upper Silurian rocks near Kendal; and the student will find a capital collection of them in the museum of that town. A more delightful neighbourhood for fossilizing than Kendal can hardly be found in England, or a more varied one. I have seen *Serpulites* more than a foot long in the deserted Silurian quarries near Ledbury.

The Secondary rocks contain true *Serpula*, and these fossils are not without a special value to the physical geologist. Some of them may be found sprawling over the interiors of bivalve shells, or covering the naked tests of sea-urchins — in both instances plainly informing us that the life-and-death conditions of the ancient sea-floors were very like those of our day. Moreover, the occurrence of these creeping worm-tubes over the dead tests of such sea-urchins as Ananchytes—one of the commonest in the Chalk—shows us that the chalky ooze must have been forming very slowly, or it would have buried up the dead animals before the sea-worms had managed to spread their tubes over and about them!

We frequently get the tubes of *Serpula* attached to fossil bivalves in the Lias and Oolitic rocks: sometimes they form dense and tortuous masses, as in the Oolitic marlstone near Banbury, and in the well-known "Serpula-bed" at Blue Wyke Scar, near Scarborough—where the geologist may obtain abundant fossils, and enjoy some of the finest coast scenery in England at the same time. The tabular Ironstone of the Gault of Kent is frequently full of annelid borings. A hard band of clay in the Gault at Folkestone, and near Charing, in the same county, is occupied with serpula tubes, which form a thin stratum two inches thick. *Serpula plexus* is always common in the Chalk; and near Norwich and Margate it frequently occurs in masses, or completely investing the larger fossil shells, such as *Inoceramus*.

In the Eocene beds the commonest fossil worm-tubes are those of *Ditrupa*, which was evidently free or unattached to objects, after the manner of the *Tentaculites*, etc., already described. It is usually found in large numbers, and appears to have been gregarious in its habits. We may get a large quantity of this fossil worm in the London Clay beds of Bognor, Hampshire. *Ditrupa plana* is the name of the common species. Ditrupa is also found in the crag beds of Suffolk, where it may have been redeposited there from denuded Eocene strata.

CHAPTER VII.

TRILOBITES AND OTHER FOSSIL CRUSTACEA.

To a young and enthusiastic geologist there is no class of fossils to which so much interest is attached as the *Trilobites*. They are extremely elegant objects, and are easily identified. Their strict limit to the primary rocks makes them geologically valuable as means of identifying strata. Even non-geologists remember their glib, half-scientific, half-popular family name, and will occasionally air it as if it were the complete key to palæontology. A good collection of well-arranged trilobites looks better in the cabinet than perhaps any other fossils. There is such a variation from the leading type that one cannot wonder the number of genera should be so great. No two are externally alike, and the deviation is sometimes so extreme that the Trilobites are no longer trilobed.

Trilobites are among the few fossils which possess the associations of folk-lore. Ammonites and Encrinite stems, Gryphea and Cycadites, share with them the feeble notice which the curious gave to them in pre-geological days when all fossils were called "petrifactions," and all were equally regarded as evidence of the universality of the Noachian Deluge. Perhaps nowhere are Trilobites more abundantly visible than in the Wenlock limestones, near Dudley. The latter have been upheaved to a very high angle, and the surfaces of the hard limestone slabs are so thickly bestrewn with fossils, that it is impossible to place the tip of one's finger without its coming into contact with some of them. These limestones are constantly clean, from weathering. They are veritably museums of Upper Silurian fossils, and although hard to extract with the hammer, the student may while away many a summer hour in gloating over these lovely treasures of the ancient deep. Trilobites are there in uncountable thousands, but nearly always in disjointed "heads" and "tails." We cannot wonder, therefore, that they should have attracted the attention of those fond of natural phenomena, although in the days long anterior to scientific explanations of them. As "Dudley Locusts," one genus of Trilobites (*Calymene*) was long known; even the fact of their standing out in relief from the limestone was noticed as very remarkable, for nothing was known in those days of sub-aërial denudation or weathering of rocks. They were named "Trilobites" as long ago as 1771, by Walch, in his "Natural History of Petrifactions," on account of the three lobes of joints which usually run along the body. Still, their crustacean origin had been guessed at by bold speculators, and even Linnæus classed them among the *Entomostraca*.

How utterly at sea the majority of naturalists were as to the true nature of these singular fossils is indicated by some of their generic names. *Agnostus*, *Asaphus*, *Calymene*, etc., the commonest of these, are only Greek words signifying "unknown," or "concealed," etc. Still, since the time of Brongniart they have been universally regarded as crustaceans, and the universal opinion is that they are allied to the *Isopoda*, only that they were legless. Dr. Henry Woodward, F.R.S., who has taken up Mr. Salter's investigations among the Trilobites with great enthusiasm, believes he has detected evidences of legs on the under side of some specimens, and his belief has recently been confirmed by the discovery of Trilobites with legs in America. Other naturalists think these members are only the remains of "calcic arches." The extinct Trilobites really represent a defunct order, and as such we usually find them arranged in systematic works on Zoology. In that case they come in as "missing links" between the *Isopoda*, of which the common woodlouse (*Oniscus*) and the shrimp-parasite (*Bopyrus*) are familiar types, and the *Merostomata* of which the well-known "king-crabs" (*Limulus*) are examples. The larval state of the *higher* classes in the same order frequently resembles the adult conditions of the *lower*. In the crustacea a very large number of genera are alike in their youngest state. From its resemblance to the adult condition of one of the lowest of the crustaceans called *Nauplius*, this state is usually called the "*Nauplius* stage." No other group of animals passes through so many metamorphoses before reaching maturity, and each of these is so well marked off from the rest, that it might be

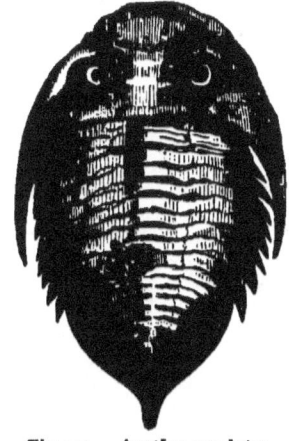

Fig. 139.—*Asaphus caudatus*.

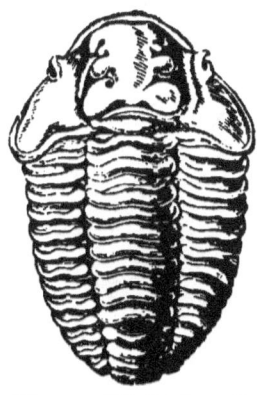

Fig. 140.—"Dudley locust" or Trilobite (*Calymene Blumenbachii*).

regarded as a generic type. Indeed, in many cases, genera have been founded on these distinctions, so that the same animal, at different periods of its life, has been regarded not only as a distinct species, but as belonging to another genus. The young of the common lobster, for instance, passes through at least *six* stages, which are so unlike each other that only careful observation has settled they are not different animals. Even when it has reached the adult condition, a lobster is so unlike what it will be when full-grown, that it might be set down as belonging to another genus. It is as if we knew nothing of the metamorphoses of the butterfly, and therefore had mistaken the caterpillar and chrysalis for animals belonging to groups wide separated from the winged insect.

The young of the recent *Limulus*, or king-crab, greatly resembles the adult Trilobites. As the king-

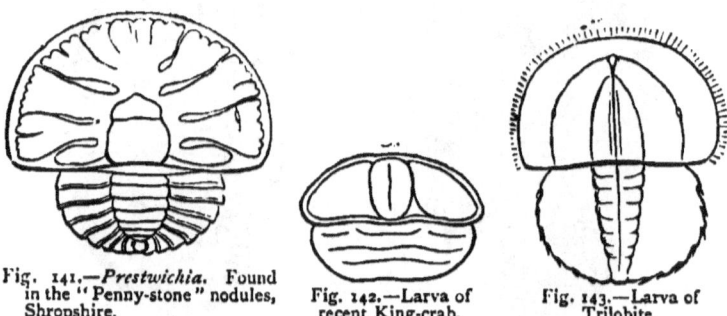

Fig. 141.—*Prestwichia.* Found in the "Penny-stone" nodules, Shropshire.

Fig. 142.—Larva of recent King-crab.

Fig. 143.—Larva of Trilobite.

crabs succeeded the latter in geological time, it may be that it was due to the Trilobites having been "advanced a stage." One genus found in the ironstone nodules of Coalbrookdale, called *Belinurus*, more nearly resembles one genus of the Trilobites (*Trinucleus*) than the king-crabs of our own days. Again, the female *Bopyrus* (Fig. 149), which parasitically attaches itself to the inner surface of the carapace of the shrimp, has a rude resemblance to the segmented body of some of the less highly organized Trilobites. The fact of its

TRILOBITES AND OTHER FOSSIL CRUSTACEA. 179

being a parasite shows that it must have undergone

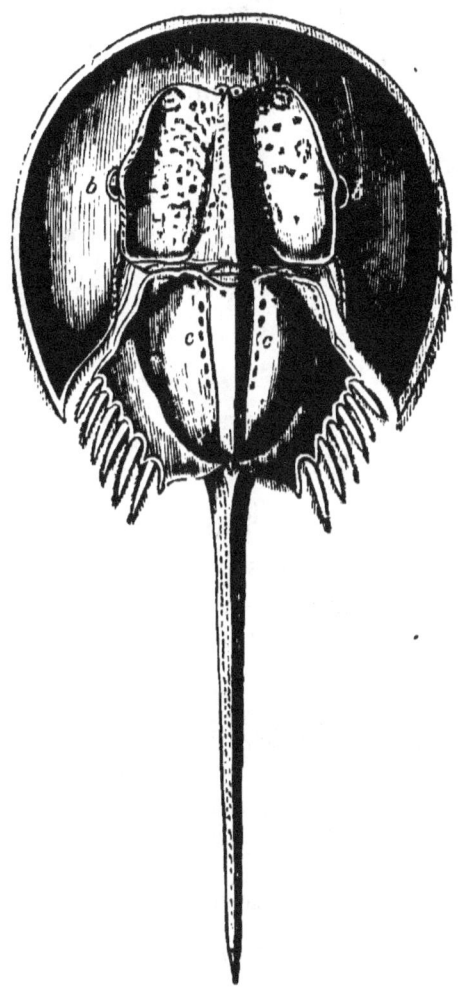

Fig. 144.—Under surface of recent King-crab (*Limulus*).

retrogradation. The figures will show that the Trilobites find their natural history place between the groups above named. Haeckel, however, places them among the "gill-footed crabs" (*Branchiopoda*), of which the water-fleas are familiar examples. He does

Fig. 145.—Fossil King-crab, from Coal measures of Coalbrookdale (*Belinurus trilobitioides*).

Fig. 146.—*Trinucleus fimbriatus*, Upper Llandeilo beds, Builth.

not tell us on what grounds this is done, for no breathing or locomotive organs have as yet certainly been found, although thousands of specimens of all the genera have been carefully examined on their under

Fig. 147.—Compound eye of fossil Trilobite (*Asaphus caudatus*) slightly magnified.
Fig. 148.—Ocelli of ditto (magnified).

sides. Again, the *compound eyes* of the Trilobites show that they were in this respect really very highly organized, and this highly developed specialization of the sense of sight certainly proves that they ought to be placed much higher among the Crustacea than we find them in Haeckel's "Systematic Survey." In many species of Trilobites the empty eye-sockets can be seen with the naked eye, notably so in *Asaphus caudatus*, in which each eye contained four hundred facets. According to Owen, *Asaphus tyrannus* possessed no fewer than six thousand eyes! The number of eyes among the Trilobites varies considerably; some specimens have none at all.

I have already referred to the fact that the Trilobites are peculiar to the Primary rocks. Although they seem to range as high as the Permian, they are chiefly confined to the strata below and including the Carboniferous limestone. No fewer than four hundred species, grouped in fifty genera, have been described from these formations, and new forms are still occasionally met with. The greater number of the species are of a Silurian age; those of the Devonian rocks are of a well-defined character; and those from the Carboniferous limestone even more distinct still. It would seem as if they reached their maximum of size, as well as of variation, during the Silurian period. The largest are *Asaphus gigas*, eighteen inches in length, found at Llandeilo; and *Paradoxides*, two feet long. On the other hand, they appear to have decreased in size as well as in numbers when we reach the Carboniferous rocks. The genus *Phillipsia*, there represented, rarely includes specimens more than three-quarters of an inch in length. It ought to be stated, however, that we know little about the embryology of the Trilobites. There can hardly be a doubt that many of the so-called species, and even genera, are larval stages in the development of the same species. I have referred to the common lobster

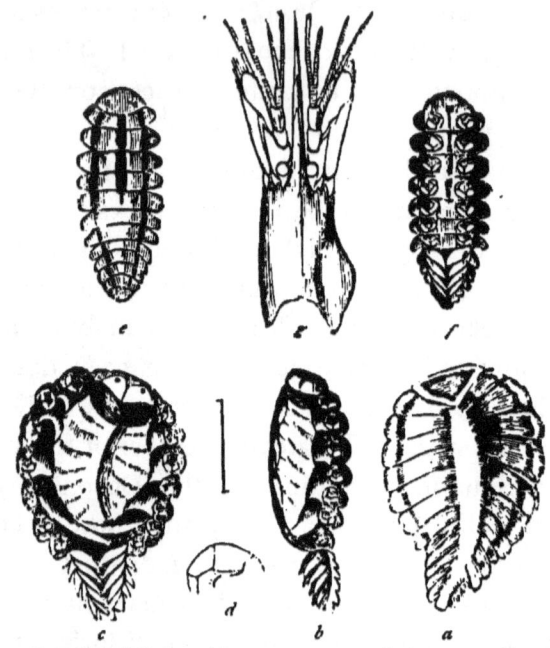

Fig. 149.—Parasite of Shrimp (*Bopyrus crangorum*); *a*, upper side; *b*, profile; *c*, under side; *d*, highly magnified and aborted foot; *e*, upper side of male *Bopyrus*, much smaller than female; *f*, lower side of ditto; *g*, part of carapace of shrimp, swelling out to show presence of parasite underneath.

as an illustration of the clearly marked characters appertaining to the various stages in the life-history of the same individual. Each of these stages is accompanied by as many "moults;" and if we reason from our general experience of the embryology of the

Crustacea, we must allow that the Trilobites were affected in the same manner. The number of larval stages they passed through depends upon the position they attained as regards organization. This was much higher than Haeckel imagines, and therefore the stages may have been numerous. It is to be expected that individuals would die and be buried in the muddy ooze in each of these intermediate states. Thus found, what more natural than to regard them as different species, and even different genera? Only a fuller knowledge of crustacean embryology will clear away a good deal of the useless nomenclature which has gathered about these interesting creatures, and it is hardly to be expected that we shall ever know their accurate life-history. Barrande, who had such splendid opportunities for studying the Trilobites, and who made equally good use of them, satisfied himself, in the case of no fewer than twenty different species of Trilobites, that they passed through larval stages, each unlike the other. In some instances he traced them from when they had only just escaped from the egg to the fully developed and mature state. In the first instance they had no joints to the body, and therefore strongly resembled one of the carapaces of the "water-fleas;" in the last they possessed ring-covered bodies, movable tails, and compound eyes. This proves that, although in their young states Trilobites resembled the *Ostracoda*, in their adult life they had proceeded much further. Parallel with the instance of the development of the lobster, all the above changes noted by Barrande in the Trilobites occurred before the animal had attained a tenth part of its full size. In Lyell's "Manual of Geology" the student will find engravings of the *Trinucleus* in three stages, each of which appears specifically distinct from the other. Another skilled observer of the Trilobites was Burmeister, who believed that all of them underwent metamorphoses. Recently the larva or young of a beautiful and highly developed Trilobite (*Conocoryphe*) has been found in this country. In the case of fossils less care has been taken than with living animals, and, in many instances, some of those who have christened species were geologists rather than naturalists. The slightest differences have been sufficient to warrant a new specific name, and thus it is more than possible that the various stages in the life-history of one and the same species may be illustrating our manuals as distinct genera and species! Even with regard to *sex* in adult individuals, little or nothing is known; although among nearly all the Crustacea these differ so extremely. Owen remarks that the difference in the head plate and the terminal spines of the tail in the two so-called species named *Asaphus caudatus* and *Asaphus longicaudatus*, may only be due to difference of sex; the inference, therefore, is that these two species represent the male and female of only one.

The earliest Trilobites, such as the eyeless *Agnostus*, are usually the simplest in structure, so that these animals are not an exception to the general palæontological rule that the simpler always precede the more complex species of the same genus or class. Nevertheless, this simple and elementary Trilobite is found in company with a more highly developed kind. *Agnostus* is usually found in large shoals, something after the manner in which the carapaces of the ancient water-fleas are met with in some of the Coal-measure shales. Owen suggests that this disposition of *Agnostus* is "as if it were the larval form of some large Trilobite." The young of all Crustacea usually associate together in shoals, and this suggestion might therefore be reasonably taken in consideration with what has already been said on the subject.

The compound eyes of Trilobites are usually thickly placed on raised half-moon-shaped ridges, and the fact that the sockets are so well preserved speaks plainly of the quiet way in which the fine mud was deposited in which the animals were buried and ultimately fossilized. Dr. Buckland spoke of these ridges as being "like a circular bastion, ranging nearly round three-fourths of a circle, each commanding so much of the horizon that where the distinct vision of one eye ceased, that of the other began." He also very sagaciously referred to the form of the ridges and their position on the head-shield as "peculiarly adapted to the uses of an animal destined to live at the bottom of the water: to look downwards was as much impossible as it was unnecessary for a creature living at the bottom; but for horizontal vision in every direction the contrivance is complete." I cannot refrain from further quoting a well-known passage from the same author, in which a logical inference is drawn from the structure of the eyes of Trilobites. "The results arising from these facts are not confined to animal physiology; they give information also regarding the condition of the ancient sea and the ancient atmosphere, and the relations of both these media to light, at that remote period when the earliest marine animals were furnished with instruments of vision in which the minute optical adaptations were the same that impart

Fig. 150.—Simplest kind of Trilobite (*Agnostus pisiformis*).

the perception of light to crustaceans now living at the bottom of the sea. . . . With regard to the atmosphere, we infer that had it differed materially from its actual condition, it might have so far affected the rays of light that a corresponding difference from the eyes of existing crustaceans would have been found in the organs on which the impressions of such rays were then received. Regarding light itself also, we learn, from the resemblance of these most ancient organizations to existing eyes, that the mutual relations of light to the eye, and of the eye to the light, were the same at the time when crustaceans endowed with the faculty of vision were first placed at the bottom of the primeval seas, as at the present moment."

That the Trilobites were bottom-feeders and haunters, there can be little doubt. The late Mr. Salter, than whom no geologist was better acquainted with Trilobites, was of opinion that they not only lived there, but fed on the organic mud, something after the manner of earth-worms. The simple structure of their mouths, and the absence of *antennæ* or feelers, indicate such a habit.

My readers will have seen from the illustrations the strong external resemblances between the earliest king-crabs, such as the *Belinurus*, and one genus of Silurian Trilobites (*Trinucleus*). The chief apparent difference is in the ends of their bodies, that of the king-crab being prolonged into the dart shape which gives to it its generic name, whilst in the *Trinucleus* it is round. But we have only to glance at figures of various kinds of Trilobites to see that they vary amongst themselves in this respect. Thus in *Asaphus caudatus* (Fig. 139), one of the commonest of Lower Silurian Trilobites, we have the pygidium, or tail, drawn into a point.

Undoubtedly the *Trinucleus* (Fig. 146) is one of the prettiest of Trilobites. It has a look which suggests the mysterious Egyptian figures of ancient courtiers! The head or cephalic shield is much developed, and on each side is prolonged into two spines half as long again as the body. Like the *Agnostus* and several others, the *Trinucleus* had no eyes. In this respect we find the various genera of Trilobites differing very much from each other. Some have a very large number, as *Asaphus tyrannus;* and thence we find them decreasing until they are absent altogether. All the genera of the order *Trinuclcidæ*, however, are not eyeless; and this illustrates the uncertainty with which the power of vision seems to have been distributed among these ancient crustaceans. Doubtless, this variation was the result of special conditions of existence, eyes being always possessed when they were required. Thus the living male *Bopyrus*, or shrimp-parasite (Fig. 149), has rudimentary eyes, whilst the female has none; but this is entirely due to the very different habits of life of the two sexes. *Trinucleus* is abundant in the Caradoc shales of Shropshire.

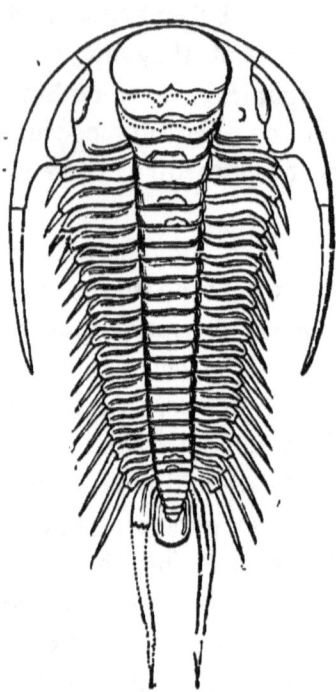

Fig. 151.—*Paradoxides Tessini.*

From the Cambrian to the Carboniferous formations we find certain Trilobites peculiar to the various

geological systems. Thus, *Paradoxides* and *Agnostus* are peculiarly Cambrian; *Trinucleus* and *Asaphus* are almost exclusively Lower Silurian; *Phacops* and *Calymene* are markedly Upper Silurian; *Brontes* and *Harpes* are among characteristic Devonian fossils; whilst *Phillipsia* and *Griffithsides* are genera of small

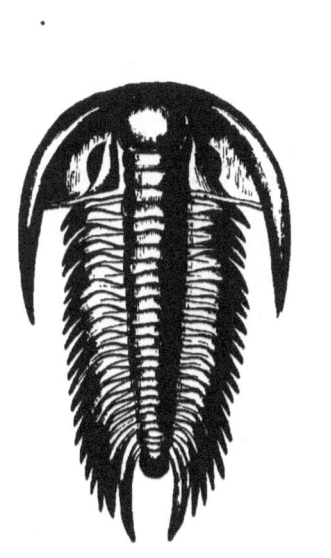
Fig. 152.—*Paradoxides Davidis.*

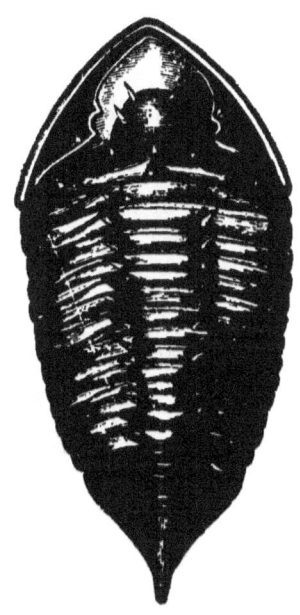
Fig. 153.—*Homalanotus.*

Trilobites—the last of their race—which are peculiar to the Carboniferous limestones.

Undoubtedly many of the fossil Tribolites we meet with in any of the above rocks are *moults*—that is, portions of the carapace thrown off after the manner of the shells of lobsters and crabs. This moulting process appears to have peeled off the external hard shell in two or three pieces. Thus, the head-piece, or cephalic shield, is usually found alone; the thorax, or ringed part, is also abundantly found separate; whilst the pygidium, or tail, is frequently met with apart from the others, although it is usually adhering to the thoracic part. Of course, animals

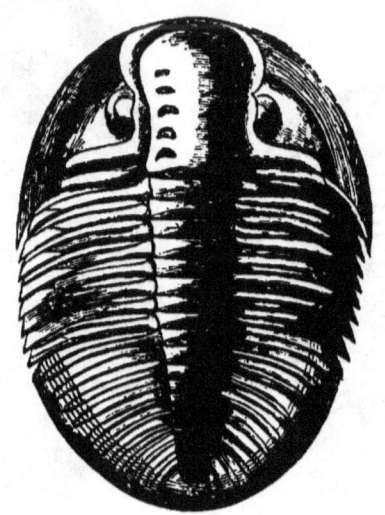

Fig. 154.—*Ogygia Buchii*.

which have died and been buried in the mud are found with all the above parts adhering to each other. The carapace or shell differed in its character in various species. In some it appears to have been very thin, in others harder. It may have been more or less chitinous, after the manner of the *elytra* of beetles, strengthened by the presence of limy matter.

In the Carboniferous Trilobites (*Phillipsia*, etc.) the carapace seems to have contained more limy matter in its composition than other species. In this genus we always find the moultings in the two parts of body and tail, and head. In the *Calymene* (Fig. 140) the thoracic or ringed part is frequently found by itself,

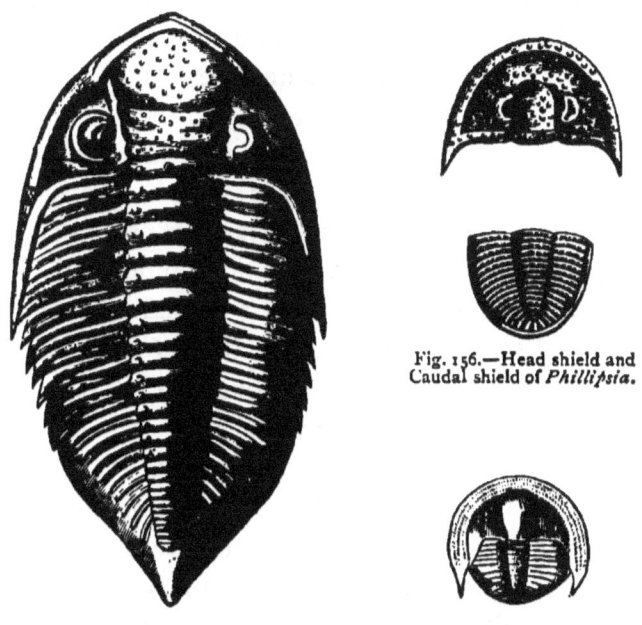

Fig. 156.—Head shield and Caudal shield of *Phillipsia*.

Fig. 155.—*Phacops caudatus*.   Fig. 157.—*Trinucleus Lloydii*.

and not seldom the rings are detached, as if the whole mechanism of the coat-of-mail-like armour had become loosened and got scattered about. Undoubtedly the chemical composition of the carapace differed accordingly as the habits of the Trilobites varied.

The Cambrian Trilobites, as a rule, differ from their Silurian descendants and representatives in having a large number of rings or segments to the thoracic (or middle) part of the body: The tail part (caudal shield) is, however, less developed than in the Silurian species. The side-lobes of some genera, *Paradoxides* and *Acidaspis*, are fringed, and, in the case of the latter, further adorned with spines. Some of these may have been merely sexual distinctions, although we are now forced to regard them as specific. Dean Buckland and many other naturalists regarded an isopod crustacean abundant in the seas around Tierra del Fuego and the Straits of Magellan, as nearly allied to this group of Trilobites. This crustacean is called *Serolis*. Its cephalic shield has compound sessile eyes, arranged in half-moon-shaped lobes exactly like those of some Trilobites. The segments or joints of the thoracic portion of the body are fringed, as in *Paradoxides*, and there is a movable caudal or tail shield, as in *Phacops caudatus* (Fig. 155), an abundant Silurian Trilobite. Only the antennæ and mouth-organs differentiate them. But these are very thin and weak, and after death may soon be detached, as various geologists believe was the case with some Trilobites. The legs are fitted for crawling about, but, as is frequent in animals living in sea-water, they are also weak and thin. The *Serolis* is a slow crawler and swimmer, and is usually found on seaweed. Some geologists have imagined that a few

Trilobites had generic relations with the common *Apus* of our ditches and ponds. Sufficient has been said, however, to show how large a middle space the numerous family of Trilobites occupy. At the one extreme they nearly touch the king-crabs—and at the other the aborted shrimp-parasites, as in the case of *Agnostus*. Perhaps the living *Serolis* better represents the average forms of Trilobites than anything else.

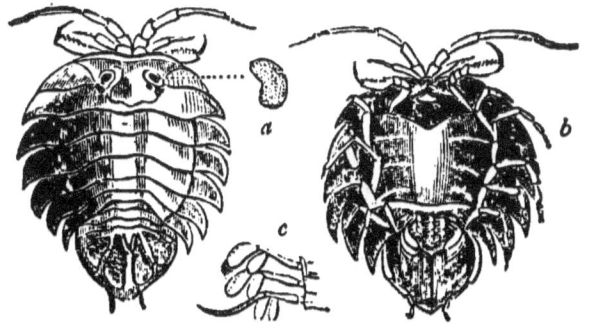

Fig. 158.—*Serolis Fabricii*. Fig. 159.—Under side of *Serolis Fabricii*.
a, eyes; *b*, feet; *c*, organs of mouth (recent).

The Cambrian strata have recently been extended upwards as high as the "May Hill" group, so as to include rocks formerly classed as Lower Silurian. They are well represented in many parts of Great Britain, notably in North Wales and the Lake districts. Trilobites of various genera may be met with in many localities which are usually visited by tourists for the sake of the scenery alone. It is one of the privileges of the geologist, that his calling

O

takes him to some of the wildest, grandest, or most beautiful scenes in nature. Although, in not a few instances, rich fossiliferous strata occur in unlovely places, amid densely populated neighbourhoods, as at the Wren's Nest, near Dudley; yet as a rule fossils are most abundant where the rocks crop out along mountain or hill sides or sea-cliffs. In searching for them he startles the grouse or the moor-fowl, and finds many a lovely mountain plant solitarily blooming. Scenes of unsurpassed loveliness are thus revealed to him, in the grandeur of rock-masses, or the panoramic stretch of the valleys below and beyond. What wonder if men who have had to toil the year round for the bread which perisheth, in dingy offices or amid the noise and bustle of machinery, should so value the week or two of summer holiday, which enables them to devote themselves to those geological pursuits which have all the charm and excitement of hunting without any of its cruelty! For, if the geologist wishes to change the area of his labours from the mountain-side to the seaside, he can do so at leisure, without interfering with his success in fossil-hunting. Some of the very best sections are those to be seen in our sea-cliffs; some of the richest fossiliferous districts are where the student may be taking in a fresh stock of health whilst he is following his bent, and is silently impressing on his memory scenes of beauty which will last as long as his own individuality! Perhaps it is this direct contract with

Nature in all her varied moods which makes such enthusiasts of geologists. Not even botanists are more devoted to their hobby; and it is undoubtedly this enthusiasm which makes geological investigation independent of companionship for success.

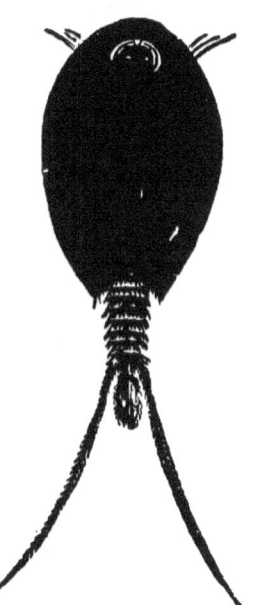

Fig. 160.—*Apus productus* (recent).

The absorption of most, if not all, of the Lower Silurian rocks into the Cambrian system has, of course, largely increased the number of localities where fossils are to be obtained. The Menevian beds near St. David's, in South Wales, are exceedingly rich in Trilobites; among which *Paradoxides Davidis*, the largest of its order, is abundant. This species sometimes attains a length of two feet, and is, therefore, strongly contrastible in this respect with the little *Agnostus* (Fig. 150) and the *Phillipsia* (Fig. 156). The South Welsh Valleys are comparatively little explored, although the geological student might do so to his double advantage, for they are equally rich in scenery and in fossils. Monmouthshire presents an area of country where we have, perhaps, a more varied geological outcrop than anywhere else in Great Britain. Near Newport a patch of Silurian strata abounds in several species of Trilobites, notably *Asaphus* and *Ogygia* (Figs. 139 and 155). Builth has been noted for the number and beauty of its *Ogygia Buchii*.

Maentrog and Port Madoc have long been celebrated for their rich yields of Trilobites. The student may obtain them, in many places, from the slates which build up the walls by the roadside, whilst in the quarries there are usually bands or seams especially full of them. Few localities are better worth a visit, for we are here within the charming circle of Snowdonia. The lower Lingula flags are well developed at Maentrog, and one Trilobite is so abundant in them that it was proposed to call them "*Olenus*" beds. Two species of the obscure little *Agnostus* are associated with it, along with various other fossils. At no great distance up the higher parts of the valley is Festiniog. A diminutive railway, with cars of the same proportion as the narrow diameter of its "permanent way," runs up one side of the valley to Festiniog, and the geological student can take advantage of it in his rambles, and thus pass over the outcrop of beds rich in Trilobites. A locality for Cambrian Trilobites is the neighbourhood of Dolgelly, a district whose magnificent scenery of wild mountain and umbrageous valley is annually drawing to it a larger number of tourists and visitors. Here *Conocoryphe*, *Agnostus*, etc., may be found in certain places in tolerable abundance. The student might advantageously work his way to Dolgelly by Tremadoc, at which place he will find abundant employment for his hammer. At the village of Penmorfa the slates are often crowded with remains of Trilobites. Garth Hill is also a capital collecting-ground. In many places the Llandeilo flags are so full of Trilobites that Sir Roderick Murchison gave them the name of "Trilobite Schists." Perhaps the neighbourhood of Builth is the best place for obtaining them. Several species of *Ogygia* occur, associated with numerous other fossils.

The Cambrian and Silurian rocks of the Lake District are not so abundant in Trilobites as those of North Wales and Shropshire, although I have found them in the rich fossiliferous shales of Applethwaite Common, and on the Lancashire side of Windermere—chiefly *Asaphus. Calymene, Homalonotus*, and others occur in the Dalton shales, of Upper Llandeilo age. In the Coniston limestone, also, we have *Illænus, Cheirurus, Agnostus*, etc., all of them well-marked genera of Trilobites.

In the Silurian proper (the *upper* Silurian of geologists only a few years ago) we find Trilobites reaching their maximum of existence, both in genera, species, and individuals; and we have tolerably certain evidence that after this epoch they began to decline until they became extinct. In the loveliest parts of North Wales, as at Conway, the Devil's Bridge (near Pentre Voelas), Craig Hir, and at Mynydd Fronfrys, about four miles from Llangollen, among the mountains, we find abundance of fossils, and among them are various species of *Phacops, Calymene*, etc. The pretty village of Woodhope, near Hereford, is another charming collecting-ground, rich in Upper Silurian fossils; and here we find *Illænus, Homalonotus, Phacops*, etc. Trilobites are also abundant in the Wenlock shales forming part of the Malvern Hills. Of the Dudley limestone and its treasury of these peculiar ancient forms of life, I have already spoken. The neighbourhood of Ludlow has also long been known as a rich storehouse of Trilobites of various species and genera.

In the Devonian beds it is only here and there we can meet with Trilobites in any abundance. One of the best localities is Newton Abbot, in Devonshire, where the limestone contains numerous Trilobites. The Pilton beds yield certain species of *Phacops* in plenty. The Trilobites are most abundant in the Middle Devonian strata of England, owing to the probable fresh-water conditions under which most of the other beds were deposited. The Carboniferous limestone, both of England and Ireland, is frequently rich in Trilobites of the genera *Phillipsia* and *Griffithsides*, named after two distinguished geologists. At Castleton, in the Peak of Derbyshire, along the outcrop of the strata forming Tre-cliff, is a band especially crowded with *Phillipsia;* and in the curious gorge to the immediate south of the cavern called "Cave Dale" (undoubtedly an ancient cavern with the roof worn off) we may find this Trilobite associated with a wonderfully abundant collection of other fossils. At Salt Hill, Clitheroe, in Lancashire, the shales which part the limestone bands are seen crowded with the evidently moulted remains of *Phillipsia*.

The large number of species, even of British Trilobites, obtained from the various strata above mentioned, are grouped into certain families. We have first the *Agnostidæ*, characterized by their small size, by the head and tail being covered with two nearly equal shields, and the possession of not more than two body-rings. This family was *eyeless*. The *Olenidæ* or *Paradoxidæ* had long bodies, with numerous free segments. The caudal or tail shield was small; the side lobes were prolonged into curved spines. A large number of the more ancient genera of Trilobites belong to this family. The *Asaphidæ* were tolerably large oval Trilobites, with smooth carapaces, and possessed about eight body-rings. *Illænus* and *Ogygia* are included in this group. The *Trinucleidæ* had a large head-shield, ending in two long spines, one on each side. The body-rings were five or six in number. The *Cheiruridæ* included seven distinct genera, which had a geological range from the Cambrian to the Devonian strata. The facial sutures of the head-shield ended on the outer margin. The number of rings or segments was eleven, and these were free at their ends. The *Calymenidæ* had carapaces roughened over with granules or tubercles, and the number of body-rings was usually thirteen. In *Homalonotus*, one of the two genera composing this family, the body-rings are not so distinctly trilobed as usual. *Phacopidæ* was a family of Trilobites with large facetted eyes. The number of body-rings is eleven. The *Lichadæ* had small head-shields, and a tail or pygidium with a broad limb. It contains only the genus *Lichas*. The *Prætidæ* includes the Carboniferous genera *Phillipsia* and *Griffithsides*. Their number of body-rings was usually nine. The carapace of *Phillipsia* is generally roughened with granules. *Acidaspidæ* had a very ornamental carapace, with eight to ten body-rings, and the segments of the side lobes (pleuræ) directed backwards. The tail had also two or three segments, furnished with prominent spines. The *Bronteidæ* had a large expanded tail or pygidium. The *Harpeidæ* were noted for the horseshoe-shaped head-shield, whose angles were greatly prolonged. The body was numerously jointed, usually with twenty-six segments. Only one genus, *Harpes*, belongs to it. Lastly, we have the *Cyphaspidæ*, whose head-shield was also prolonged into spines, and the carapace marked by spiny or pitted surface ornamentations. The number of body-rings varied in the different genera from ten to twenty-two. These are among the less common of the Trilobites.

I have given the principal place to Trilobites

among the fossil crustacea on account of their singular interest and beauty; but nearly all other living groups of this family are represented in the fossil state. We have some occurring in the latter condition which have long been extinct, as the *Eurypteridæ*, for instance. Its members were both abundant and huge of size during the Upper Silurian and Devonian

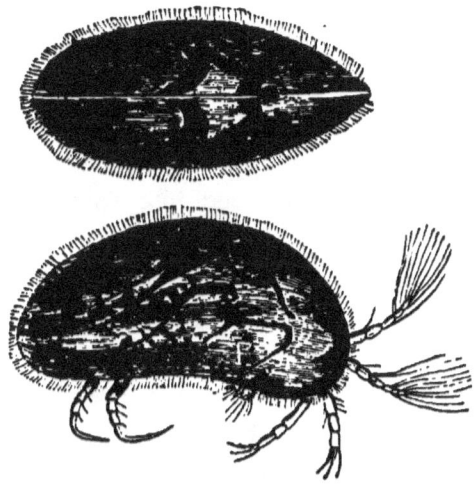

Fig. 161.—Recent *Entomostracan* (magnified). The upper figure shows the two valve-like parts of the crust.

periods. Specimens of this group may be seen in nearly all our British museums. The *Phyllopoda* were among the first crustaceans to appear in the early seas, and were represented by *Hymenocaris*. The *Entomostraca* are the lowest organized among this varied class of animals, and from the Lower Silurian rocks upwards and onwards into the seas, lakes, and rivers of modern times, we rarely lose sight of them. The shales overlying the Coal-seams frequently look as if somebody had sown millions of pins' heads there: these are the fossil *Cyprides*, allied to the water-fleas seen in our modern ponds and tarns. Shales, slates, and thin limestones not unfrequently owe their fissile character to the abundance of Entomostracans of various kinds.

The large and beautiful *Estheria*—a form still existing, and delighting in brackish water, and whose two shells so much resemble those of a bivalve mollusc (even in the recent state) that a young student may easily be deceived into thinking he has found another sort of animal—occurs first in the Devonian rocks, and is also found in the Carboniferous and Permian series. In the upper Trias of Warwickshire and Leicestershire it is not unfrequent; indeed, it is one of the few fossils found in these strata, which are so rich in evidences of physical action—rain-drops, sun-cracks, ripple-marks, etc.—and so poor in palæontological souvenirs.

To the naturalist there are few classes of the world-wide (and also *old* world) group of crustacea more interesting than the *Cirripedia*, of which our modern acorn-shells (*Balanus*), seen clustering after their sessile fashion on the rocks, to the detriment of naked feet when bathing—and the stalked kinds (*Lepas*) seen attached to fragments of old wreck-wood which has long been floating about and is at length cast ashore,

TRILOBITES AND OTHER FOSSIL CRUSTACEA. 203

In these animals, curious and wonderful as they are in their power of adaptation, we find a class which are zoologically more highly organized in their *larval* state than in their adult condition. The doctrine of evolution admits of *retrogression* as well as of *progression*, and the Cirripedia are all, without an exception, illustrations of the former. Consequently, for the philosophical student to find fossil specimens of a group illustrating *retrogression* is an interesting fact.

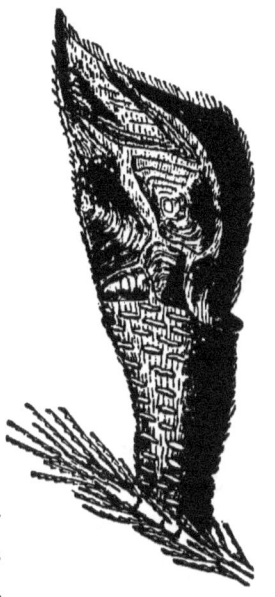

Fig. 162.—*Scalpellum vulgare* (recent).

It would appear as if the *stalked* barnacles (*Lepadidæ*) preceded in geological time the sessile kinds. Thus we find a genus of the former so far back as the Upper Silurian rocks, in which *Turrilepas* occurs. In the Rhætic strata we have *Pollicipes;* we come across them frequently in true marine strata (and all of this group are of a thoroughly marine character), through the Oolites, into the White Chalk, where Darwin mentioned thirty-two species as having been dis-

Fig. 163.—*Balanus porcatus.*

Figs. 162, 163.—Specimens of recent stalked and sessile Barnacles.

covered. The White Chalk of Norfolk has, I believe, proved richest in these stalked cirripedial forms. The peculiar angular and striated plates are by no means uncommon in the Chalk-pits about Norwich, and they are found fossilized (generally on the outside) on the flint nodules as well.

Real *sessile* Cirripedes occur first in the Lias. *Verruca stromia* is common (in detached plates) in the Coralline and Red Crags. Species of sessile barnacles still in existence—as, for instance, *Balanus porcatus*, etc.—cover the upper surfaces of all the large stones at the bottom of the Red Crag strata near Ipswich and Felixstowe; and so firmly do they cling that I have frequently seen the pauper-broken flints (obtained thence) in fragments, with their share of thickly coated fossil barnacle-shells still adhering to them—thanks to the strong precipitation of iron-oxide which cemented them more firmly than ever they intended to their original settling-place more than a quarter of a million of years ago!

What we call *true* crustaceans are hardly represented by that early "shrimp," the *Hymenocaris*. All zoologists know that the true crustacea are now separated into the long-bodied kinds (*Macrura*), such as the lobsters and crayfish; and the short-bodied kinds (*Brachyura*), as represented by our modern edible crab. Somewhere half-way between these we may place the *Anomura*, of which the soft-bellied, hard-clawed, and evidently anomalous "hermit-crabs" are examples.

It has frequently been pointed out that by carefully studying the embryological development of any individual up to its adult state, we may get a glimpse of the stages through which the genus or species, or even the family, has passed in its evolutional develop-

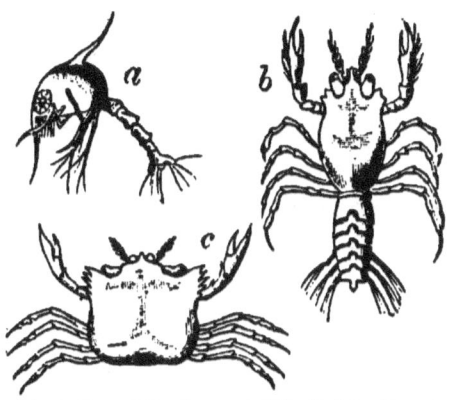

Fig. 164.—Phases in the Larval Development of the Crab: *a*, Zœa stage; *b*, advanced (or *megalopa*) stage; *c*, earliest completed stage.

ment. Thus the young larvæ of the common crab—whose aborted and contracted body is popularly known as the "apron"—in the first three or four of its early stages, has a properly jointed body like the lobster. The long-bodied crustaceans preceded the short-bodied ones in order of geological time; so that we have here an indication that the short-bodied crabs are descended from long-bodied and lobster-like ancestors.

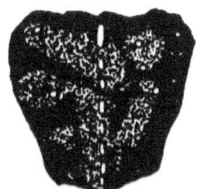

Fig. 165.—Carapace of *Notopocorystes*. (Cambridge Greensand).

The short-bodied crustaceans (called *Brachyura* on

that account) have not been found in rocks of older formation than the Lower Oolite. There we get a generic form, named by Dr. H. Woodward *Paliœnachus*. The long-bodied crustacea (*Macrura*) had appeared in the stage of creation before the end of the Primary period, as *Anthrapalæmon*—the *Phyllopods* (a lower group) having preceded them.

In many English localities the fossil crustacea are very beautifully preserved, and are unquestionably among the gems of the cabinet when properly worked out. In the Oolitic and Cretaceous rocks we have the well-known generic type *Eryon*, not at all uncommon. The chalk of Hertfordshire has yielded to a friend of mine (who was geologically inclined, and wanted a "hobby") a number of *new* forms of fossil crayfishes. The real fact was—they wanted hunting up. When the student has learned to recognize crustacean structure, and he sees a bit of it cropping out in the chalk, he must work away with his pocket-knife and tooth-brush until the whole of the probably buried-up crustacean is developed. Chalk is a capital rock for allowing of this; the harder Oolitic limestone is not so easily persuaded to give up its dead.

When we came to the Tertiary formations, especially to the Eocene—or rather, the London Clay representative of that interesting formation—the higher-developed fossil crustaceans are not uncommon, and, in places, even plentiful. The London Clay of the Isle of Sheppey is a sort of crustacean cemetery. How abundant they are there may be best stated by saying that Sheppey *fossil* lobsters may be bought in the Strand geologist's shop for sixpence each—a good deal cheaper than the price of the *recent* lobsters in the other shops, a door or two away.

Still, at Sheppey, and elsewhere, these fossil crustaceans have to be dug out of the clay, or else the collector takes advantage of the weather and the waves having washed them out of exposed cliffs.

In Suffolk we are very advantageously placed in this respect. The weather and the waves washed all the harder Eocene fossil crustacea out of the London Clay, perhaps during the Eocene period, and they were collected together in hollows and other protected places. The area these fossils occupied subsequently became a sea-floor, and the old derivative fossil crustaceans were thus covered up by the dead shells of a later period, and were even subjected to the indignity of having their petrified corpses made use of as settling-places for Red-Crag barnacles (retrograde representatives of the class of which they were aristocrats)!

Anyhow, you can get any number of fossil crabs and lobsters—*Brachyura, Anomoura*, and *Macrura*—in the heaps of phosphatic nodules collected together and awaiting carting, in the neighbourhood of the "coprolite" pits about Ipswich and Felixtowe. The commonest of these fossil crustaceans are *Xanthopsis, Thenops, Zantholites, Hoploparia, Archæo-*

carabus, *Dromilites* (possibly a fossil hermit-crab), etc. . Some of these derivative specimens are very perfect, others are water-worn; but all are imbedded in what was once a phosphatic paste. Singularly enough, marine phosphate deposits are frequently remarkable for their fossil crustaceans; as, for instance, the Greensand "coprolites" of Cambridgeshire, where we have an abundance of the carapaces of *Notopocorystes*. In the Silurian formation we have certain thin beds of phosphorite, or phosphate of lime, more or less associated with Trilobites, and perhaps partly produced by their subsequent chemical transformation; for we have to remember that the carapaces of crustaceans are remarkable for the quantity of phosphate of lime which enters into their composition.

CHAPTER VIII.

FOSSIL SEA-MATS (POLYZOA).

FEW people, possessed of natural history tastes, can have examined the odds and ends thrown upon the sea-beaches of the watering-places in the summer without noticing that the larger seaweeds, and even the bases of the numerous corallines, are matted or encrusted with peculiarly lovely lace-like organisms, which bleach to a pure white when dead. A magnifying glass shows clusters of cells, the residences of tiny and relatively highly organized little creatures which live together in a neighbourly fashion—all of them the descendants of an original ancestor, like the "ham" of an early Saxon chief. The cells are variously shaped, adorned or defended by spines, etc., so that species can easily be multiplied. A good deal of lime is employed in the walls and partitions of these dwellings, hence their durability after death. Some genera are remarkable for the relatively large quantity of lime used in their common structure or Polyzoaria, as, for instance, *Eschara*, etc.

Others are largely chitinous, as the common sea-mats (*Flustra*), whose seaweed-like fronds often appear as algæ in seaside albums, but which are really an innumerable colony of little cells placed back to back.

Fig. 166.—Recent Polyzoon (*Membranipora*), encrusting Sea-weed.

Stones, rocks, oyster and other shells are frequently invested with the spreading growth of these lovely organisms. And in this respect we find their habits have not altered since the Silurian period, for numbers of the pretty corals, shells, etc., in the limestones of the Silurian, Devonian, Carboniferous, Permian, Oolite, Chalk, and Crag formations are more or less covered with fossil Polyzoa. Indeed, in the Crag beds we often find univalves so thickly encrusted with growths of these animals that the mollusca must have been finally killed by the mouths of their shells being closed. Recent fronds of the *Laminaria* seaweed just thrown up are sure to be

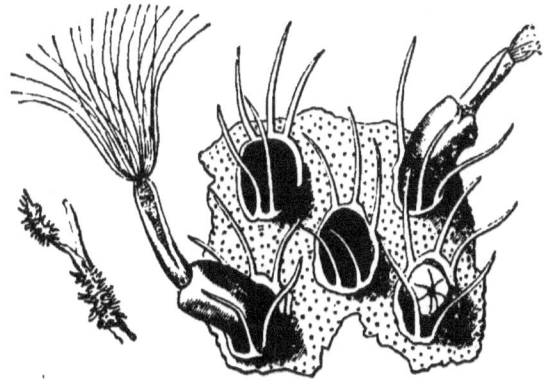

Fig. 167.—Recent Polyzoon, showing Polyps protruded (magnified).

found with living patches of these lace-like organisms upon them. Let the observer snip off a strip with such a colony upon it, and place it in sea-water. If it is of a dull glassy appearance, and not an opaque white, the colony is probably alive. When the strip is placed in a zoophyte-trough, after a short time, the observer will see suddenly popping out of each cell a cluster of lily-like petals, sixteen or more in number.

These are the ciliated tentacles, and a higher power (say a half-inch objective) will show the cilia actively at work on the lobe-like tentacles, so that the sea-water is thrown into a state of microscopical commotion thereby, and particles of floating matter are seen whirled about, and finally gathered by the vortex into the mouth of one of the little creatures, whose diaphanous body enables us to trace its passage to the stomach. The slightest jerk, or even the falling of a shadow, is quite sufficient to cause these zoophytes to withdraw within the protection of their cells—to reappear immediately afterwards.

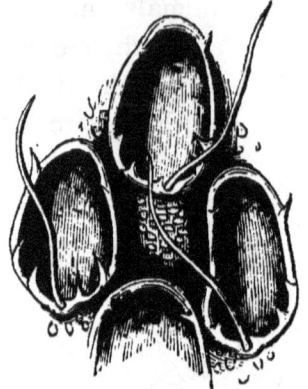

Fig. 168.—Cells of *Membranipora* (magnified, 60).

All of the Polyzoa are really highly organized creatures, possessed of a mouth, stomach, intestinal canal, anus, and nervous and muscular systems. They are very nearly related to the *Ascidia* or "sea-squirts" (especially to those social groups of the latter family we see clustered on seaweeds, such as *Botryllus*). The absence of any solid parts in the "sea-squirt" family has of course prevented our finding any traces of them in the fossil state. This is to be regretted, especially as the tadpole-shaped young of these Ascidians so much resemble the internal organization of the lowest of the Vertebrates—the order of fishes represented by the Lancelet (*Amphioxus lanceolatus*) —that we may regard them as a bridge connecting the Invertebrate and Vertebrate divisions of the

Fig. 169.—Common Sea-Mat (*Flustra truncata*), natural size, recent.

animal kingdom. Indeed, the larvæ of the Ascidians are so much more highly organized than the adults that Professor Ray Lankester and others regard the Ascidia as *degraded* Vertebrates! The geologist hardly doubts that sea-squirts were in existence in the earlier seas of the globe. Had we any fossil evidences of them, they might be serviceable in tracing the original connection between the Invertebrates and the Vertebrates.

These sea-mats are also related to another group of animals which, as we have already seen, played a very active part in the seas of the Palæozoic epoch—the Lamp-shells or *Brachiopoda*. In fact, sea-mats,

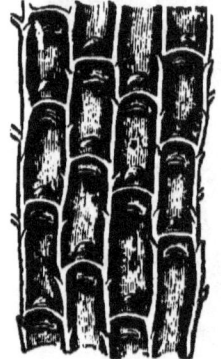

Fig. 170.—Cells of *Flustra* (magnified 60).

Fig. 171.—Social Ascidians (*Botryllus*), on Sea-weed (natural size).

sea-squirts, and lamp-shells are all grouped in the division *Molluscoida*.

It is a common error to associate the sea-mats with the Corallines. In reality these two groups of animals are widely separated by zoological characters, although not unfrequently they greatly resemble each other as far as external characters go.

The most beautiful, and perhaps also the most extensive, of the ancient sea-mats were the *Fenestellidæ*.

FOSSIL SEA-MATS.

They abound in the marine deposits of all the Palæozoic rocks, from the Lower Silurian upwards. The

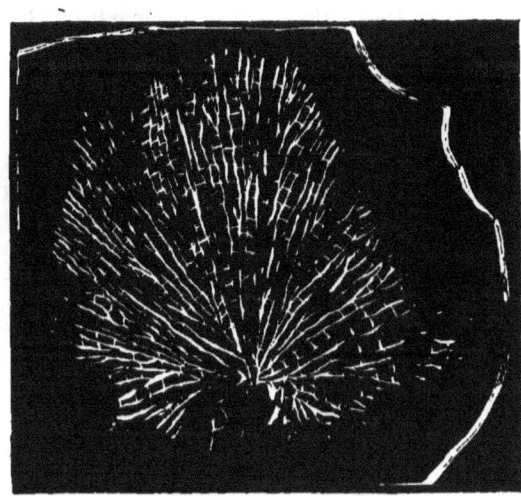

Fig. 172.—*Fenestella plebeia.*

geologist finds them creeping over shells and encrinite stems, and they are often spread out in a fan shape.

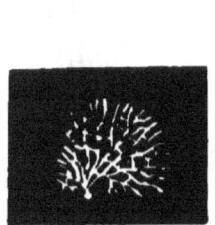 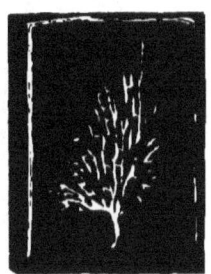 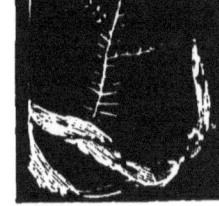

Figs. 173, 174.—*Fenestella plebeia* (Carboniferous limestone, Halkyn, etc.).   Fig. 175.—*Glauconome flexicarinata.*

The limestone shales of the Silurian and Carboniferous formation contain them in great plenty, as is indicated by the fact that Mr. G. R. Vine obtained, by washing from six to eight tons of Wenlock shale, a vast number of specimens of fossil Polyzoa, among which the genera

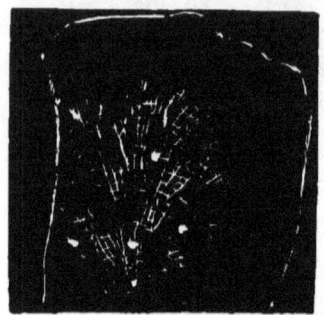
Fig. 176.—*Fenestella nodulosa* (Carboniferous limestone and shales).

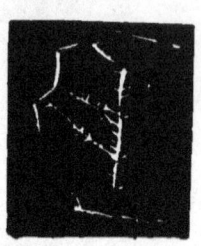
Fig. 177.—*Glauconome elegans.*

Stomatopora, *Spiropora*, *Glauconome*, *Hornera*, *Fenestella*, etc., were abundant. Certain localities are distinguished for the abundance of fossil sea-mats they

Fig. 178.—*Vincularia.*

Fig. 179.—*Retepora* (magnified).

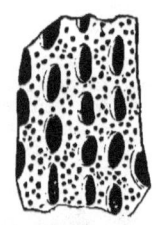
Fig. 180.—Portion of *Polypora* (magnified).

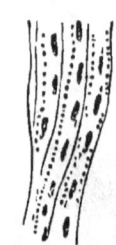
Fig. 181.—*Fenestella membranacea* (magnified).

have yielded, but it is really because there have been enthusiastic geologists to work them. Mr. Vine has astonished palæontologists by the great number of new species he has obtained by carefully washing, sifting, etc., deposits likely to contain Polyzoa in nearly all our British marine strata. Mr. John Young, F.G.S. of Glasgow, has similarly worked the Lower Carboniferous beds of Scotland, and has carefully brought to light a wonderful variety. Hairmyres is perhaps the best hunting-ground for these delicate little fossils in Scotland, and the Halkyn Mountains in Wales. But they are easiest seen on the surfaces

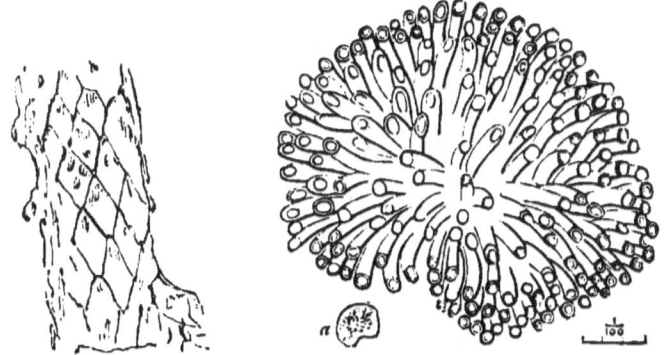

Fig. 182.—*Polypora tuberculata*, showing arrangement of cells.

Fig. 183.—*Diastopora Oolitica*: *a*, natural size.

of the thin dark bands of shale which frequently occur in all limestones.

The Oolitic limestones are frequently rich in Polyzoa, of which perhaps *Diastopora* is the commonest genus, and *Bidiastopora*, *Eschara*, and *Idmonea* the next.

In the Chalk (a deep-sea deposit—and the Polyzoa seem to love clear water, as is proved by the abundance of recent species on the "Gulf-weed") the sea-mats attain their minimum of beauty. About two hundred species are said to have been already described from this important formation, most of them belonging to the genus *Eschara*. I have found that the best objects on which to look for Cretaceous fossil sea-mats are the naked tests of such sea-urchins as Ananchytes and Galerites. Very few of these fossils, excavated from the Norfolk Chalk, and then carefully and tenderly washed, but have a sprinkling of fossil

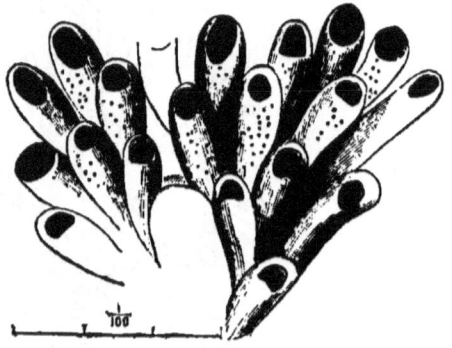

Fig. 184.—Cells of *Diastopora Oolitica* (magnified).

sea-mats over them. Not a few may be found completely invested with them (all but the base), looking as if the "fairy-loaves," as they are called, had been packed away in delicate Honiton lace, and all had been fossilized together. We find these Cretaceous sea-mats actually silicified, which shows what a great chemical change is often included in fossilization.

We do not lose sight of fossil sea-mats in our British Eocene deposits, but the place to find Tertiary species in superabundance is the "Coralline" Crag, which took its geological name from their numerical abundance, in the early zoological days when sea-mats and sea-firs (*Hydrozoa* and *Polyzoa*) were grouped together as "corallines."

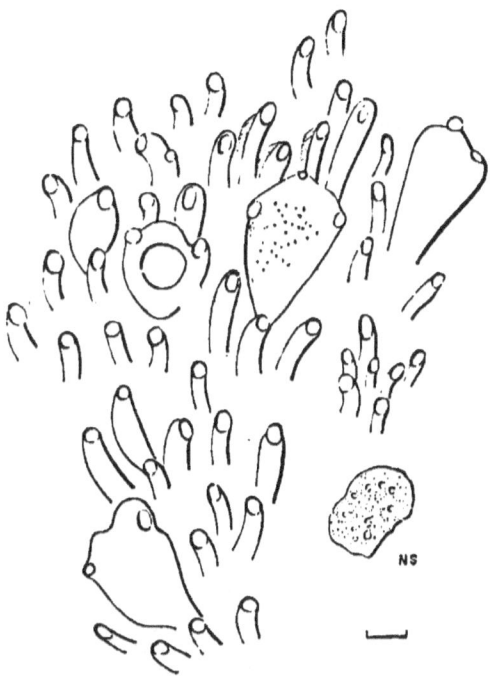

Fig. 185.—*Diastopora ventricosa*; NS (natural size).

The "re-deposited" Coralline or White Crag is best seen in the neighbourhood of Aldborough and Orford, in Suffolk, where it is about eighty feet thick, and of a pretty cream-colour. The fossils in this bed are abundant, but every one is encrusted with a growth of fossil Polyzoa, many of them allied to, if not identical with, existing kinds, such as *Cellepora*,

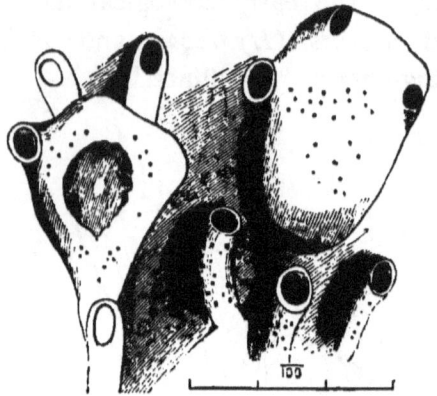

Fig. 186.—*Diastopora ventricosa* (highly magnified).

Membranipora, Hornera, etc. Others are locally extinct, and can only be found in warmer seas. Near

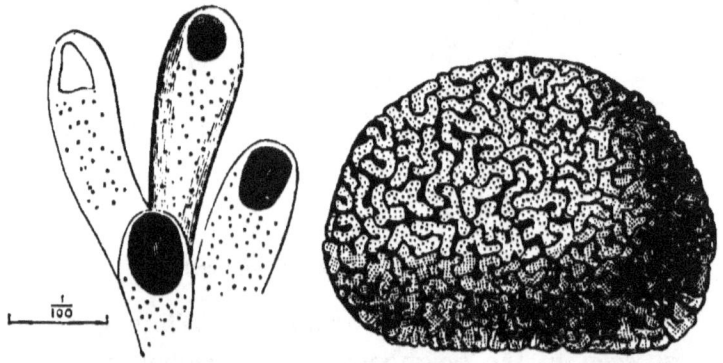

Fig. 187.—Cells of *Diastopora Oolitica* (highly magnified).

Fig. 188.—*Fascicularia aurantium* (Coralline and Red Crags).

Orford the young geologist will find plenty of round balls, which, when split open, reveal a radiated structure, each surface of this convoluted and radiated structure showing the latticed appearance of a sea-mat. This is *Fascicularia aurantium*. Other common kinds (about which Professor Busk wrote a monograph for the Palæontological Society) are several species of *Hornera*, of which the most beautiful, perhaps, is *H. reteporacea;* several species of *Alveolaria*, the finest and largest being *A. semiovata ;* of *Eschara*, and *Cellepora*. Some of the latter species are branched and resemble corals ; others, as *Cellepora edax*, have crept over, covered, and suffocated the inhabitants of univalve shells. *Hydractinia* is also found in the fossil state in the Coralline Crag, covering shells in a similar manner. Other abundant sea-mats are various species of *Lepralia* (found covering the interiors of empty bivalves), *Heteropora*, and others which the collector will not fail to gather about Orford and Aldborough, in greater abundance than his powers to remove them will prove available.

CHAPTER IX.

FOSSIL LAMP-SHELLS (BRACHIOPODA).

REFERENCE has already been made to this class of fossils as being by far the most numerous in the Primary rocks. The limestones are not unfrequently wholly composed of their ancient shells. They are also very abundant in the Secondary strata, although less numerous than in those preceding them; whilst in the Tertiary marine deposits they are much scarcer, and in the Recent or present period comparatively rare. Thus the Geological Record presents us with the interesting spectacle of the rise, growth, decline, and fall of one very large class of marine animals.

Notwithstanding this inability on the part of the Brachiopoda to compete successfully in the struggle for existence with the more highly organized mollusca, it is very singular how persistently certain genera have maintained their distinctive features through periods of time as vast as that which has extended from the Silurian epoch to the present day, like the *Lingula* genus, for instance, has done. One can hardly distinguish the fossil Lingulas, found so abundantly in the Lingula Flags (whence the name of the latter deposit), from those still living, and possessed of the same kind of peduncle or anchoring appendage, as well as the same semi-horny structure of shell. The pretty *Terebratula striata*, found not uncommonly in the Chalk near Norwich, is believed to be even specifically identical with a form still living in British seas, but known by another name. Mr. Thomas Davidson, F.R.S., in his exceedingly lucid papers on "What is a Brachiopod?" published in the *Geological Magazine* for 1877, says, "What wonderful changes have been operating during the incalculable number of ages in which the creation and extinction of a large number of genera and thousands of species have taken place! Some few only of the primordial, or first created genera, such as *Lingula, Discina,* and *Crania*, have fought their way and struggled for existence through the entire sequence of geological time; many were destined to a comparatively ephemeral existence, while others had a greater or lesser prolongation of reproduction."

Fig. 189.—*Lingular anatina*, (recent), showing peduncle.

It seems as if the very name of this order contains a fossil *idea*—that these animals employed their long coiled arms for locomotive purposes. Such was the origin of the term *Brachiopoda*, or "arm-footed." And, although Professor King endeavoured to change the name to *Palliobranchiata* (or "mantle-gilled"), the

Fig. 190.—*Lingula* (Silurian formation).

latter somehow has not "stuck." Suffice it to say, therefore, that the long arms of the *Brachiopoda*—so distinctive a feature in their anatomy and physiology—are only labial appendages to the mouth, bringing food by means of their currents, and air as well; but are never employed as locomotive organs.

The young of the *Brachiopoda*, like those of such well-known bivalves as the common oyster, are free-

Fig. 191.—*Lingula Lewisii* (Silurian formation).

Fig. 192.—*Leptæna transversalis* (Silurian).

swimmers. In this stage they are believed by some to show evidences of annelid affinity—just as Mr. Harmer has recently demonstrated that young Polyzoa show affinities with the *Rotiferæ*. It is interesting thus to see the hitherto unstudied stages of embryological development enabling the naturalist to join hands across a space which the boldest investigator would not have dreamed of half a century ago!

The common name of "lamp-shells," given both to fossil and recent species of Brachiopoda, is due to the resemblance of the two valves, ventral and dorsal (minus the *handle*), to an old Etruscan or Roman

Fig. 193.—*Atrypa reticularis*, showing internal spiral coil (Silurian formation).

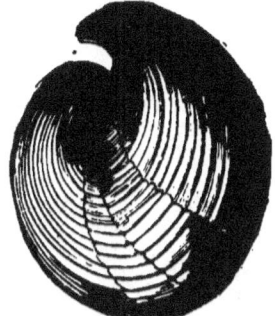

Fig. 194.—*Obolus*, showing internal loop.

Fig. 195.—*Pentamerus Knightii* (Upper Silurian limestone).

lamp. The ventral valve is the larger, and usually has a perforation in the upturned beak, exactly like that through which the wick passed in the ancient

Fig. 196.—*Pentamerus*, showing internal plates.

Fig. 197.—*Orthis elegantula* (Silurian).

lamps. Older naturalists were, of course, more affected by external appearances than by internal structure—even supposing they took any notice of the

Q

latter—and by them this group of fossils were called *Lampades*.

The *structure* of the shells of Brachiopoda (as

Fig. 198.—*Craniæ*, showing exterior and interior of shells.

Dr. Carpenter has clearly shown) is different from that of the bivalves or Lamellibranchiate mollusca,

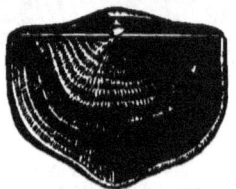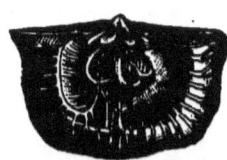

Fig. 199.—*Strophomena depressa*, showing exterior and interior of valves (Silurian).

although it represents one stage in the formation of the shells of the latter—that of the outer layer.

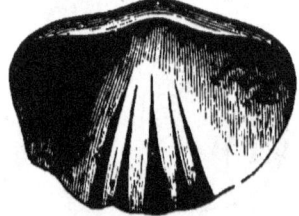

Fig. 200.—*Strophomena rugosa*.

Fig. 201.—*Rhynchonella pugnus* (Carboniferous limestone).

Owing to the large size of the " arms" (as they are still technically called) of most of the Brachiopods, the interior of the valves contain remarkable structures, which are useful to the palæontologist in enabling him to classify these fossils. In many genera there is a limy, *brittle*, and delicate structure, assuming either the shape of "plates," "loops," or "spirals." Very frequently we get fossils in which

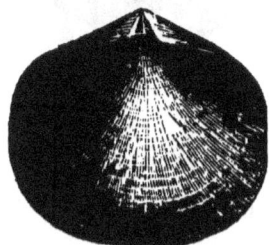

Fig. 202.—*Orthis striatula* (Devonian).

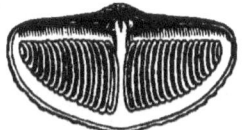

Fig. 203.—Interior of *Spirifer*, showing spiral coils.

these are still preserved, and the experienced worker among the limestones of the Palæozoic rocks knows that the "chert-bands"—that is, the accumulation of

Fig. 204.—*Spirifer trigonalis*, showing internal coil where portion of shell is removed (Carboniferous limestone).

Fig. 205.—*Spirifer speciosus* (Devonian).

chemically combined silica and lime (analogous to the flint-bands and nodules of the Chalk)—are the best places in which to look for the *internal* spirals, loops, plates, etc., of the fossil Brachiopods. For in such places the outer shell has been dissolved away, and the internal and more delicate "skeleton" has been preserved, and is now perhaps encrusted with microscopical crystals of silica.

In all cases, this internal loop, spiral, or whatever shape it may have assumed, is merely the mechanical

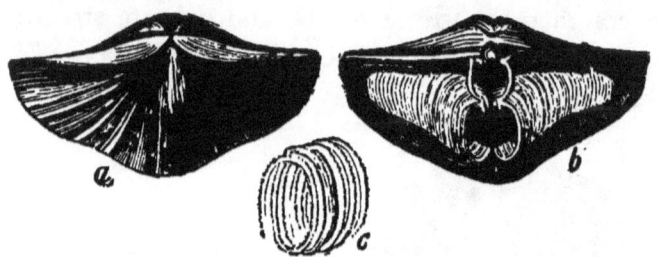

Fig. 206.—*Spirifer striatus*: *a*, exterior of shell; *b*, interior, showing spiral coils; *c*, portion of coil (Carboniferous limestone).

support of the brachial or labial coils, about which remarks have already been made.

Not unfrequently this internal loop (as in some *Terebratulæ*) occupies more than half of the interior

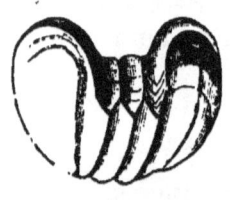  

Fig. 207.—*Rhynchonella pleurodon* (Carboniferous limestone). Fig. 208.—*Terebratula hastata* (Carboniferous limestone). Fig. 209.—*Spirifer cuspidatus* (Carboniferous limestone).

of the shell. In the *Spiriferæ* there are two conical coils or spires (whence the name of the genus—"spire-bearing"), the apices of which are on each side. In the *Pentamerus* we have it developed as a series of *plates*, dividing the interior into five parts, like chambers; so that this ancient genus of Brachiopods takes its name from the circumstance. In the *Rhynchonellidæ* there are two internal short, slender, and curved plates. What we have to note, however, is

Fig. 210.—*Rhyachonella* (Carboniferous limestone).

Fig. 211.—*Productus punctata* (Carboniferous limestone).

that all of these mechanical structures are merely adaptations, to better enable the " arms " to do their work effectively. It is in the *smaller* or dorsal valve

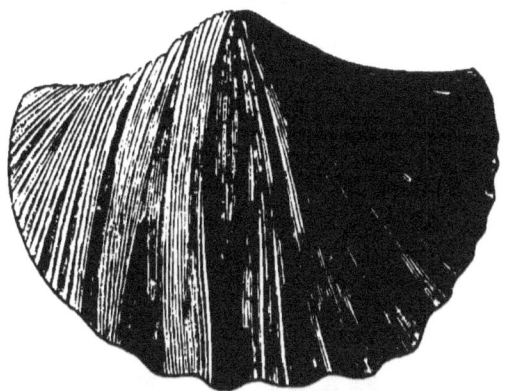

Fig. 212.—*Productus giganteus* (Carboniferous limestone).

that this skeleton is usually seen. No skeleton is found within the genera *Lingula, Lingulella, Obolus, Discina, Crania,* etc. In the *Terebratulæ* it is often largely developed, and assumes such a variety of forms that it proves useful for classificatory purposes. The spiral coils are found in *Spirifer, Spiriferina, Athyris, Retzia, Merista,* etc. In the *Rhynchonellidæ*

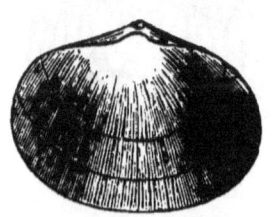

Fig. 213.—*Orthis resupinata* (Carboniferous limestone).

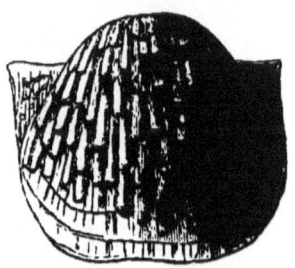

Fig. 214.—*Productus scabriculus* (Carboniferous limestone).

the fleshy arms are usually supported by the pair of short plates alluded to, and sometimes by spirally coiled ribbons, closely pressed together, and having the apices of the flattened spires meeting *within*, instead of the reverse way, as in the *Spiriferæ*. This structure is best and most commonly found in *Atrypa*.

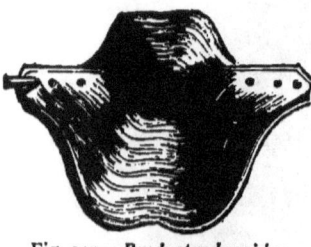

Fig. 215.—*Productus horridus* (Permian limestone).

The enormous size of the plates inside the *Pentamerus* is finely seen in the large and beautiful Upper Silurian fossil *Pentamerus Knightii*, which frequently splits open with great ease along the planes or faces of these internal divisions.

The *Cranias* are easily identified, for they are

found adhering like limpets, by the entire surface of the ventral valves, to other fossils. This family has had a wonderfully long range in geological time, for species belonging to it are not uncommon in the Silurian rocks, and the genus has lived on ever since into our own time, and is still to be found in British seas, particularly in the marine lochs of Western Scotland.

The valves of *Strophomena*—abundant in the Silurian rocks—are semicircular in shape, and the two valves vary, being sometimes flat or concave or convex. It is the type of a family of Brachiopods to which the well-known genera *Orthis*, *Leptæna*, *Streptorhychus*, etc., belong.

The *Productus* family is a very important and a very interesting one. These fossils usually occur in great specific abundance, so that if we meet with one or two individuals we may expect to find others. Indeed, the *living* Brachiopods are still distinguished by their social or gregarious habits. Where they do occur, they live in abundance. One of the pleasantest rewards of the dredger in Oban Bay and thereabouts is to bring up a clinker with half a dozen living *Terebratulina caput-serpentis*. What a sensation it is to see in the flesh a representative of one of the oldest and most continuously unbroken families of the globe! It is like raising a ghost unawares. One of the best-known of living Brachiopods is the Australian *Waldheimia Australis*. We see it in every museum, and in most private collections ; and it can be bought very cheaply, which is perhaps a still better proof of its commonness. This Brachiopod can be gathered by handsfull in the reefs of the Australian coasts. Evidently, in the "good old times" (which must be the last lingering memory of the Brachiopods), this habit of living together not only characterized the race, but had very important geological results. Who can visit the bold Eglwysey rocks, in the Vale of Llangollen, for instance, and see how the white limestone is in places composed entirely of the valves *Productus Llangolliensis*, without feeling that if it had not been for the abundance and gregarious habits of this Brachiopod in the early Carboniferous seas, those very rocks would never have been in existence ? The same may be said of the Carboniferous limestone near Buxton, where the huge *Productus giganteus*—not unfrequently as large as a child's head—builds up the rock wholesale. *Rhynchonella Wilsonii* in the Silurian limestones, and *Rhynchonella socialis* (deservedly so called) in the Oolites, have performed the same geological feat.

The *Productidæ* are very easy to make out, notwithstanding their strong specific differentiations. The two shells are either concavo-convex, as in *Productus giganteus*, *P. Martini*, *P. cora*, etc., or round above and flat beneath, as in *Productus punctatus*, etc. The valves are, moreover, frequently adorned with spines, as in *Productus spinosus* (armed with them like a conchological hedgehog), or the well-known *Productus horridus* of the Permian rocks—the latter found in good condition near Tynemouth. Another feature about the valves of the *Productus* family is that they are "auriculated," which means that the shells are more or less drawn out on either side of the hinge-line. The *Productidæ* have been extinct ever since the close of the Primary or Palæozoic epoch. A microscopical examination of the shells of any species of *Productus* would alone enable a student to identify it, if only on account of the peculiar "canals" which are present.

Speaking of this group of fossils, Mr. Etheridge says—"The significance or importance of *Productus* as a Carboniferous genus cannot be overlooked when determining, through its species, definite horizons in these rocks. It is ubiquitous; in no region on the globe, where Carboniferous rocks are developed, do we not find this characteristic shell, and in vast abundance—in the Polar regions, Australia, New Zealand, Van Dieman's Land, India, America (in fifteen states), throughout Europe, and in Africa."

The space in the hinge-line between the two shells (deltidium) has to be taken into account in the endeavour to identify species. This is largest developed in *Spirifera deltoidea*—of the Carboniferous limestone—and is not an uncommon fossil at Castleton, in the Peak District of Derbyshire, —surely, one of the most delightful for a young geologist to "break ground" on, to be found within the narrow circle of the present British seas.

Terebratulidæ is a well-known group of fossil Brachiopods, which have been in existence from the Devonian period without losing their distinctive characters up to the present day. The genus reached its climax during the Oolitic period, when nearly seventy species were in existence. *Waldheimia Australis*—the antipodal representative—seems to be doing well and flourishing yet, as though the country which is still the abode of Marsupials (the *low-pressure*

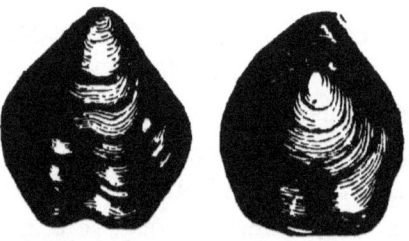

Fig. 216.—*Terebratula biplicata* (Oolite).

Secondary type of Mammalian life that preceded the high-pressure forms of the Tertiary and Recent periods) were a belated geological area both as regards sea and land. What an abundance of species of *Terebratula* occur in the limestone of all the geological periods! *Terebratula hastata* swarms in many localities in the Carboniferous limestone. About Castleton, Derbyshire, and near Clitheroe, Lancashire, we get it in every stage of growth, and with remnants of its ancient radiating colour-bands still adorning it. The noble *Pentamerus Knightii* of the Aymestry limestone used to be so abundant that it was used to mend the roads with. *Terebratula sella* is no less abundant in the Oolite; *T. carnea* and *T. globosa*, equally so in the White Chalk of England, in almost every Chalk-pit. *T. grandis*, of the Suffolk White Coralline Crag, is the hugest and finest of all, but uncommon enough for the young geologist to be

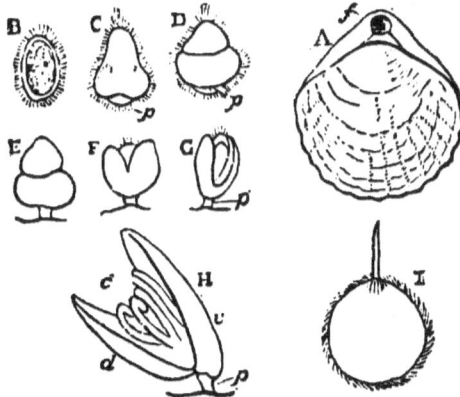

Fig. 217.—Diagram showing the various stages of development in a recent Brachiopod, from *b*, *c*, larval stages, etc., to *a*, adult animal.

delighted when he finds a specimen with both valves still united.

The fossil Brachiopoda have undergone great changes. In the Cambrian, Silurian, and Devonian slates we find them chiefly as casts, the fossils being natural casts of the interior of the shells, and the slates retaining the impressions of the external ribs and other markings. On the top of Snowdon, and elsewhere, we find them imbedded in volcanic ashes, which accumulated on the ancient Silurian sea-bed. The original lime of the shells has in all these instances been dissolved away by the action of percolating water.

The Upper Silurian rocks, limestones, and shales are perhaps the best hunting-grounds for fossil Brachiopoda. More than a hundred species are found

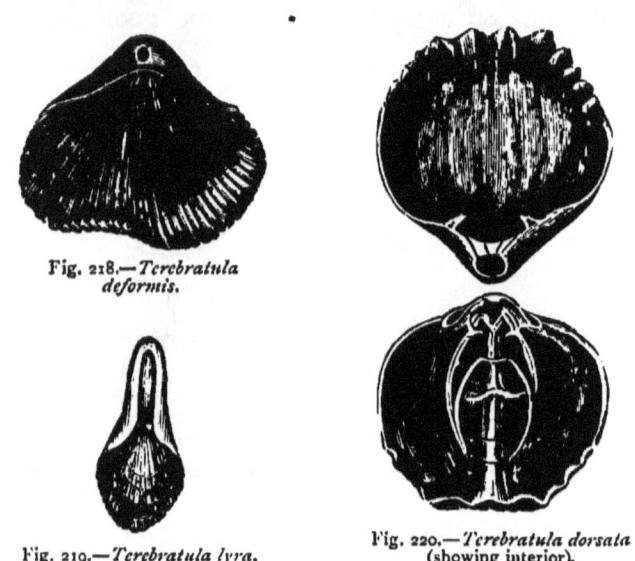

Fig. 218.—*Terebratula deformis.*

Fig. 219.—*Terebratula lyra.*

Fig. 220.—*Terebratula dorsata* (showing interior).

in them, and there is not a single locality where these rocks are quarried (that I know of) where fossil Brachiopoda cannot be obtained. Some districts are especially noted for them—the Wren's Nest, near Dudley; Aymestry; Woolhope; the Malverns; Girvan, in Ayrshire, etc. They are not less common in the Devonian and Carboniferous limestones as regards individuals. The most notable form in the Devonian rocks is *Calceola*, which occurs in such numbers near Torquay and Newton that the rocks are technically called "Calceola-beds." Every geological formation,

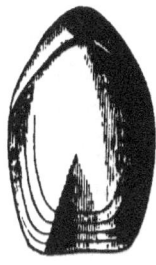 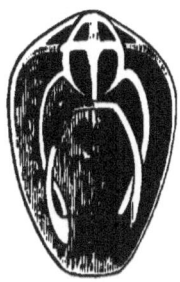

Fig. 221.—*Terebratula*, one valve showing large internal loop.

and most subdivisions, have their suite of peculiar Brachiopods. The coins of the later Roman empire do not succeed each other more rapidly than do these

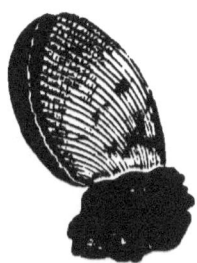  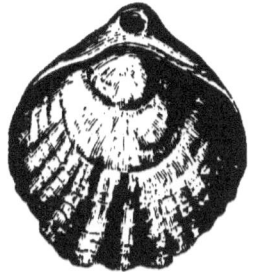

Fig. 222.—Recent species of *Terebratula*.

Fig. 223.—*Terebratula caput-serpentis* (recent, but supposed to be identical with *T. striata* of the Chalk).

Fig. 224.—*Terebratula dorsata* (exterior).

fossils in the rocks of Palæozoic age. Hence their great value to the geologist in helping him to diagnose the strata where he happens to find them. Another peculiarity about the Palæozoic Brachiopods is their world-wide character—many of the same species distinguish Australian and American limestones and shales which are characteristic of British rocks. Altogether this is a most interesting series of animal forms, and one which has played no small share in the formation of the stratified rocks of the earth's crust—living on through long periods of geological time; silent witnesses of those great world-throes and world-changes, each appearing at the time destructive, but all of which were combined to make our world such as we find it to-day.

CHAPTER X.

FOSSIL MOLLUSCA (PALÆOZOIC, OR PRIMARY).
BIVALVES AND UNIVALVES.

IT does not need much mental preparation to perceive that the hard parts of those animals popularly called "shell-fish" must have contributed very largely to "fossil remains." They are so abundant, so widely spread, so wonderfully adapted to almost every physical condition of the earth's surface—terrestrial, fresh-water, brackish water, shallow and deep seas,—to cold, temperate, and tropical regions alike—that it is not surprising the geologist pays great attention to the suggestions which fossil mollusca give him. Moreover, mollusca are, perhaps, among the most permanent and stereotyped, and the least inclined to change, of animal forms. The fossil fresh-water mussels which flourished in the extensive lakes of the Old Red Sandstone period (*Anodonta Jukesii*) do not differ in any important character from the Swan mussels (*Anodon*), so abundant in English lakes and rivers at the present time; the *Paludina* of the Wealden epoch, and the *Planorbis* of the Eocene, are so like species of the same genera now abundant in any of our streams and ponds, that the least informed student would identify the relationship at once.

Perhaps this wonderful persistence of type in fresh-water mollusca is to be found in the fact that fresh-water conditions experience less change in physical environment than any other. The water of the Old Red Sandstone lakes may have been exposed

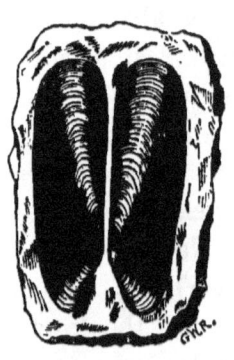
Fig. 225.—*Orthonota parallela.*

Fig. 226.—*Murchisonia gracilis.*

to warmer conditions than those of Great Britain now, but in the deeper parts the bivalve mollusca would find almost similar conditions that modern fresh-water bivalves would be able to select, if they chose to do so.

The *composition* of the shells of bivalve mollusca is not always the same. Indeed, we may somewhat definitely separate them into two classes, according to the chemical composition of their shells—*calcitic* and *arragonitic*. To the modern student of mollusca this may not seem of the same importance it is to the geologist. To the latter, this difference in the composition of the limy shells of bivalves is frequently of great value; for the valves composed of the limy mineral *arragonite* are liable to be decomposed by the action of percolating water through the rocks in which they are imbedded much sooner than those constructed of calcite. Hence the geological student finds the remains of fossil mollusca possessed of shells composed of arragonite chiefly, if not entirely, as *casts*. Calcite is a more stable or endurable form of lime than arragonite—hence the reason why mollusca whose shells are formed of arragonite are found as casts, whilst those whose shells are of calcite appear to be unchanged.

Shells are useful to the geologist, also, in quietly but emphatically convincing him of the former conditions of marine and fresh-water deposition of strata. He finds them bored by marine sponges. Or they may be covered, inside and out, with the tubes of marine worms or Polyzoa, or spat of ancient oysters —in which case he knows these fossil bivalves died, and their parts separated, before the contemporary creatures which made use of them for a mechanical foothold could spread there. Such conditions quite correspond to those he sees going on nowadays at the seaside.

Bivalves and univalves are the most abundant of

the mollusca, and their hard parts or shells are among the most valuable and durable of all the "medals of creation." But doubtless there were sea-slugs in the ancient seas, just as there are now, but as they possess no hard parts (except teeth), they have not contributed in any notable way to fossil remains. When we study the fossil mollusca, we see that the univalves have been more modified than the bivalves. Mr. J. Starkie Gardner has also noticed this fact. He states that, as regards bivalve mollusca, there does not seem to be any broad rule of progression. The contrary is the case with the univalves or Gasteropods. In them, says Mr. Gardner, there is a most unmistakable and pronounced tendency to elongate the canal. He therefore thinks that the presence in greater or less numbers, or the absence, of spindle-shaped or fusiform shells possessed of lengthened canals, would be an infallible test of the geological age of any group of Gasteropods, from the Oolitic rocks to the Eocene. Thus, the Cones and the Cowries are among the most highly differentiated of Gasteropods, and they are also the latest introduced.

The mollusca have a geological value in determining the physical conditions of ancient seas. Where bivalves abound, as in the different strata of the Oolite, we have evidence of shallow water, and this is usually supplemented by other facts. Not unfrequently the univalves bear similar testimony, for many littoral or shallow-water genera have a very high geological antiquity.

One broad fact also strikes the geological student: the specific and numerical abundance of mollusca, bivalve and univalve, is greatest in the most recent formations, and least in the oldest ; whereas the specific and numerical abundance of the Brachiopods is just the reverse—greatest in the oldest deposits, and scantiest in the latest formed.

The shells of bivalves may be regarded as hollow cones. The *umbo* or beak is the apex of such cone. The shells are frequently unequal-sided, one being more elongated than the other. The mouth of the animal within the shell is uniformly on that side of the body indicated by the umbo or beak ; hence this is called the *anterior* or front part of the shell. The two valves are hinged together by projections and notches which accurately fit each other, and these are technically called "teeth." Their number, size, and position have to be carefully noted, for they are among the chief means of diagnozing genera and species.

Inside the shells of all bivalves, fossil as well as recent, the student will observe well-defined scars, which indicate where the mantle of the animal was attached. In some mollusca the mantle is in two halves or lobes which are united along their edges, so that a siphon is necessary to admit water to the gills. Such bivalve mollusca are usually sand and mud dwellers, and during life are imbedded in an upright position, with the siphon projecting above the muddy bottom where they are protected. These siphons can be lengthened or shortened at the will of the animal, by means of special muscles. These muscles leave their marks on the interior of the shell, so that a naturalist can readily tell a Siphonate mollusc from an Asiphonate kind. In the latter, the scar left by the mantle's attachment is unbroken; in the former, it is indented into a sort of bay or *sinus*. Scars are also left by the adductor muscles, which close the two shells and defend the animal from enemies.

Singularly enough, there is a geological peculiarity about the two kinds of bivalves just mentioned.

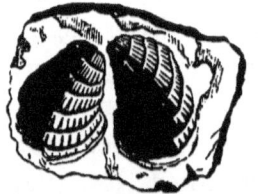

Fig. 227.—*Cardiola interrupta* (Silurian).

Fig. 228.—*Pterinea subfalcata* (Silurian).

The siphon-bearing (*Siphonate*) mollusca get more numerous in the Secondary rocks than they were in the Primary, whilst they are far more numerous in the Tertiary strata than in the Secondary. The Primary and early Secondary rocks are marked by a preponderance of siphonless (*Asiphonate*) bivalves.

Fossil bivalves first make their appearance in the Lower Tremadoc rocks, where about twelve species have been found. The univalves first appear in the Arenig rocks. In the neighbourhood of St. David's four genera are met with, among which are the ancient forms of *Pleurotomaria* and *Euomphalus*.

But neither bivalves nor univalves are very abundant in our British Cambrian rocks. Perhaps the district of Ty-Obry, North Wales, is one of the best for finding this class of fossils, among which are *Palæarca socialis*, and species of *Ctenodonta*. These are, in reality, very highly organized bivalves, and the fact that they are among the oldest known indicates, if evolution be true, that many other simpler forms must have preceded them.

Fig. 229.—*Ctenodonta contracta*.

In the Silurian rocks the true mollusca grow more abundant; and in the Upper Silurian, although there are few species, these are individually abundant. Both in the Cambrian and Silurian rocks (except in the limestones of the latter) the fossils exist as *casts*. The lime of the true shells has long been dissolved away, and only the impressions left in the rocks where they were originally imbedded. These impressions have often been filled in by infiltration of some other material, so that natural casts of them have thus been taken. Nevertheless, vast numbers of the fossils in these older rocks are only to be met with as *impressions*. Many of them are very clear and beautiful; others are not only obscure, but often pulled out of shape by having partaken in the molecular movements resulting in "cleavage."

The most abundant of these early genera of mollusca, besides those already named, are—*Patella* (the limpet, whose simple cone is an index of the degree in which all univalve shells have been modified), *Bellerophon* (a "heteropod," or free-swimming gasteropod), *Natica* (which has been in existence ever since, and is still abundant in British seas), *Murchisonia*, *Holopella*, *Loxonema*, *Cyclonema*, *Ophileta*, *Orthonota*, *Ambonychia*, *Pterinea*, *Myacites*, *Cardiola*, *Nuclea*, etc. In the Middle Silurian rocks which crop up about Eastnor, in the Malverns (a locality not likely to be soon forgotten for its quiet beauty), one bivalve, *Nuclea Eastnori*, is common. Several small quarries may be visited in Eastnor Park where these fossils are to be obtained. Near Bronsil a large species of Pterinea occurs.

The Upper Silurian rocks almost everywhere yield plenty of fossil mollusca. In the hardened Wenlock shales about Llangollen, *Cardiola interruptæ* is most abundant; the casts showing that the two opened valves were not separated. The Ludlow beds in the quarry on the side of the river opposite the picturesque old castle, are crowded with *Ctenodonta* and *Orthonota*. In the Wenlock limestone of Shropshire and South Staffordshire that splendid fossil univalve *Euomphalus rugosus* is abundant.

The Middle Devonian strata of North Devon occur in about the most varied and picturesque portion of that charming county. I have found a little botany an excellent help-meet to fossil-hunting, for they can both be pursued together. Nowhere is this twofold pursuit more delightful than along the coasts of North Devon. At the Little Hangman, the rocks in places are fossiliferous, although only to be met with as casts. Here is that singular and easily recognized bivalve *Megalodon*, and large mussel *Natica*, etc. The quarry at Hagginton Hill abounds with fossils, and the pedestrian will frequently meet with them as he hammers his way along from Ilfracombe to Combe Martin. At Pilton and Barnstaple the Upper Devonian rocks yield abundance of *Avicula*, *Cucculea*, *Modiola*, etc. Perhaps the richest locality for obtaining these are the rocks on the summit of the hill at Baggy Point: Braunton, Marwood, and other localities, also yield them. Top Orchard quarry has long been a recognized Devonian hunting-ground.

The Devonian limestone also contains fossil mollusca. The ancestors of the common cockle (*Cardium*) first appear here. *Loxonema Murchisonia*, etc., are found in the limestone at Plymouth, Chudleigh, Newton Abbot, and elsewhere.

Fossil fresh-water mussels, nearly allied to the common swan mussels of our rivers, are in abundance in the Old Red Strata of Kiltorcan, in Ireland. The species (*Anodonta Jukesii*) was named after the late director of the Irish geological survey. This fossil bivalve is also found in strata of similar age in Scotland.

The Carboniferous formation, in all its divisions, contains plenty of fossil mollusca. In places these are overwhelmingly abundant. The limestone yields several species of *Natica*. At Castleton, in the Peak

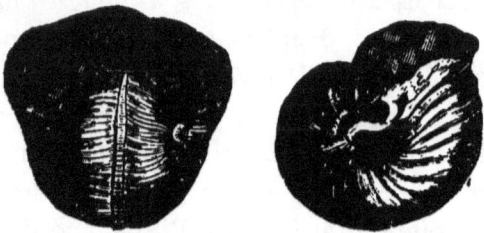

Fig. 230.—*Bellerophon hiulcus* (Carboniferous limestone).

of Derbyshire, these fossils are very beautifully preserved, and often of large size. The largest species, however, is to be met with in the neighbourhood of

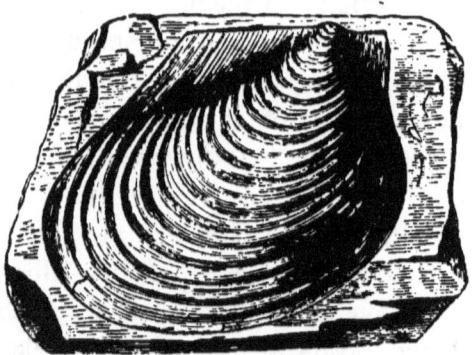

Fig. 231.—*Posidonia* (Carboniferous).

Clitheroe, in Lancashire, associated with *Bellerophon*. Both are met with as solid casts, often besprinkled with small crystals of calcite; and the geologist will see them ornamenting the window-sills of the cottages, or conspicuously placed in the "rockeries" of the gardens. *Euomphalus pentangulatus* is another abundant Carboniferous univalve, and one of the most beautiful.

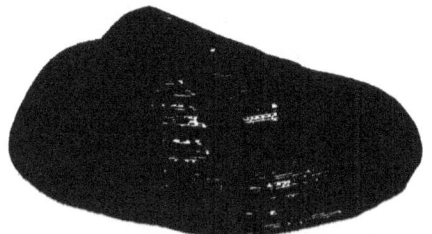

Fig. 232.—*Anthracosia robusta*.

It is very easily hammered out of the rock, where its hollow coil leaves a pretty impression. At Castleton it is extremely abundant, and may be met with in every stage of development; but, in point of fact, it is one of the most abundant and characteristic of the Carboniferous limestone fossils. *Pleurotomaria carinata* is abundant in places, as at Castleton—one of the best localities in Great Britain for the exquisite state in which the fossils are preserved. I have met

Fig. 233.—*Pleurotomaria carinata* (Carboniferous limestone).

with *Pleurotomaria* there with the zigzag markings still quite distinct. *Capulus* or *Calyptrea*, *Naticopsis*, *Murchisonia*, *Solarium*, *Nerita*, *Posidonomya*, *Sanguinolites*, *Pinna*, *Pecten*, *Cardiomorpha*, etc., are not unfrequent. In the black Carboniferous limestone of the Isle of Man *Sanguinolites* is locally very plentiful.

The Yoredale shales, and also the true Lower Coal Measures, often contain an abundance of fossil marine mollusca. Of these *Posidonomya* and *Aviculo-pecten papyraceus* are most numerous. The former is a small, thin bivalve; the latter of much larger size. In the black shales which crop out in the gorges and valleys near Hebden Bridge and Tod-

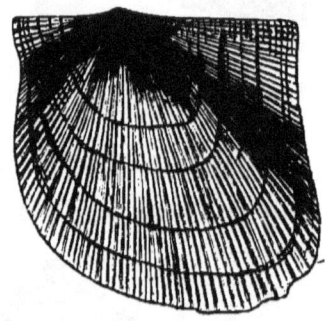

Fig. 234.—*Aviculo-pecten papyraceus* (Carboniferous formation).

Fig. 235.—*Euomphalus pentangulata* (Carboniferous limestone).

morden, *Aviculo-pecten* is converted into iron-pyrites, and the black shales look as if they had been gilded all over with pictures of this fossil. In the shales of the coal-seams in the Lower Measures near Oldham, and also in a similar situation in strata of about the same age at Halifax, *Aviculo-pecten* is uncompressed, and usually converted into carbonate of iron ore. This fossil is quite as abundant in the shales of this age in Ireland as in England. At the pretty spa of Lisdoonvarna, county Clare, it crowds them everywhere and the chemical decomposition of the pyrites, these fossils were originally converted into, has probably originated the sulphur springs.

Fresh-water mollusca take the place of the marine forms in the Upper Coal Measures. The most abundant is the genus *Anthracosia*, or "fossil mussel." Its dark-brown shells, often much flattened and crushed, may be found in the greatest abundance on the shale-heaps which accumulate near the coal-pits in Lancashire, Cheshire, and Yorkshire. In the colleries near Wigan several species may be obtained; one kind, *A. robusta*, so named on account of its greater size, is most abundant about the pits where the "Arley mine" is worked for coal. These Anthracosia are sometimes so numerous that the surfaces of the shale are completely covered thereby. Not unfrequently they are converted into argillaceous iron ore, and can then be picked out of the soft shale like nuts. At times they form bands of ironstone, rich enough to be worked and smelted, as at Carron, in Scotland, where the celebrated "Blackband" ironstone is formed of nothing but minerally altered mussel-shells. The geological student can hardly go to a coal-pit in Lancashire and Yorkshire, especially in the neighbourhoods of Manchester and Barnsley, without finding plenty of Anthracosia.

The Permian rocks of England are nowhere particularly rich in fossils—except, perhaps, a few localities near Tynemouth, where nests of minute Rissoa-like univalves are found. *Bakevellia* and *Schizodus* are the characteristic bivalves. The former used to be met with in great abundance in the Permian marls at Collyhurst, Manchester, but the place is now completely built over. The best Permian fossil-bearing localities are in Durham. About one-half of the fossil animals found in the Permian strata of Great Britain are mollusca, which fact is a fair index to the comparatively rapid manner this group had developed since its first scanty representation in the Cambrian formation. Some important genera first appear in the Permian, most notable among which, perhaps, is the genus *Mytilus*, or the true mussel family.

CHAPTER XI.

FOSSIL MOLLUSCA (MESOZOIC, OR SECONDARY).

FOSSIL mollusca increase very rapidly, both in species and numbers, as we explore the strata of the Secondary formations. They are absent from the Trias of Great Britain, the greater part of whose beds seem to have been formed along the bottoms of large lakes, something like the existing Dead Sea, whose waters were too salt for Mollusca to live in. In the Rhætic beds, however, which overlie the upper Trias, and which seem to have been formed under semi-marine or brackish-water conditions, bivalves are very abundant, and some of them are quite characteristic, such as *Cardium Rhæticum, Pecten Valoniensis, Avicula contorta, Ostrea liassica.* The student will find them in any quantity in the rocks forming the bold headland of Penarth, just beyond Cardiff, and also at Aust Cliff, on the opposite side the Severn estuary to Chepstow. At the latter place the grey Rhætic strata succeed the red Trias, and the ground is strewn with fallen blocks of the former, where some splendid fossilizing may be had—bones, teeth, and spines of fish, saurians, etc., as well as fossil shells being abundant. It is in this formation (a part of which was formerly known as the "White Lias") that the well-known but curious "Landscape marble" occurs at Cotham. Practically, we may say that the Rhætic series extends diagonally across England, from Redcar, on the north Yorkshire coast, to Lyme Regis. In many places its beds have been exposed, as near Leicester, where shells may be got. Somersetshire, however, is perhaps the best county for specimens, those obtained from near Watchet having found their way into most collections. Among other localities where Rhætic fossils can be hammered out are Queen Camel, near Yeovil, Westbury, Puriton, Shepton Mallet, Wedmore, and Beer Crocombe.

The strata of the Lias frequently teem with fine and well-preserved specimens of fossil mollusca, so that it is both difficult and tedious to enumerate localities for finding them, either in this formation or the Oolite, of which the Lias is now usually regarded as the lowest member. A good many modern genera of mollusca first make their appearance here, such as *Corbis*, *Astarte*, *Limnœa*, *Lithodomus*, and *Teredo*. The last two are curious on account of their habits, *Lithodomus* being a burrower, and Teredo (the genus of modern "ship-worms") a borer into wood, etc.

In the Oolite proper the now widespread genus

of bivalves, *Venus,* commenced its existence, together with *Trigonia* (still surviving in Australian seas), *Isocardia, Tellina, Corbula, Panopœa, Bulla, Paludina,* etc., all of which are well-known modern forms. The naturalist is as much interested, when studying the life-history of the globe as revealed by geology, in observing where the different kinds of families of animals and plants first make their appearance, as a genealogist is in tracing the commencement, development, and alliances of some illustrious aristocratic houses.

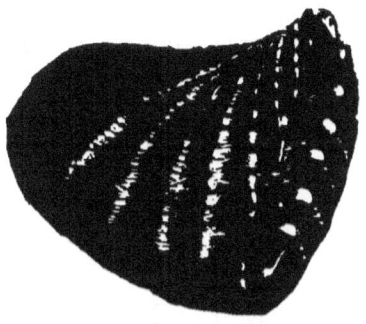

Fig. 236.—*Trigonia costata* (Oolite).

Commonest among the genera of Liassic and Oolitic univalve and bivalve mollusca are (in addition to those above-mentioned)—*Purpurina, Cerithium, Nerinea, Apporhais, Potamides, Modiola, Ostrea, Gryphœa, Exogyra, Gervillea, Pholadomya, Anatina, Lima, Hippodium, Pecten, Cucullœa, Avicula,* etc. Some of these are splendid fossils; and there are few cabinets, and perhaps no museums, which do not possess *Lima gigantea, Avicula Cygnipes, Hippodium ponderosum, Trigonia clavellata,* etc.

If the student cannot afford to travel in search of specimens to the spots where they are actually found, he can obtain them nowadays by various means, in exchange for those of his own neighbourhood. Or let him cultivate the acquaintance of the nearest stone-mason's yard, the proprietor whereof will set him up with plenty of "rotten stuff," unworkable because of the hollows and casts of fossil shells, but dearer to the young geologist than a gold-mine on that account! Fragments of Portland Oolite may always be got in any large stone-mason's yard, and they contain an abundance of fossil (casts), *Nerinæa*, *Cerithium*, and *Trigonia*, all of which are usually casts

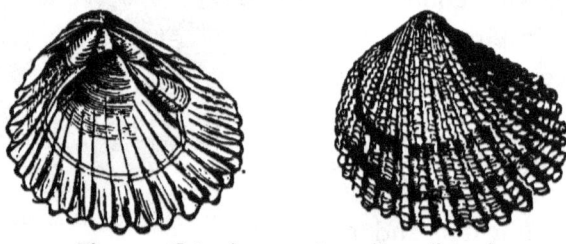

Fig. 237.—*Trigonia margaritacea* (Australia seas).

of the *interiors* of these shells; so they have a very different appearance from the more gracefully shaped and ornamented exteriors.

Tourists in the north-west of Scotland will find some interesting and varied geologizing in Western Scotland and the Hebrides; and in various places the Lias beds yield fossils, as along the Sound of Mull, Tobermory, the Isle of Skye, Eigg, Muck, etc., where there are fragmentary patches and outliers of once very extensive Lias and Oolitic strata, which probably extended from continuous fossilferous strata.

In Northamptonshire numerous fossil mollusca can be collected in the refuse of the iron-mines near Northampton town, and also at Kingsthorpe, Durton, and Blisworth. No fewer than one hundred and twenty-five species have been catalogued from the last neighbourhood. The "Northampton Sands" are very rich in this class of fossils, having yielded one hundred and forty-one species of bivalves, and thirty species of univalves.

The Oolitic strata of Yorkshire will similarly

Fig. 238.—*Gryphæa incurva* (Oolite).

reward the student, and these are all easily accessible from the various watering-places, such as Scarborough, Whitby, and Filey. Among other localities which are richly fossiliferous are Cloughton Wyke, Hundale, Hayburn Wyke, Gristhorpe, Cayton Bey, Pickering.

In Lincolnshire the Oolitic beds are cut through by the railway from Spalding to Lincoln, and in proceeding to the latter place from Grantham we see them forming the hills which flank the railway on the right-hand side. Numerous quarries, for road-material, limestone, and ironstone, are opened in them, where plenty of fossil mollusca can be collected. Perhaps the best collecting-grounds for Oolitic fossils in Lincolnshire are at Weldon, Wakerley, the neighbourhood of Stamford (as at Squire's Stone quarry), Wild's Ford, Kingscliffe, Stibbington, Whittering, Wrawly, Brigg, Market Rasen, and Horncastle.

We naturally turn to the West of England, how-

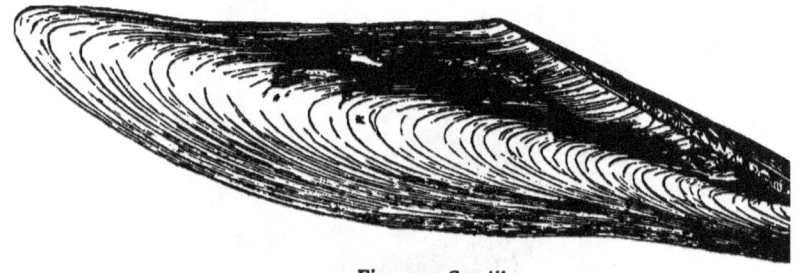

Fig. 239.—*Gervillea*.

ever, for Oolitic fossils. The great Oolite formation extends from the middle of Lincolnshire to Gloucestershire, and quarries for various purposes are opened in it more or less along its entire course, where fossils abound, among which bivalves and univalves are the most numerous. There are also plenty of places in Bedfordshire (as in Cowper's county), Rutlandshire, Buckinghamshire, and Oxfordshire, as well as Gloucestershire (which last county is nothing if not Oolitic), Somersetshire, Wiltshire, Dorsetshire, etc.

Mr. Robert Damon's excellent book on the geology of the latter coast supplies the tourist with more good fossiliferous localities than he will have time to visit, unless he has got nothing else to do, and both time and means to indulge his fossil-hunting propensities. Of course, all the strata at Kimmeridge Bay are classic ground for their geological interest. Both here and the neighbourhood of Weymouth fossil mollusca abound, *Trigoniæ* being particularly plentiful

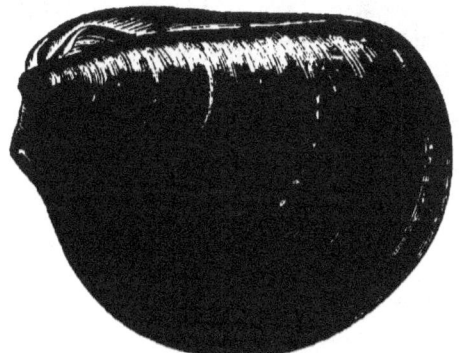

Fig. 240.—*Plapostom Giganteum* (Lias).

at Weymouth, Osmington. At Sandsfoot Castle we get the great *Limas*, and at Highworth. At Portland these fossils are so plentiful that one stratum of *Trigonia gibbosa* goes by the name of the Trigonia bed. The same series contains a stratum crowded with another fossil bivalve, *Exogyra bruntrutana*.

Between Swanage and Bridport the geologist gradually passes from the Eocene, through the Cretaceous, down to the lower strata of the Oolite. The

Fuller's earth at Langton, five miles west of Weymouth, contains plenty of small elongated fossil oysters, *Ostrea acuminata*. The Forest marble of the neighbourhood yields *Avicula, Lima, Pholadomya, Pecten, Trigonia, Myacites, Turbos, Eulimas*, etc. In the quarry at Well Down, *Ostrea Sowerbyi* and *Avicula costata* are especially common.

Fig. 241.—*Hippopodium ponderosum* (Oolite).

The stony cliffs of the back-water channel near the village of Radipole are composed of Cornbrash, crowded with bivalves and univalves, the commonest being *Pholadomya bucardium* and *Avicula edimata*. There are numerous quarries in the neighbourhood where similar fossils may be obtained.

The beautiful Vale of Wardour, Wiltshire, has long been famous for its yield of Oolitic fossils, and the geological structure of the district has been described in the "Transactions of the Geologists' Association." Among the commonest of the fossils belonging to the classes we are now considering are *Cerithium Portlandicum*, and other species of this genus of univalves; several species of *Trigonia, Ostrea, Cardium dissimile*, etc. The neighbourhood of Swindon is richly fossiliferous, *Trigonia, Lima, Ostrea*, and *Perna* being very common. The Upper Oolites continue into Buckinghamshire, where the limestones are usually full of fossils, such as *Natica, Trigonia, Cyprina, Cypricardia, Pleuromya, Mytilus,* etc.

Mr. Etheridge, F.R.S., states that the Oolitic (or Jurassic) rocks of Great Britain have yielded up to the present time no fewer than ninety-five genera, and one thousand three hundred and sixty-eight species of fossil bivalves alone. Indeed, they are by far the most abundant forms of ancient life met with in these rocks, although both Ammonites and Belemnites, and, in some localities, even Brachiopods, are also very numerously represented; some species of *Avicula, Hinnites, Lima, Ostrea, Pecten, Perna, Pinna, Astarte, Trigonia, Modiola, Cucculæa, Pholadomya,* etc., have a very long upward range. The total number of the Oolitic Gasteropods (according to the same high authority) is seventy-six genera, and one thousand and fifteen species. The most numerously represented of these genera are *Alaria, Cerithium, Chemnitzia, Nerinæa, Pleurotomaria, Trochus,* and *Turbo.*

In the uppermost strata of the Oolitic formation are the fresh-water beds at Purbeck, so crowded with the still living *Paludina* as to constitute the famous "Purbeck marble," formerly used in interior church work. Associated with this univalve are *Planorbis, Melania, Limnæa, Physa, Cyclus, Corbula,* and other well-known recent genera. Lulworth Cove is a capital hunting-ground for them.

The Wealden Clay, Sussex, has in places beds of

so-called "Sussex marble," also formed chiefly of a species of *Paludina*, which can hardly be distinguished from that which still abounds in English rivers. In the Isle of Wight the Wealden is also fossiliferous, especially near Sandown, the commonest fossil being a fresh-water bivalve *Unio Valdensis*.

At Punfield, in Dorsetshire, fresh-water shells, such as *Cyrena*, *Cyclas*, *Unio*, etc., are mixed with oyster-shells, indicating brackish-water conditions.

The Cretaceous, or Chalk formation, includes the Neocomian (better known, perhaps, as Lower Greensand), the Gault and Upper Greensand, and the Upper or Grey and White Chalk beds. At Specton and Tealby, in Lincolnshire, there is a bed of clay five hundred feet thick belonging to the former subdivision, and this is remarkable for a very large bivalve, *Pecten cinctus*, which is sometimes as much as a foot in diameter; *Perna Mulletii* is another characteristic fossil. The Lower Cretaceous beds are extensively developed in Surrey, Kent, Sussex, Oxfordshire, Bedfordshire, Hampshire, Wiltshire, Norfolk, etc. At Atherfield, in the Isle of Wight, the common fossils are *Perna, Arca, Astarte, Panopœa, Gervillea, Trigonia caudata, Exogyra sinuata*, etc. Near Maidstone there are numerous fossiliferous localities; the quarries where the well-known "Kentish rag" is worked are good fossiliferous places, where *Exogyra* and *Trigonia* more or less abound. Other localities are Godalming, Godstone, Folkestone,

Wotton, Sevenoaks, Nutfield, Pulborough, and Petersfield. Near Folkestone there occur layers of a siliceous limestone often full of *Ostrea, Arca, Lima, Exogyra, Panopæa,* and *Pecten.*

At Shotover Hill, near Oxford, there are strata of this age which contain *Unio, Cyrena, Paludina,* and other fresh-water forms. In Bedfordshire (as, for instance, at Patton, Woburn, Ampthill, Sandy, Wicken, and Upware) the sands are worked in order to get at a "coprolite" bed, which is frequently as much as two feet thick. These "coprolite" workings

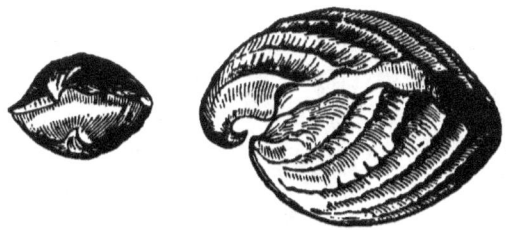

Fig. 242.—*Inoceramus sulcatus* (Gault).

are capital places for fossils, all phosphatized, or converted into phosphate of lime, and most of them of considerable interest and importance, because they have been "derived" or washed out of the older formations where they were originally deposited, such as the various strata of the Oolite and Wealden. *Ostrea, Gervillea, Exogyra, Gryphæa,* etc., are very common.

The fossils of the Gault have always been admired on account of their great beauty; many of them still retain, when dug out of the stiff clay, the rainbow hues of the nacre or mother-of-pearl coating. But the shells are fragile, and the tints evanescent, unless means are taken to preserve them. The commonest of the bivalve and univalve fossils are *Inoceramus sulcatus*, *Plicatula*, *Dentalium*, *Rostellaria*, etc. Outcrops of Gault clay, containing fossils, are worked at Barnwell, near Cambridge, but the chief hunting-ground has long been Copt Point, Folkestone, which is classic on that account. In Norfolk, the Red Chalk of Hunstanton—which stands forth in such vivid relief from the green strata below and the grey chalk above it—is usually regarded as of the same age as the Gault. It is in places full of small Belemnites, like those obtained from the Gault, and contains numerous *Inocerami* and *Ostrea*.

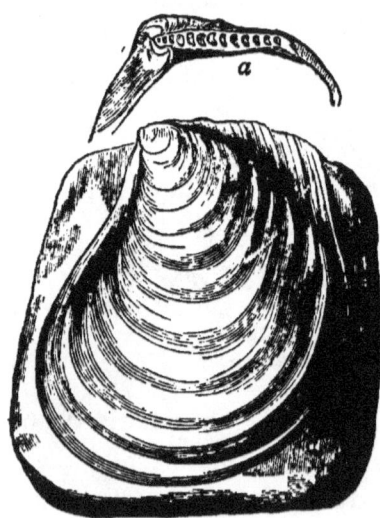

Fig. 243.—*Inoceramus Cuvieri* (Lower Chalk).

The Greensand of Cambridge rests on the Gault, and is crowded with fossils which have been washed out of that deposit. The Upper Greensand occurs in Devon, Somerset, Sussex, Kent, Isle of Wight, Dorsetshire, etc. Its chief fossils are *Pecten asper, Pecten Beaveri, Pecten quinquecostatus, Exogyra conica, Ostrea carinata.* The Warminster and Blackdown beds are also well known collecting-grounds for fossils of this period.

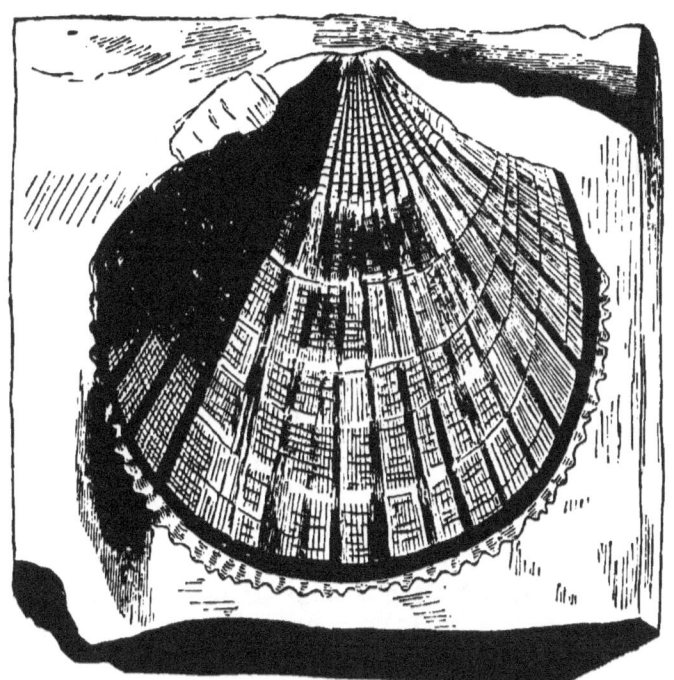

Fig. 244.—*Pecten Beaveri* (Greensand).

The Upper Chalk strata are always favourite fossil-collecting beds to a young geologist. The fossils look so pretty, when properly cleaned, in their white matrix; and, moreover, the eyes of the ardent youth are not so likely to be fatigued or repelled by the glaring whiteness of the chalk quarries in the hot summer sunshine, as they will be in later life. In Kent, Sussex, Dorset, Suffolk, Norfolk, Lincolnshire, Hertfordshire, etc., as well as the North of Ireland, every Chalk-pit contains fossils, more or less. True, both bivalves and univalves are comparatively rare, for these indicate that the strata they are found in were deposited in shallow water, whereas all the fossils incident in the Chalk, and especially in the Upper Chalk, bespeak deep water. Perhaps the earlier

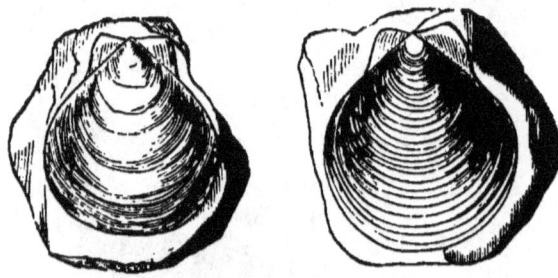

Fig. 245.—*Pecten orbicularis* (Chalk).

geologists thought the White Chalk was originally formed in deeper water than it is now known to have been; but it must still be regarded as a deep-sea deposit, in comparison with the varying strata of the Oolite.

The Lower White Chalk, perhaps, contains more fossil bivalves than the Upper. Some of them attain a large size, such as *Inoceramus Cuvieri* and *Inoceramus Lamarcki*, whose vertically fibrous structure reveals to the student the presence of the smallest fragment.

Inoceramus sulcatus and *Inoceramus concentricus* are also abundant forms, and they often serve to distinguish a block of Lower White Chalk from the Upper, where they are either uncommon or absent.

In the Chalk one of the commonest and most beautiful fossils is the bivalve *Spondylus spinosa*, which

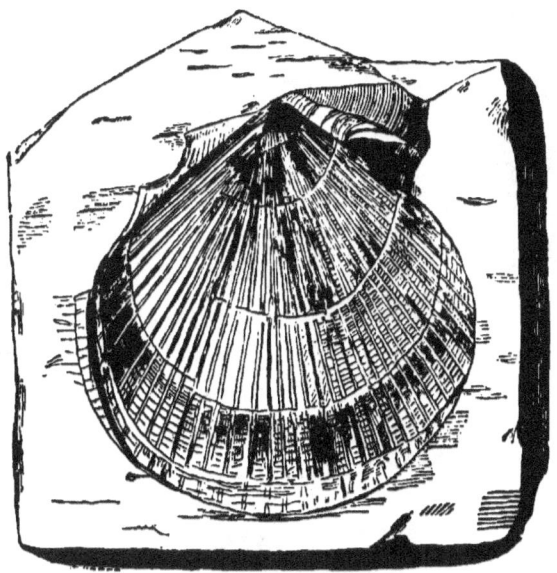

Fig. 246.—*Pecten interstriatus* (Greensand).

also rejoices in the other names of *Plagiostoma spinosa* and *Lima spinosa*, much to the unnecessary bewilderment of the student. It is difficult to extract it with its long spines intact, but patience, and the fortunate softness of the moist chalk when the fossil is first extracted, as well as the clever use of a camel's-hair brush to laboriously wash away the chalk matrix, will bring the collector off triumphantly. *Ostrea vescicularis* is a very abundant fossil in the Upper Chalk. It is found in every stage of development, from the young spat no bigger than a pin's head, to a grotesque and many-layered old *Ostrea*. One learns a good deal of the conditions of the deep sea-bed where chalk was formed, from such fossils as *O. vescicularis*. I know of no other fossil so apt to bewilder the young geologist, for its external shapes are various. The fact is, it could find few or no solid objects amid the slimy,

Fig. 247.—*Pecten inequvisival* (Greensand).

Fig. 248.—*Pecten asper* (Greensand).

muddy ooze (now white chalk) of the Cretaceous sea-bed, to which its valves could be attached. It

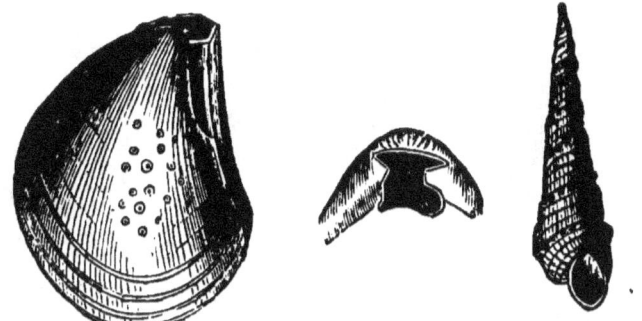

Fig. 249.—*Dianchora striata* (Cretaceous).

Fig. 250.—*Turitella granulata* (Greensand).

was thankful to settle down as spat on any surface

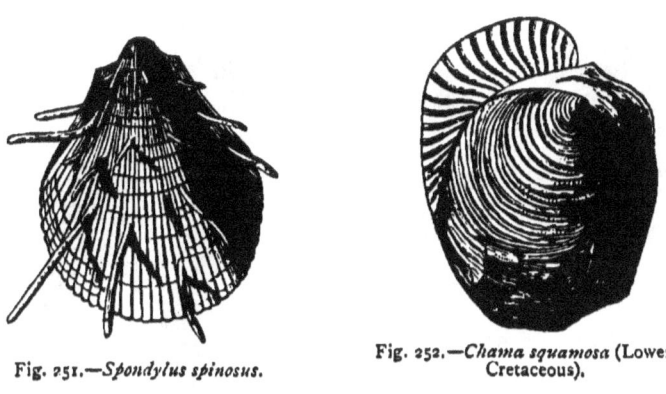

Fig. 251.—*Spondylus spinosus.*

Fig. 252.—*Chama squamosa* (Lower Cretaceous).

Fig. 253.—*Gervillea anceps* (Greensand).

which presented itself—whether a dead "fairy-loaf," the bone of a decomposed cuttle-fish (Belemnite), the dead shell of an Ammonite, etc.—where it settled, there it grew, adapting its expanding shell to the object it

 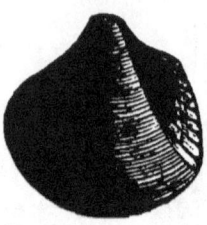 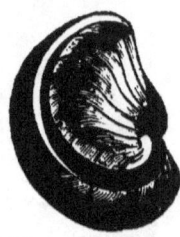

Fig. 254.—*Ostrea vescicularis* (Chalk).   Fig. 255.—*Cardium Lillanum* (Greensand).   Fig. 256.—*Exogyra conica* (Greensand).

was attached to; and so in the Chalk-pits near Norwich we find this very common fossil more than half

 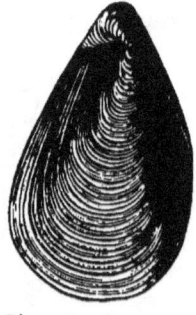 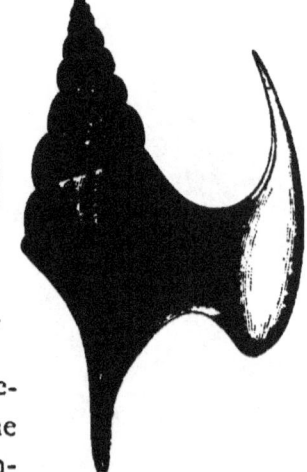

Fig. 257.—*Pecten quadricostatus.*   Fig. 258.—*Inoceramus concentricus.*

encircling the solid shafts of Belemnites, or actually taking the impression of some coiled Ammonite.

Fig. 259.—*Rostellaria Parkinsonii.*

Other bivalve mollusca of the Chalk are the graceful *Inoceramus mytiloides* and *I. labiatus*, the latter not unfrequent near Dover, whilst the former is found generally in the Lower White Chalk.

CHAPTER XII.

FOSSIL MOLLUSCA (CAINOZOIC, OR TERTIARY).

NOWHERE is a knowledge of fossil bivalves and univalves of such great importance as in the Tertiary strata. All other kinds of fossils are few in comparison with their abundance.

The pursuit of Tertiary geology takes the student into some of the most delightful spots in southern and eastern England, and to wide stretches of heath and common which still remain unenclosed. The sandy nature of the strata of many Tertiary formations tends to a "hungriness" of surface soil, especially in districts south of the Thames, where the morainic matter, or Boulder-clay of the Glacial period, is not strewn over the older deposits.

In Dorsetshire and Hampshire the Lower and Middle Eocene beds are frequently rich in fossil plants (as in the clay-pits on the west side of Bournemouth). The vertical strata of "pipe-clays," with their beautifully preserved fossil plants, are also well known at Alum Bay, Isle of Wight.

The Thanet Sands may be seen resting on the Chalk in the large pit close by Charlton Station, near Woolwich, and some fine fossils characteristic of this deposit may be obtained there, such as *Turritella, Cyprina, Aporrhairs, Corbula*, etc.

The Woolwich and Reading beds are excavated into, or else they naturally crop out in various places about London, as at Woolwich, Blackheath, Reading,

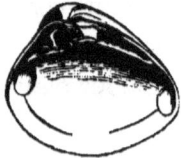

Fig. 260.—*Cyrena antiqua.*

etc. Banks of fossil oysters (*Ostrea bellorvacina*) are found; Bromley being perhaps the best place to get them. *Melania, Cyrena cuneiformis*, and other mollusca, all of which indicate brackish-water conditions, are plentiful near Woolwich and New Charlton. These and other fossils are also found near Dulwich, Lewisham, and Peckham.

The London Clay is of course the thickest and most important member of our English Eocene formation. Fossils, however, only occur in it here and there, and at different horizons. The Isle of Sheppey has long been famous as the best collecting-ground, but univalve and bivalve mollusca, such as *Voluta nodosa*, *Phorus extensus*, *Rostellaria ampla*, *Leda amygdaloides*, *Cryptodon*, etc., are found at Highgate. Some of these, and other fossils, are also met with near Hungerford, Basingstoke, Bognor, Finchley, Holloway, Ipswich, and Harwich ; especially in the cement stones, which, near Harwich and Ipswich, are often full of *Modiola* and *Cyrena*. The Harwich cement-stones are rich in fossil wood, showing structure when cut and polished ; and large fragments of this wood are often seen perforated and honey-combed by a species

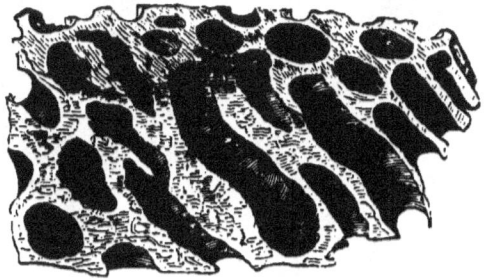

Fig. 261.—Wood perforated by the tubes of *Teredo*.

of the same kind of boring-mollusc (*Teredo*) as that which has earned for itself the modern name of "ship-worm." In the Suffolk crags, the bewildered student frequently finds contorted and serpentinely intertwined masses, and he wonders what they are, little thinking they are the filled-up *Teredo*-borings in the fossil woods of the London Clay. The fossil wood was washed out of the latter deposit by denudation, was then gradually dissolved away, so that eventually

T

the casts of the *Teredo*-borings alone were left to tell of the many changes through which re-deposited fossils frequently have to pass before they reach their final resting-place.

Bracklesham Bay, in Sussex, has long been famous for its remarkable series of Eocene strata, some of them full of shells. At Whitecliff Bay we have deposits of about the same age, in which fossil mollusca are abundant. The large and beautiful bivalve

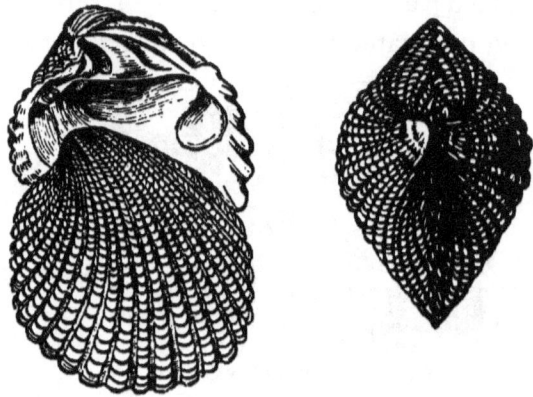

Fig. 262.—*Cardita imbricata* (Eocene).

Cardita planicosta gives its name to the stratum where it swarms, in company with the univalve *Turitella imbricataria*.

The Barton Clay is a higher deposit than the last mentioned, and it is perhaps the most renowned hunting-ground of the entire Eocene formation. It takes its name from Barton, on the Hampshire coast, and there, and also at Hordwell, the geologist will find an abundance of the most beautifully preserved fossils, among which, perhaps, the choicest are *Voluta lucatrix, Typhis pungens, Rostellaria rimosa, Crassatella,* and other genera which remind him of tropical seas.

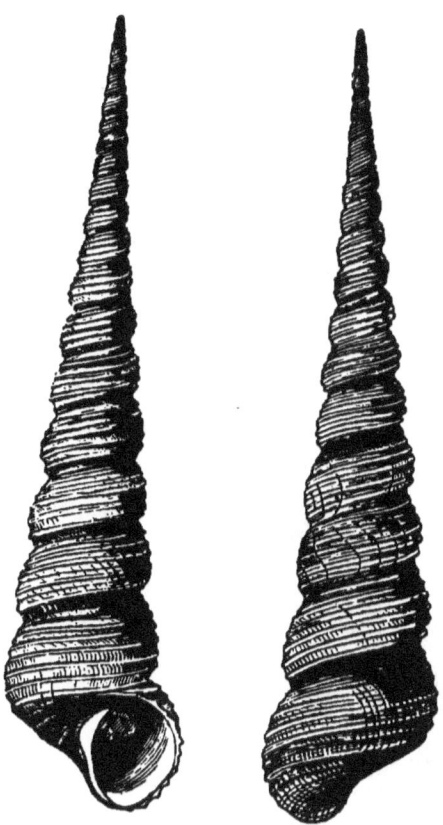

Fig. 263.—*Turritella.*

Yarmouth, in the Isle of Wight, is a good place to put up at for a few days in order to work the Upper

Eocene beds of the district. The Hempstead Beds (sometimes regarded as Lower Miocene) run along the coast, and are especially well developed at the locality whence they take their name. The sea-bed there (at low water) is seen to be formed of stiff bluish clay, intercalated in which are strata of harder masses, probably hardened by diffused iron and lime, and by others formed of nothing but shells. All the shells, bivalve and univalve, belong to *fresh-water* species, such as *Paludina lenta* (which occurs in enormous numbers in the harder interstratified masses), *Melania, Melanopsis, Cyrena, Corbula, Cyclas, Unio*, etc.

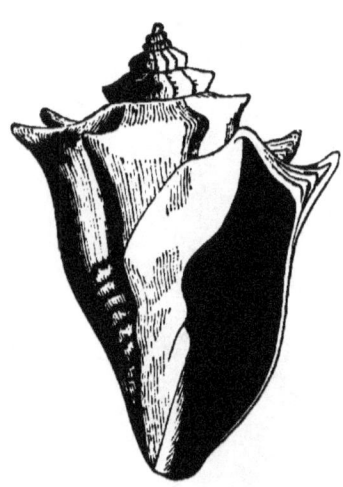

Fig. 264.—*Voluta athleta* (Eocene).

On the coast side of Yarmouth, towards Alum Bay—a distance thence to the latter place of about seven or eight miles—the geologist finds plenty of work, quite sufficient climbing, and a delightful sea view. The fossils lie strewn about the *talus* of the cliffs in all directions. They are so innumerable that the collector gives up all endeavour to identify them, and simply "boxes them." They have been washed out of the beds in which they were originally deposited, and the wash of the rain-water has strewn them thus over almost the entire face of the cliff. What myriads of *Cerithium, Rissoa, Hydrobia, Melania,* etc.!

This lovely Isle of Wight is surely the "garden" of English geology! Where else in Great Britain, within so short a space, can the young geological student see so much, collect so many objects, or be able to roam over such a variety of geological and geographical scenic features? From the Wealden and Greensand to the great backbone of Chalk, which runs through the length of the little island, right up through all the most interesting deposits of Lower, Middle, and Upper Eocene—here we have a perfect "thumb-nail" geological sketch. Some of the Upper Eocene beds are not found elsewhere in Great Britain, as the local names they bear testify. The Isle of Wight will long be "classic ground" to the geologist, not only for its variety of geological formations and plethoric abundance of fossils, but also because of dear old Dr. Mantells' book upon it—which, if any young and ardent student happens to read it, he will straightway go, on the first opportunity, and verify what that "grand old man" had to tell them about!

Cowes is a good place (rather too good for a quiet and economic student) to put up at, if he wishes to work the "Fluvio-marine" series. Thence he will make his way to Osborne (which would be sacred ground to him apart from the fact that it is the Queen's home), and there he finds an abundance of fossil shells, and possibly some of the *Chara* fruits which Sir Charles Lyell made famous. *Limnea longiscata, Paludina lenta* (which continued to live right on to the time when the Norwich Crag was formed in the later Pliocene age), *Melania excavata, Planorbis*, etc.—all are to be found at Osborne in profuse abundance. At Bembridge and Headon, in the marls and shell-limestones, we have more than enough of *Melania turritissima, Cerithium mutabile, Cyrena pulchra, Ostrea Vectensis;* land shells, such as *Helix globosa, Bulimus ellipticus* (actually forming a limestone by its remains), and fresh-water shells, such as *Limnea* and the beautiful *Planorbis discus.*

With the exception of the Hempstead strata (Isle of Wight), we have only doubtful and scanty remnants of Miocene deposit in Great Britain, and these are hardly worth mentioning so far as fossil collecting is concerned.

Perhaps the most interesting of them in this respect are found in Suffolk, especially in the neighbourhood of Felixstowe—a pretty sea-side watering-place—and that of Ipswich. This is a splendid county for Pliocene fossils, locally and indeed generally known as "crag." The cliffs at the former place are simply masses of shells, and in the district there are plenty of "coprolite pits"—places where the small phosphatic nodules (formerly believed to be the fossil fæces of animals, whence their name) are worked. More than two million pounds' worth of these "coprolites" have been excavated and converted into artificial manures since the late Professor Henslow found out what they were, nearly forty years ago. The "coprolites" are richest at the base of the shell-crags, where they form part of a bed in which we get the remains of mastodon, tapir, hipparion, rhinoceros, deer, etc.; also roundish and elongated

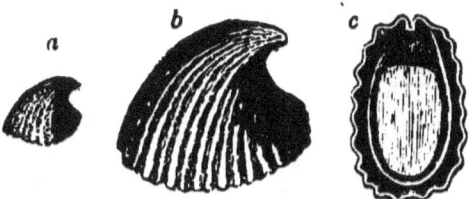

Fig. 265.—*Emarginulai fissura* : *a*, natural size; *b*, magnified; *c*, lower side (Crag and recent).

masses of coffee-coloured sandstones, which the visitor will find lying in heaps near every coprolite pit.

Very singular are these roundish masses of sandstone, most of which are about the size of one's fist. From Foxhall, the bed containing them (which usually lies directly on the London clay) extends to Felixstowe, and heaps of them may be seen by the roadside, waiting to be broken up for road-mending. They are very curious, for they represent a lost geological formation, older than the Coralline Crag (for they are also found *under* the latter), which is probably of late Miocene age. The rounded specimens go by the name of "box-stones"—a term which has been given to them by the quarrymen. You strike them with a sharp blow of the hammer, and about one in every ten or so will break in halves, revealing the cast of a fossil shell, etc., within. When neatly broken, they form very interesting geological specimens. Among the fossil shells thus found enclosed are *Pectunculus, Cardium, Cassidaria, Isocardium, Buccinum*, etc. These "box-stones" are the

Fig. 266.—*Pecten varius* (Crag and recent).

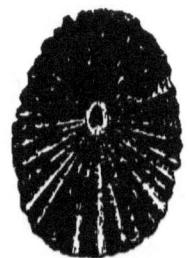

Fig. 267.—*Fissurella Græca* (Crag and recent).

broken up and rolled remains of a bed of sandstone, which once covered part of Suffolk, and which still underlies Diest, Antwerp, Brussels, and other places in Belgium, on the other side the German Ocean. These "box-stones" were broken up and rounded before the Pliocene period began, as is indicated by the fact that they are often found coated on their upper surfaces with fossil Barnacles, which clustered and spread over their surfaces as they lay on the floor of the shallow Red Crag sea. At Trimley,

Nacton, Bucklesham, Foxhall, Waldringfield, and thereabouts, these stones are very abundant. In the Ipswich museum there may be seen an almost perfect fauna, recovered from this missing and fragmentary British Miocene deposit.

The Pliocene beds in England lie almost entirely on the east coast. A deposit of this period has lately been discovered in Cornwall, and there are also patches in Aberdeenshire; but the shells are too meagre and fragmentary in these outlying localities to refer the fossil-collecting student to them, especially when he

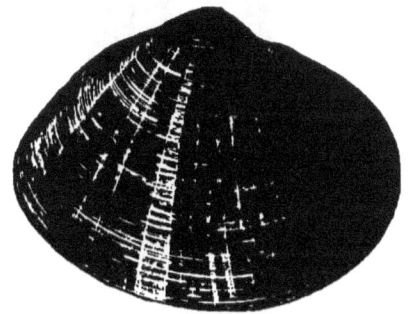

Fig. 268.—*Mactra*.

Fig. 269.—*Trochus* (Crag and recent).

has access to the wonderfully rich Pliocene formations of Norfolk, Suffolk, and Essex, where everybody knows them by the name of "crags." The crag beds are richest near the coast, as at Walton-on-the-Naze, Felixstowe, Orford, and Aldborough, although they extend inland, and "crag" pits are very common in the neighbourhood of Ipswich; and about Norwich we have the "crag" (latest formed of the entire series) which takes the name of that ancient and picturesque city. The places where the crag-pits are usually richest in fossil shells are on the heaths and commons so numerous in Suffolk and elsewhere, for the crags produce what the farmers call very "hungry land," and such unprofitable areas have therefore remained longer in their wild state than would have been the case had the soil been fertile.

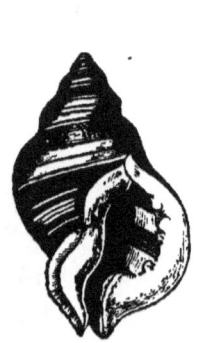 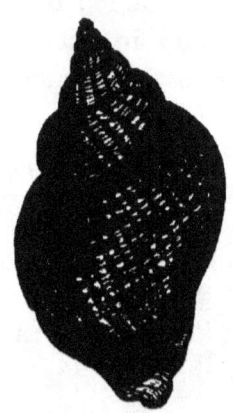

Fig. 270.—*Purpura lapillus* (Crag and recent).

Fig. 271.—*Buccinum undulatum* (Crag beds and recent).

But these heaths are glorious places in the early summer-time, when the sky is full of lark music, and the gorse and broom bushes are ablaze with aromatic yellow blossom, and the delicate crosiers of the bracken fern are everywhere bursting from the ground.

Then, again, I know of no formation which more impresses the young student with the full meaning and significance of fossils than the Crag. Here they are in the profusest abundance—young and old, large and small, millions upon millions on every hand! They can be taken out with the fingers—no hammering is required; and if the collector has come pro-

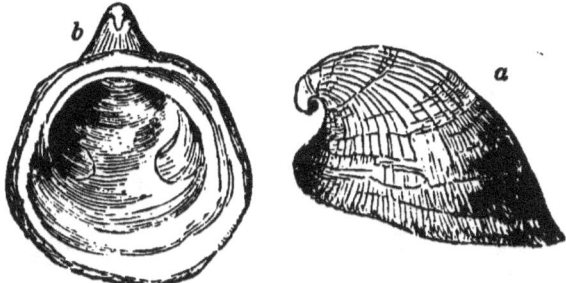

Fig. 272.—*Pileopsis ungarica.*

vided with a wire-gauzed tray to sift the finer material, he will get all the lovely little shells, and plenty of foramenifera, etc., as well. Thirty or forty species of fossils can be collected in a very short time.

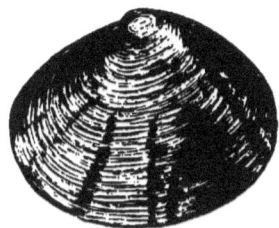

Fig. 273.—*Tellina crassa* (Crag and recent).

Fig. 274.—*Pectunculus glycimeris* (Red Crag and recent).

Geologists recognize *three* of these Crags—the Coralline, which is the oldest; the Red Crag; and the Norwich Crag. The Coralline Crag is divided into two main parts, with a third subordinate bed. The lowest of these consists of a series of calcareous sands, rich in fossil shells. The second bed is more solid, and is formed of the remains of shells, etc., cemented, together with fossil Polyzoa, into a rock so hard that it can sometimes be quarried for a building stone. The third and uppermost layer consists of a few feet

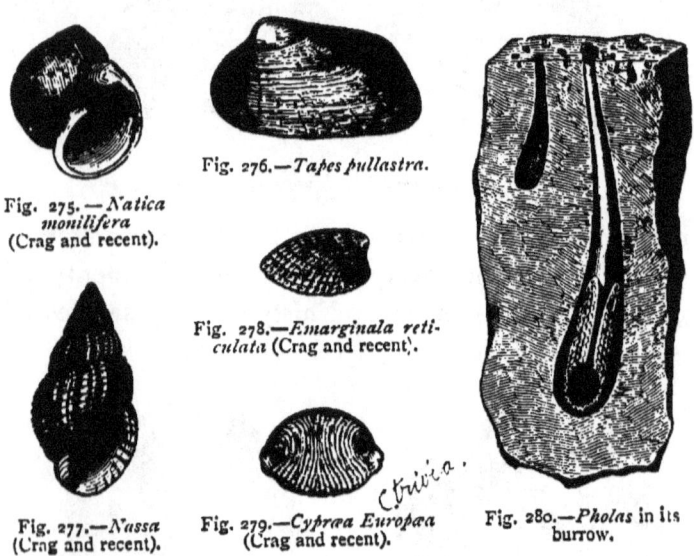

Fig. 275.—*Natica monilifera* (Crag and recent).

Fig. 276.—*Tapes pullastra*.

Fig. 277.—*Nassa* (Crag and recent).

Fig. 278.—*Emarginala reticulata* (Crag and recent).

Fig. 279.—*Cypræa Europæa* (Crag and recent).

Fig. 280.—*Pholas* in its burrow.

of the abraded material of the last bed, reconstructed in shallow water, and bearing strong marks of current bedding. The thickness of the rockier stratum has been calculated at about eighty feet, but there is reason to believe this is too great an estimate. In the neighbourhood of Sudbourne, and especially in one or two pits in the park, near to the hall, the Coralline Crag is in a state of high perfection, the bivalve shells imbedded in it being frequently found double. At Gedgrave, Gomer, and the neighbourhood, by digging a few feet we come upon the original and undisturbed Coralline Crag, very rich in molluscan remains. As we ascend from the lower areas where this bed occurs, and come to the higher grounds, we reach the out-crop of the second or rocky Coralline Crag. Many pits are exposed in it in the neighbourhood of Orford and Sudbourne. For obtaining fossils, the Aldborough section is perhaps better than those of the same beds at Orford. Mr. Searles Wood, sen., considered that nothing among the fossil shells yet obtained from the Coralline Crag indicated the latter to have been formed under a greater depth of water than from thirty to forty fathoms.

Professor Prestwich thinks that after the Coralline Crag sea had attained its greatest depth, a change took place, and a bed of comminuted shells was spread over the deep-sea bed. Further elevation exposed the seabed to the action of tides and currents, to the denudation of the lower beds, and heaping up the Bryozoa and Mollusca of the later deposits in banks. The water continued to get shallower, until a continuance of the elevatory movement gradually raised the Coralline Crag above the sea, where it was exposed to the considerable denuding action which removed so large a portion of it. During the Red Crag period immediately succeeding, the Coralline Crag was broken up into islands and reefs, among and around which the Red Crag was deposited during a period of slow subsidence.

Professor Prestwich thinks that the more southern species of mollusca which had migrated thus far north during the later Miocene period, and whilst the Belgian deposits were forming, were replaced in the Coralline Crag by an assemblage partly northern and partly southern. That is to say, we have undoubtedly proofs of a slow but sure migration of northern forms. This may have resulted from a general lowering of the temperature, or by the setting in of fresh currents from a northerly direction, owing to the subsidence of land in that direction. Among the common northern species of mollusca are *Astarte sulcata, Glycimeris siliqua, Tellina calcarea, Buccinopsis Dalei, Emarginula crassa.* Professor Prestwich is further of opinion that there are different zones in the Coralline Crag, to be distinguished by the occurrence of characteristic shells. Mr. Searles Wood described 322 species of Coralline Crag shells; whilst five more species of Brachiopoda bring up the number to 327. The late Dr. Woodward based certain calculations on the data

Fig. 281.—*Cyprina Islandica* (Crag formations and recent).

thus supplied. Thus he regarded 159 species as extinct, the recent forms numbering 168, or a percentage of rather more than half. Of these he considered 139 species to be still living in British seas, whilst twenty-seven species were confined to southern, and two to northern seas.

The Red Crag is formed of a succession of beds, varying from two and three to nearly twenty feet in thickness. The layers are composed of sand and shells, and many sections show them inclined at a considerably high angle. This structure is altogether different from that known as "false bedding," although the latter occurs to a considerable extent in the Red Crag. In Bawdsey Cliff, and also in the cliff at Felixstowe, this oblique lamination is very distinctly shown. Geologists regard this phenomenon as the accumulations of a foreshore. At Sutton the Red Crag is bedded or banked up against an older Coralline Crag cliff. Mr. Wood regarded the Red Crag as the "remains of an extensive series of banks that were more or less dry at every tide, and that were from time to time partially swept away and re-accumulated; every bed representing some of this destruction and re-accumulation, since the top of every preceding bed is planed off evenly to form a floor for the next above, in the base of which small pebbles and small rolled phosphatic nodules often abound, in some cases forming thin bands. In the channels which permeated these banks there seems to have accumulated those portions of the Red Crag which exhibit the true features, often very extreme, of false bedding." The beds of phosphatic stones (commonly termed "coprolites") for which the Red Crag is so much worked on the left bank of the Orwell, are seldom found beneath such sections of the beached-up Crag.

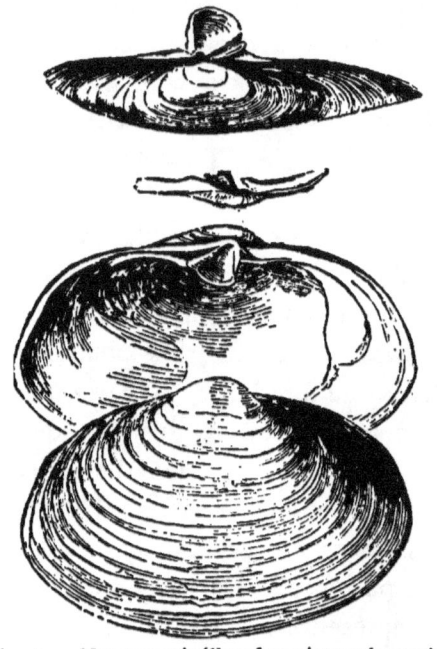

Fig. 282.—*Mya arenaria* (Crag formations and recent).

Mr. Searles Wood, sen., pointed out that the Red Crag at Walton-on-the-Naze was the oldest bed. The reasons rest on the universal absence of certain shells abundant in other parts of the Red Crag, among others, of *Fusus antiquus, Tellina obliqua, Tellina prætenuis,* etc. This distinction of the Walton Crag has been carried far enough for it to be regarded as possessing some affinity with the Coralline Crag. The *Fusus contrarius* is abundant there, and the bivalves are often found with both shells together. The most perfect fossils are found here. Great difficulty exists in determining the relative ages of the Red Crag strata in different localities, owing to the manner in which the shell beds have been taken up and re-deposited. In the Red Crag at Butley, near Orford, northern forms of mollusca prevail, the commonest shell being very large-sized specimens of *Tellina obliqua*.

In a pit in Tattingstone Park, about four miles from Ipswich, the Red Crag may be seen overlying the Coralline Crag. A thin seam of pebbles marks the junction of the two beds, indicating a brief period between the depositions, and showing that the Red and Coralline Crags were not continuous. The places where the sections are best exposed are on

Fig. 283. — *Astarte Omalii* (Coralline and Red Crags).

the slopes of the hills along the rivers Deben and Orwell, in addition to the coast sections at Bawdsey and Felixstowe. At the latter place is a fine section thirty feet in height. As a rule, it occupies excavated hollows of the Coralline Crag, wrapping round the reefs of the latter, and filling up the hollows between them so as to lie nearly level. Professor Prestwich divides the

U

Red Crag into two series—the lower, characterized by oblique lamination; and the upper by persistent horizontal bedding. The lower part is much richer in shells than the upper. The most abundant in the Red Crag are the Common cockle, *Cardium angustatum, Pectunculus glycimeris, Tellina crassa, T. obliqua, Mytilus edulis, Pecten opercularis, Cyprina islandica, Lucina borealis, Cardita senilis, Purpura tetragona, P. lapillus, Trophon* (or *Fusus*) *antiquus, T. contrarius, Nassa reticosa, N. granulata, Astarte Omallii, Cyprœa Europœa,* etc. In many places, as at Tattingstone, Bentley (in the pits near the station), Foxhall, Bucklesham, and elsewhere, the strata teem with *Pectunctulus, Trophon contrarius, Cardita senilis, Nassa,* etc.

Fig. 284.—*Purpura tetragona* (Crag beds).

The number of species of fossil mollusca belonging to the Red Crag is two hundred and thirty-four, of which two hundred and sixteen are still in existence. In addition to this number, we must include about forty extraneous species. About one hundred and fifty of the above species are still living in British seas, whilst of the remainder, thirty-two are southern forms, and twenty-three northern—a total of nine more northern species than are found in the Coralline Crag, thus far indicating a refrigeration of the climate.

In the base of the Red Crag, the large angular flint nodules are usually found thickly encrusted with barnacle shells. The septarian nodules are perforated with holes, bored by various boring mollusca, such as *Pholas, Saxicava*, and we frequently find the fossil shells of these borers in the holes they excavated. It

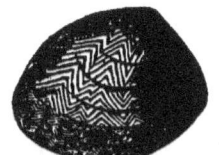

Fig. 286.—*Nucula Cobboldiæ* (Red and Norwich Crags).

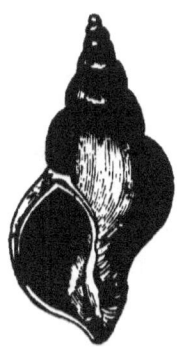

Fig. 285.—*Voluta Lamberti* (Coralline and Red Crags).

Fig. 287.—*Trophon Contrarius* (Red Crag).

is in this part of the Red Crag that the phosphatic stones, or "coprolites," are usually found in greatest abundance.

A large number of mollusca, which lived in the sea that covered East Suffolk during the Crag period, are now living further south, in the Atlantic or the Mediterranean, having been driven from these areas by the increasing cold, which here reached its maximum during the Glacial epoch.

The best places to obtain Red Crag fossils are pits at Wherstead, Tattingstone, Bentley, Foxhall, Boyton, places near Woodbridge, Bucklesham, Walton, the Felixstowe cliffs, Bawdsey, Chillesford, Sudbourne, Butley, Aldborough, etc.

The Norwich Crag was formerly called the "Mammaliferous crag." But it has been shown that the mammalian remains are older than the shells associated with them. In Suffolk this crag occurs at Thorpe, near Aldborough, at Bulcamp, and Chillesford. Sir Charles Lyell gave to it the name of "Fluvio-marine Crag," on account of the large percentage of land, fresh-water, and brackish-water shells it contains. It is usually regarded as nearly synchronous with the Red Crag, and as a fluvio-marine extension of the latter. The shells of the Norwich Crag are remarkable for their littoral, or shallow water character. The most abundant fossils are *Littorina littorea, Purpura lapillus, Cardium edule, Mytilus edulis, Cerithium tricinctum, Turritella communis, Natica monilifera, Tellina prætenuis, T. obliqua,* etc. At the base of the railway cutting, about a mile from Aldborough station, we have found undoubtedly Red Crag shells associated with others we regard as equally undoubted Norwich Crag forms, indicating that here may be the junction of the two formations. This stratum lies in a denuded hollow of the harder and more consolidated strata of the Coralline Crag. From Thorpe Common, near Aldborough, the true Norwich Crag extends to the city whence it derives its name. Its greatest thickness is about eight to ten feet. This crag is distinguished by its abundance of recent forms, and the general absence of southern types of shells, thus showing that the cold was increasing. The total number of species of mollusca catalogued from it is one hundred and forty, of which one hundred and twenty-three are still living; seventeen are supposed to be extinct. Of the above number, one hundred and one species are still living in British seas, twelve are Arctic and North American, eight Mediterranean, and two species Asiatic, the latter being *Corbicula fluminalis* and *Paludina unicolor*. From the fact that twenty species of shells belonging to the Norwich Crag are not found either in the Red or Coralline Crags, Dr. Gwyn Jeffreys thinks that there is some difference in their geological age, the Norwich Crag being more recent than the Red Crag, and its shells of a more arctic character.

In 1865, the bed which had previously gone by the name of the Norwich Crag was shown to be composed of two deposits, usually separated by ten or fifteen feet of sand, etc. The upper bed is distinguished by a general absence of shore shells, such as *Littorina* and *Purpura*, and by the presence of shells affecting deeper water, and also by the greater preponderance of arctic or northern forms. After the formation of the Norwich Crag, the depression continued so as to bring the sea over its site, and it was along its floor that this Upper Norwich Crag was deposited. Hence it obtains a more extensive geographical distribution than the lower, or true "Fluvio-marine" Crag. In Norfolk it extends to about eight miles beyond Norwich; and in Suffolk it is so well displayed at Chillesford that it sometimes goes by the name of the Chillesford Crag. At Aldeby, near Beccles, this crag is exposed in some brick-pits, and such shells as *Mya arenaria* are found abundantly, with both valves attached, standing upright in the sands as when they were alive. At Chillesford, in the stackyard near Mr. Crisp's house, this crag is seen to its best advantage, full of shells, many of them of a northern type, such as *Mya truncata, Cardium Greenlandicum, Astarte borealis*, etc. There can be no doubt that much confusion still prevails in the catalogue of the Norwich Crag shells, owing to the manner in which both the upper and lower crags were formerly confounded. In the pits on Thorpe and Sizewell Commons, near Aldborough, the ordinary Norwich Crag fossils are abundant; whilst the brick-pits at Aldeby yield most beautifully preserved Upper Norwich, or Chillesford Crag.

The Norwich Crag is seen resting on the Chalk at Thorpe, near Norwich, where the shell bed is about four feet thick. The bank of fallen or accumulated sand and shells will give the geologist plenty of "boxing" to do, for the fossils are extremely abundant, although usually in a very fragile state. The Norwich Crag also crops up in the pretty river-side calling place, Postwick Grove ; and at Whitlingham, on the other side the river. Bramerton, however, has long been regarded as the best place to get fossils at. They are here in a remarkably good state of preservation, and there will be no difficulty in getting a score or more species. The Crag lies on the top of the chalk, and if the geologist lays bare the latter, he will see it drilled again and again by boring mollusca, showing that it was once the bare bed of the sea.

Beyond Norwich there are several good places where the later Pliocene shells may be collected, as at Wroxham, Belaugh, Coltishall, Horstead, etc., all in exceedingly picturesque districts, and not far from the now celebrated "broads." Beds of shells also occur on the Norfolk coast, between Cromer and Sherringham, and at Weybourn, Runton, and Trimmingham.

CHAPTER XIII.

FOSSIL CEPHALOPODS.

I DON'T know any British fossils more common than some of those which come in for treatment in the present chapter. In China a few (like *Orthoceras* and *Ammonites*) are used in medicine, for the simple reason that nobody there knows anything about their origin, and their mysterious abundance is taken as an indication of the generative powers of the earth! Even in Britain they have gained a place in folk-lore, and some have been immortalized in poetry, like the "snake-stones" (*Ammonites communis*), in Scott's "Marmion." In the Eastern Counties, where they abound—although the specimens found there do not rightly belong to the place, for they are "derivatives," torn out of their parent rocks and brought thither during the Glacial period by ice agency, and re-deposited in the boulder-clays—they are known by the name of "thunder-bolts."

Thunder was always more dreadful to uneducated people than lightning, and all over the world there has been a great desire to find the source of that mystical power—the "thunder-bolt."

In Kent, Cambridgeshire, and elsewhere, the rounded masses of iron pyrites originally formed in

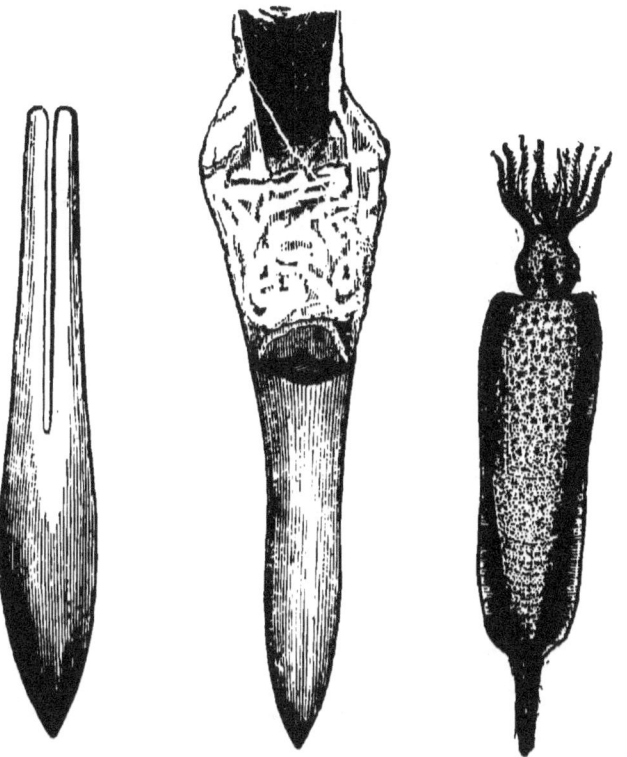

Fig. 288.—*Belemnites hastata* (Lias).   Fig. 289.—*Belemnites puzosianus* (guard and part of phragmacone).   Fig. 290.— Restoration of an ancient Belemnite.

the chalk, and subsequently denuded out of it, are called by this name. When broken, such masses (about as big as one's fist, or less) have a *radiated* structure. I have had them brought to me even by skilful astronomers with F.R.A.S. behind their names, as "meteorites." Can we wonder, therefore, if less educated people call them by their other name of "thunder-bolts"?

Of course, lightning sometimes kills one of a herd

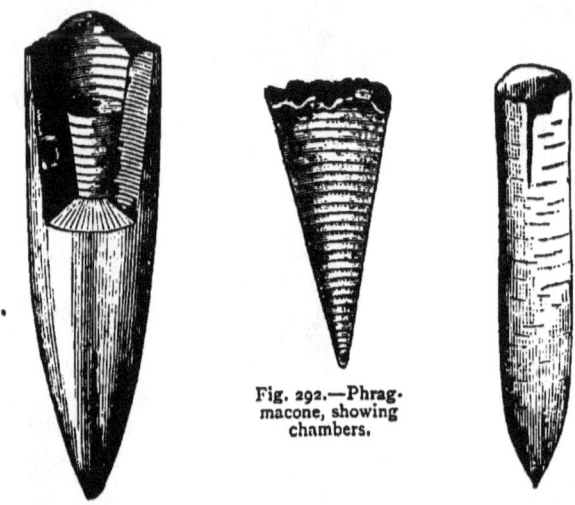

Fig. 291.—*Belemnites abbreviatus*, showing phragmacone.

Fig. 292.—Phragmacone, showing chambers.

Fig. 293.—*Belemnites mucronata* (chalk).

of cattle. I have a vivid remembrance of a veterinary surgeon, of such eminence that I dared not contradict him then, who triumphantly brought a real "thunder-bolt." A cow had been killed by lightning, and this "thunder-bolt" was found just underneath her. Where were your "scientists"? There was the dead cow; here was the object known for centuries as the "thunder-bolt"! Could cause and effect be more closely associated?

I "shut up." What is the use of arguing with a man who has made his mind up that he is right and everybody else is wrong?

The fact is, as just stated, the boulder-clay forming the subsoil of the Eastern Counties abounds with

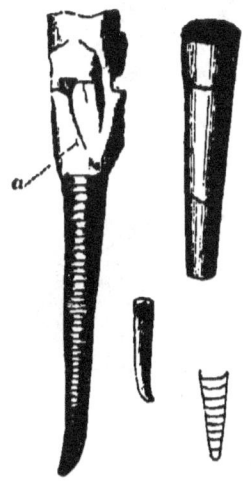

Fig. 294.—*Orthoceras*, showing body-chamber at *a*.

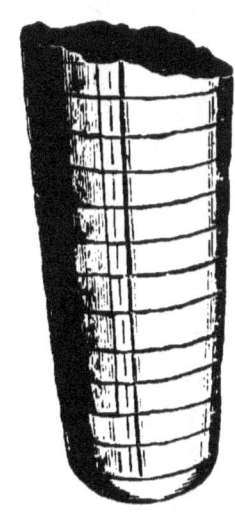

Fig. 295.—*Orthoceras laterale*.

derivative Oolitic Belemnites. These may be picked up on the surface. The poor old cow happened to have one underneath her when she died (I have not the slightest doubt she had frequently laid down on them before), and in this way the "thunder-bolt" theory received extra support!

Popularly speaking, both Ammonites and Belemnites should be regarded as belonging to that group of animals which, rightly or wrongly, has for years occupied the leading position of the Invertebrates. Nautiluses and "cuttle-fishes" still figure at the top

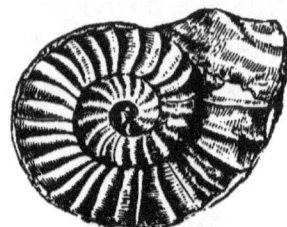

Fig. 297.—*Lituites articulatus.*

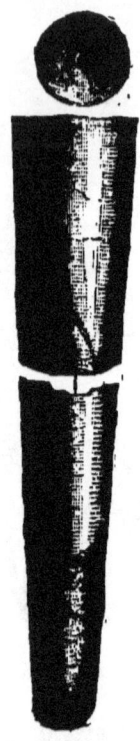

Fig. 296.—*Orthoceras*, upper part shows chamber perforated by siphuncle.

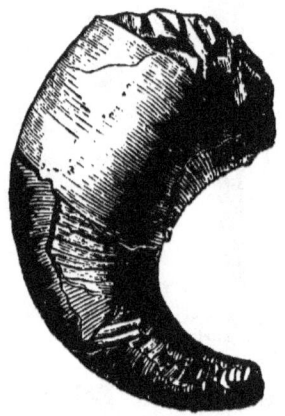

Fig. 298.—*Cyrtoceras Murchisoni* (Silurian).

of this division, and many students accept that position as indicating their higher zoological rank. Many philosophical naturalists doubt this, but meantime we must accept it, for classification purposes at least.

My readers are fully aware that those parts most precious to the geologist—viz. those which resisted decay because of their hardness and earthy composition, such as shells, corals, spines, tests, etc.—do not

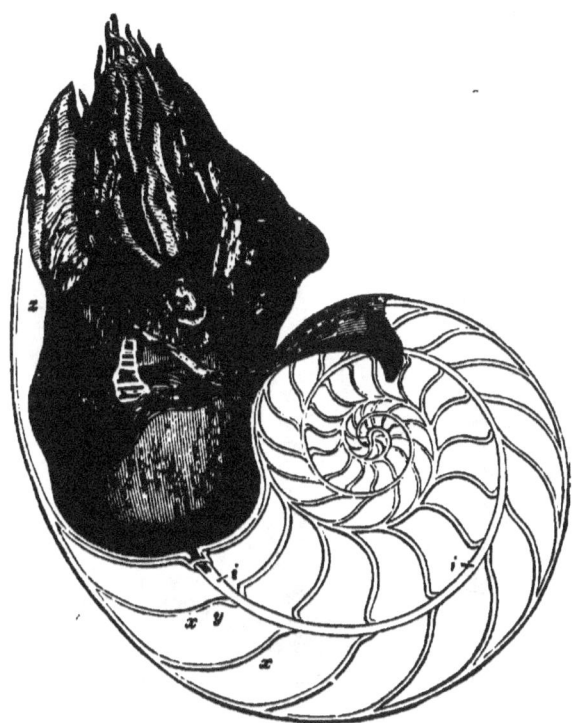

Fig. 299.—The Pearly Nautilus, with animal in last chamber; (recent, chambers in section to show structure).—i, siphuncle; $x\,y$, chambers; z, body-chamber.

necessarily represent the most important parts of the animal economy. The geologist has still to be thankful for those shreds of evidence which not long since were regarded by conchologists and others as the sole ends of knowledge. Not much more than a quarter of a century ago, conchologists were careful only to collect *shells;* they hardly cared for the *creatures* to whom those shells originally belonged, and many knew very little of their life-histories, now the most valuable part of them.

Whatever may be the actual zoological position of the *Cephalopoda* (to which these *Orthoceratites, Ammo-*

Fig. 300.—Exterior of Shell of Pearly Nautilus (recent).

nites, Belemnites, etc., belong), there is no question that they stand at the head of the Mollusca. This is evident from their high organization, their well-developed eyes, nervous and muscular systems, hydrostatic apparatus, etc. Thanks to our public aquaria, most people are acquainted with the appearance of such representatives of the order as the cuttle-fish or octopus, and can readily understand why the order is named *Cephalopoda*, because of the arrangement of the arms or feet, or whatever we like to call them, around the head. A few members of the order have their hard structures or shells outside their bodies—as the Nautilus, for instance; but the majority of them have the solid parts inside, which are called "cuttle-bones," "pens," etc. In the modern seas the shelled Cephalopoda (such as the Nautilus) are exceedingly rare, and the cuttle-fishes both abundant and widely dispersed. In the seas of the Palæozoic epoch the reverse of this was the case—the Nautilus family abounded; the cuttle-fishes had not come into existence. All the *Cephalopoda* are carnivorous in their habits now, and there is every reason to believe they were always so.

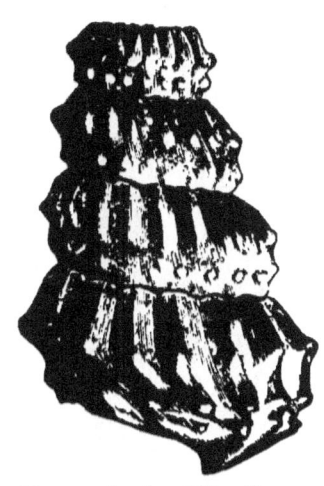

Fig. 301.—Portion of *Turrilitæ*.

We may practically divide the *Cephalopoda* into two divisions, for the benefit of the geological student anxious to be acquainted with the fossil remains of each group. First, there are those possessed of shells, such as the Nautilus and Ammonite family; and second, those which had hard internal structures, like those represented in the Secondary rocks by the numerous Belemnites, and in modern seas by the "cuttle-bones."

The lovely shell of the modern striped *Nautilus pompilius* is well known, and may be seen in any

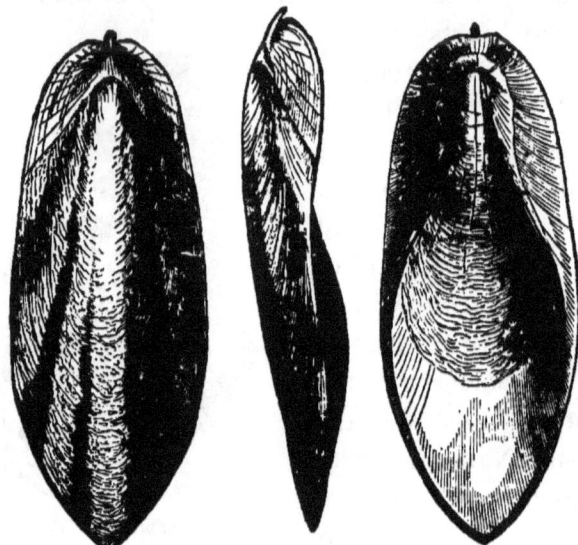

Fig. 302.—Internal shells of recent Cuttle-fish.

museum. Its architectural and mechanical structure appears to be the same nowadays as it was in the early Palæozoic ages of the globe. There is a series of chambers united by a tube called the *siphuncle* running through the centre of them. The last chamber is the largest, and is called the body-chamber, because it was last occupied by the body of the creature. Each chamber was formerly filled by the animal, which retired from it as it grew larger, and formed another with more room; but it maintained its organic connection with all of these deserted chambers by means of the siphuncle.

These shelled Cephalapods (*Tetrabranchiate* or "four-gilled") are separated in the Nautilus and Ammonite families. In the former, the divisions (*septa*) of the chambers are simple and curved, and the edges (*sutures*) plain, whilst the siphuncle usually runs through the middle (*central*), as above described. In a few instances, however, the siphuncle is *ventral*, or at the base of the chambers.

Fig. 303.—*Clymenia*.

In the Ammonites, on the contrary, the septa are folded and very complex, and the sutures are zigzagged, foliated, or irregularly lobed; the siphuncle or air-tube is on the *outside* of the chamber (dorsal).

These are very well-marked and easily recognized points of difference. It is as well to remember them, for, as far as *external* appearance goes, it is singular (as Dr. Nicholson has shown) how one group mimics the other, the real fact being that they were built up on the same external architectural lines. Thus, in the

X

Nautilus family we have—(1) the straight-shelled group called, on this account, *Orthoceras;* (2) another with the shell bent on itself, as *Ascoceras;* (3) a curved shell, *Cyrtoceras;* (4) a spiral form, *Trochoceras;* (5) a discoidal kind, *Gyroceras;* (6) discoidal and produced, *Lituites;* (7) and the involute, as represented by the Nautilus itself.

In the Ammonite family all of these external shapes are repeated. Thus the straight ammonital form

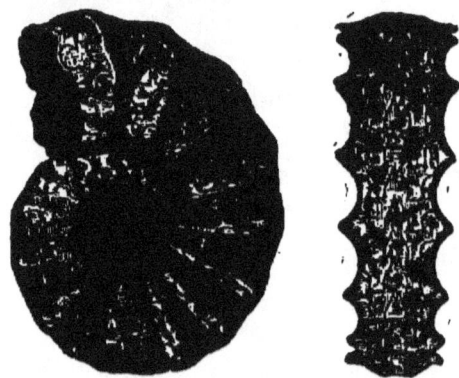

Fig. 304.—*Ceratites nodosus.*

is represented by (1) *Baculites;* (2) *Ptychoceras;* (3) *Taxoceras;* (4) *Turrilites;* (5) *Crioceras;* (6) *Ancyloceras;* and (7) the ordinary Ammonites.

The Nautilus family, however, was by far the earliest to appear in the seas of the globe, and many of its genera had died out before the true Ammonites appeared, although the *Goniatites* are found in Silurian rocks.

Practically, therefore, we may regard the Nautilus family as being essentially Palæozoic, and the Ammonites as characteristic of the Secondary period.

The *Nautilidæ* include the following well-known genera of fossils, *Lituites, Trochoceras, Gomphoceras, Orthoceras, Trochoceras, Phragmoceras, Cyrtoceras, Clymenia*, etc.

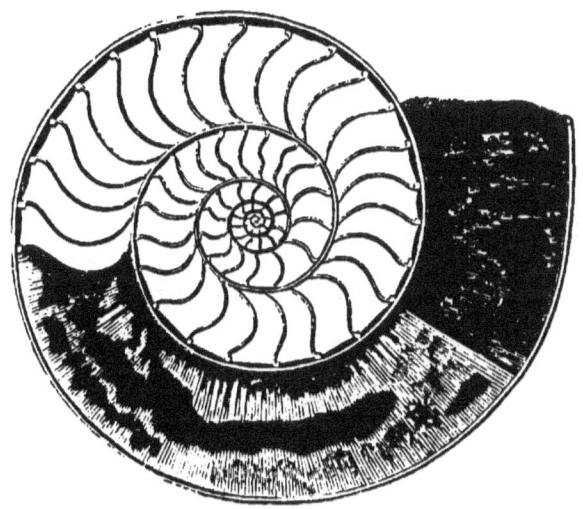

Fig. 305.—Section of Shell of Ammonite, showing the large body-whorl, or last chamber.

In the *Ammonitidæ* we have the well-known *Goniatites, Ceratites, Turrilites, Baculites, Hamites, Scaphites, Ptychoceras, Ancyloceras*, etc.

We find these beautiful fossils of all sizes (although some so-called species are doubtless the young stages in the development of the larger kinds), as well as possessing wonderfully numerous kinds of external ornamentation. Ammonites range in size from the lovely *Ammonites lautus* of the Gault, not bigger than a threepenny-bit, to the *A. giganteus* of the Upper Oolite, as large as a cart-wheel.

The *Cephalopoda* first make their appearance in the Lower Tremadoc rocks. One form, *Cyrtoceras precox*, found at Llanerch, west of Tremadoc, is the oldest known. *Orthoceras sericeum* appears in the Upper Tremadoc strata at St. David's, Llanwern, and elsewhere. The *Orthoceratites* (as this genus is usually

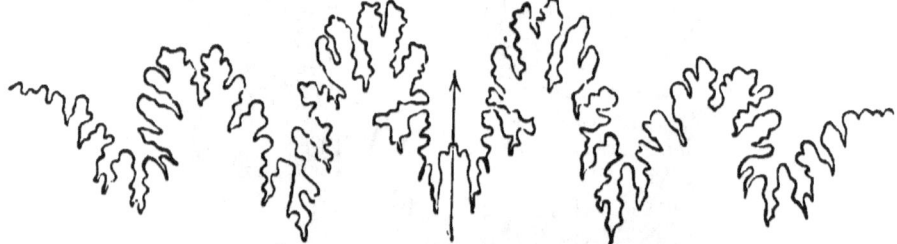

Fig. 306.—Plan of foliation of edges of chamber of Ammonite.

called when we speak of it in the plural) are most numerous in the Upper Silurian beds, as at Woolhope, Wenlock, and Ludlow. At the latter locality they are very numerous, and some species attain a large size. About thirty species of *Orthoceras* and Nautilus are known from the Wenlock formation alone; twenty-four species of *Orthoceras* occur in the higher Ludlow series. The Aymestry limestone is singularly rich in places, in various kinds of *Nautilidæ*. Indeed, whenever the Upper Silurian strata are fossiliferous, the geologist is sure to find numbers of this group present.

The Devonian limestones cropping up in the neighbourhood of Torquay and Newton Abbot, and also the Upper Devonian rocks at Petherwin, in Cornwall, have yielded about sixty species of fossil *Cephalopoda*. At Petherwin the chief kind is the

Fig. 307.—Section of Liassic Ammonite, showing chambers filled with spar.

beautiful *Clymenia*, of which eleven species are there met with. *Goniatites* is another genus not uncommon at Petherwin, although not so numerously represented, as far as species go, as Torquay. The richly coloured red and yellow limestones at the latter place are cut and polished, and then present a very lovely appearance, being crowded with fossil, corals, shells, etc.; and not unfrequently we see a white, vertebrate-looking organism cut through—this will doubtless be an *Orthoceras*.

In the Carboniferous limestone this family attains its maximum development, for no fewer than one hundred and sixty-nine species have been described from this and associated deposits, up to and including the Millstone Grit. In this list we find fifty-nine species of *Goniatites*, forty-eight of *Orthoceras*, thirty-six of *Nautilus*, and seventeen of *Discites* (which is usually regarded as a sub-genus of *Nautilus*). Some of the individuals attain a gigantic size. I have found fossil Nautili in Derbyshire and the Isle of Man which required a strong man easily to lift them. And, especially in the Irish Carboniferous limestone, specimens of *Orthoceras* are met with as thick as a man's thigh.

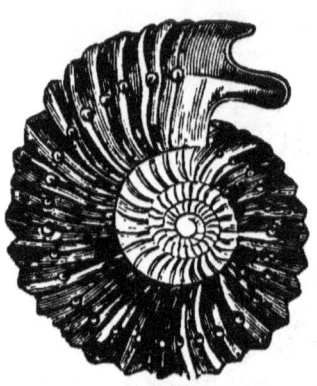

Fig. 308.—Beaked Ammonite.

Perhaps the commonest of the Carboniferous limestone *Goniatites* is *G. sphæricus*. It abounds at Castleton, in the Peak of Derbyshire—at places in swarms. Higher up the series, in the Yoredale shales at Todmorden and Hebden Bridge, there are thin

FOSSIL CEPHALOPODS. 311

bands of black limestone completely made up of small Goniatites. In the shales which overlie the

Fig. 309.—*Ammonites bifrons.*   Fig. 310.—Side view of ditto

impure coal-seams in the Millstone Grit of Yorkshire

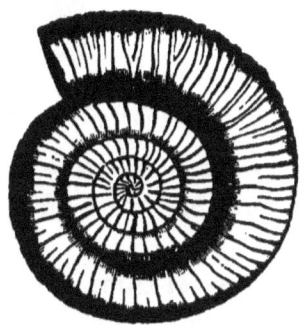

Fig. 311.—*Ammonites communis.*   Fig. 312.—Side view of ditto.

and Lancashire—best seen, perhaps, in the neighbourhood of Halifax and Oldham, we have a splendid fossil, *Goniatites Listeri*, as large as the palm of one's hand, and frequently converted into iron pyrites.

The *Ceratites* of the Muschelkalk (Trias) of Germany is nearly allied to the Ammonites, and is a member of the latter family. The edges of the chamber-divisions in *Ceratites* are not so intricately folded as in the *Ammonites* proper, and, singularly enough, many of the *young* in some species of

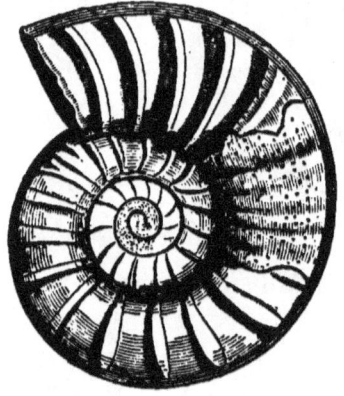

Fig. 313.—*Ammonites obtusus*.   Fig. 314.—Side view of ditto.

Ammonites pass through a Ceratite stage, in that their sutures are less complex then than during their adult life.

About five hundred species of Ammonites have been already figured and described, as occurring in the formations from the Lias up to and including the Chalk. Palæontologists have roughly separated them into six great groups as follows :—(1) Those where

FOSSIL CEPHALOPODS. 313

the external or dorsal edges of the shell are marked by an entire ridge or *keel;* (2) those in which the back is crenated ; (3) those having the back sharp ; (4) those with the back channelled ; (5) those with the back squared ; and (6) those with the back round or convex.

The Lias and Oolite abound in Ammonites.

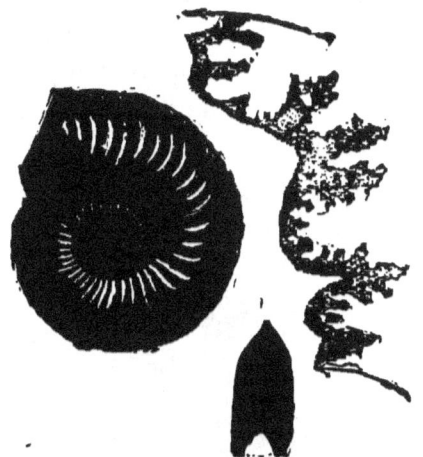

Fig. 315.—*Ammonites amaltheus*, with a plan of foliation of chambers, and section of back of shell.

About two hundred species have been found in the Lias strata alone, and they are so persistent that thirteen zones are distinguished by the presence of certain species of them, which have a limited range.

The name of "snakestone" is given to them at Whitby, where Ammonites of many kinds abound. They are found in blue nodules, which, when broken open, reveal the coiled-up ringed shell, wonderfully resembling a snake in such species as *Ammonites communis*, and still more wonderfully resembling one when they put a "head" on, with eyes in—as they sometimes do.

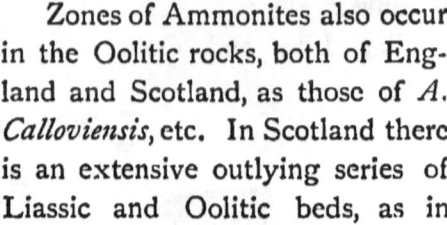

Fig. 316.—*Ammonites varicosus.*

Zones of Ammonites also occur in the Oolitic rocks, both of England and Scotland, as those of *A. Calloviensis*, etc. In Scotland there is an extensive outlying series of Liassic and Oolitic beds, as in Skye, and other islands, and in Sutherlandshire— remnants of a vast sheet of Secondary strata which probably once completely covered the Western High-

Fig. 317.—*Ammonites Cooperi.*

lands, where they have long been removed by denudations. In the Oolitic strata of Sutherland an impure coal is worked, as at Brora, and there the roof over the coal is literally crowded with the elegant *Ammonites Jason.*

Mr. W. Hudleston, F.R.S., has remarked on the *suddenness* with which about forty species of Ammonites make their appearance in the Kelloways rock of Yorkshire. He thinks it due to a "regular invasion." Fossil *Nautili* are not unfrequent, both in Lias and Oolite; and some very pretty ones, cut and uncut, are offered for sale at Whitby, Scarborough, Lyme

Fig. 318.—*Ammonites Mantellii.*

Regis, Weymouth, and other seaside places where fossiliferous strata occur, and where people come with a little scientific taste, more leisure, and most money. The group of Ammonites technically known as *Ornati* occur plentifully near Scarborough. At Cayton Bay, Filey, and Pickering, in Yorkshire, we have well-known localities for very large Ammonites, such as the easily recognized *Ammonites excavatus, A. vertebralis, A. perarmatus, A. plicatilis,* etc.

The Cotteswold district is a capital one for
"snake-stone" hunting. There we find beds full of
Ammonites Parkinsoni and *A. Humphresianus*.

In the neighbourhood of Kimmeridge Bay—where
lie the strata forming that division of the Oolite which
takes its name from the locality—there are numerous
fossil Ammonites, all flattened, and usually of a
creamy-white colour. We often get fragments both
of the Kimmeridge and Oxford Clays in the Boulder
Clays of the Eastern Counties (where they have been

Fig. 319.—*Ammonites falcatus.*

Fig. 320.—*Ammonites lautus.*

brought by ice-action), and they are sometimes so
full of these and other Secondary fossils that the
student may study the Dorsetshire, Oxfordshire, and
Lincolnshire Oolites (or their representatives) without
leaving his own parish.

Of course, in the neighbourhood of Portland we
may see any number of huge, bulky Ammonites in
the rockeries of gardens. These large types are
found plentifully in the Portland stone, although only
as natural casts.

Mr. Robert Etheridge, F.R.S., in his presidential address to the Geographical Society of London, stated that "the whole of the Secondary rocks, from the base of the Lias to the highest Chalk, have been subdivided and specialized by the *Ammonitidæ*—a classification holding good for Europe, India, and America, many species being the same both in the eastern and western hemispheres."

Perhaps the commonest species of Nautilus in the Inferior Oolite is the elegantly shaped *Nautilus hexa-*

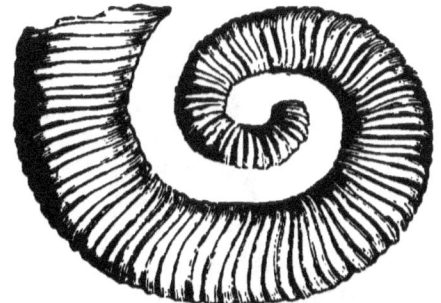

Fig. 321.—*Crioceras.*

gonus. It is found in the "Cornbrash" of Northamptonshire, Kellaways rock, and other subformations.

I ought to mention that certain fossils called *Trigonellites* are found in the Secondary strata, and that they have always been regarded as the "opercula," or "doors" of Ammonites. The late Charles Moore, F.G.S., of Bath, was strongly against this notion.

In those subdivisions of the Oolite which are of

purely argillaceous or *clayey* origin, the fossil Ammonites still retain their pearly, iridescent nacre, or "mother-of-pearl" coating. This is the case with them in the Oxford Clay, and also in the Gault—a subdivision of the Cretaceous or Chalk formation. Indeed, in the latter the fossils are perhaps more

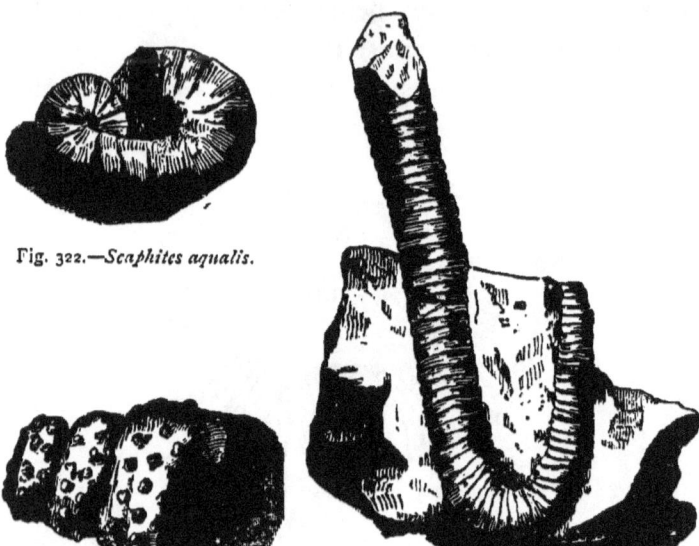

Fig. 322.—*Scaphites aqualis.*

Fig. 323.—Fragment of *T. tuberculatus.*

Fig. 324.—*Hamites attenuatus.*

beautifully preserved in this respect than in any other formation, although I have laid open *Strophomena* and other fossil Brachiopods in the Wenlock Shales (another clayey deposit), which showed distinct nacreous lustre at first, but immediately vanished on exposure to the air.

The Gault near Folkestone is a magnificent storehouse of fossil Cephalopoda. Both on the beach and in the brick pits on the common any quantity of fossils can be obtained. The Ammonite family seems

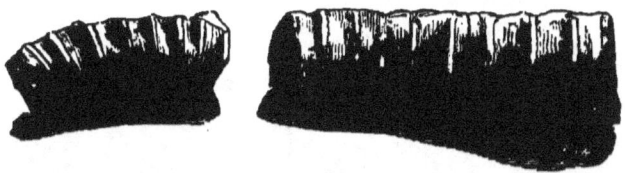

Fig. 325.—Fragments of *Hamites attenuatus*.

to run into strange and fantastic external forms in the Cretaceous strata, commencing with the Lower Greensand, and passing upwards through the Gault,

Fig. 326.—*Turrilites Bergerii*.

Fig. 327.—*Turrilites undulatus*.

Upper Greensand, and Lower Chalk. The regularly coiled Ammonites now become irregular. Sometimes they are only partly coiled, as in *Crioceras ;* at others hooked at one end, as in *Hamites*, or coiled up at both ends, as in *Scaphites*, or they may be quite straight, as in *Baculites*. The Gault is remarkable

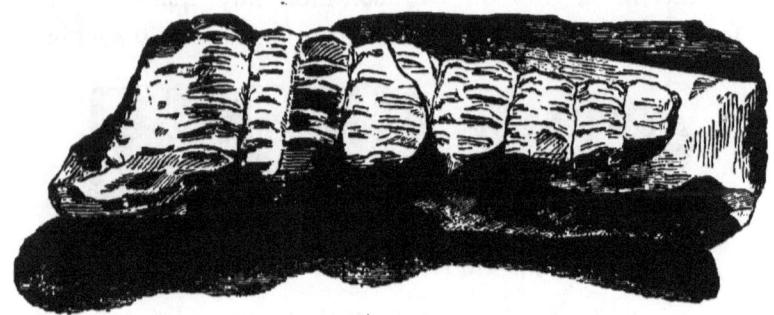

Fig. 328.—*Turrilites costatus*.

for its abundance of these types. In the Lower Chalk they are represented chiefly by the spiral form

Fig. 329.—*Turrilites tuberculatus*.

Turrilites. At Atherton, in the Isle of Wight, these fossils occur in abundance. In the South of England generally, wherever the chalk marl is worked, many of these forms of *Ammonitidæ* will be found. A good many true Ammonites range to the very highest part of the Norfolk Chalk, which is, perhaps, the highest horizon in England—such as *Ammonites Rhotomagensis*, etc.

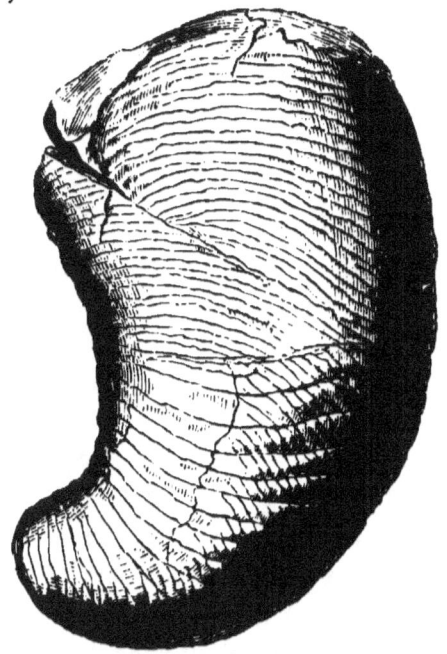

Fig. 330.—*Phragmoceras ventricosum.*

The *Belemnites* belong to the *Dibranchiate* (or two-gilled) division of *Cephalopoda*. The fossils known by this name are the hard internal parts or "guards" of an extinct family of cuttle-fishes. It will be seen, in a perfect Belemnite, that the upper and thicker

Y

part is usually hollow; sometimes, however, it is occupied by an inverted conical object, divided into nearly horizontal chambers. The latter is called the *phragmacone*. Its chambers are usually traversed by a tube or siphuncle, as in those of the Nautilus, and the internal parts of the extinct animals which formed the Belemnites were chiefly contained within the last-formed chamber, as the body of the whole animal is in the Nautilus. The true Belemnites only occur in Secondary rocks of this country. In the Chalk we have a sub-genus termed *Belemnitella*, which may be distinguished from the former by the slit in the upper part of the guard. It is clearly seen in that most abundant and widely distributed Chalk species *Belemnitella mucronata.*

In the Lias and Oolite, Belemnites are marvellously abundant. Near Whitby the limestone frequently appears as if wholly composed of them. Scores are often seen on the surface of a single slab. No fewer than one hundred and fifteen species have been described from the Oolitic rocks of Great Britain alone. There is as great variety in their sizes as in the other families of Cephalopods. For instance, we have some species in the Lias whose "guards" are a foot and a half long; and others, like *Belemnites minima*, found plentifully in the Lower Cretaceous strata—and particularly in the Gault—only about an inch long.

Genuine cuttle-fishes, allied to existing genera,

are also met with, chiefly in the Oxford and Kimmeridge Clays, where they have been so well preserved that even their "ink-bags" are fossilized—clays being always the best preserving grounds for fossils. After the long periods of time which have elapsed since the ancient creatures secreted the pigment, it is still avail-

Fig. 331.—*Baculites vertebralis*: *c*, cast of detached chamber.

able, and I have seen sketches in sepia made entirely from the fossil ink of extinct cuttle-fishes!

The limits of space prevent me doing more than merely sketching the outlines of the history and affinities of our most interesting and common fossils. The student who collects will soon learn more about them; particularly in the magnificent volumes published by the Palæontographical Society of Great Britain, which form one of those unconscious monuments of English voluntary science, the rest of the world can only wonder at.

One common lesson is written upon the rocks of all geological ages by these palæontological characters —that in the midst of life we are literally in death! That the platforms, on which the *vitality* of animals was temporarily exercised during one period, had their foundations laid down, and were built up, by the *death* and extinction of the species of a preceding period! "Upwards and onwards" has been the motto of the Organic Life of the globe,—in spite of those "fallings, off, vanishings," of which Retrogradation takes particular note. One cannot reverently study these incomings and outgoings of the life-forms of succeeding epochs without feeling that "one Divine Purpose runs" throughout the ages, connecting and uniting them into a single great Life-scheme, of which we as yet see only the tangled and disjoined portions!

INDEX.

A

Abundance of fossils, 3
Acorn-shells, 202; larval changes of, 203
Actinocrinus, 117, 127
Agelacrinus, 131
Allman on graptolites, 40, 44, 45
Ammonites, 300, 305; number of species, 312; zones of, 314
Ammonitidæ, 307; in Kelloways rock, 315; localities for, 315, 316; at Portland, 316; variation in, 319; in Chalk, 321
Ananchytes, 151
Anodonta Jukesii, 239
Anthracosia, 251; in ironstone, 251
Apiocrinites, 128, 129
Aporose corals, 63, 64, 67
Arenicolites, 164
Ascidia and sea-mats, 212; larva of, 213; relation to brachiopoda, 214
Aspidophyllum, 87
Astræa, 69, 79
Australian *Brachiopoda*, 231, 232, 234
Aymestry limestone corals, 77

B

Barnacles in Silurian, Rhætic, Oolite, and Chalk strata, 203; in Coralline and Red Crag, 204
Barton Clay, fossils of, 274
Beith, corals at, 87
Belemnites, 321; structure of, 322; in Lias and Oolite, 322; their relation to cuttle-fishes, 323
Benthall Edge, corals at, 76
Black Head, Carboniferous limestone at, 17
Blastoidia, position of, 112
Boring sponges, 13
Box-stones, 279; fossils in, 280; localities for finding, 281
Brachiopoda, 222; life-histories of, 223; geological antiquity of, 223; erroneous notions concerning, 224; larval stages of, 224
Bracklesham, Tertiary fossils of, 274
Bradford (Wilts), encrinites in clay, 117, 128
Bray Head, *Oldhamia* at, 37, 38
Brittle-stars, 132; structure of, 134

C

Cambrian fossil worm-tracks, etc., 163
—— mollusca, 245
—— rocks, Lower, sponges in, 11
—— rocks, *Oldhamia* at, 37
—— star-fishes, 131
—— trilobites, 189, 192
Cambridgeshire coprolites, 208
Carboniferous corals, 65, 69, 82, 87, 88, 89; of Scotland, 85
—— crinoids, 126

Carboniferous encrinites, 115, 122
—— limestones, 29; foraminifera in, 30, 31
—— mollusca, 248; localities for finding, 248, 249, 250, 251
—— polyzoa, 217
—— trilobites, 191, 198, 199
—— worm-tracks, 166
Carpenter, encrinites dredged by, 104, 122
Carpenter, Dr., on shells of brachiopods, 226
Carrick mountain, *Oldhamia* at, 37
Carruthers on graptolites, 44, 47
Cephalopoda, zoological position of, 302; division of, 303; shelled, 305; first appearance of, 308; Carboniferous, 310; localities for, 310, 311
—— Gault, 319, 320
Ceratites, 312
Chain-coral, 74, 79
Chalk fossils, character of, 265, 266; Lower, 266
Chalk, white corals of, 95; sponges in, 16; foraminifera, 30; encrinites, 123, 129
Chert, 21
Choanites, 25
Cladograptus, 47
Cladophora, 46
Cliffs of Mohr, worm-track in flags of, 166, 167
Climacograptus, 48, 50
Clitheroe, encrinite heads in seams, 127
Cœnenchyma, 68
Comatula, 108
Coniston limestone corals, 81
Corals, ancient, genera of one species, 82
—— recent and fossil, 55; classification of, 58; abundant, 73, 74, 75, 76, 78, 79, 80, 81, 83, 84, 85, 87, 88, 89; in flints, 95
Coral-reefs, 69, 70, 77, 83, 90, 94
Coralline Crag, 284, 285, 286; northern shells in, 286; Dr. Woodward on shells of, 287
Corallines, 35

Cornulites, 170
Cowes, fluvio-marine fossils at, 271
Crag beds, 281; abundance of fossils in, 283; division of, 283
—— corals in, 97
—— fossils, localities for, 289, 290, 292
—— polyzoa, 219; localities for, 219
Cretaceous corals, 90
—— echinoderms, 152, 153, 156, 157
—— foraminifera, 30
—— mollusca, 262; localities for finding, 262, 263, 270
—— polyzoa, 217, 218, 221
—— sponges, 16, 18, 25
—— strata, single-corals characteristic, 94
—— star-fishes, 137
Crinoid, recent, 104; Palæozoic described, 113
Crotalocrinus described, 125
Crustacea, classification of, 205; larval changes of, 205; geological appearance of, 205; localities for finding fossil, 206, 207; cretaceous, 206
Cruziana, what it is, 159
Crytograptus, 47
Cyathaxinia, 88
Cyathocrinus, 127
Cyathophyllum, 78, 79, 82
Cyprides in coal measures, 202
Cystidea, position of, 112, 130, 131

D

Dendrograptus, 47
Devonian *brachiopoda*, 237
—— *cephalopoda*, 309; localities for, 309
—— corals, 82, 83, 84, 85
—— encrinites, 115; comparatively rare, 126
—— mollusca, 246, 247; localities of finding, 247
—— trilobites, 198
Dichograptus, 47

INDEX.

Dicranograptus, 48
Didymograptus, 47
Diplograptus, 47, 50
Dissolution of spicules, 11
Ditrupa, 173
Dudley limestone corals, 73
Dumfriesshire, graptolites of, 49

E

Earliest trilobites eyeless, 184
Echinodermata, inter-relations of different forms, 107; their young condition, 110; structure of, 144, 146; of fossil, 147, 149
Echinozoa, 105
Echinus, 109
Eglwyseg corals, 87
Eifel Mountains, crinoids in, 126
"Encrinital limestone," 118
—— marble, 120
Encrinite, description of an, 112
Encrinites, 98; zoological position of, 99; living, 107; abundant, 115, 118, 120, 121, 122, 124, 127, 128
—— effects of muddy water on, 115
—— Primary, 115
—— Secondary, 128
Encrinus moniliformis, 128
Eozoon Canadense, 28
Estheria, 202
Etheridge, Mr., on sponges, 19; on *Productus*, 233; on *Ammonitidæ*, 317
Euplectella aspergillum, 11
Eurypteridæ, 201

F

Fascicularia aurantium, 221
Favosites, 79, 82, 84
Feather-star, 107
Felixstowe, fossil lobsters at, 207; fossil shells at, 278
"Fire-stone," 25
"Five-fingers" star-fish, 132
"Flint-meal," 20, 23

Flint nodules, formation of, 34
Flints, sponges in, 20, 23; encrinites on, 123
Fossil cephalopods, 296; folk-lore of, 296
—— worms, 158
Fossils, abundance of, 3; doubtful classification, 14; popular names, 26
Foraminifera, 28, 29; in carboniferous limestone, 30; in white chalk, 30; to prepare, 50
Fusulina limestone, 29
Fusus contrarius, 289

G

Gault echinoderms, 153
—— fossils of, 263
Gasteropoda, differentiation of, 242
Girvan, corals at, 82
"Glass-rope" sponge, 18
Glyptocrinus, 124
Goniaster, 132
Goniatites, in Yoredale shales, 116,
Gonotheca, 41, 42, 44
Graptolites, 38; zoological position of, 40; structure of, 42; abundant at, 50, 51, 52, 53; in shales, 54
Graptolithus, 47
Gravel flints, sponges in, 27
Greensand echini, 153
—— fossil mollusca of, 263; localities for, 264, 265
—— sponges in, 19, 25, 26

H

Hafod, corals at, 88, 89
Halysites, 78, 79, 84
Hampstead beds, fossils of, 276
Heliolites, 62, 78, 81, 82, 83
Hexactinellidæ, 11, 12, 23, 24, 25
Hinde on sponge spicules, 19
Hopkinson on graptolites, 40, 41, 46
Hunstanton, corals at, 94

Hunting-grounds for Silurian star-fish, 138, 139; for Rhætic star-fish, 140; for Lias star-fish, 141; for Oolitic star-fish, 141; for Chalk star-fish, 142
Hyalonema, 18
Hymenocaris, 201, 204

I

Ipswich, crag corals near, 97; fossil lobsters at, 207; coprolite pits at, 207
Ireland, corals in, 87

J

Jaws of modern worms, 162; of fossil, 162

K

Kentish rag, sponges in, 19
Kirkby - Lonsdale, worm - tracked flags of 161, 167

L

Lamp-shells, 222; origin of name, 225; description of valves of, 225; structure of shells of, 226; internal structure of, 227; loops and spirals in, 228
Lapworth on graptolites, 40
Lessons taught by fossils, 324
Lias corals, 90
—— encrinites, 128
—— mollusca of, 254; in Scotland, 256
—— star-fishes, 137
Liassic ammonites, 313
—— rocks, eozoon in, 28; foraminifera in, 29
"Lily Encrinite," 128
Limestone, foraminifera in, 28
Lincolnshire, Oolite strata of, 257; quarries in, 258
Lithistidæ, 11, 12, 19, 23, 25, 26

Lithostrotion, 88
Llangollen corals, 87
Locomotive organs of star-fish, 123
Longmynd rocks, worm tracks in, 166
London Clay, encrinites, 129
—— fossils of, 272; localities for, 273; fossil wood in, 273
Lonsdalia, 87, 88
Ludlow rocks, sponges in, 10

M

Madrepores, 67
Malvern Hills, corals in, 78
Manon, 26
Marble, encrinite, 120
Marsupites of Chalk, 112, 129, 131
Microscope, use in geology, 27
Microzoa, 18
"Millepore-bed," 91
Moffat, graptolites at, 49, 50
Mold, *Lonsdalia* at, 87
Monactinellidæ, 11
Montilivaltia, 91
Moseley, Professor, on corals, 60
Mollusca, antiquity of, 239; composition of shells of, 240; calcitic and arragonitic structures in shells of, 241; geological value of, 241; structure of shells of, 243; interior scars and markings in, 243; siphonate and asiphonate kinds of, 244; first appearance of, in time, 244; geological localities for first species of, 244
—— fossil (Palæozoic), 239; Secondary, 253; Tertiary, 271
Mullock Hill, corals at, 84

N

Nautili in Yoredale shales, 116
Nautilus family, division of, 306, 307
—— fossil, in Oolite, 317
—— *pompilius*, 394
Nicholson on graptolites, 44, 46

INDEX.

Northamptonshire, fossil mollusca of, 257
Norwich, corals near, 96
—— Crag, 292; fossils of, 292, 293; division of, 293; localities for fossils in, 294, 295
Nummulite limestone, 29

O

Oldhamia, 35
Omphyma, 78, 79
Oolite, Great, sponges in, 19
—— fresh-water beds of, 251; fossils in, 261
—— mollusca of, 255; localities for, 258, 259, 260
—— Yorkshire, fossils of, 257
Oolitic corals, 91
—— crustacea, 206
—— echinoderms, 154; localities for, 154–6
—— encrinites, 117, 128
—— polyzoa, 217
Old Red Sandstone lakes, the, 240
Ossicles of encrinites, 114
Orthoceratites, in Yoredale shales, 116
Ostrea vesicularis, 268, 269, 270

P

Palæchinus, structure of, 153
Palæontographical Society, 324
Paludina, Wealden, 239
Paramoudra, 26
Peak district, encrinites in, 118
"Pear encrinite," 128
Pentacrinus, 113, 128
Pentamerus Knightii, 78, 235
Pentremites, 130, 132
Perforata, 66
"Periwinkle Rocks," 38
Permian mollusca, 251; localities for, 252
Phillipsastræa, 89
Phosphorite, 208
Phosphate, sponges converted into, 26

Pliocene fossils, 278
Planorbis, Eocene, 240
Platycrinus, 127
Pleurograptus, 48
Polyzoa, appearance of living, 211; their relation to *Brachiopoda*, 214; localities for fossil kinds, 215–217; in Coralline Crags, 284
Portland stone sponges, 19
Poteriocrinus, 122, 127
Prestwich on the Crags, 285
Productidæ, 232
Productus giganteus, 232
—— *Llangolliensis*, 232
Pyritized encrinites, 128
Purbeck limestone sponges, 16

R

Radiata, 104
Radiolarians, 18, 32
Ramsey Island, graptolites in, 48, 53
Rastrites, 43, 47
Reef-building corals, 69
"Rose encrinite," 125
Rhabdophora, 40, 46
Rhætic mollusca, 253; localities for, 253, 254
Rhodocrinus, 125, 127
Rhynchonellidæ, 229
Rhynchonella socialis, 232
—— *Wilsonii*, 232
Rugosa, 62, 64

S

Saccosoma, 129; of Oolite, 112
Salenia, 152
Scarborough, corals near, 91
"Screwstones," 119
Sea mats, 209; structure of, 210; distribution of fossil, 211
Secondary corals, 90
Serpula, 170; in Oolite, 172; in Chalk, 173
Sertularians, modern, structure of, 41
Silurian *cephalopoda*, 308

Silurian corals, 70, 83
—— encrinites, 115, 117, 124, 125
—— foraminifera, 31
—— fossil mollusca, 245; alterations in appearance of, 245; impressions of, 245; localities for finding, 246
—— fossil worms, 168, 170, 171, 172
—— graptolites, 38, 48, 49, 52
—— sponges, 13
—— star-fishes, 138
—— trilobites, 189, 192
Siphonia, 12, 25
Sorby, Dr., on corals, 64
Spirifera, 228
Spirorbis, 169, 170
Spongites, 21, 22
Sponge-flesh (*sarcode*), 6, 8
Sponge gravels, 26
Sponges, boring, 13
—— calcareous, 10, 14, 16
—— Carboniferous, 17
—— chitinous, 10
—— compound animals, 7
—— Cretaceous, 16, 18, 25
—— Flint, 20
—— Great Oolite, 19
—— Greensand, 19, 25, 26
—— in Lower Cambrian rocks, 11
—— in Ludlow rocks, 10
—— Kentish Rag, 19
—— Portland stone, 19
—— Purbeck limestone, 16
—— recent, 13, 19
—— siliceous, 11
—— Silurian, 13, 17
—— spicules of, 9, 10, 18, 19
Star-fishes, 130; deep sea, 136
Starkie Gardner on modification of mollusca, 242
"St. Cuthbert's Beads," 128
Strophomena, 231
Stroud, corals near, 93
Swansea, zaphrentis at, 86

T

Tabulata, 58
Tentaculites, 170

Terebratulidæ, 228, 234
Terebratula hastata, 234
—— *grandis*, 235
Tertiary corals, 96
—— crustacea, 206; at Sheppey, 207
—— mollusca, 271; importance of, 271; in Thanet sands, 272; localities for, 272
Tetractinellidæ, 11, 12
Thamnastræa, 91
Thecosmilia, 93
Thomson, James, discovery of sponge spicules, 18; on corals, 85
—— Sir Wyville, encrinites dredged, 104, 122
Thunder-bolt, story of a, 298
Thunder-bolts, 296, 297
Tortoise-encrinites of Chalk, 112
Trilobites, 174; folk-lore of, 175; etymology of, 176; relations of, 176; metamorphoses of, 177; their relation to king-crabs, 178; resemblance of larva of king-crab to, 178; compound eyes of, 180, 185; sizes of, 181; Barrande on larval stages of, 183; Owen on sexes in, 184; Buckland on eyes of, 185; bottom feeders, 187; Salter on, 187; relations of species of to shrimp, parasite (*Bopyrus*), 188; moulting of, 189; relation to recent *serolis*, 192, 193; to recent *apus*, 193; localities for finding, 194, 199; classification of, 199, 200
Trigonellites, 317
Tubed worms, 162

U

Upper Silurian *Brachiopoda*, 237; localities for, 236

V

Ventriculites, 12, 21, 24
"Venus' flower-basket," 11, 12, 24

INDEX.

W

Wales, North and South, graptolites in, 52, 53
—— North, corals, 80, 87
Wandering worms, 163.
Water-vascular system of echinozoa, 107
Wealden, 261 ; fossil mollusca of, 262
Wenlock Edge coral-reef, 70, 77
—— corals abundant, 75, 82
Wight, Isle of, a good fossilizing place, 271
Windermere, graptolites at, 51
Wood, Mr., 127
—— Searles, on the Crags, 285 ; 286, 287, 288
Woodocrinus, 127
Woolhope Valley corals, 78

Woolwich and Reading beds, fossils of, 272
Worm-tracks, modern, 159 ; fossil, 159 ; indicative of subsidence, 160 ; in millstone grit, 165
Worm-tubes, 164, 165
Wren's Nest, corals at, 71, 74

Y

Yarmouth (Isle of Wight), a good locality, 275, 276
Yoredale beds, encrinites in, 116
Young, Mr. J., on microzoa, 18

Z

Zaphrentis, 79, 85

THE END.

PRINTED BY WILLIAM CLOWES AND SONS, LIMITED, LONDON AND BECCLES.

[*December*, 1888.

A LIST OF BOOKS
PUBLISHED BY
CHATTO & WINDUS,
214, PICCADILLY, LONDON, W.

Sold by all Booksellers, or sent post free for the published price by the Publishers.

EDITION DE LUXE OF A FRENCH CLASSIC.
Abbé Constantin (The). By LUDOVIC HALEVY, of the French Academy. Translated into English. With 36 Photogravure Illustrations by GOUPIL & Co., after the Drawings of Madame MADELEINE LEMAIRE. Only 250 copies of this choice book have been printed (in large quarto) for the English market, each one numbered. The price may be learned from any Bookseller.

About.—The Fellah: An Egyptian Novel. By EDMOND ABOUT. Translated by Sir RANDAL ROBERTS. Post 8vo, illustrated boards, 2s.; cloth limp, 2s. 6d.

Adams (W. Davenport), Works by:
A Dictionary of the Drama. Being a comprehensive Guide to the Plays, Playwrights, Players, and Playhouses of the United Kingdom and America, from the Earliest to the Present Times. Crown 8vo, half-bound, 12s. 6d. [*Preparing.*
Quips and Quiddities. Selected by W. DAVENPORT ADAMS. Post 8vo, cloth limp, 2s. 6d.

Advertising, A History of, from the Earliest Times. Illustrated by Anecdotes, Curious Specimens, and Notices of Successful Advertisers. By HENRY SAMPSON. With Coloured Frontispiece and Illustrations. Crown 8vo, cloth gilt, 7s. 6d.

Agony Column (The) of "The Times," from 1800 to 1870. Edited, with an Introduction, by ALICE CLAY. Post 8vo, cloth limp, 2s. 6d.

Aïdé (Hamilton), Works by:
Post 8vo, illustrated boards, 2s. each.
Carr of Carrlyon. | Confidences.

Alexander (Mrs.), Novels by:
Post 8vo, illustrated boards, 2s. each.
Maid, Wife, or Widow?
Valerie's Fate.

Allen (Grant), Works by:
Crown 8vo, cloth extra, 6s. each.
The Evolutionist at Large. Second Edition, revised.
Vignettes from Nature.
Colin Clout's Calendar.

Crown 8vo, cloth extra, 6s. each; post 8vo, illustrated boards., 2s. each.
Strange Stories. With a Frontispiece by GEORGE DU MAURIER.
The Beckoning Hand. With a Frontispiece by TOWNLEY GREEN.

Post 8vo, illustrated boards, 2s. each.
Babylon: A Romance.
In all Shades.

Crown 8vo, cloth extra, 3s. 6d. each.
For Maimie's Sake: A Tale of Love and Dynamite.
The Devil's Die. [*Shortly.*
Philistia. Crown 8vo, cloth extra, 3s. 6d.; post 8vo, illust. boards, 2s.
This Mortal Coil. Three Vols., crown 8vo.

Architectural Styles, A Handbook of. Translated from the German of A. ROSENGARTEN, by W. COLLETT-SANDARS. Crown 8vo, cloth extra, with 639 Illustrations, 7s. 6d.

Arnold.—Bird Life in England. By EDWIN LESTER ARNOLD, Crown 8vo, cloth extra, 6s.

Artemus Ward:
Artemus Ward's Works: The Works of CHARLES FARRER BROWNE, better known as ARTEMUS WARD. With Portrait and Facsimile. Crown 8vo, cloth extra, 7s. 6d.
The Genial Showman: Life and Adventures of Artemus Ward. By EDWARD P. HINGSTON. With a Frontispiece. Cr. 8vo, cl. extra, 3s. 6d.

Art (The) of Amusing: A Collection of Graceful Arts, Games, Tricks, Puzzles, and Charades. By FRANK BELLEW. With 300 Illustrations. Cr. 8vo, cloth extra, 4s. 6d.

Ashton (John), Works by:
Crown 8vo, cloth extra, 7s. 6d. each.
A History of the Chap-Books of the Eighteenth Century. With nearly 400 Illustrations, engraved in facsimile of the originals.
Social Life In the Reign of Queen Anne. From Original Sources. With nearly 100 Illustrations.
Humour, Wit, and Satire of the Seventeenth Century. With nearly 100 Illustrations.
English Caricature and Satire on Napoleon the First. With 115 Illustrations.
Modern Street Ballads. With 57 Illustrations.
*** Also a Large Paper Edition of the last (only 100 printed: all numbered), bound in half-parchment. The price of the special copies may be learned from any Bookseller.

Bacteria.—A Synopsis of the Bacteria and Yeast Fungi and Allied Species. By W. B. GROVE, B.A. With 87 Illusts. Crown 8vo, cl. extra, 3s. 6d.

Bankers, A Handbook of London; together with Lists of Bankers from 1677. By F. G. HILTON PRICE. Crown 8vo, cloth extra, 7s. 6d.

Bardsley(Rev.C.W.),Works by:
English Surnames: Their Sources and Significations. Third Edition, revised. Crown 8vo, cl. ex., 7s. 6d.
Curiosities of Puritan Nomenclature. Second Edition. Crown 8vo, cloth extra, 6s.

Bartholomew Fair, Memoirs of. By HENRY MORLEY. With 100 Illusts. Crown 8vo, cloth extra, 7s. 6d.

Beaconsfield, Lord: A Biography. By T. P. O'CONNOR, M.P. Sixth Edition, with a New Preface. Crown 8vo, cloth extra, 7s. 6d.

Beauchamp. — Grantley Grange: A Novel. By SHELSLEY BEAUCHAMP. Post 8vo, illust. bds., 2s.

Beautiful Pictures by British Artists: A Gathering of Favourites from our Picture Galleries. All engraved on Steel in the highest style of Art. Edited, with Notices of the Artists, by SYDNEY ARMYTAGE, M.A. Imperial 4to, cloth extra, gilt and gilt edges 21s.

Bechstein. — As Pretty as Seven, and other German Stories. Collected by LUDWIG BECHSTEIN. With Additional Tales by the Brothers GRIMM, and 100 Illusts. by RICHTER. Small 4to, green and gold, 6s. 6d.; gilt edges, 7s. 6d.

Beerbohm. — Wanderings in Patagonia; or, Life among the Ostrich Hunters. By JULIUS BEERBOHM. With Illusts. Crown 8vo, cloth extra, 3s. 6d.

Belgravia for 1888. One Shilling Monthly. Two New Serial Stories began in BELGRAVIA for JANUARY: Undercurrents, by the Author of "Phyllis;" and The Blackhall Ghosts, by SARAH TYTLER.
*** *Bound Volumes from the beginning are kept in stock, cloth extra, gilt edges, 7s. 6d. each; cases for binding Vols., 2s. each.*

Belgravia Holiday Number, published Annually in JULY; and Belgravia Annual, published Annually in NOVEMBER. Each Complete in itself. Demy 8vo, with Illustrations, 1s. each.

Bennett (W.C.,LL.D.),Works by:
Post 8vo, cloth limp, 2s. each.
A Ballad History of England
Songs for Sailors.

Besant (Walter) and James Rice, Novels by. Crown 8vo, cloth extra, 3s. 6d. each; post 8vo, illust. boards, 2s. each; cloth limp, 2s. 6d. each.
Ready-Money Mortiboy.
My Little Girl.
With Harp and Crown.
This Son of Vulcan.
The Golden Butterfly.
The Monks of Thelema.
By Celia's Arbour.
The Chaplain of the Fleet.
The Seamy Side.
The Case of Mr. Lucraft, &c.
'Twas in Trafalgar's Bay, &c.
The Ten Years' Tenant, &c.

Besant (Walter), Novels by:
Crown 8vo, cloth extra, 3s. 6d. each;
post 8vo, illust. boards, 2s. each;
cloth limp, 2s. 6d. each.
All Sorts and Conditions of Men: An Impossible Story. With Illustrations by FRED. BARNARD.
The Captains' Room, &c. With Frontispiece by E. J. WHEELER.
All In a Garden Fair. With 6 Illustrations by HARRY FURNISS.
Dorothy Forster. With Frontispiece by CHARLES GREEN.
Uncle Jack, and other Stories.
Children of Gibeon.

Crown 8vo, cloth extra, 3s. 6d. each.
The World Went Very Well Then. With Illustrations by A. FORESTIER.
Herr Paulus: His Rise, his Greatness, and his Fall. With a NEW PREFACE.

Fifty Years Ago. With 137 full-page Plates and Woodcuts. Demy 8vo, cloth extra, 16s.
The Eulogy of Richard Jefferies: A Memoir. With Photograph Portrait. Cr. 8vo, cl. extra, 6s.
For Faith and Freedom. With Illustrations by A. FORESTIER. Three Vols., crown 8vo. [*Shortly.*

The Art of Fiction. Demy 8vo, 1s.

COMPLETION OF THE
Library Edition of the Novels of
Besant and Rice.
The whole 12 Volumes, printed from new type on a large crown 8vo page, and handsomely bound in cloth, are now ready, price Six Shillings each.
1. Ready-Money Mortiboy. With Etched Portrait of JAMES RICE.
2. My Little Girl.
3. With Harp and Crown.
4. This Son of Vulcan.
5. The Golden Butterfly. With Etched Portrait of WALTER BESANT.
6. The Monks of Thelema.
7. By Celia's Arbour.
8. The Chaplain of the Fleet.
9. The Seamy Side.
10. The Case of Mr. Lucraft, &c.
11. 'Twas In Trafalgar's Bay, &c.
12. The Ten Years' Tenant, &c.

Betham-Edwards (M.), Novels by:
Felicia. Cr. 8vo, cloth extra, 3s. 6d.; post 8vo, illust. bds., 2s.
Kitty. Post 8vo, illust. bds., 2s.

Bewick (Thomas) and his Pupils. By AUSTIN DOBSON. With 95 Illusts. Square 8vo, cloth extra, 10s. 6d.

Birthday Books:—
The Starry Heavens: A Poetical Birthday Book. Square 8vo, handsomely bound in cloth, 2s. 6d.
The Lowell Birthday Book. With Illusts. Small 8vo, cloth extra, 4s. 6d.

Blackburn's (Henry) Art Handbooks. Demy 8vo, Illustrated, uniform in size for binding.
Academy Notes, separate years, from 1875 to 1887, each 1s.
Academy Notes, 1888. With numerous Illustrations. 1s.
Academy Notes, 1875-84. Complete in One Volume, with about 700 Facsimile Illustrations. Cloth limp, 6s.
Grosvenor Notes, 1877. 6d.
Grosvenor Notes, separate years, from 1878 to 1887, each 1s.
Grosvenor Notes, 1888. With numerous Illusts. 1s.
Grosvenor Notes, Vol. I., 1877-82. With upwards of 300 Illustrations. Demy 8vo, cloth limp, 6s.
Grosvenor Notes, Vol. II., 1883-87. With upwards of 300 Illustrations. Demy 8vo, cloth limp, 6s.
The New Gallery, 1888. With numerous Illustrations. 1s.
The English Pictures at the National Gallery. 114 Illustrations. 1s.
The Old Masters at the National Gallery. 128 Illustrations. 1s. 6d.
A Complete Illustrated Catalogue to the National Gallery. With Notes by H. BLACKBURN, and 242 Illusts. Demy 8vo, cloth limp, 3s.

The Paris Salon, 1888. With 300 Facsimile Sketches. Demy 8vo, 3s.

Blake (William): Etchings from his Works. By W. B. SCOTT. With descriptive Text. Folio, half-bound boards, India Proofs, 21s.

Boccaccio's Decameron; or, Ten Days' Entertainment. Translated into English, with an Introduction by THOMAS WRIGHT, F.S.A. With Portrait and STOTHARD'S beautiful Copperplates. Cr. 8vo, cloth extra, gilt, 7s. 6d.

Bourne (H. R. Fox), Works by:
English Merchants: Memoirs in Illustration of the Progress of British Commerce. With numerous Illustrations. Cr. 8vo, cloth extra, 7s. 6d.
English Newspapers: Chapters in the History of Journalism. Two Vols., demy 8vo, cloth extra, 25s.

Bowers'(G.) Hunting Sketches:
Oblong 4to, half-bound boards, 21s. each
Canters In Crampshire.
Leaves from a Hunting Journal. Coloured in facsimile of the originals.

BOOKS PUBLISHED BY

Boyle (Frederick), Works by:
Crown 8vo, cloth extra, 3s. 6d. each; post 8vo, illustrated boards, 2s. each.
Camp Notes: Stories of Sport and Adventure in Asia, Africa, America.
Savage Life: Adventures of a Globe-Trotter.

Chronicles of No-Man's Land. Post 8vo, illust. boards, 2s.

Brand's Observations on Popular Antiquities, chiefly Illustrating the Origin of our Vulgar Customs, Ceremonies, and Superstitions. With the Additions of Sir HENRY ELLIS. Crown 8vo, with Illustrations, 7s. 6d.

Bret Harte, Works by:
Bret Harte's Collected Works. Arranged and Revised by the Author. Complete in Five Vols., crown 8vo, cloth extra, 6s. each.
Vol. I. COMPLETE POETICAL AND DRAMATIC WORKS. With Steel Portrait, and Introduction by Author.
Vol. II. EARLIER PAPERS—LUCK OF ROARING CAMP, and other Sketches—BOHEMIAN PAPERS — SPANISH AND AMERICAN LEGENDS.
Vol. III. TALES OF THE ARGONAUTS—EASTERN SKETCHES.
Vol. IV. GABRIEL CONROY.
Vol. V. STORIES — CONDENSED NOVELS, &c.
The Select Works of Bret Harte, in Prose and Poetry. With Introductory Essay by J. M. BELLEW, Portrait of the Author, and 50 Illustrations. Crown 8vo, cloth extra, 7s. 6d.
Bret Harte's Complete Poetical Works. Author's Copyright Edition. Printed on hand-made paper and bound in buckram. Cr. 8vo, 4s. 6d.
Gabriel Conroy: A Novel. Post 8vo, illustrated boards, 2s.
An Heiress of Red Dog, and other Stories. Post 8vo illust. boards, 2s.
The Twins of Table Mountain. Fcap. 8vo, picture cover, 1s.
Luck of Roaring Camp, and other Sketches. Post 8vo, illust. bds., 2s.
Jeff Briggs's Love Story. Fcap. 8vo, picture cover, 1s.
Flip. Post 8vo, illust. bds., 2s.; cl. 2s. 6d.
Californian Stories (including THE TWINS OF TABLE MOUNTAIN, JEFF BRIGGS'S LOVE STORY, &c.) Post 8vo, illustrated boards, 2s.
Maruja A Novel. Post 8vo, illust. boards, 2s.; cloth limp, 2s. 6d.
The Queen of the Pirate Isle. With 28 original Drawings by KATE GREENAWAY, Reproduced in Colours by EDMUND EVANS. Sm, 4to, bds., 5s.
A Phyllis of the Sierras, &c. Post 8vo, Illust. bds., 2s. cloth limp, 2s. 6d.

Brewer (Rev. Dr.), Works by:
The Reader's Handbook of Allusions, References, Plots, and Stories. Twelfth Thousand. With Appendix, containing a COMPLETE ENGLISH BIBLIOGRAPHY. Cr. 8vo, cloth 7s, 6d.
Authors and their Works, with the Dates: Being the Appendices to "The Reader's Handbook," separately printed. Cr. 8vo, cloth limp, 2s.
A Dictionary of Miracles: Imitative, Realistic, and Dogmatic. Crown 8vo, cloth extra, 7s. 6d.; half-bound, 9s.

Brewster (Sir David), Works by:
More Worlds than One: The Creed of the Philosopher and the Hope of the Christian. With Plates. Post 8vo, cloth extra, 4s. 6d.
The Martyrs of Science: Lives of GALILEO, TYCHO BRAHE, and KEPLER. With Portraits. Post 8vo, cloth extra, 4s. 6d.
Letters on Natural Magic. A New Edition, with numerous Illustrations, and Chapters on the Being and Faculties of Man, and Additional Phenomena of Natural Magic, by J. A. SMITH. Post 8vo, cl. ex., 4s. 6d.

Brydges. — Uncle Sam at Home. By HAROLD BRYDGES. Post 8vo, illust. boards, 2s.; cloth, 2s. 6d.

Buchanan's (Robert) Works:
Crown 8vo, cloth extra, 6s. each.
Ballads of Life, Love, and Humour. With a Frontispiece by ARTHUR HUGHES.
Selected Poems of Robert Buchanan. With a Frontispiece by T. DALZIEL.
The Earthquake; or, Six Days and a Sabbath.
The City of Dream: An Epic Poem. With Two Illusts. by P. MACNAB. Second Edition.

Robert Buchanan's Complete Poetical Works. With Steel-plate Portrait. Crown 8vo, cloth extra, 7s. 6d.

Crown 8vo, cloth extra, 3s. 6d. each; post 8vo, illust. boards, 2s. each.
The Shadow of the Sword.
A Child of Nature. With a Frontispiece.
God and the Man. With Illustrations by FRED. BARNARD.
The Martyrdom of Madeline. With Frontispiece by A. W. COOPER.
Love Me for Ever. With a Frontispiece by P. MACNAB.
Annan Water. | **The New Abelard.**
Foxglove Manor.

CHATTO & WINDUS, PICCADILLY. 5

BUCHANAN (ROBERT), *continued*—
Crown 8vo, cloth extra, 3s. 6d. each;
post 8vo, illustrated boards, 2s. each.
Matt: A Story of a Caravan.
The Master of the Mine.
The Heir of Linne. Cheaper Edition.
Crown 8vo, cloth extra, 3s. 6d.

Burnett (Mrs.), Novels by:
Surly Tim, and other Stories. Post 8vo, illustrated boards, 2s.
Fcap. 8vo, picture cover, 1s. each.
Kathleen Mavourneen.
Lindsay's Luck.
Pretty Polly Pemberton.

Burton (Captain).—The Book of the Sword: Being a History of the Sword and its Use in all Countries, from the Earliest Times. By RICHARD F. BURTON. With over 400 Illustrations. Square 8vo, cloth extra, 32s.

Burton (Robert):
The Anatomy of Melancholy. A New Edition, complete, corrected and enriched by Translations of the Classical Extracts. Demy 8vo, cloth extra, 7s. 6d.
Melancholy Anatomised: Being an Abridgment, for popular use, of BURTON'S ANATOMY OF MELANCHOLY. Post 8vo, cloth limp, 2s. 6d.

Byron (Lord):
Byron's Letters and Journals. With Notices of his Life. By THOMAS MOORE. Cr. 8vo, cloth extra, 7s. 6d.
Prose and Verse, Humorous, Satirical, and Sentimental, by THOMAS MOORE; with Suppressed Passages from the Memoirs of Lord Byron. Edited, with Notes and Introduction, by R. HERNE SHEPHERD. Crown 8vo, cloth extra, 7s. 6d.

Caine (T. Hall), Novels by:
Crown 8vo, cloth extra, 3s. 6d. each; post 8vo, illustrated boards, 2s. each.
The Shadow of a Crime.
A Son of Hagar.

The Deemster: A Romance of the Isle of Man. Fourth Edition, crown 8vo, cloth extra, 3s. 6d.

Cameron (Commander).—
The Cruise of the "Black Prince" Privateer. By V. LOVETT CAMERON, R.N., C.B. With Two Illustrations by P. MACNAB. Crown 8vo, cl. ex., 5s.; post 8vo, illustrated boards, 2s.

Cameron (Mrs. H. Lovett), Novels by:
Crown 8vo, cloth extra, 3s. 6d. each post 8vo, illustrated boards, 2s. each.
Juliet's Guardian. | Deceivers Ever.

Carlyle (Thomas):
On the Choice of Books. By THOMAS CARLYLE. With a Life of the Author by R. H. SHEPHERD. New and Revised Edition, post 8vo, cloth extra, Illustrated, 1s. 6d.
The Correspondence of Thomas Carlyle and Ralph Waldo Emerson, 1834 to 1872. Edited by CHARLES ELIOT NORTON. With Portraits. Two Vols., crown 8vo, cloth extra, 24s.

Chapman's (George) Works:
Vol. I. contains the Plays complete, including the doubtful ones. Vol. II., the Poems and Minor Translations, with an Introductory Essay by ALGERNON CHARLES SWINBURNE. Vol. III., the Translations of the Iliad and Odyssey. Three Vols., crown 8vo, cloth extra, 18s.; or separately, 6s. each.

Chatto & Jackson.—A Treatise on Wood Engraving, Historical and Practical. By WM. ANDREW CHATTO and JOHN JACKSON. With a Additional Chapter by HENRY G. BOHN; and 450 fine Illustrations. A Reprint of the last Revised Edition. Large 4to, half-bound, 28s.

Chaucer:
Chaucer for Children: A Golden Key. By Mrs. H.R. HAWEIS. With Eight Coloured Pictures and numerous Woodcuts by the Author. New Ed., small 4to, cloth extra, 6s.
Chaucer for Schools. By Mrs. H. R. HAWEIS. Demy 8vo, cloth limp, 2s. 6d.

Chronicle (The) of the Coach: Charing Cross to Ilfracombe. By J.D CHAMPLIN. With 75 Illustrations by EDWARD L. CHICHESTER. Square 8vo, cloth extra, 7s. 6d.

Clodd.— Myths and Dreams. By EDWARD CLODD, F.R.A.S., Author of "The Story of Creation," &c. Crown 8vo, cloth extra, 5s.

Cobban.—The Cure of Souls: A Story. By J. MACLAREN COBBAN. Post 8vo, illustrated boards, 2s.

Coleman (John), Works by:
Curly: An Actor's Story. Illustrated by J. C. DOLLMAN. Crown 8vo, 1s.; cloth, 1s. 6d.
Players and Playwrights I have Known. Two Vols., demy 8vo, cloth extra, 24s.

Collins (Wilkie), Novels by:
Crown 8vo, cloth extra, 3s. 6d. each;
post 8vo, illustrated boards, 2s. each;
cloth limp, 2s. 6d. each.
Antonina. Illust. by Sir JOHN GILBERT.
Basil. Illustrated by Sir JOHN GILBERT and J MAHONEY.
Hide and Seek. Illustrated by Sir JOHN GILBERT and J. MAHONEY.
The Dead Secret. Illustrated by Sir JOHN GILBERT.
Queen of Hearts. Illustrated by Sir JOHN GILBERT.
My Miscellanies. With a Steel-plate Portrait of WILKIE COLLINS.
The Woman In White. With Illustrations by Sir JOHN GILBERT and F. A. FRASER.
The Moonstone. With Illustrations by G. DU MAURIER and F. A. FRASER.
Man and Wife. Illust. by W. SMALL.
Poor Miss Finch. Illustrated by G. DU MAURIER and EDWARD HUGHES.
Miss or Mrs.? With Illustrations by S. L. FILDES and HENRY WOODS.
The New Magdalen. Illustrated by G. DU MAURIER and C. S. REINHARDT.
The Frozen Deep. Illustrated by G. DU MAURIER and J. MAHONEY.
The Law and the Lady. Illustrated by S. L. FILDES and SYDNEY HALL.
The Two Destinies.
The Haunted Hotel. Illustrated by ARTHUR HOPKINS.
The Fallen Leaves.
Jezebel's Daughter.
The Black Robe.
Heart and Science: A Story of the Present Time.
"I Say No."
The Evil Genius.

Little Novels. Cr. 8vo, cl. ex., 3s. 6d.
The Legacy of Cain. Three Vols., crown 8vo.

Collins (Mortimer), Novels by:
Crown 8vo, cloth extra, 3s. 6d. each; post 8vo, illustrated boards, 2s. each.
Sweet Anne Page. | Transmigration.
From Midnight to Midnight.

A Fight with Fortune. Post 8vo, illustrated boards, 2s.

Collins (Mortimer & Frances), Novels by:
Crown 8vo, cloth extra, 3s. 6d. each; post 8v), illustrated boards, 2s. each.
Blacksmith and Scholar.
The Village Comedy.
You Play Me False.

Post 8vo, illustrated boards, 2s. each,
Sweet and Twenty. | Frances.

Collins (C. Allston).—The Bar Sinister: A Story. By C. ALLSTON COLLINS. Post 8vo, illustrated bds., 2s.

Colman's Humorous Works:
"Broad Grins," "My Nightgown and Slippers," and other Humorous Works, Prose and Poetical, of GEORGE COLMAN. With Life by G. B. BUCKSTONE, and Frontispiece by HOGARTH. Crown 8vo cloth extra, gilt, 7s. 6d.

Colquhoun.—Every Inch a Soldier: A Novel. By M. J. COLQUHOUN. Cheaper Edition. Post 8vo, illustrated boards, 2s. [Shortly.

Convalescent Cookery: A Family Handbook. By CATHERINE RYAN. Crown 8vo, 1s.; cloth, 1s. 6d.

Conway (Moncure D.), Works by:
Demonology and Devil-Lore. Two Vols., royal 8vo, with 65 Illusts., 28s.
A Necklace of Stories. Illustrated by W. J. HENNESSY. Square 8vo, cloth extra, 6s.
Pine and Palm: A Novel. Cheaper Edition. Post 8vo, illustrated boards, 2s. [Shortly.

Cook (Dutton), Novels by:
Leo. Post 8vo, illustrated boards, 2s.
Paul Foster's Daughter. Crown 8vo, cloth extra, 3s. 6d.; post 8vo, illustrated boards, 2s.

Copyright.—A Handbook of English and Foreign Copyright in Literary and Dramatic Works. By SIDNEY JERROLD. Post 8vo, cl., 2s. 6d.

Cornwall.—Popular Romances of the West of England; or, The Drolls, Traditions, and Superstitions of Old Cornwall. Collected and Edited by ROBERT HUNT, F.R.S. New and Revised Edition, with Additions, and Two Steel-plate Illustrations by GEORGE CRUIKSHANK. Crown 8vo, cloth extra, 7s. 6d.

Craddock.—The Prophet of the Great Smoky Mountains. By CHARLES EGBERT CRADDOCK. Post 8vo illust. bds., 2s. cloth limp, 2s. 6d.

Cruikshank (George):
The Comic Almanack. Complete in TWO SERIES: The FIRST from 1835 to 1843; the SECOND from 1844 to 1853. A Gathering of the BEST HUMOUR of THACKERAY, HOOD, MAYHEW, ALBERT SMITH, A'BECKETT, ROBERT BROUGH, &c. With 2,000 Woodcuts and Steel Engravings by CRUIKSHANK, HINE, LANDELLS, &c. Crown 8vo, cloth gilt, two very thick volumes, 7s. 6d. each.

CHATTO & WINDUS, PICCADILLY. 7

CRUIKSHANK (GEORGE), continued—
The Life of George Cruikshank. By
BLANCHARD JERROLD, Author of
"The Life of Napoleon III.," &c.
With 84 Illustrations. New and
Cheaper Edition, enlarged, with Additional Plates, and a very carefully
compiled Bibliography. Crown 8vo,
cloth extra, 7s. 6d.

Cumming (C. F. Gordon), Works by:
Demy 8vo, cloth extra, 8s. 6d. each.
In the Hebrides. With Autotype Facsimile and numerous full-page Illusts.
In the Himalayas and on the Indian Plains. With numerous Illustrations.

Via Cornwall to Egypt. With a Photogravure Frontispiece. Demy 8vo, cloth extra, 7s. 6d.

Cussans.—Handbook of Heraldry; with Instructions for Tracing Pedigrees and Deciphering Ancient MSS., &c. By JOHN E. CUSSANS. Entirely New and Revised Edition, illustrated with over 400 Woodcuts and Coloured Plates. Crown 8vo, cloth extra, 7s. 6d.

Cyples.—Hearts of Gold: A Novel. By WILLIAM CYPLES. Crown 8vo, cloth extra, 3s. 6d.; post 8vo, illustrated boards, 2s.

Daniel. — Merrie England In the Olden Time. By GEORGE DANIEL. With Illustrations by ROBT. CRUIKSHANK. Crown 8vo, cloth extra, 3s. 6d.

Daudet.—The Evangelist; or, Port Salvation. By ALPHONSE DAUDET. Translated by C. HARRY MELTZER. With Portrait of the Author. Crown 8vo, cloth extra, 3s. 6d.; post 8vo, illust. boards, 2s.

Davenant.—Hints for Parents on the Choice of a Profession or Trade for their Sons. By FRANCIS DAVENANT, M.A. Post 8vo, 1s.; cloth limp, 1s. 6d.

Davies (Dr. N. E.), Works by:
Crown 8vo, 1s. each; cloth limp, 1s. 6d. each.
One Thousand Medical Maxims.
Nursery Hints: A Mother's Guide.
Aids to Long Life. Crown 8vo, 2s.; cloth limp, 2s. 6d.

Davies' (Sir John) Complete Poetical Works, including Psalms I. to L. in Verse, and other hitherto Unpublished MSS., for the first time Collected and Edited, with MemorialIntroduction and Notes, by the Rev. A. B. GROSART, D.D. Two Vols., crown 8vo, cloth boards, 12s.

De Maistre —A Journey Round My Room. By XAVIER DE MAISTRE. Translated by HENRY ATTWELL. Post 8vo, cloth limp, 2s. 6d.

De Mille.—A Castle In Spain: A Novel. By JAMES DE MILLE. With a Frontispiece. Crown 8vo, cloth extra, 3s. 6d.; post 8vo, illust. bds., 2s.

Derwent (Leith), Novels by:
Crown 8vo, cloth extra, 3s. 6d. each; post 8vo, illustrated boards, 2s. each.
Our Lady of Tears. | Circe's Lovers.

Dickens (Charles), Novels by Post 8vo, illustrated boards, 2s. each.
Sketches by Boz. | Nicholas Nickleby
Pickwick Papers. | Oliver Twist.

The Speeches of Charles Dickens 1841-1870. With a New Bibliography, revised and enlarged. Edited and Prefaced by RICHARD HERNE SHEPHERD. Cr. 8vo, cloth extra, 6s.—Also a SMALLER EDITION, in the Mayfair Library. Post 8vo, cloth limp, 2s. 6d.
About England with Dickens. By ALFRED RIMMER. With 57 Illustrations by C. A. VANDERHOOF, ALFRED RIMMER, and others. Sq. 8vo, cloth extra, 7s. 6d.

Dictionaries:
A Dictionary of Miracles: Imitative, Realistic, and Dogmatic. By the Rev. E. C. BREWER, LL.D. Crown 8vo, cloth extra, 7s. 6d.; hf.-bound, 9s.
The Reader's Handbook of Allusions, References, Plots, and Stories. By the Rev. E. C. BREWER, LL.D. With an Appendix, containing a Complete English Bibliography. Eleventh Thousand. Crown 8vo, 1,400 pages, cloth extra, 7s. 6d.
Authors and their Works, with the Dates. Being the Appendices to "The Reader's Handbook," separately printed. By the Rev. Dr BREWER. Crown 8vo, cloth limp, 2s.
A Dictionary of the Drama: Being a comprehensive Guide to the Plays, Playwrights, Players, and Playhouses of the United Kingdom and America, from the Earliest to the Present Times. By W. DAVENPORT ADAMS. A thick volume, crown 8vo, halfbound, 12s. 6d. [In preparation.

BOOKS PUBLISHED BY

DICTIONARIES, continued—
Familiar Short Sayings of Great Men. With Historical and Explanatory Notes. By SAMUEL A. BENT, M.A. Fifth Edition, revised and enlarged. Cr. 8vo, cloth extra, 7s. 6d.
The Slang Dictionary: Etymological, Historical, and Anecdotal. Crown 8vo, cloth extra, 6s. 6d.
Women of the Day: A Biographical Dictionary. By FRANCES HAYS. Cr. 8vo, cloth extra, 5s.
Words, Facts, and Phrases: A Dictionary of Curious, Quaint, and Out-of-the-Way Matters. By ELIEZER EDWARDS. New and Cheaper Issue. Cr. 8vo, cl. ex., 7s. 6d.; hf.-bd., 9s.

Diderot.—The Paradox of Acting. Translated, with Annotations, from Diderot's "Le Paradoxe sur le Comédien," by WALTER HERRIES POLLOCK. With a Preface by HENRY IRVING. Cr. 8vo, in parchment, 4s. 6d.

Dobson (W. T.), Works by:
Post 8vo, cloth limp, 2s. 6d. each.
Literary Frivolities, Fancies, Follies, and Frolics. [cities.
Poetical Ingenuities and Eccentri-

Donovan (Dick), Detective Stories by:
Post 8vo, illustrated boards, 2s. each; cloth limp, 2s. 6d. each.
The Man-hunter: Stories from the Note-book of a Detective.
Caught at Last! [Shortly.

Doran.—Memories of our Great Towns; with Anecdotic Gleanings concerning their Worthies and their Oddities. By Dr. JOHN DORAN, F.S.A. With 38 Illusts. New and Cheaper Edit. Cr. 8vo, cl. extra, 7s. 6d.

Drama, A Dictionary of the.
Being a comprehensive Guide to the Plays, Playwrights, Players, and Playhouses of the United Kingdom and America, from the Earliest to the Present Times. By W. DAVENPORT ADAMS. (Uniform with BREWER'S "Reader's Handbook.") Crown 8vo, half-bound, 12s. 6d. [In preparation.

Dramatists, The Old. Cr. 8vo, cl. ex., Vignette Portraits, 6s. per Vol.
Ben Jonson's Works. With Notes Critical and Explanatory, and a Biographical Memoir by WM. GIFFORD. Edit. by Col. CUNNINGHAM. 3 Vols.
Chapman's Works. Complete in Three Vols. Vol. I. contains the Plays complete, including doubtful ones; Vol. II., Poems and Minor Translations, with Introductory Essay by A. C. SWINBURNE; Vol. III., Translations of the Iliad and Odyssey.

DRAMATISTS, THE OLD, continued—
Crown 8vo, cloth extra, Vignette Portraits, 6s. per Volume.
Marlowe's Works. Including his Translations. Edited, with Notes and Introduction, by Col. CUNNINGHAM. One Vol.
Massinger's Plays. From the Text of WILLIAM GIFFORD. Edited by Col. CUNNINGHAM. One Vol.

Dyer. — The Folk - Lore of Plants. By Rev. T. F. THISELTON DYER, M.A. Crown 8vo, cloth extra, 6s. [Shortly.

Early English Poets. Edited, with Introductions and Annotations, by Rev. A. B. GROSART, D.D. Crown 8vo, cloth boards, 6s. per Volume.
Fletcher's (Giles, B D.) Complete Poems. One Vol.
Davies' (Sir John) Complete Poetical Works. Two Vols.
Herrick's (Robert) Complete Collected Poems. Three Vols.
Sidney's (Sir Philip) Complete Poetical Works. Three Vols.

Edgcumbe. — Zephyrus: A Holiday in Brazil and on the River Plate. By E. R. PEARCE EDGCUMBE. With 41 Illusts. Cr. 8vo, cl. extra, 5s.

Edwardes (Mrs. A.), Novels by:
A Point of Honour. Post 8vo, illustrated boards, 2s.
Archie Lovell. Crown 8vo, cloth extra, 3s. 6d.; post 8vo, illust. bds., 2s.

Eggleston.—Roxy: A Novel. By EDWARD EGGLESTON. Post 8vo, illust. boards, 2s.

Emanuel.—On Diamonds and Precious Stones: their History, Value, and Properties; with Simple Tests for ascertaining their Reality. By HARRY EMANUEL, F.R.G.S. With numerous Illustrations, tinted and plain. Crown 8vo, cloth extra, gilt, 6s.

Ewald (Alex. Charles, F.S.A.), Works by:
The Life and Times of Prince Charles Stuart, Count of Albany, commonly called the Young Pretender. From the State Papers and other Sources. New and Cheaper Edition, with a Portrait, crown 8vo, cloth extra, 7s. 6d.
Stories from the State Papers. With an Autotype Facsimile. Crown 8vo, cloth extra, 6s.
Studies Re-studied: Historical Sketches from Original Sources. Demy 8vo, cloth extra, 12s.

Englishman's House, The: A Practical Guide to all interested in Selecting or Building a House; with full Estimates of Cost, Quantities, &c. By C. J. RICHARDSON. Fourth Edition. With Coloured Frontispiece and nearly 600 Illustrations. Crown 8vo, cloth extra, 7s. 6d.

Eyes, Our: How to Preserve Them from Infancy to Old Age. By JOHN BROWNING, F.R.A.S., &c. Sixth Edition (Eleventh Thousand). With 58 Illustrations. Crown 8vo, cloth, 1s.

Familiar Short Sayings of Great Men. By SAMUEL ARTHUR BENT, A.M. Fifth Edition, Revised and Enlarged. Crown 8vo, cloth extra, 7s. 6d.

Faraday (Michael), Works by:
Post 8vo, cloth extra, 4s. 6d. each.
The Chemical History of a Candle: Lectures delivered before a Juvenile Audience at the Royal Institution. Edited by WILLIAM CROOKES, F.C.S. With numerous Illustrations.
On the Various Forces of Nature, and their Relations to each other: Lectures delivered before a Juvenile Audience at the Royal Institution. Edited by WILLIAM CROOKES, F.C.S. With numerous Illustrations.

Farrer (James Anson), Works by:
Military Manners and Customs. Crown 8vo, cloth extra, 6s.
War: Three Essays, Reprinted from "Military Manners." Crown 8vo, 1s.; cloth, 1s. 6d.

Fin-Bec. — The Cupboard Papers: Observations on the Art of Living and Dining. By FIN-BEC. Post 8vo, cloth limp, 2s. 6d.

Fireworks, The Complete Art of Making; or, The Pyrotechnist's Treasury. By THOMAS KENTISH. With 267 Illustrations. A New Edition, Revised throughout and greatly Enlarged. Crown 8vo, cloth extra, 5s.

Fitzgerald (Percy), Works by:
The World Behind the Scenes. Crown 8vo, cloth extra, 3s. 6d.
Little Essays: Passages from the Letters of CHARLES LAMB. Post 8vo, cloth limp, 2s. 6d.
A Day's Tour: A Journey through France and Belgium. With Sketches in facsimile of the Original Drawings. Crown 4to picture cover, 1s.
Fatal Zero: A Homburg Diary. Cr. 8vo, cloth extra, 3s. 6d.; post 8vo, illustrated boards, 2s.

FITZGERALD (PERCY), continued—
Post 8vo, illustrated boards, 2s. each.
Bella Donna. | Never Forgotten.
The Second Mrs. Tillotson.
Seventy-five Brooke Street
Polly. | The Lady of Brantome.

Fletcher's (Giles, B.D.) Complete Poems: Christ's Victorie in Heaven, Christ's Victorie on Earth, Christ's Triumph over Death, and Minor Poems. With Memorial-Introduction and Notes by the Rev. A. B. GROSART, D.D. Cr. 8vo, cloth bds., 6s.

Fonblanque.—Filthy Lucre: A Novel. By ALBANY DE FONBLANQUE. Post 8vo, illustrated boards, 2s.

Francillon (R. E.), Novels by:
Crown 8vo, cloth extra, 3s. 6d. each; post 8vo, illust. boards, 2s. each.
One by One. | A Real Queen.
Queen Cophetua.
Olympia. Post 8vo, illust. boards, 2s.
Esther's Glove. Fcap. 8vo, 1s.
King or Knave: A Novel. Cheaper Edition. Crown 8vo, cloth extra, 3s. 6d. [Shortly.
Romantic Stories of the Legal Profession. Crown 8vo, cloth extra, 6s. [Shortly.

Frederic. — Seth's Brother's Wife: A Novel. By HAROLD FREDERIC. Cheaper Ed. Post 8vo, illust. bds., 2s.

French Literature, History of. By HENRY VAN LAUN. Complete in 3 Vols., demy 8vo, cl. bds., 7s. 6d. each.

Frere.—Pandurang Hari; or, Memoirs of a Hindoo. With a Preface by Sir H. BARTLE FRERE, G.C.S.I., &c. Crown 8vo, cloth extra, 3s. 6d.; post 8vo, illustrated boards, 2s.

Friswell.—One of Two: A Novel. By HAIN FRISWELL. Post 8vo, illustrated boards, 2s.

Frost (Thomas), Works by:
Crown 8vo, cloth extra, 3s. 6d. each.
Circus Life and Circus Celebrities.
The Lives of the Conjurers.
The Old Showmen and the Old London Fairs.

Fry's (Herbert) Royal Guide to the London Charities, 1887-8. Showing their Name, Date of Foundation, Objects, Income, Officials, &c. Published Annually. Cr. 8vo, cloth, 1s. 6d.

Gardening Books:
A Year's Work In Garden and Greenhouse: Practical Advice to Amateur Gardeners as to the Management of the Flower, Fruit, and Frame Garden. By GEORGE GLENNY. Post 8vo, 1s. cloth limp, 1s. 6d.

GARDENING BOOKS, *continued—*
Post 8vo, 1s. each; cl. limp, 1s. 6d. each.
Our Kitchen Garden: The Plants we Grow, and How we Cook Them. By TOM JERROLD.
Household Horticulture: A Gossip about Flowers. By TOM and JANE JERROLD. Illustrated.
The Garden that Paid the Rent. By TOM JERROLD.

My Garden Wild, and What I Grew there. By F. G. HEATH. Crown 8vo, cloth extra, 5s.; gilt edges, 6s.

Garrett.—The Capel Girls: A Novel.
By EDWARD GARRETT. Cr. 8vo, cl. ex., 3s. 6d.; post 8vo, illust. bds., 2s.

Gentleman's Magazine (The)
for 1888. 1s. Monthly. In addition to the Articles upon subjects in Literature, Science, and Art, for which this Magazine has so high a reputation, "Science Notes," by W. MATTIEU WILLIAMS, F.R.A.S., and "Table Talk," by SYLVANUS URBAN, appear monthly.
* *Bound Volumes for recent years are kept in stock, cloth extra, price* 8s. 6d. *each; Cases for binding,* 2s. *each.*

Gentleman's Annual (The).
Published Annually in November. In illuminated cover. Demy 8vo, 1s. The Number for 1888 is entitled "By Devious Ways," by T. W. SPEIGHT.

German Popular Stories.
Collected by the Brothers GRIMM, and Translated by EDGAR TAYLOR. Edited, with an Introduction, by JOHN RUSKIN. With 22 Illustrations on Steel by GEORGE CRUIKSHANK. Square 8vo, cloth extra, 6s. 6d.; gilt edges, 7s. 6d.

Gibbon (Charles), Novels by:
Crown 8vo, cloth extra, 3s. 6d. each post 8vo, illustrated boards, 2s. each.
Robin Gray.
What will the World Say?
Queen of the Meadow.
The Flower of the Forest.
In Honour Bound.
Braes of Yarrow.
A Heart's Problem.
The Golden Shaft.
Of High Degree.
Loving a Dream.

Post 8vo, illustrated boards, 2s. each.
For Lack of Gold.
For the King. | In Pastures Green.
In Love and War.
By Mead and Stream.
Fancy Free. | A Hard Knot.
Heart's Delight.

Gilbert (William), Novels by:
Post 8vo, illustrated boards, 2s. each.
Dr. Austin's Guests.
The Wizard of the Mountain.
James Duke, Costermonger.

Gilbert (W. S.), Original Plays
by: In Two Series, each complete in itself, price 2s. 6d. each.
The FIRST SERIES contains—The Wicked World—Pygmalion and Galatea — Charity — The Princess — The Palace of Truth—Trial by Jury.
The SECOND SERIES contains—Broken Hearts—Engaged—Sweethearts—Gretchen—Dan'l Druce—Tom Cobb—H.M.S. Pinafore—The Sorcerer—The Pirates of Penzance.

Eight Original Comic Operas. Written by W. S. GILBERT. Containing: The Sorcerer—H.M.S. "Pinafore"—The Pirates of Penzance—Iolanthe — Patience — Princess Ida — The Mikado—Trial by Jury. Demy 8vo, cloth limp, 2s. 6d.

Glenny.—A Year's Work in Garden and Greenhouse:
Practical Advice to Amateur Gardeners as to the Management of the Flower, Fruit, and Frame Garden. By GEORGE GLENNY. Post 8vo, 1s.; cloth, 1s. 6d.

Godwin.—Lives of the Necromancers.
By WILLIAM GODWIN. Post 8vo, limp, 2s.

Golden Library, The:
Square 16mo (Tauchnitz size), cloth limp, 2s. per Volume.
Bayard Taylor's Diversions of the Echo Club.
Bennett's (Dr. W. C.) Ballad History of England.
Bennett's (Dr.) Songs for Sailors.
Godwin's (William) Lives of the Necromancers.
Holmes's Autocrat of the Breakfast Table. Introduction by SALA.
Holmes's Professor at the Breakfast Table.
Hood's Whims and Oddities. Complete. All the original Illustrations.
Jesse's (Edward) Scenes and Occupations of a Country Life.
Leigh Hunt's Essays: A Tale for a Chimney Corner, and other Pieces. With Portrait, and Introduction by EDMUND OLLIER.
Mallory's (Sir Thomas) Mort d'Arthur: The Stories of King Arthur and of the Knights of the Round Table. Edited by B. MONTGOMERIE RANKING.
Square 16mo, 2s. per Volume.
Pascal's Provincial Letters. A New Translation, with Historical Introduction and Notes, by T. M'CRIE, D.D.
Pope's Poetical Works. Complete.
Rochefoucauld's Maxims and Moral Reflections. With Notes, and Introductory Essay by SAINTE-BEUVE.

Golden Treasury of Thought, The: An ENCYCLOPÆDIA OF QUOTATIONS from Writers of all Times and Countries. Selected and Edited by THEODORE TAYLOR. Crown 8vo, cloth gilt and gilt edges, 7s. 6d.

Graham. — The Professor's Wife: A Story. By LEONARD GRAHAM. Fcap. 8vo, picture cover, 1s.

Greeks and Romans, The Life of the, Described from Antique Monuments. By ERNST GUHL and W. KONER. Translated from the Third German Edition, and Edited by Dr. F. HUEFFER. 545 Illusts. New and Cheaper Edition, large crown 8vo, cloth extra, 7s. 6d.

Greenaway (Kate) and Bret Harte.—The Queen of the Pirate Isle. By BRET HARTE. With 25 original Drawings by KATE GREENAWAY, Reproduced in Colours by E. EVANS. Sm. 4to, bds., 5s.

Greenwood (James), Works by: Crown 8vo, cloth extra, 3s. 6d. each.
The Wilds of London.
Low-Life Deeps: An Account of the Strange Fish to be Found There.

Dick Temple: A Novel. Post 8vo, illustrated boards, 2s.

Habberton (John), Author of "Helen's Babies," Novels by:
Post 8vo, illustrated boards, 2s. each; cloth limp, 2s. 6d. each.
Brueton's Bayou.
Country Luck.

Hair (The): Its Treatment in Health, Weakness, and Disease. Translated from the German of Dr. J. PINCUS. Crown 8vo, 1s.; cloth, 1s. 6d.

Hake (Dr. Thomas Gordon), Poems by:
Crown 8vo, cloth extra, 6s. each.
New Symbols.
Legends of the Morrow.
The Serpent Play.

Maiden Ecstasy. Small 4to, cloth extra, 8s.

Hall.—Sketches of Irish Character. By Mrs. S. C. HALL. With numerous Illustrations on Steel and Wood by MACLISE, GILBERT, HARVEY, and G. CRUIKSHANK. Medium 8vo, cloth extra, gilt, 7s. 6d.

Halliday.—Every-day Papers. By ANDREW HALLIDAY. Post 8vo, illustrated boards, 2s.

Handwriting, The Philosophy of. With over 100 Facsimiles and Explanatory Text. By DON FELIX DE SALAMANCA. Post 8vo, cl. limp, 2s. 6d.

Hanky-Panky: A Collection of Very Easy Tricks, Very Difficult Tricks, White Magic, Sleight of Hand, &c. Edited by W. H. CREMER. With 200 Illusts. Crown 8vo, cloth extra, 4s. 6d.

Hardy (Lady Duffus). — Paul Wynter's Sacrifice: A Story. By Lady DUFFUS HARDY. Post 8vo, illust. boards, 2s.

Hardy (Thomas).—Under the Greenwood Tree. By THOMAS HARDY, Author of "Far from the Madding Crowd." With numerous Illustrations. Crown 8vo, cloth extra, 3s. 6d.; post 8vo, illustrated boards, 2s.

Harwood.—The Tenth Earl. By J. BERWICK HARWOOD. Post 8vo, illustrated boards, 2s.

Haweis (Mrs. H. R.), Works by:
The Art of Dress. With numerous Illustrations. Small 8vo, illustrated cover, 1s.; cloth limp, 1s. 6d.
The Art of Beauty. New and Cheaper Edition. Crown 8vo, cloth extra. Coloured Frontispiece and Illusts. 6s.
The Art of Decoration. Square 8vo, handsomely bound and profusely Illustrated, 10s. 6d.
Chaucer for Children: A Golden Key. With Eight Coloured Pictures and numerous Woodcuts. New Edition, small 4to, cloth extra, 6s.
Chaucer for Schools. Demy 8vo, cloth limp, 2s. 6d.

Haweis (Rev. H. R.).—American Humorists: WASHINGTON IRVING, OLIVER WENDELL HOLMES, JAMES RUSSELL LOWELL, ARTEMUS WARD, MARK TWAIN, and BRET HARTE. By Rev. H. R. HAWEIS, M.A. Cr. 8vo, 6s.

Hawthorne.—Tanglewood Tales for Girls and Boys. By NATHANIEL HAWTHORNE. With numerous fine Illustrations by GEORGE WHARTON EDWARDS. Large 4to, cloth extra, 10s. 6d.

Hawthorne (Julian), Novels by. Crown 8vo, cloth extra, 3s. 6d. each; post 8vo, illustrated boards, 2s. each.

Garth.	Sebastian Strome.
Ellice Quentin.	Dust.
Fortune's Fool.	Beatrix Randolph

HAWTHORNE (JULIAN), *ntinued—*
Post 8vo, illustrated boards, 2s. each.
Miss Cadogna. | Love—or a Name.
Prince Saroni's Wife.

Mrs. Gainsborough's Diamonds.
Fcap. 8vo, illustrated cover, 1s.
David Poindexter's Disappearance.
Crown 8vo, cloth extra, 3s. 6d.
A Dream and a Forgetting. By
JULIAN HAWTHORNE. Cr. 8vo, picture cover, 1s.; cloth, 1s. 6d.
The Spectre of the Camera. Crown 8vo, cloth extra, 3s. 6d.

Hays.—Women of the Day: A Biographical Dictionary of Notable Contemporaries. By FRANCES HAYS. Crown 8vo, cloth extra, 5s.

Heath (F. G.). — My Garden Wild, and What I Grew There. By FRANCIS GEORGE HEATH, Author of "The Fern World," &c. Crown 8vo, cloth extra, 5s.; cl. gilt, gilt edges, 6s.

Helps (Sir Arthur), Works by:
Post 8vo, cloth limp, 2s. 6d. each.
Animals and their Masters.
Social Pressure.

Ivan de Biron: A Novel. Crown 8vo, cloth extra, 3s. 6d.; post 8vo, illustrated boards, 2s.

Henderson.—Agatha Page: A Novel. By ISAAC HENDERSON. With a Photograph Frontispiece from a Picture by F. MOSCHELES. 2 Vols., crown 8vo.

Herman.—One Traveller Returns: A Romance. By HENRY HERMAN and D. CHRISTIE MURRAY. Crown 8vo, cloth extra, 6s.

Herrick's (Robert) Hesperides, Noble Numbers, and Complete Collected Poems. With Memorial-Introduction and Notes by the Rev. A. B. GROSART, D.D., Steel Portrait, Index of First Lines, and Glossarial Index, &c. Three Vols., crown 8vo, cloth, 18s.

Hesse-Wartegg (Chevalier Ernst von), Works by:
Tunis: The Land and the People. With 22 Illusts. Cr. 8vo, cl. ex., 3s. 6d.
The New South-West: Travelling Sketches from Kansas, New Mexico, Arizona, and Northern Mexico. With 100 fine Illustrations and Three Maps. Demy 8vo, cloth extra, 14s. [*In preparation.*

Hoey.—The Lover's Creed. By Mrs. CASHEL HOEY. With Frontispiece by P. MACNAB. Post 8vo, illustrated boards, 2s.

Hindley (Charles), Works by:
Tavern Anecdotes and Sayings: Including the Origin of Signs, and Reminiscences connected with Taverns. Coffee Houses, Clubs, &c. With Illustrations. Crown 8vo, cloth extra, 3s. 6d.
The Life and Adventures of a Cheap Jack. By One of the Fraternity. Edited by CHARLES HINDLEY. Crown 8vo, cloth extra, 3s. 6d.

Holmes (O. Wendell), Works by:
The Autocrat of the Breakfast-Table. Illustrated by J. GORDON THOMSON. Post 8vo, cloth limp, 2s. 6d.—Another Edition in smaller type, with an Introduction by G. A. SALA. Post 8vo, cloth limp, 2s.
The Professor at the Breakfast-Table; with the Story of Iris. Post 8vo, cloth limp, 2s.

Holmes. — The Science of Voice Production and Voice Preservation: A Popular Manual for the Use of Speakers and Singers. By GORDON HOLMES, M.D. With Illustrations. Crown 8vo, 1s.; cloth, 1s. 6d.

Hood (Thomas):
Hood's Choice Works, in Prose and Verse. Including the Cream of the COMIC ANNUALS. With Life of the Author, Portrait, and 200 Illustrations. Crown 8vo, cloth extra, 7s. 6d.
Hood's Whims and Oddities. Complete. With all the original Illustrations. Post 8vo, cloth limp, 2s.

Hood (Tom), Works by:
From Nowhere to the North Pole: A Noah's Arkæological Narrative. With 25 Illustrations by W. BRUNTON and E. C. BARNES. Square crown 8vo, cloth extra, gilt edges, 6s.
A Golden Heart: A Novel. Post 8vo, illustrated boards, 2s.

Hook's (Theodore) Choice Humorous Works, including his Ludicrous Adventures, Bons Mots, Puns and Hoaxes. With a New Life of the Author, Portraits, Facsimiles, and Illusts. Cr. 8vo, cl. extra, gilt, 7s. 6d.

Hooper.—The House of Raby: A Novel. By Mrs. GEORGE HOOPER. Post 8vo, illustrated boards, 2s.

Horse (The) and his Rider: An Anecdotic Medley. By "THORMANBY." Crown 8vo, cloth extra, 6s.

Hopkins—"'Twixt Love and Duty:" A Novel. By TIGHE HOPKINS. Crown 8vo, cloth extra, 6s.; post 8vo, illustrated boards, 2s.

CHATTO & WINDUS, PICCADILLY. 13

Horne.—Orion : An Epic Poem,
in Three Books. By RICHARD HEN-
GIST HORNE. With Photographic
Portrait from a Medallion by SUM-
MERS. Tenth Edition, crown 8vo,
cloth extra, 7s.

Hunt (Mrs. Alfred), Novels by:
Crown 8vo, cloth extra, 3s. 6d. each;
post 8vo, illustrated boards, 2s. each.
Thornicroft's Model.
The Leaden Casket.
Self-Condemned.
That other Person.

Hunt.—Essays by Leigh Hunt.
A Tale for a Chimney Corner, and
other Pieces. With Portrait and Introduction by EDMUND OLLIER. Post
8vo, cloth limp, 2s.

Hydrophobia: an Account of M.
PASTEUR'S System. Containing a
Translation of all his Communications
on the Subject, the Technique of his
Method, and the latest Statistical
Results. By RENAUD SUZOR, M.B.,
C.M. Edin., and M.D. Paris, Commis-
sioned by the Government of the
Colony of Mauritius to study M.
PASTEUR'S new Treatment in Paris.
With 7 Illusts. Cr. 8vo, cloth extra, 6s.

Indoor Paupers. By ONE OF
THEM. Crown 8vo, 1s.; cloth, 1s. 6d.

Ingelow.—Fated to be Free: A
Novel. By JEAN INGELOW. Crown
8vo, cloth extra, 3s. 6d.; post 8vo,
illustrated boards, 2s.

Irish Wit and Humour, Songs
of. Collected and Edited by A. PER-
CEVAL GRAVES. Post 8vo, cloth limp,
2s. 6d.

James.—A Romance of the
Queen's Hounds. By CHARLES JAMES.
Post 8vo, picture cover, 1s.; cl., 1s. 6d.

Janvier.—Practical Keramics
for Students. By CATHERINE A.
JANVIER. Crown 8vo, cloth extra, 6s.

Jay (Harriett), Novels by:
Post 8vo, illustrated boards, 2s. each.
The Dark Colleen.
The Queen of Connaught.

Jefferies (Richard), Works by:
Nature near London. Crown 8vo,
cl. ex., 6s.; post 8vo, cl. limp, 2s. 6d.
The Life of the Fields. Post 8vo,
cloth limp, 2s. 6d.
The Open Air. Crown 8vo, cloth
extra, 6s.

The Eulogy of Richard Jefferies.
By WALTER BESANT. With a Photograph Portrait and facsimile of Signature. Cr. 8vo, cl. ex., 6s.

Jennings (H. J.), Works by:
Curiosities of Criticism. Post 8vo,
cloth limp, 2s. 6d.
Lord Tennyson: A Biographical
Sketch. With a Photograph-Por-
trait. Crown 8vo, cloth extra, 6s.

Jerrold (Tom), Works by:
Post 8vo, 1s. each; cloth, 1s. 6d. each.
The Garden that Paid the Rent.
Household Horticulture: A Gossip
about Flowers. Illustrated.
Our Kitchen Garden: The Plants
we Grow, and How we Cook Them.

Jesse.—Scenes and Occupa-
tions of a Country Life. By EDWARD
JESSE. Post 8vo, cloth limp, 2s.

Jeux d'Esprit. Collected and
Edited by HENRY S. LEIGH. Post 8vo,
cloth limp, 2s. 6d.

"John Herring," Novels by
the Author of:
Crown 8vo, cloth extra, 3s. 6d. each.
Red Spider. | Eve.

Jones (Wm., F.S.A.), Works by:
Crown 8vo, cloth extra, 7s. 6d. each.
Finger-Ring Lore: Historical, Le-
gendary, and Anecdotal. With over
Two Hundred Illustrations.
Credulities, Past and Present; in-
cluding the Sea and Seamen, Miners,
Talismans, Word and Letter Divina-
tion, Exorcising and Blessing of
Animals, Birds, Eggs, Luck, &c.
With an Etched Frontispiece.
Crowns and Coronations: A History
of Regalia in all Times and Coun-
tries. One Hundred Illustrations.

Jonson's (Ben) Works. With
Notes Critical and Explanatory, and
a Biographical Memoir by WILLIAM
GIFFORD. Edited by Colonel CUN-
NINGHAM. Three Vols., crown 8vo,
cloth extra, 18s.; or separately, 6s. each.

Josephus, The Complete Works
of. Translated by WHISTON. Containing both "The Antiquities of the
Jews" and "The Wars of the Jews."
Two Vols., 8vo, with 52 Illustrations
and Maps, cloth extra, gilt, 14s.

Kempt.—Pencil and Palette:
Chapters on Art and Artists. By ROBERT
KEMPT. Post 8vo, cloth limp, 2s. 6d.

Kershaw.—Colonial Facts and
Fictions: Humorous Sketches. By
MARK KERSHAW. Post 8vo, illustrated
boards, 2s.; cloth, 2s. 6d.

King (R. Ashe), Novels by:
Crown 8vo, cloth extra, 3s. 6d. each;
post 8vo, illustrated boards, 2s. each.
A Drawn Game.
"The Wearing of the Green."

Kingsley (Henry), Novels by:
Oakshott Castle. Post 8vo, illustrated boards, 2s.
Number Seventeen. Crown 8vo, cloth extra, 3s. 6d.

Knight.—The Patient's Vade Mecum: How to get most Benefit from Medical Advice. By WILLIAM KNIGHT, M.R.C.S., and EDWARD KNIGHT, L.R.C.P. Crown 8vo, 1s.; cloth, 1s. 6d.

Lamb (Charles):
Lamb's Complete Works, in Prose and Verse, reprinted from the Original Editions, with many Pieces hitherto unpublished. Edited, with Notes and Introduction, by R. H. SHEPHERD. With Two Portraits and Facsimile of Page of the "Essay on Roast Pig." Cr. 8vo, cl. extra, 7s. 6d.
Poetry for Children, and Prince Dorus. By CHARLES LAMB. Carefully reprinted from unique copies. Small 8vo, cloth extra, 5s.
Little Essays: Sketches and Characters by CHARLES LAMB. Selected from his Letters by PERCY FITZGERALD. Post 8vo, cloth limp, 2s. 6d.

Lane's Arabian Nights.—The Thousand and One Nights: commonly called, in England, "THE ARABIAN NIGHTS' ENTERTAINMENTS." A New Translation from the Arabic with copious Notes, by EDWARD WILLIAM LANE. Illustrated by many hundred Engravings on Wood, from Original Designs by WM. HARVEY. A New Edition, from a Copy annotated by the Translator, edited by his Nephew, EDWARD STANLEY POOLE. With a Preface by STANLEY LANE-POOLE. Three Vols., demy 8vo, cloth extra, 7s. 6d. each.

Lares and Penates; or, The Background of Life. By FLORENCE CADDY. Crown 8vo, cloth extra, 6s.

Larwood (Jacob), Works by:
The Story of the London Parks. With Illusts. Cr. 8vo, cl. ex., 3s. 6d.

Post 8vo, cloth limp, 2s. 6d. cae
Forensic Anecdotes.
Theatrical Anecdotes.

Leigh (Henry S.), Works by:
Carols of Cockayne. A New Edition, printed on fcap. 8vo, hand-made paper, and bound in buckram, 5s.
Jeux d'Esprit. Collected and Edited by HENRY S. LEIGH. Post 8vo, cloth limp, 2s. 6d.

Leys.—The Lindsays: A Romance of Scottish Life. By JOHN K. LEYS. Cheaper Edition. Post 8vo, illustrated boards, 2s. [Shortly.

Life in London; or, The History of Jerry Hawthorn and Corinthian Tom. With the whole of CRUIKSHANK'S Illustrations, in Colours, after the Originals. Cr. 8vo, cl. extra, 7s. 6d.

Linskill.—In Exchange for a Soul. By MARY LINSKILL, Author of "The Haven Under the Hill," &c. Cheaper Edit. Post 8vo, illust. bds., 2s.

Linton (E. Lynn), Works by:
Post 8vo, cloth limp, 2s. 6d. each.
Witch Stories.
The True Story of Joshua Davidson
Ourselves: Essays on Women.
Crown 8vo, cloth extra, 3s. 6d. each; post 8vo, illustrated boards, 2s. each.
Patricia Kemball.
The Atonement of Leam Dundas.
The World Well Lost.
Under which Lord?
"My Love!" | Ione.
Post 8vo, illustrated boards, 2s. each.
With a Silken Thread.
The Rebel of the Family.
Paston Carew, Millionaire and Miser. Crown 8vo, cl. extra, 3s. 6d.

Longfellow's Poetical Works. Carefully Reprinted from the Original Editions. With numerous fine Illustrations on Steel and Wood. Crown 8vo, cloth extra, 7s. 6d.

Long Life, Aids to: A Medical, Dietetic, and General Guide in Health and Disease. By N. E. DAVIES, L.R.C.P. Cr. 8vo, 2s.; cl. limp, 2s. 6d.

Lucy.—Gideon Fleyce: A Novel. By HENRY W. LUCY. Crown 8vo, cl. ex., 3s. 6d.; post 8vo, illust. bds., 2s.

Lusiad (The) of Camoens. Translated into English Spenserian Verse by ROBERT FFRENCH DUFF Demy 8vo, with Fourteen full-page Plates, cloth boards, 18s

Macalpine (Avery), Novels by:
Teresa Itasca, and other Stories. Crown 8vo, bound in canvas, 2s. 6d.
Broken Wings. With Illustrations by W. J. HENNESSY. Crown 8vo, cloth extra, 6s.

McCarthy (Justin, M.P.), Works by:

A History of Our Own Times, from the Accession of Queen Victoria to the General Election of 1880. Four Vols. demy 8vo, cloth extra, 12s. each.—Also a POPULAR EDITION, in Four Vols. cr. 8vo, cl. extra, 6s. each. —And a JUBILEE EDITION, with an Appendix of Events to the end of 1886, complete in Two Vols., square 8vo, cloth extra, 7s. 6d. each.

A Short History of Our Own Times. One Vol., crown 8vo, cloth extra, 6s.

History of the Four Georges. Four Vols. demy 8vo, cloth extra, 12s. each. [Vol. I. now ready.

Crown 8vo, cloth extra, 3s. 6d. each; post 8vo, illustrated boards, 2s. each.

Dear Lady Disdain.
The Waterdale Neighbours.
A Fair Saxon.
Miss Misanthrope.
Donna Quixote.
The Comet of a Season.
Maid of Athens.
Camiola: A Girl with a Fortune.

Post 8vo, illustrated boards, 2s. each.
Linley Rochford.
My Enemy's Daughter.

"The Right Honourable:" A Romance of Society and Politics. By JUSTIN MCCARTHY, M.P., and Mrs. CAMPBELL-PRAED. New and Cheaper Edition, crown 8vo, cloth extra, 6s.

McCarthy (Justin H., M.P.), Works by:

An Outline of the History of Ireland, from the Earliest Times to the Present Day. Cr. 8vo, 1s.; cloth, 1s. 6d.
Ireland since the Union: Sketches of Irish History from 1798 to 1886. Crown 8vo, cloth extra, 6s.
England under Gladstone, 1880-85. Second Edition, revised. Crown 8vo, cloth extra, 6s.
Doom! An Atlantic Episode. Crown 8vo, 1s.; cloth, 1s. 6d.
Our Sensation Novel. Edited by JUSTIN H. MCCARTHY. Crown 8vo, 1s.; cloth, 1s. 6d.
Hafiz in London. Choicely printed. Small 8vo, gold cloth, 3s. 6d.

Magician's Own Book (The):

Performances with Cups and Balls, Eggs, Hats, Handkerchiefs, &c. All from actual Experience. Edited by W. H. CREMER. With 200 Illustrations. Crown 8vo, cloth extra, 4s. 6d.

MacDonald.—Works of Fancy and Imagination.

By GEORGE MACDONALD, LL.D. Ten Volumes, in handsome cloth case, 21s — Vol. 1. WITHIN AND WITHOUT. THE HIDDEN LIFE.—Vol. 2. THE DISCIPLE. THE GOSPEL WOMEN. A BOOK OF SONNETS. ORGAN SONGS.—Vol. 3. VIOLIN SONGS. SONGS OF THE DAYS AND NIGHTS. A BOOK OF DREAMS. ROADSIDE POEMS. POEMS FOR CHILDREN. Vol. 4. PARABLES. BALLADS. SCOTCH SONGS.— Vols. 5 and 6. PHANTASTES: A Faerie Romance.—Vol. 7. THE PORTENT.— Vol. 8. THE LIGHT PRINCESS. THE GIANT'S HEART. SHADOWS.—Vol. 9. CROSS PURPOSES. THE GOLDEN KEY. THE CARASOYN. LITTLE DAYLIGHT.— Vol. 10. THE CRUEL PAINTER. THE WOW O' RIVVEN. THE CASTLE. THE BROKEN SWORDS. THE GRAY WOLF. UNCLE CORNELIUS.

The Volumes are also sold separately in Grolier-pattern cloth, 2s. 6d. each.

Macdonell.—Quaker Cousins:

A Novel. By AGNES MACDONELL. Crown 8vo, cloth extra, 3s. 6d.; post 8vo, illustrated boards, 2s.

Macgregor. — Pastimes and Players.

Notes on Popular Games. By ROBERT MACGREGOR. Post 8vo, cloth limp, 2s. 6d.

Mackay.—Interludes and Undertones;

or, Music at Twilight. By CHARLES MACKAY, LL.D. Crown 8vo, cloth extra, 6s.

Maclise Portrait-Gallery (The)

of Illustrious Literary Characters; with Memoirs—Biographical, Critical, Bibliographical, and Anecdotal—illustrative of the Literature of the former half of the Present Century. By WILLIAM BATES, B.A. With 85 Portraits printed on an India Tint. Crown 8vo, cloth extra, 7s. 6d.

Macquoid (Mrs.), Works by:

Square 8vo, cloth extra, 7s. 6d. each.
In the Ardennes. With 50 fine Illustrations by THOMAS R. MACQUOID.
Pictures and Legends from Normandy and Brittany. With numerous Illusts. by THOMAS R. MACQUOID.
Through Normandy. With 90 Illustrations by T. R. MACQUOID.
Through Brittany. With numerous Illustrations by T. R. MACQUOID.
About Yorkshire. With 67 Illustrations by T. R. MACQUOID.

Post 8vo, illustrated boards, 2s. each.
The Evil Eye, and other Stories.
Lost Rose.

Magic Lantern (The), and its Management: including full Practical Directions for producing the Limelight, making Oxygen Gas, and preparing Lantern Slides. By T. C. HEPWORTH. With 10 Illustrations. Crown 8vo, 1s.; cloth, 1s. 6d.

Magna Charta. An exact Facsimile of the Original in the British Museum, printed on fine plate paper, 3 feet by 2 feet, with Arms and Seals emblazoned in Gold and Colours. 5s.

Mallock (W. H.), Works by:
The New Republic; or, Culture, Faith and Philosophy in an English Country House. Post 8vo, cloth limp, 2s. 6d.; Cheap Edition, illustrated boards, 2s.
The New Paul and Virginia; or, Positivism on an Island. Post 8vo, cloth limp, 2s. 6d.
Poems. Small 4to, in parchment, 6s.
Is Life worth Living? Crown 8vo, cloth extra, 6s.

Mallory's (Sir Thomas) Mort d'Arthur: The Stories of King Arthur and of the Knights of the Round Table. Edited by B. MONTGOMERIE RANKING. Post 8vo, cloth limp, 2s.

Man - Hunter (The): Stories from the Note-book of a Detective. By DICK DONOVAN. Post 8vo, illustrated boards, 2s.; cloth, 2s. 6d.

Mark Twain, Works by:
The Choice Works of Mark Twain. Revised and Corrected throughout by the Author. With Life, Portrait, and numerous Illust. Cr. 8vo, cl. ex, 7s. 6d.
The Innocents Abroad; or, The New Pilgrim's Progress: Being some Account of the Steamship "Quaker City's" Pleasure Excursion to Europe and the Holy Land. With 234 Illustrations. Crown 8vo, cloth extra, 7s. 6d.—Cheap Edition (under the title of "MARK TWAIN'S PLEASURE TRIP"), post 8vo, illust. boards, 2s.
Roughing It, and The Innocents at Home. With 200 Illustrations by F. A. FRASER. Cr. 8vo, cl. ex., 7s. 6d.
The Gilded Age. By MARK TWAIN and CHARLES DUDLEY WARNER. With 212 Illustrations by T. COPPIN Crown 8vo, cloth extra, 7s. 6d.
The Adventures of Tom Sawyer With 111 Illustrations. Crown 8vo, cloth extra, 7s. 6d.—Cheap Edition post 8vo, illustrated boards, 2s.
The Prince and the Pauper. With nearly 200 Illustrations. Crown 8vo, cloth extra, 7s. 6d.—Cheap Edition, post 8vo, illustrated boards, 2s.
A Tramp Abroad. With 314 Illusts. Cr. 8vo, cloth extra, 7s. 6d.—Cheap Edition, post 8vo illust. bds., 2s.

MARK TWAIN'S WORKS, *continued*—
The Stolen White Elephant, &c. Crown 8vo, cloth extra, 6s.; post 8vo, illustrated boards, 2s.
Life on the Mississippi. With about 300 Original Illustrations. Crown 8vo, cloth extra, 7s. 6d.—Cheap Edition, post 8vo, illustrated boards, 2s.
The Adventures of Huckleberry Finn. With 174 Illustrations by E. W. KEMBLE. Crown 8vo, cloth extra, 7s. 6d.—Cheap Edition, post 8vo, illustrated boards, 2s.
Mark Twain's Library of Humour. With numerous Illustrations. Crown 8vo, cloth extra, 7s. 6d.

Marlowe's Works. Including his Translations. Edited, with Notes and Introductions, by Col. CUNNINGHAM. Crown 8vo, cloth extra, 6s.

Marryat (Florence), Novels by:
Crown 8vo, cloth extra, 3s. 6d. each; post 8vo, illustrated boards, 2s. each.
Open! Sesame! | Written In Fire.
Post 8vo, illustrated boards, 2s. each.
A Harvest of Wild Oats.
Fighting the Air.

Massinger's Plays. From the Text of WILLIAM GIFFORD. Edited by Col. CUNNINGHAM. Crown 8vo, cloth extra, 6s.

Masterman.—Half a Dozen Daughters: A Novel. By J. MASTERMAN. Post 8vo, illustrated boards, 2s.

Matthews.—A Secret of the Sea, &c. By BRANDER MATTHEWS. Post 8vo, illust. bds., 2s.; cloth, 2s. 6d.

Mayfair Library, The:
Post 8vo, cloth limp, 2s. 6d. per Volume.
A Journey Round My Room. By XAVIER DE MAISTRE. Translated by HENRY ATTWELL.
Quips and Quiddities. Selected by W. DAVENPORT ADAMS.
The Agony Column of "The Times," from 1800 to 1870. Edited, with an Introduction, by ALICE CLAY.
Melancholy Anatomised: A Popular Abridgment of "Burton's Anatomy of Melancholy."
The Speeches of Charles Dickens.
Literary Frivolities, Fancies, Follies, and Frolics. By W. T. DOBSON.
Poetical Ingenuities and Eccentricities. Selected and Edited by W. T. DOBSON.
The Cupboard Papers. By FIN-BEC.
Original Plays by W. S. GILBERT. FIRST SERIES. Containing: The Wicked World — Pygmalion and Galatea—Charity—The Princess—The Palace of Truth—Trial by Jury.

CHATTO & WINDUS, PICCADILLY. 17

MAYFAIR LIBRARY, continued—
Post 8vo, cloth limp, 2s. 6d. per Vol.
Original Plays by W. S GILBERT. SECOND SERIES. Containing: Broken Hearts — Engaged — Sweethearts — Gretchen — Dan'l Druce — Tom Cobb — H.M.S. Pinafore — The Sorcerer — The Pirates of Penzance.
Songs of Irish Wit and Humour. Collected and Edited by A. PERCEVAL GRAVES.
Animals and their Masters. By Sir ARTHUR HELPS.
Social Pressure. By Sir A. HELPS.
Curiosities of Criticism. By HENRY J. JENNINGS.
The Autocrat of the Breakfast-Table By OLIVER WENDELL HOLMES. Illustrated by J. GORDON THOMSON.
Pencil and Palette. By ROBERT KEMPT.
Little Essays: Sketches and Characters. By CHAS. LAMB. Selected from his Letters by PERCY FITZGERALD.
Forensic Anecdotes; or, Humour and Curiosities of the Law and Men of Law. By JACOB LARWOOD.
Theatrical Anecdotes. By JACOB LARWOOD. [LEIGH.
Jeux d'Esprit. Edited by HENRY S.
True History of Joshua Davidson. By E. LYNN LINTON.
Witch Stories. By E. LYNN LINTON.
Ourselves: Essays on Women. By E. LYNN LINTON. [MACGREGOR.
Pastimes and Players. By ROBERT
The New Paul and Virginia. By W. H. MALLOCK.
New Republic. By W. H. MALLOCK.
Puck on Pegasus. By H. CHOLMONDELEY-PENNELL.
Pegasus Re-Saddled. By H. CHOLMONDELEY-PENNELL. Illustrated by GEORGE DU MAURIER.
Muses of Mayfair Edited by H. CHOLMONDELEY-PENNELL.
Thoreau: His Life and Aims. By H. A. PAGE.
Puniana. By the Hon. HUGH ROWLEY.
More Puniana. By the Hon. HUGH ROWLEY.
The Philosophy of Handwriting. By DON FELIX DE SALAMANCA.
By Stream and Sea. By WILLIAM SENIOR. [THORNBURY.
Old Stories Re-told. By WALTER
Leaves from a Naturalist's Note-Book. By Dr. ANDREW WILSON.

Mayhew.—London Characters and the Humorous Side of London Life. By HENRY MAYHEW. With numerous Illusts. Cr. 8vo, cl. extra, 3s. 6d.

Medicine, Family.—One Thousand Medical Maxims and Surgical Hints, for Infancy, Adult Life, Middle Age, and Old Age. By N. E. DAVIES, L.R.C.P. Lond. Cr. 8vo, 1s.; cl., 1s. 6d.

Menken.—Infelicia: Poems by ADAH ISAACS MENKEN. A New Edition, with a Biographical Preface, numerous Illustrations by F. E. LUMMIS and F. O. C. DARLEY, and Facsimile of a Letter from CHARLES DICKENS. Beautifully printed on small 4to ivory paper, with red border to each page, and handsomely bound. Price 7s. 6d.

Mexican Mustang (On a), through Texas, from the Gulf to the Rio Grande. A New Book of American Humour. By A. E. SWEET and J. ARMOY, KNOX, Editors of "Texas Siftings." With 265 Illusts. Cr. 8vo, cl.extra, 7s.6d.

Middlemass (Jean), Novels by: Post 8vo, illustrated boards, 2s. each.
Touch and Go. | Mr. Dorillion.

Miller.—Physiology for the Young; or, The House of Life: Human Physiology, with its application to the Preservation of Health. For Classes and Popular Reading. With numerous Illusts. By Mrs. F. FENWICK MILLER. Small 8vo, cloth limp, 2s. 6d.

Milton (J. L.), Works by:
Sm. 8vo, 1s. each; cloth ex., 1s. 6d. each.
The Hygiene of the Skin. A Concise Set of Rules for the Management of the Skin; with Directions for Diet, Wines, Soaps, Baths, &c.
The Bath in Diseases of the Skin.
The Laws of Life, and their Relation to Diseases of the Skin.

Molesworth (Mrs.).—Hathercourt Rectory. By Mrs. MOLESWORTH, Author of "The Cuckoo Clock," &c. Cr. 8vo, cl. extra, 4s. 6d.; post 8vo, illustrated boards, 2s.

Moncrieff.—The Abdication; or, Time Tries All. An Historical Drama. By W. D. SCOTT-MONCRIEFF. With Seven Etchings by JOHN PETTIE, R.A., W. Q. ORCHARDSON, R.A., J. MACWHIRTER, A.R.A., COLIN HUNTER, A.R.A., R. MACBETH, A.R.A., and TOM GRAHAM, R.S.A. Large 4to, bound in buckram, 21s.

Moore (Thomas):
Byron's Letters and Journals; with Notices of his Life. By THOMAS MOORE. Cr. 8vo, cloth extra, 7s. 6d.
Prose and Verse, Humorous, Satirical, and Sentimental, by THOMAS MOORE; with Suppressed Passages from the Memoirs of Lord Byron. Edited, with Notes and Introduction, by R. HERNE SHEPHERD. With a Portrait. Cr. 8vo, cloth extra, 7s. 6d.

Novelists. — Half-Hours with the Best Novelists of the Century: Choice Readings from the finest Novels. Edited, with Critical and Biographical Notes, by H. T. MACKENZIE BELL. Crown 8vo, cl. ex., 3s. 6d. [Preparing.

Murray (D. Christie), Novels by. Crown 8vo, cloth extra, 3s. 6d. each; post 8vo, illustrated boards, 2s. each.
A Life's Atonement. | A Model Father.
Joseph's Coat. | Coals of Fire.
By the Gate of the Sea.
Val Strange. | Hearts.
The Way of the World.
A Bit of Human Nature.
First Person Singular.
Cynic Fortune.
Old Blazer's Hero. With Three Illustrations by A. McCormick. Crown 8vo, cloth ex., 6s.—Cheaper Edition, post 8vo, illust. boards, 2s. [Shortly.
One Traveller Returns. By D. Christie Murray and H. Herman. Cr. 8vo, cl. ex., 6s.

Nursery Hints: A Mother's Guide in Health and Disease. By N. E. Davies, L.R.C.P. Cr.8vo, 1s.; cl., 1s.6d.

O'Connor.—Lord Beaconsfield: A Biography. By T. P. O'Connor, M.P. Sixth Edition, with a New Preface, bringing the work down to the Death of Lord Beaconsfield. Crown 8vo, cloth extra, 7s. 6d.

O'Hanlon (Alice), Novels by:
The Unforeseen. Post 8vo, illustrated boards, 2s.
A Freak of Fate. 3 vols.,cr.8vo. [Shortly

Ohnet. — Doctor Rameau: A Novel. By Georges Ohnet, Author of "The Ironmaster," &c. Translated from the French by F. Cashel Hoey. Crown 8vo, cl. ex., 6s. [Preparing.

Oliphant (Mrs.) Novels by:
Whiteladies. With Illustrations by Arthur Hopkins and H. Woons. Crown 8vo, cloth extra, 3s. 6d.; post 8vo, illustrated boards, 2s.
Crown 8vo, cloth extra, 4s. 6d. each.; post 8vo, illustrated boards, 2s. each.
The Primrose Path.
The Greatest Heiress in England.

O'Reilly.—Phœbe's Fortunes: A Novel. With Illustrations by Henry Tuck. Post 8vo, illustrated boards, 2s.

O'Shaughnessy (A.), Works by:
Songs of a Worker. Fcap. 8vo, cloth extra, 7s. 6d.
Music and Moonlight. Fcap. 8vo, cloth extra, 7s. 6d.
Lays of France. Cr.8vo, cl. ex.,10s. 6d.

Ouida, Novels by. Crown 8vo, cloth extra, 3s. 6d. each; post 8vo, illustrated boards, 2s. each.
Held in Bondage. | Under Two Flags.
Strathmore. | Cecil Castlemaine's Gage.
Chandos

Ouida, continued—
Crown 8vo, cloth extra, 3s. 6d. each; post 8vo, illustrated boards, 2s. each.
Idalia. | Friendship.
Tricotrin. | Moths. | Bimbi.
Puck. | Pipistrello.
Folle Farine. | In Maremma.
TwoLittleWooden | A Village Commune.
Shoes.
A Dog of Flanders. | Wanda.
Pascarel. | Frescoes. [ine.
Signa. | Ariadne. | Princess Naprax-
In a Winter City. | Othmar.
Wisdom, Wit, and Pathos, selected from the Works of Ouida by F. Sydney Morris. Sm.cr.8vo,cl.ex.,5s.
Cheaper Edition, illust. bds., 2s.

Page (H. A.), Works by:
Thoreau: His Life and Aims: A Study. With Portrait. Post 8vo,cl.limp, 2s.6d.
Lights on the Way: Some Tales within a Tale. By the late J. H. Alexander, B.A. Edited by H. A. Page. Crown 8vo, cloth extra, 6s.
Animal Anecdotes. Arranged on a New Principle. Cr. 8vo, cl. extra, 5s.

Parliamentary Elections and Electioneering in the Old Days (A History of). Showing the State of Political Parties and Party Warfare at the Hustings and in the House of Commons from the Stuarts to Queen Victoria. Illustrated from the original Political Squibs, Lampoons, Pictorial Satires, and Popular Caricatures of the Time. By Joseph Grego, Author of "Rowlandson and his Works," "The Life of Gillray," &c. A New Edition, crown 8vo, cloth extra, with Coloured Frontispiece and 100 Illustrations, 7s. 6d. [Preparing.

Pascal's Provincial Letters. A New Translation, with Historical Introduction and Notes, by T. M'Crie, D.D. Post 8vo, cloth limp, 2s.

Patient's (The) Vade Mecum: How to get most Benefit from Medical Advice. By W. Knight, M.R.C.S., and E.Knight,L.R.C.P. Cr.8vo,1s.; cl. 1/6.

Paul Ferroll:
Post 8vo, illustrated boards, 2s. each.
Paul Ferroll: A Novel.
Why Paul Ferroll Killed his Wife.

Payn (James), Novels by. Crown 8vo, cloth extra, 3s. 6d. each; post 8vo, illustrated boards, 2s. each.
Lost Sir Massingberd.
Walter's Word.
Less Black than we're Painted.
By Proxy. | High Spirits.
Under One Roof.
A Confidential Agent.

PAYN (JAMES), *continued—*
Crown 8vo, cloth extra, 3s. 6d. each;
post 8vo, illustrated boards, 2s. each.
Some Private Views.
A Grape from a Thorn.
From Exile. | The Canon's Ward.
The Talk of the Town.
Holiday Tasks.

Post 8vo, illustrated boards, 2s. each.
Kit: A Memory. | Carlyon's Year.
A Perfect Treasure.
Bentinck's Tutor.|Murphy's Master.
The Best of Husbands.
For Cash Only.
What He Cost Her. | Cecil's Tryst.
Fallen Fortunes. | Halves.
A County Family. | At Her Mercy.
A Woman's Vengeance.
The Clyffards of Clyffe.
The Family Scapegrace.
The Foster Brothers.| Found Dead.
Gwendoline's Harvest.
Humorous Stories.
Like Father, Like Son.
A Marine Residence.
Married Beneath Him.
Mirk Abbey. | Not Wooed, but Won.
Two Hundred Pounds Reward.

Crown 8vo, cloth extra, 3s. 6d. each.
In Peril and Privation: Stories of Marine Adventure Re-told. With 17 Illustrations.
Glow-Worm Tales.
The Mystery of Mirbridge. [*Shortly.*

Paul.—Gentle and Simple. By MARGARET AGNES PAUL. With a Frontispiece by HELEN PATERSON. Cr. 8vo, cloth extra, 3s. 6d.; post 8vo, illustrated boards, 2s.

Pears.—The Present Depression in Trade: Its Causes and Remedies. Being the "Pears" Prize Essays (of One Hundred Guineas). By EDWIN GOADBY and WILLIAM WATT. With an Introductory Paper by Prof. LEONE LEVI, F.S.A., F.S.S. Demy 8vo, 1s.

Pennell (H. Cholmondeley), Works by:
Post 8vo, cloth limp, 2s. 6d. each.
Puck on Pegasus. With Illustrations.
Pegasus Re-Saddled. With Ten full-page Illusts. by G. DU MAURIER.
The Muses of Mayfair. Vers de Société, Selected and Edited by H. C. PENNELL.

Phelps (E. Stuart), Works by:
Post 8vo, 1s. each; cl. limp, 1s. 6d. each.
Beyond the Gates. By the Author of "The Gates Ajar."
An Old Maid's Paradise.
Burglars in Paradise.

Jack the Fisherman. With Twenty-two Illustrations by C. W. REED. Cr. 8vo, picture cover, 1s.; cl. 1s. 6d.

Pirkis (C. L.), Novels by:
Trooping with Crows. Fcap. 8vo, picture cover, 1s. [boards, 2s.
Lady Lovelace. Post 8vo, illustrated

Planché (J. R.), Works by:
The Pursuivant of Arms; or, Heraldry Founded upon Facts. With Coloured Frontispiece and 200 Illustrations. Cr. 8vo, cloth extra, 7s. 6d.
Songs and Poems, from 1819 to 1879. Edited, with an Introduction, by his Daughter, Mrs. MACKARNESS. Crown 8vo, cloth extra, 6s.

Plutarch's Lives of Illustrious Men. Translated from the Greek, with Notes Critical and Historical, and a Life of Plutarch, by JOHN and WILLIAM LANGHORNE. Two Vols., 8vo, cloth extra, with Portraits, 10s. 6d.

Poe (Edgar Allan):—
The Choice Works, in Prose and Poetry, of EDGAR ALLAN POE. With an Introductory Essay by CHARLES BAUDELAIRE, Portrait and Facsimiles. Crown 8vo, cl. extra, 7s. 6d.
The Mystery of Marie Roget, and other Stories. Post 8vo, illust.bds.,2s.

Pope's Poetical Works. Complete in One Vol. Post 8vo, cl. limp, 2s.

Praed (Mrs. Campbell-).—"The Right Honourable:" A Romance of Society and Politics. By Mrs. CAMPBELL-PRAED and JUSTIN MCCARTHY, M.P. Cr. 8vo, cloth extra, 6s.

Price (E. C.), Novels by:
Crown 8vo, cloth extra, 3s. 6d. each; post 8vo, illustrated boards, 2s. each.
Valentina. | The Foreigners.
Mrs. Lancaster's Rival.
Gerald. Post 8vo, illust. boards, 2s.

Princess Olga—Radna; or, The Great Conspiracy of 1881. By the Princess OLGA. Cr. 8vo, cl. ex., 6s.

Proctor (Rich. A.), Works by:
Flowers of the Sky. With 55 Illusts. Small crown 8vo, cloth extra, 4s. 6d.
Easy Star Lessons. With Star Maps for Every Night in the Year, Drawings of the Constellations, &c. Crown 8vo, cloth extra, 6s.
Familiar Science Studies. Crown 8vo, cloth extra, 7s. 6d.
Saturn and its System. New and Revised Edition, with 13 Steel Plates. Demy 8vo, cloth extra, 10s. 6d.
Mysteries of Time and Space. With Illusts. Cr. 8vo, cloth extra, 7s. 6d.
The Universe of Suns, and other Science Gleanings. With numerous Illusts. Cr. 8vo, cloth extra, 7s. 6d.
Wages and Wants of Science Workers. Crown 8vo, 1s. 6d.

Rabelais' Works. Faithfully Translated from the French, with variorum Notes, and numerous characteristic Illustrations by GUSTAVE DORÉ. Crown 8vo, cloth extra, 7s. 6d.

Rambosson.—Popular Astronomy. By J. RAMBOSSON, Laureate of the Institute of France. Translated by C. B. PITMAN. Crown 8vo, cloth gilt, numerous Illusts., and a beautifully executed Chart of Spectra, 7s. 6d.

Reade (Charles), Novels by:
Cr. 8vo, cloth extra, illustrated, 3s. 6d. each; post 8vo, illust. bds., 2s. each.
Peg Woffington. Illustrated by S. L. FILDES, A.R.A.
Christie Johnstone. Illustrated by WILLIAM SMALL.
It is Never Too Late to Mend. Illustrated by G. J. PINWELL.
The Course of True Love Never did run Smooth. Illustrated by HELEN PATERSON.
The Autobiography of a Thief; Jack of all Trades; and James Lambert. Illustrated by MATT STRETCH.
Love me Little, Love me Long. Illustrated by M. ELLEN EDWARDS.
The Double Marriage. Illust. by Sir JOHN GILBERT, R.A., and C. KEENE.
The Cloister and the Hearth. Illustrated by CHARLES KEENE.
Hard Cash. Illust. by F. W. LAWSON.
Griffith Gaunt. Illustrated by S. L. FILDES, A.R.A., and WM. SMALL.
Foul Play. Illust. by DU MAURIER.
Put Yourself in His Place. Illustrated by ROBERT BARNES.
A Terrible Temptation. Illustrated by EDW. HUGHES and A. W. COOPER.
The Wandering Heir. Illustrated by H. PATERSON, S. L. FILDES, A.R.A., C. GREEN, and H. WOODS, A.R.A.
A Simpleton. Illustrated by KATE CRAUFORD. [COULDERY.
A Woman-Hater. Illust. by THOS.
Singleheart and Doubleface: A Matter-of-fact Romance. Illustrated by P. MACNAB.
Good Stories of Men and other Animals. Illustrated by E. A. ABBEY, PERCY MACQUOID, and JOSEPH NASH.
The Jilt, and other Stories. Illustrated by JOSEPH NASH.
Readiana. With a Steel-plate Portrait of CHARLES READE.

Bible Characters: Studies of David, Nehemiah, Jonah, Paul, &c. Fcap. 8vo, leatherette, 1s.

Reader's Handbook (The) of Allusions, References, Plots, and Stories. By the Rev. Dr. BREWER. Fifth Edition, revised throughout, with a New Appendix, containing a COMPLETE ENGLISH BIBLIOGRAPHY. Cr. 8vo, 1,400 pages, cloth extra, 7s. 6d.

Richardson. — A Ministry of Health, and other Papers. By BENJAMIN WARD RICHARDSON, M.D., &c. Crown 8vo, cloth extra, 6s.

Riddell (Mrs. J. H.), Novels by:
Crown 8vo, cloth extra, 3s. 6d. each; post 8vo, illustrated boards, 2s. each.
Her Mother's Darling.
The Prince of Wales's Garden Party.
Weird Stories.

Post 8vo, illustrated boards, 2s. each.
The Uninhabited House.
Fairy Water.
The Mystery in Palace Gardens.

Rimmer (Alfred), Works by.
Square 8vo, cloth gilt, 7s. 6d. each.
Our Old Country Towns. With over 50 Illustrations.
Rambles Round Eton and Harrow. With 50 Illustrations.
About England with Dickens. With 58 Illustrations by ALFRED RIMMER and C. A. VANDERHOOF.

Robinson (F. W.), Novels by:
Crown 8vo, cloth extra, 3s. 6d. each; post 8vo, illustrated boards, 2s. each.
Women are Strange.
The Hands of Justice.

Robinson (Phil), Works by:
Crown 8vo, cloth extra, 7s. 6d. each.
The Poets' Birds.
The Poets' Beasts.
The Poets and Nature: Reptiles, Fishes, and Insects. [Preparing.

Rochefoucauld's Maxims and Moral Reflections. With Notes, and an Introductory Essay by SAINTE-BEUVE. Post 8vo, cloth limp, 2s.

Roll of Battle Abbey, The; or, A List of the Principal Warriors who came over from Normandy with William the Conqueror, and Settled in this Country, A.D. 1066-7. With the principal Arms emblazoned in Gold and Colours. Handsomely printed, 5s.

Rowley (Hon. Hugh), Works by:
Post 8vo, cloth limp, 2s. 6d. each.
Puniana: Riddles and Jokes. With numerous Illustrations.
More Puniana. Profusely Illustrated.

Runciman (James), Stories by:
Post 8vo, illustrated boards, 2s. each; cloth limp, 2s. 6d. each.
Skippers and Shellbacks.
Grace Balmaign's Sweetheart.
Schools and Scholars.

Russell (W. Clark), Works by:
Crown 8vo, cloth extra, 6s. each; post 8vo, illustrated boards, 2s. each.
Round the Galley-Fire.
In the Middle Watch.
A Voyage to the Cape.

On the Fo'k'sle Head. Post 8vo, illustrated boards, 2s.

Crown 8vo, cloth extra, 6s. each.
A Book for the Hammock.
The Mystery of the "Ocean Star," &c.

*** The above Six Books may also be had in a handsome cloth box, under the general title of "CLARK RUSSELL'S SEA BOOKS," price 36s.

Sala.—Gaslight and Daylight.
By GEORGE AUGUSTUS SALA. Post 8vo, illustrated boards, 2s.

Sanson.—Seven Generations of Executioners: Memoirs of the Sanson Family (1688 to 1847). Edited by HENRY SANSON. Cr. 8vo, cl. ex. 3s. 6d.

Saunders (John), Novels by:
Crown 8vo, cloth extra, 3s. 6d. each; post 8vo, illustrated boards, 2s. each.
Bound to the Wheel.
Guy Waterman. | Lion in the Path.
The Two Dreamers.
One Against the World. Post 8vo, illustrated boards, 2s.

Saunders (Katharine), Novels by. Cr. 8vo, cloth extra, 3s. 6d. each; post 8vo, illustrated boards, 2s. each.
Margaret and Elizabeth.
The High Mills.
Heart Salvage. | Sebastian.

Joan Merryweather. Post 8vo, illustrated boards, 2s.
Gideon's Rock. Crown 8vo, cloth extra, 3s. 6d.

Science-Gossip: An Illustrated Medium of Interchange for Students and Lovers of Nature. Edited by J. E. TAYLOR, F.L.S., &c. Devoted to Geology, Botany, Physiology, Chemistry, Zoology, Microscopy, Telescopy, Physiography, &c. Price 4d. Monthly; or 5s. per year, post free. Vols. I. to XIV. may be had at 7s. 6d. each; and Vols. XV. to date, at 5s. each. Cases for Binding, 1s. 6d. each.

"Secret Out" Series, The:
Cr. 8vo, cl. ex., Illusts., 4s. 6d. each.
The Secret Out: One Thousand Tricks with Cards, and other Recreations; with Entertaining Experiments in Drawing-room or "White Magic." By W. H. CREMER. 300 Illusts.
The Art of Amusing: A Collection of Graceful Arts, Games, Tricks, Puzzles, and Charades By FRANK BELLEW. With 300 Illustrations.
Hanky-Panky: Very Easy Tricks, Very Difficult Tricks, White Magic, Sleight of Hand. Edited by W. H. CREMER. With 200 Illustrations.
Magician's Own Book: Performances with Cups and Balls, Eggs, Hats, Handkerchiefs, &c. All from actual Experience. Edited by W. H. CREMER. 200 Illustrations.

Seguin (L. G.), Works by:
Crown 8vo, cloth extra, 6s. each.
The Country of the Passion Play, and the Highlands and Highlanders of Bavaria. With Map and 37 Illusts.
Walks in Algiers and its Surroundings. With 2 Maps and 16 Illusts.

Senior.—By Stream and Sea.
By W. SENIOR. Post 8vo, cl. limp, 2s. 6d.

Seven Sagas (The) of Prehistoric Man. By JAMES H. STODDART, Author of "The Village Life." Crown 8vo, cloth extra, 6s.

Shakespeare:
The First Folio Shakespeare.—MR. WILLIAM SHAKESPEARE'S Comedies, Histories, and Tragedies. Published according to the true Originall Copies. London, Printed by ISAAC IAGGARD and ED. BLOUNT. 1623.—A Reproduction of the extremely rare original, in reduced facsimile, by a photographic process—ensuring the strictest accuracy in every detail. Small 8vo, half-Roxburghe, 7s. 6d.
The Lansdowne Shakespeare. Beautifully printed in red and black, in small but very clear type. With engraved facsimile of DROESHOUT'S Portrait. Post 8vo, cloth extra, 7s. 6d.
Shakespeare for Children: Tales from Shakespeare. By CHARLES and MARY LAMB. With numerous Illustrations, coloured and plain, by J. MOYR SMITH. Cr. 4to, cl. gilt, 6s.
The Handbook of Shakespeare Music. Being an Account of 350 Pieces of Music, the compositions ranging from the Elizabethan Age to the Present Time. By ALFRED ROFFE. 4to, half-Roxburghe, 7s.
A Study of Shakespeare. By ALGERNON CHARLES SWINBURNE. Crown 8vo, cloth extra, 8s.

Sharp.—Sanpriel: A Novel. By WILLIAM SHARP. Crown 8vo. cloth extra, 6s. [*Shortly.*

Shelley.—The Complete Works in Verse and Prose of Percy Bysshe Shelley. Edited, Prefaced and Annotated by RICHARD HERNE SHEPHERD. Five Vols., crown 8vo, cloth boards, 3s. 6d. each.

Poetical Works, in Three Vols.
Vol. I. An Introduction by the Editor; The Posthumous Fragments of Margaret Nicholson; Shelley's Correspondence with Stockdale; The Wandering Jew (the only complete version); Queen Mab, with the Notes; Alastor, and other Poems; Rosalind and Helen; Prometheus Unbound; Adonais, &c.
Vol. II. Laon and Cythna (as originally published, instead of the emasculated "Revolt of Islam"); The Cenci; Julian and Maddalo (from Shelley's manuscript); Swellfoot the Tyrant (from the copy in the Dyce Library at South Kensington); The Witch of Atlas; Epipsychidion; Hellas.
Vol. III. Posthumous Poems, published by Mrs. SHELLEY in 1824 and 1839; The Masque of Anarchy (from Shelley's manuscript); and other Pieces not brought together in the ordinary editions.

Prose Works, in Two Vols.
Vol. I. The Two Romances of Zastrozzi and St. Irvyne; the Dublin and Marlow Pamphlets; A Refutation of Deism; Letters to Leigh Hunt, and some Minor Writings and Fragments.
Vol. II. The Essays; Letters from Abroad; Translations and Fragments, Edited by Mrs. SHELLEY, and first published in 1840, with the addition of some Minor Pieces of great interest and rarity, including one recently discovered by Professor DOWDEN. With a Bibliography of Shelley, and an exhaustive Index of the Prose Works.

** Also a LARGE-PAPER EDITION, to be had in SETS only, at 52s. 6d. for the Five Volumes.

Sheridan:—
Sheridan's Complete Works, with Life and Anecdotes. Including his Dramatic Writings, printed from the Original Editions, his Works in Prose and Poetry, Translations, Speeches, Jokes, Puns, &c. With a Collection of Sheridaniana. Crown 8vo, cloth extra, gilt, with 10 full-page Tinted Illustrations, 7s. 6d.

Sheridan's Comedies: The Rivals, and The School for Scandal. Edited, with an Introduction and Notes to each Play, and a Biographical Sketch of Sheridan, by BRANDER MATTHEWS. With Decorative Vignettes and 10 full-page Illusts. Demy 8vo, half-parchment, 12s. 6d.

Sheridan (General).—Personal Memoirs of General P. H. Sheridan: The Romantic Career of a Great Soldier, told in his Own Words. With 22 Portraits and other Illustrations, 27 Maps and numerous Facsimiles of Famous Letters. Two Vols. of 500 pages each, demy 8vo, cloth extra, 24s.

Sidney's (Sir Philip) Complete Poetical Works, including all those in "Arcadia." With Portrait, Memorial Introduction, Notes, &c., by the Rev. A. B. GROSART, D.D. Three Vols., crown 8vo, cloth boards, 18s.

Signboards: Their History. With Anecdotes of Famous Taverns and Remarkable Characters. By JACOB LARWOOD and JOHN CAMDEN HOTTEN. Crown 8vo, cloth extra, with 100 Illustrations, 7s. 6d.

Sims (George R.), Works by:
Post 8vo, illustrated boards, 2s. each; cloth limp, 2s. 6d. each.
Rogues and Vagabonds.
The Ring o' Bells.
Mary Jane's Memoirs.
Mary Jane Married.

The Dagonet Reciter and Reader: Being Readings and Recitations in Prose and Verse, selected from his own Works by G. R. SIMS. Post 8vo, portrait cover, 1s.; cloth, 1s. 6d.

Sister Dora: A Biography. By MARGARET LONSDALE. Popular Edition, Revised, with additional Chapter, a New Dedication and Preface, and Four Illustrations. Sq. 8vo, picture cover, 4d.; cloth, 6d.

Sketchley.—A Match in the Dark. By ARTHUR SKETCHLEY. Post 8vo, illustrated boards, 2s.

Slang Dictionary, The: Etymological, Historical, and Anecdotal. Crown 8vo, cloth extra, gilt, 6s. 6d.

Smith (J. Moyr), Works by:
The Prince of Argolis: A Story of the Old Greek Fairy Time. Small 8vo, cloth extra, with 130 Illusts., 3s. 6d.
Tales of Old Thule. With numerous Illustrations. Cr. 8vo, cloth gilt, 6s.
The Wooing of the Water Witch. With Illustrations. Small 8vo, 6s.

Society in London. By A FOREIGN RESIDENT. Crown 8vo, 1s.; cloth, 1s. 6d.

Society out of Town. By A FOREIGN RESIDENT, Author of "Society in London." Crown 8vo, cloth extra, 6s. [*Preparing.*

Society in Paris: The Upper Ten Thousand. By Count PAUL VASILI. Trans. by RAPHAEL LEDOS DE BEAUFORT. Cr. 8vo, cl. ex., 6s. [*Preparing.*

Spalding.—Elizabethan Demonology: An Essay in Illustration of the Belief in the Existence of Devils, and the Powers possessed by Them. By T. A. SPALDING, LL.B. Cr. 8vo, cl. ex., 5s.

Speight (T. W.), Novels by:
The Mysteries of Heron Dyke. With a Frontispiece by M. ELLEN EDWARDS. Crown 8vo, cloth extra, 3s. 6d.; post 8vo, illustrated bds., 2s.
Wife or No Wife? Cr. 8vo, picture cover, 1s.; cloth, 1s. 6d.
The Golden Hoop. Post 8vo, illust. boards, 2s.
By Devious Ways. Demy 8vo, 1s.

Spenser for Children. By M. H. TOWRY. With Illustrations by WALTER J. MORGAN. Crown 4to, with Coloured Illustrations, cloth gilt, 6s.

Staunton.—Laws and Practice of Chess; Together with an Analysis of the Openings, and a Treatise on End Games. By HOWARD STAUNTON. Edited by ROBERT B. WORMALD. New Edition, small cr. 8vo, cloth extra, 5s.

Stedman (E. C.), Works by:
Victorian Poets. Thirteenth Edition, revised and enlarged. Crown 8vo, cloth extra, 9s.
The Poets of America. Crown 8vo, cloth extra, 9s.

Sterndale.—The Afghan Knife: A Novel. By ROBERT ARMITAGE STERNDALE. Cr. 8vo, cloth extra, 3s. 6d.; post 8vo, illustrated boards, 2s.

Stevenson (R. Louis), Works by:
Travels with a Donkey in the Cevennes. Sixth Ed. Frontispiece by W. CRANE. Post 8vo, cl. limp, 2s. 6d.
An Inland Voyage. With Front. by W. CRANE. Post 8vo, cl. lp., 2s. 6d.
Familiar Studies of Men and Books. 2nd Edit. Cr. 8vo, buckram extra, 6s.
New Arabian Nights. Crown 8vo, buckram extra, 6s.; post 8vo, illust. boards, 2s.
The Silverado Squatters. With Frontispiece. Crown 8vo, buckram extra, 6s. Cheap Edition, post 8vo, picture cover, 1s.; cloth, 1s. 6d.
Prince Otto: A Romance. Fourth Edition. Crown 8vo, buckram extra, 6s.; post 8vo, illustrated boards, 2s.
The Merry Men, and other Tales and Fables. Cr. 8vo, buckram ex., 6s.
Underwoods: Poems. Post 8vo, cl. ex. 6s.
Memories and Portraits. Second Edition. Cr. 8vo, buckram extra, 6s.
Virginibus Puerisque, and other Papers. A New Edition, Revised. Fcap. 8vo, buckram extra, 6s.

St. John.—A Levantine Family. By BAYLE ST. JOHN. Post 8vo, illustrated boards, 2s.

Stoddard.—Summer Cruising in the South Seas. By CHARLES WARREN STODDARD. Illust. by WALLIS MACKAY. Crown 8vo, cl. extra, 3s. 6d.

Stories from Foreign Novelists. With Notices of their Lives and Writings. By HELEN and ALICE ZIMMERN. Frontispiece. Crown 8vo, cloth extra, 3s. 6d.; post 8vo, illust. bds., 2s.

Strange Manuscript (A) found in a Copper Cylinder. With 19 full-page Illustrations by GILBERT GAUL. Third Edition. Cr. 8vo, cl. extra, 5s.

Strutt's Sports and Pastimes of the People of England; including the Rural and Domestic Recreations, May Games, Mummeries, Shows, &c., from the Earliest Period to the Present Time. With 140 Illustrations. Edited by WM. HONE. Cr. 8vo, cl. extra, 7s. 6d.

Suburban Homes (The) of London: A Residential Guide to Favourite London Localities, their Society, Celebrities, and Associations. With Notes on their Rental, Rates, and House Accommodation. With Map of Suburban London. Cr. 8vo, cl. ex., 7s 6d.

Swift's Choice Works, in Prose and Verse. With Memoir, Portrait, and Facsimiles of the Maps in the Original Edition of "Gulliver's Travels." Cr. 8vo, cloth extra, 7s. 6d.

Swinburne (Algernon C.), Works by:
Selections from the Poetical Works of Algernon Charles Swinburne. Fcap. 8vo, cloth extra, 6s.
Atalanta in Calydon. Crown 8vo, 6s.
Chastelard. A Tragedy. Cr. 8vo, 7s.
Poems and Ballads. FIRST SERIES. Fcap. 8vo, 9s. Cr. 8vo, same price.
Poems and Ballads. SECOND SERIES. Fcap. 8vo, 9s. Cr. 8vo, same price.
Notes on Poems and Reviews. 8vo, 1s.
Songs before Sunrise. Cr. 8vo, 10s. 6d.
Bothwell: A Tragedy. Cr. 8vo, 12s. 6d.
Songs of Two Nations. Cr. 8vo, 6s.
Essays and Studies. Crown 8vo, 12s.
Erechtheus: A Tragedy. Cr. 8vo, 6s.
Note on Charlotte Bronte. Cr. 8vo, 6s.
A Study of Shakespeare. Cr. 8vo, 8s.
Songs of the Springtides. Cr. 8vo, 6s.
Studies in Song. Crown 8vo, 7s.
Mary Stuart: A Tragedy. Cr. 8vo, 8s.
Tristram of Lyonesse, and other Poems. Crown 8vo, 9s.
A Century of Roundels. Small 4to, 8s.
A Midsummer Holiday, and other Poems. Crown 8vo, 7s.
Marino Faliero: A Tragedy. Cr. 8vo, 6s.
A Study of Victor Hugo. Cr. 8vo, 6s.
Miscellanies. Crown 8vo, 12s.
Locrine: A Tragedy. Crown 8vo, 6s.
Mr. Swinburne's New Volume of Poems. Crown 8vo, 6s. [Shortly.

BOOKS PUBLISHED BY

Symonds.—Wine, Women, and Song: Mediæval Latin Students' Songs. Now first translated into English Verse, with Essay by J. ADDINGTON SYMONDS. Small 8vo, parchment, 6s.

Syntax's (Dr.) Three Tours: In Search of the Picturesque, in Search of Consolation, and in Search of a Wife. With the whole of ROWLANDSON'S droll page Illustrations in Colours and a Life of the Author by J. C. HOTTEN. Med. 8vo, cloth extra, 7s. 6d.

Taine's History of English Literature. Translated by HENRY VAN LAUN. Four Vols., small 8vo, cloth boards, 30s.—POPULAR EDITION, Two Vols., crown 8vo, cloth extra, 15s.

Taylor's (Bayard) Diversions of the Echo Club: Burlesques of Modern Writers. Post 8vo, cl. limp, 2s.

Taylor (Dr. J. E., F.L.S.), Works by. Crown 8vo, cloth ex., 7s. 6d. each.
The Sagacity and Morality of Plants: A Sketch of the Life and Conduct of the Vegetable Kingdom. Coloured Frontispiece and 100 Illust.
Our Common British Fossils, and Where to Find Them: A Handbook for Students. With 331 Illustrations.
The Playtime Naturalist: A Book for Home and School. With 366 Illustrations. Crown 8vo, cloth extra, 5s. [*Preparing.*]

Taylor's (Tom) Historical Dramas: "Clancarty," "Jeanne Darc," "'Twixt Axe and Crown," "The Fool's Revenge," "Arkwright's Wife," "Anne Boleyn," "Plot and Passion." One Vol., cr. 8vo, cloth extra, 7s. 6d.
*** The Plays may also be had separately, at 1s. each.

Tennyson (Lord): A Biographical Sketch. By H. J. JENNINGS. With a Photograph Portrait. Crown 8vo, cloth extra, 6s.

Thackerayana: Notes and Anecdotes. Illustrated by Hundreds of Sketches by WILLIAM MAKEPEACE THACKERAY, depicting Humorous Incidents in his School-life, and Favourite Characters in the books of his every-day reading. With Coloured Frontispiece. Cr. 8vo, cl. extra, 7s. 6d.

Thomas (Bertha), Novels by: Crown 8vo, cloth extra, 3s. 6d. each; post 8vo, illustrated boards, 2s. each.
Cressida. | Proud Maisie.
The Violin-Player.

Thomas (M.).—A Fight for Life: A Novel. By W. MOY THOMAS. Post 8vo, illustrated boards, 2s.

Thomson's Seasons and Castle of Indolence. With a Biographical and Critical Introduction by ALLAN CUNNINGHAM, and over 50 fine Illustrations on Steel and Wood. Crown 8vo, cloth extra, gilt edges, 7s. 6d.

Thornbury (Walter), Works by: Haunted London. Edited by EDWARD WALFORD, M.A. With Illustrations by F. W. FAIRHOLT, F.S.A. Crown 8vo, cloth extra, 7s. 6d.
The Life and Correspondence of J. M. W. Turner. Founded upon Letters and Papers furnished by his Friends and fellow Academicians. With numerous Illusts. in Colours, facsimiled from Turner's Original Drawings. Cr. 8vo, cl. extra, 7s. 6d.
Old Stories Re-told. Post 8vo, cloth limp, 2s. 6d. CHEAPER EDITION, illustrated boards, 2s.
Tales for the Marines. Post 8vo, illustrated boards, 2s.

Timbs (John), Works by: Crown 8vo, cloth extra, 7s. 6d. each.
The History of Clubs and Club Life in London. With Anecdotes of its Famous Coffee-houses, Hostelries, and Taverns. With many Illusts.
English Eccentrics and Eccentricities: Stories of Wealth and Fashion, Delusions, Impostures, and Fanatic Missions, Strange Sights and Sporting Scenes, Eccentric Artists, Theatrical Folk, Men of Letters, &c. With nearly 50 Illusts.

Trollope (Anthony), Novels by: Crown 8vo, cloth extra, 3s. 6d. each; post 8vo, illustrated boards, 2s. each.
The Way We Live Now.
Kept in the Dark.
Frau Frohmann. | Marion Fay.
Mr. Scarborough's Family.
The Land-Leaguers.
Post 8vo, illustrated boards, 2s. each.
The Golden Lion of Granpere.
John Caldigate. | American Senator

Trollope (Frances E.), Novels by Crown 8vo, cloth extra, 3s. 6d. each; post 8vo, illustrated boards, 2s. each.
Like Ships upon the Sea.
Mabel's Progress. / Anne Furness

Trollope (T. A.).—Diamond Cut Diamond, and other Stories. By T. ADOLPHUS TROLLOPE. Post 8vo, illustrated boards, 2s.

Trowbridge.—Farnell's Folly: A Novel. By J. T. TROWBRIDGE. Post 8vo, illustrated boards, 2s.

Turgenieff. — Stories from Foreign Novelists. By IVAN TURGENIEFF, and others. Cr. 8vo, cloth extra, 3s. 6d.; post 8vo, illustrated boards, 2s.

CHATTO & WINDUS, PICCADILLY.   25

Tytler (C. C. Fraser-).—Mistress Judith: A Novel. By C. C. FRASER-TYTLER. Cr. 8vo, cloth extra, 3s. 6d.; post 8vo, illust. boards, 2s.

Tytler (Sarah), Novels by:
Crown 8vo, cloth extra, 3s. 6d. each; post 8vo, illustrated boards, 2s. each.
What She Came Through.
The Bride's Pass. | Noblesse Oblige.
Saint Mungo's City. | Lady Bell.
Beauty and the Beast.
Citoyenne Jacqueline.

Crown 8vo, cloth extra, 3s. 6d. each.
The Huguenot Family. With Illusts.
Buried Diamonds.

Disappeared: A Romance. Post 8vo, illustrated boards, 2s.
The Blackhall Ghosts: A Novel. 3 Vols., crown 8vo.

Van Laun.—History of French Literature. By H. VAN LAUN. Three Vols., demy 8vo, cl. bds., 7s. 6d. each.

Villari.—A Double Bond: A Story. By LINDA VILLARI. Fcap. 8vo, picture cover, 1s.

Walford (Edw., M.A.), Works by:
The County Families of the United Kingdom. Containing Notices of the Descent, Birth, Marriage, Education, &c., of more than 12000, distinguished Heads of Families, their Heirs Apparent or Presumptive, the Offices they hold or have held, their Town and Country Addresses, Clubs, &c. Twenty-seventh Annual Edition, for 1888, cloth gilt, 50s.
The Shilling Peerage (1888). Containing an Alphabetical List of the House of Lords, Dates of Creation, Lists of Scotch and Irish Peers, Addresses, &c. 32mo, cloth, 1s.
The Shilling Baronetage (1888). Containing an Alphabetical List of the Baronets of the United Kingdom, short Biographical Notices, Dates of Creation, Addresses, &c. 32mo, cloth, 1s.
The Shilling Knightage (1888). Containing an Alphabetical List of the Knights of the United Kingdom, short Biographical Notices, Dates of Creation, Addresses,&c. 32mo,cl.,1s.
The Shilling House of Commons (1888). Containing a List of all the Members of Parliament, their Town and Country Addresses, &c. New Edition, embodying the results of the recent General Election. 32mo, cloth, 1s.
The Complete Peerage, Baronetage, Knightage, and House of Commons (1888). In One Volume, royal 32mo, cloth extra, gilt edges, 5s.

WALFORD'S (EDW.) WORKS, continued—
Haunted London. By WALTER THORNBURY. Edited by EDWARD WALFORD, M.A. With Illustrations by F. W. FAIRHOLT, F.S.A. Crown 8vo, cloth extra, 7s. 6d.

Walton and Cotton's Complete Angler; or, The Contemplative Man's Recreation; being a Discourse of Rivers, Fishponds, Fish and Fishing, written by IZAAK WALTON; and Instructions how to Angle for a Trout or Grayling in a clear Stream, by CHARLES COTTON. With Original Memoirs and Notes by Sir HARRIS NICOLAS, and 61 Copperplate Illustrations. Large crown 8vo, cloth antique, 7s. 6d.

Walt Whitman, Poems by. Selected and edited, with an Introduction, by WILLIAM M. ROSSETTI. A New Edition, with a Steel Plate Portrait. Crown 8vo, printed on handmade paper and bound in buckram, 6s.

Wanderer's Library, The:
Crown 8vo, cloth extra, 3s. 6d. each.
Wanderings In Patagonia; or, Life among the Ostrich-Hunters. By JULIUS BEERBOHM. Illustrated.
Camp Notes: Stories of Sport and Adventure in Asia, Africa, and America. By FREDERICK BOYLE.
Savage Life. By FREDERICK BOYLE.
Merrie England in the Olden Time. By GEORGE DANIEL. With Illustrations by ROBT. CRUIKSHANK.
Circus Life and Circus Celebrities. By THOMAS FROST.
The Lives of the Conjurers. By THOMAS FROST.
The Old Showmen and the Old London Fairs. By THOMAS FROST.
Low-Life Deeps. An Account of the Strange Fish to be found there. By JAMES GREENWOOD.
The Wilds of London. By JAMES GREENWOOD.
Tunis: The Land and the People. By the Chevalier de HESSE-WARTEGG. With 22 Illustrations.
The Life and Adventures of a Cheap Jack. By One of the Fraternity Edited by CHARLES HINDLEY.
The World Behind the Scenes. By PERCY FITZGERALD.
Tavern Anecdotes and Sayings: Including the Origin of Signs, and Reminiscences connected with Taverns, Coffee Houses, Clubs, &c By CHARLES HINDLEY. With Illusts.
The Genial Showman: Life and Adventures of Artemus Ward. By E. P. HINGSTON. With a Frontispiece.
The Story of the London Parks. By JACOB LARWOOD. With Illusts.
London Characters. By HENRY MAYHEW. Illustrated.

WANDERER'S LIBRARY, THE, continued—
Crown 8vo, cloth extra, 3s. 6d. each.
Seven Generations of Executioners: Memoirs of the Sanson Family (1688 to 1847). Edited by HENRY SANSON.
Summer Cruising in the South Seas. By C. WARREN STODDARD. Illustrated by WALLIS MACKAY.

Warner.—A Roundabout Journey. By CHARLES DUDLEY WARNER, Author of "My Summer in a Garden." Crown 8vo, cloth extra, 6s.

Warrants, &c.:—
Warrant to Execute Charles I. An exact Facsimile, with the Fifty-nine Signatures, and corresponding Seals. Carefully printed on paper to imitate the Original, 22 in. by 14 in. Price 2s.
Warrant to Execute Mary Queen of Scots. An exact Facsimile, including the Signature of Queen Elizabeth, and a Facsimile of the Great Seal. Beautifully printed on paper to imitate the Original MS. Price 2s.
Magna Charta. An exact Facsimile of the Original Document in the British Museum, printed on fine plate paper, nearly 3 feet long by 2 feet wide, with the Arms and Seals emblazoned in Gold and Colours. 5s.
The Roll of Battle Abbey; or, A List of the Principal Warriors who came over from Normandy with William the Conqueror, and Settled in this Country, A.D. 1066-7. With the principal Arms emblazoned in Gold and Colours. Price 5s.

Wayfarer, The: Journal of the Society of Cyclists. Published at short intervals. Price 1s. The Numbers for OCT., 1886, JAN., MAY, and OCT., 1887, and FEB., 1888, are now ready.

Weather, How to Foretell the, with the Pocket Spectroscope. By F. W. CORY, M.R.C.S. Eng., F.R.Met. Soc., &c. With 10 Illustrations. Crown 8vo, 1s.; cloth, 1s. 6d.

Westropp.—Handbook of Pottery and Porcelain; or, History of those Arts from the Earliest Period. By HODDER M. WESTROPP. With numerous Illustrations, and a List of Marks. Crown 8vo, cloth limp, 4s. 6d.

Whist. — How to Play Solo Whist: Its Method and Principles Explained, and its Practice Demonstrated. With Illustrative Specimen Hands in red and black, and a Revised and Augmented Code of Laws. By ABRAHAM S. WILKS and CHARLES F. PARDON. Crown 8vo, cloth extra, 3s. 6d.

Whistler's (Mr.) "Ten o'Clock." Uniform with his "Whistler v. Ruskin: Art and Art Critics." Cr. 8vo, 1s.

Williams (W. Mattieu, F.R.A.S.), Works by:
Science Notes. See the GENTLEMAN'S MAGAZINE. 1s. Monthly.
Science in Short Chapters. Crown 8vo, cloth extra, 7s. 6d.
A Simple Treatise on Heat. Crown 8vo, cloth limp, with Illusts., 2s. 6d.
The Chemistry of Cookery. Crown 8vo, cloth extra, 6s.

Wilson (Dr. Andrew, F.R.S.E.), Works by:
Chapters on Evolution: A Popular History of Darwinian and Allied Theories of Development. 3rd ed. Cr. 8vo, cl. ex., with 259 Illusts., 7s. 6d.
Leaves from a Naturalist's Notebook. Post 8vo, cloth limp, 2s. 6d.
Leisure-Time Studies, chiefly Biological. Third Edit., with New Preface. Cr. 8vo, cl. ex., with Illusts., 6s.
Studies in Life and Sense. With numerous Illusts. Cr. 8vo, cl. ex., 6s.
Common Accidents, and How to Treat them. By Dr. ANDREW WILSON and others. With numerous Illusts. Cr. 8vo, 1s.; cl. limp, 1s. 6d.

Winter (J. S.), Stories by:
Post 8vo, illustrated boards, 2s. each.
Cavalry Life.
Regimental Legends.

Women of the Day: A Biographical Dictionary of Notable Contemporaries. By FRANCES HAYS. Crown 8vo, cloth extra, 5s.

Wood.—Sabina: A Novel. By Lady WOOD. Post 8vo, illust. bds., 2s.

Wood (H. F.), Detective Stories by:
The Passenger from Scotland Yard: Crown 8vo, cloth extra, 6s.; post 8vo, illustrated boards, 2s.
The Englishman of the Rue Caïn. Crown 8vo, cloth ex., 6s. [Shortly.

Words, Facts, and Phrases: A Dictionary of Curious, Quaint, and Out-of-the-Way Matters. By ELIEZER EDWARDS. New and cheaper issue, cr. 8vo, cl. ex., 7s. 6d.; half-bound, 9s.

Wright (Thomas), Works by:
Crown 8vo, cloth extra, 7s. 6d. each.
Caricature History of the Georges. (The House of Hanover.) With 400 Pictures, Caricatures, Squibs, Broadsides, Window Pictures, &c.
History of Caricature and of the Grotesque in Art, Literature, Sculpture, and Painting. Profusely Illustrated by F.W. FAIRHOLT, F.S.A.

Yates (Edmund), Novels by:
Post 8vo, illustrated boards, 2s. each.
Castaway. | The Forlorn Hope.
Land at Last.

NEW NOVELS.

A Strange Manuscript found in a Copper Cylinder. Illustrated by GILBERT GAUL. Cr. 8vo, 5s.
The Legacy of Cain. By WILKIE COLLINS. 3 Vols., cr. 8vo.
For Faith and Freedom. By WALTER BESANT. 3 Vols., cr. 8vo. [*Shortly.*
The Englishman of the Rue Caïn. By H. F. WOOD. Crown 8vo, cloth extra, 6s. [*Shortly.*
Romantic Stories of the Legal Profession. By R. E. FRANCILLON. Cr. 8vo, cloth extra, 6s. [*Shortly.*

Doctor Rameau. By GEORGES OHNET. Crown 8vo, cloth extra, 6s. [*Shortly.*
This Mortal Coil. By GRANT ALLEN. 3 vols., crown 8vo.
The Blackhall Ghosts. By SARAH TYTLER. 3 Vols., cr. 8vo.
Agatha Page. By ISAAC HENDERSON. 2 Vols., crown 8vo.
A Freak of Fate. By ALICE O'HANLON. 3 vols., crown 8vo. [*Shortly.*
Sanpriel. By WILLIAM SHARP. Crown 8vo, cloth extra, 6s. [*Shortly.*

THE PICCADILLY NOVELS.

Popular Stories by the Best Authors. LIBRARY EDITIONS, many Illustrated, crown 8vo, cloth extra, 3s. 6d. each.

BY GRANT ALLEN.
Philistia.
For Maimie's Sake.
The Devil's Die.

BY THE AUTHOR OF "JOHN HERRING."
Red Spider. | Evo.

BY W. BESANT & JAMES RICE.
Ready-Money Mortiboy.
My Little Girl.
The Case of Mr. Lucraft.
This Son of Vulcan.
With Harp and Crown.
The Golden Butterfly.
By Celia's Arbour.
The Monks of Thelema.
'Twas in Trafalgar's Bay.
The Seamy Side.
The Ten Years' Tenant.
The Chaplain of the Fleet.

BY WALTER BESANT.
All Sorts and Conditions of Men.
The Captains' Room.
All in a Garden Fair.
Dorothy Forster. | Uncle Jack.
Children of Gibeon.
The World Went Very Well Then.

BY ROBERT BUCHANAN.
Child of Nature.
God and the Man.
The Shadow of the Sword.
The Martyrdom of Madeline.
Love Me for Ever.
Annan Water. | The New Abelard.
Matt. | Foxglove Manor.
The Master of the Mine.
The Heir of Linne.

BY HALL CAINE.
The Shadow of a Crime.
A Son of Hagar. | The Deemster.

BY MRS. H. LOVETT CAMERON.
Deceivers Ever. | Juliet's Guardian.

BY MORTIMER COLLINS.
Sweet Anne Page. | Transmigration.
From Midnight to Midnight.

MORTIMER & FRANCES COLLINS.
Blacksmith and Scholar.
The Village Comedy.
You Play me False.

BY WILKIE COLLINS.
Antonina. | The Frozen Deep.
Basil. | The Law and the
Hide and Seek. | Lady.
The Dead Secret. | The Two Destinies
Queen of Hearts. | Haunted Hotel.
My Miscellanies. | The Fallen Leaves
Woman in White. | Jezebel's Daughter
The Moonstone. | The Black Robe.
Man and Wife. | Heart and Science
Poor Miss Finch. | "I Say No."
Miss or Mrs.? | Little Novels.
New Magdalen. | The Evil Genius.

BY DUTTON COOK.
Paul Foster's Daughter.

BY WILLIAM CYPLES.
Hearts of Gold.

BY ALPHONSE DAUDET.
The Evangelist; or, Port Salvation.

BY JAMES DE MILLE.
A Castle in Spain.

BY J. LEITH DERWENT.
Our Lady of Tears.
Circe's Lovers.

BY M. BETHAM-EDWARDS.
Felicia.

BY MRS. ANNIE EDWARDES.
Archie Lovell.

BY PERCY FITZGERALD
Fatal Zero.

BY R. E. FRANCILLON.
Queen Cophetua.
One by One.
A Real Queen.
King or Knave?
Prefaced by Sir BARTLE FRERE
Pandurang Hari.

BY EDWARD GARRETT.
The Capel Girls.

PICCADILLY NOVELS, continued—
BY CHARLES GIBBON.
Robin Gray.
What will the World Say?
In Honour Bound.
Queen of the Meadow.
The Flower of the Forest.
A Heart's Problem.
The Braes of Yarrow.
The Golden Shaft.
Of High Degree.
Loving a Dream.

BY THOMAS HARDY.
Under the Greenwood Tree.

BY JULIAN HAWTHORNE.
Garth.
Ellice Quentin.
Sebastian Strome.
Dust.
Fortune's Fool.
Beatrix Randolph.
David Poindexter's Disappearance.
The Spectre of the Camera.

BY SIR A. HELPS.
Ivan de Biron.

BY MRS. ALFRED HUNT
Thornicroft's Model.
The Leaden Casket.
Self-Condemned.
That other Person.

BY JEAN INGELOW.
Fated to be Free.

BY R. ASHE KING.
A Drawn Game.
"The Wearing of the Green."

BY HENRY KINGSLEY.
Number Seventeen.

BY E. LYNN LINTON.
Patricia Kemball.
Atonement of Leam Dundas.
The World Well Lost.
Under which Lord?
"My Love!"
Ione.
Paston Carew.

BY HENRY W. LUCY.
Gideon Fleyce.

BY JUSTIN McCARTHY.
The Waterdale Neighbours.
A Fair Saxon.
Dear Lady Disdain.
Miss Misanthrope.
Donna Quixote.
The Comet of a Season.
Maid of Athens.
Camiola.

BY MRS. MACDONELL.
Quaker Cousins.

BY FLORENCE MARRYAT.
Open! Sesame! | Written in Fire.

PICCADILLY NOVELS, continued—
BY D. CHRISTIE MURRAY.
Life's Atonement. | Coals of Fire.
Joseph's Coat. | Val Strange.
A Model Father. | Hearts.
By the Gate of the Sea.
The Way of the World.
A Bit of Human Nature.
First Person Singular.
Cynic Fortune.

BY MRS. OLIPHANT.
Whiteladies.

BY OUIDA.
Held in Bondage. | Two Little Wooden
Strathmore. | Shoes.
Chandos. | In a Winter City
Under Two Flags. | Ariadne.
Idalia. | Friendship
Cecil Castle- | Moths.
maine's Gage. | Pipistrello.
Tricotrin. | A Village Com-
Puck. | mune.
Folle Farine. | Bimbi.
A Dog of Flanders | Wanda.
Pascarel. | Frescoes.
Signa. [ine.| In Maremma.
Princess Naprax-| Othmar.

BY MARGARET A. PAUL.
Gentle and Simple.

BY JAMES PAYN.
Lost Sir Massing- | A Grape from a
berd. | Thorn.
Walter's Word. | Some Private
Less Black than | Views. [Ward.
We're Painted. | The Canon's
By Proxy. | Talk of the Town.
High Spirits. | Glow-worm Tales.
Under One Roof. | In Peril and Pri-
A Confidential | vation.
Agent. | Holiday Tasks.
From Exile.

BY E. C. PRICE.
Valentina. | The Foreigners.
Mrs. Lancaster's Rival.

BY CHARLES READE.
It is Never Too Late to Mend.
Hard Cash. | Peg Woffington.
Christie Johnstone.
Griffith Gaunt. | Foul Play.
The Double Marriage.
Love Me Little, Love Me Long.
The Cloister and the Hearth.
The Course of True Love.
The Autobiography of a Thief.
Put Yourself in His Place.
A Terrible Temptation.
The Wandering Heir. | A Simpleton.
A Woman-Hater. | Readiana.
Singleheart and Doubleface.
The Jilt.
Good Stories of Men and other Animals.

BY MRS. J. H. RIDDELL.
Her Mother's Darling.
Prince of Wales's Garden-Party.
Weird Stories.

PICCADILLY NOVELS, *continued*—
BY F. W. ROBINSON.
Women are Strange.
The Hands of Justice.
BY JOHN SAUNDERS.
Bound to the Wheel.
Guy Waterman. | Two Dreamers.
The Lion in the Path.
BY KATHARINE SAUNDERS.
Margaret and Elizabeth.
Gideon's Rock. | Heart Salvage.
The High Mills. | Sebastian.
BY T. W. SPEIGHT.
The Mysteries of Heron Dyke.
BY R. A. STERNDALE.
The Afghan Knife.
BY BERTHA THOMAS.
Proud Maisie. | Cressida.
The Violin-Player
BY ANTHONY TROLLOPE.
The Way we Live Now.
Frau Frohmann. | Marion Fay.

PICCADILLY NOVELS, *continued*—
ANTHONY TROLLOPE, *continued*,
Kept in the Dark.
Mr. Scarborough's Family.
The Land-Leaguers.
BY FRANCES E. TROLLOPE.
Like Ships upon the Sea.
Anne Furness.
Mabel's Progress.
BY IVAN TURGENIEFF, &c.
Stories from Foreign Novelists.
BY SARAH TYTLER
What She Came Through.
The Bride's Pass.
Saint Mungo's City
Beauty and the Beast.
Noblesse Oblige
Citoyenne Jacqueline.
The Huguenot Family.
Lady Bell. | Buried Diamonds.
BY C. C. FRASER-TYTLER.
Mistress Judith.

CHEAP EDITIONS OF POPULAR NOVELS.
Post 8vo, illustrated boards, 2s. each.

BY EDMOND ABOUT.
The Fellah.
BY HAMILTON AÏDÉ.
Carr of Carrlyon. | Confidences.
BY MRS. ALEXANDER.
Maid, Wife, or Widow?
Valerie's Fate.
BY GRANT ALLEN.
Strange Stories.
Philistia.
Babylon.
In all Shades.
The Beckoning Hand.
BY SHELSLEY BEAUCHAMP.
Grantley Grange.
BY W. BESANT & JAMES RICE.
Ready-Money Mortiboy.
With Harp and Crown.
This Son of Vulcan. | My Little Girl.
The Case of Mr. Lucraft.
The Golden Butterfly.
By Celia's Arbour.
The Monks of Thelema.
'Twas in Trafalgar's Bay.
The Seamy Side.
The Ten Years' Tenant.
The Chaplain of the Fleet.
BY WALTER BESANT.
All Sorts and Conditions of Men.
The Captains' Room.
All in a Garden Fair.
Dorothy Forster.
Uncle Jack.
Children of Gibeon.

BY FREDERICK BOYLE.
Camp Notes. | Savage Life.
Chronicles of No-man's Land.
BY BRET HARTE.
An Heiress of Red Dog.
The Luck of Roaring Camp.
Californian Stories.
Gabriel Conroy. | Flip.
Maruja. | A Phyllis of the Sierras.
BY ROBERT BUCHANAN.
The Shadow of | The Martyrdom
the Sword. | of Madeline.
A Child of Nature. | Annan Water.
God and the Man. | The New Abelard.
Love Me for Ever. | Matt.
Foxglove Manor. |
The Master of the Mine.
BY MRS. BURNETT.
Surly Tim.
BY HALL CAINE.
The Shadow of a Crime.
A Son of Hagar.
BY COMMANDER CAMERON.
The Cruise of the "Black Prince."
BY MRS. LOVETT CAMERON
Deceivers Ever. | Juliet's Guardian.
BY MACLAREN COBBAN.
The Cure of Souls.
BY C. ALLSTON COLLINS.
The Bar Sinister.
BY WILKIE COLLINS.
Antonina. | Queen of Hearts.
Basil. | My Miscellanies.
Hide and Seek. | Woman in White.
The Dead Secret. | The Moonstone.

BOOKS PUBLISHED BY

CHEAP POPULAR NOVELS, continued—
WILKIE COLLINS, continued.
Man and Wife. | Haunted Hotel.
Poor Miss Finch. | The Fallen Leaves.
Miss or Mrs.? | Jezebel's Daughter
New Magdalen. | The Black Robe.
The Frozen Deep. | Heart and Science
Law and the Lady. | "I Say No."
The Two Destinies | The Evil Genius.
BY MORTIMER COLLINS.
Sweet Anne Page. | From Midnight to
Transmigration. | Midnight.
A Fight with Fortune.
MORTIMER & FRANCES COLLINS.
Sweet and Twenty. | Frances.
Blacksmith and Scholar.
The Village Comedy.
You Play me False.
BY M. J. COLQUHOUN.
Every Inch a Soldier.
BY MONCURE D. CONWAY.
Pine and Palm.
BY DUTTON COOK.
Leo. | Paul Foster's Daughter.
BY C. EGBERT CRADDOCK.
The Prophet of the Great Smoky
Mountains.
BY WILLIAM CYPLES.
Hearts of Gold.
BY ALPHONSE DAUDET.
The Evangelist; or, Port Salvation.
BY JAMES DE MILLE.
Castle in Spain.
BY J. LEITH DERWENT.
Our Lady of Tears. | Circe's Lovers.
BY CHARLES DICKENS.
Sketches by Boz. | Oliver Twist.
Pickwick Papers. | Nicholas Nickleby
BY DICK DONOVAN.
The Man-Hunter.
Caught at Last!
BY MRS. ANNIE EDWARDES.
A Point of Honour. | Archie Lovell.
BY M. BETHAM-EDWARDS.
Felicia. | Kitty.
BY EDWARD EGGLESTON.
Roxy.
BY PERCY FITZGERALD.
Bella Donna. | Never Forgotten.
The Second Mrs. Tillotson.
Polly. | Fatal Zero.
Seventy-five Brooke Street.
The Lady of Brantome.
BY ALBANY DE FONBLANQUE.
Filthy Lucre.
BY R. E. FRANCILLON.
Olympia. | Queen Cophetua.
One by One. | A Real Queen.
BY HAROLD FREDERIC.
Seth's Brother's Wife.
Prefaced by Sir H. BARTLE FRERE.
Pandurang Hari.
BY HAIN FRISWELL.
One of Two.
BY EDWARD GARRETT.
The Capel Girls.

CHEAP POPULAR NOVELS, continued—
BY CHARLES GIBBON.
Robin Gray. | The Flower of the
For Lack of Gold, | Forest.
What will the | Braes of Yarrow.
World Say? | The Golden Shaft.
In Honour Bound. | Of High Degree.
In Love and War. | Fancy Free.
For the King. | Mead and Stream
In Pastures Green | Loving a Dream.
Queen of the Mea- | A Hard Knot.
dow. | Heart's Delight.
A Heart's Problem |
BY WILLIAM GILBERT.
Dr. Austin's Guests. | James Duke.
The Wizard of the Mountain.
BY JAMES GREENWOOD.
Dick Temple.
BY JOHN HABBERTON.
Brueton's Bayou. | Country Luck.
BY ANDREW HALLIDAY
Every-Day Papers.
BY LADY DUFFUS HARDY.
Paul Wynter's Sacrifice.
BY THOMAS HARDY.
Under the Greenwood Tree.
BY J. BERWICK HARWOOD.
The Tenth Earl.
BY JULIAN HAWTHORNE.
Garth. | Sebastian Strome
Ellice Quentin. | Dust.
Prince Saroni's Wife.
Fortune's Fool. | Beatrix Randolph.
Miss Cadogna. | Love—or a Name.
BY SIR ARTHUR HELPS.
Ivan de Biron.
BY MRS. CASHEL HOEY.
The Lover's Creed.
BY TOM HOOD.
A Golden Heart.
BY MRS. GEORGE HOOPER.
The House of Raby.
BY TIGHE HOPKINS.
'Twixt Love and Duty.
BY MRS. ALFRED HUNT.
Thornicroft's Model.
The Leaden Casket.
Self-Condemned.
That other Person.
BY JEAN INGELOW.
Fated to be Free.
BY HARRIETT JAY.
The Dark Colleen.
The Queen of Connaught.
BY MARK KERSHAW
Colonial Facts and Fictions.
BY R. ASHE KING
A Drawn Game.
"The Wearing of the Green."
BY HENRY KINGSLEY
Oakshott Castle.
BY JOHN LEYS.
The Lindsays.
BY MARY LINSKILL.
In Exchange for a Soul.
BY E. LYNN LINTON.
Patricia Kemball.
The Atonement of Leam Dundas.

CHATTO & WINDUS, PICCADILLY. 31

CHEAP POPULAR NOVELS, *continued*—
E. LYNN LINTON, *continued*—
The World Well Lost.
Under which Lord?
With a Silken Thread.
The Rebel of the Family.
"My Love." | Ione.
  BY HENRY W. LUCY.
Gideon Fleyce.
  BY JUSTIN McCARTHY.
Dear Lady Disdain | Miss Misanthrope
The Waterdale | Donna Quixote.
Neighbours. | The Comet of a
My Enemy's | Season.
Daughter. | Maid of Athens.
A Fair Saxon. | Camiola.
Linley Rochford.
  BY MRS. MACDONELL.
Quaker Cousins.
  BY KATHARINE S. MACQUOID.
The Evil Eye. | Lost Rose.
  BY W. H. MALLOCK.
The New Republic.
  BY FLORENCE MARRYAT.
Open! Sesame. | Fighting the Air.
A Harvest of Wild | Written in Fire.
Oats.
  BY J. MASTERMAN.
Half-a-dozen Daughters.
  BY BRANDER MATTHEWS.
A Secret of the Sea.
  BY JEAN MIDDLEMASS.
Touch and Go. | Mr. Dorillion.
  BY MRS. MOLESWORTH.
Hathercourt Rectory.
  BY D. CHRISTIE MURRAY.
A Life's Atonement | Hearts.
A Model Father. | Way of the World.
Joseph's Coat. | A Bit of Human
Coals of Fire. | Nature.
By the Gate of the | First Person Sin-
Sea. | gular.
Val Strange. | Cynic Fortune.
Old Blazer's Hero.
  BY ALICE O'HANLON.
The Unforeseen.
  BY MRS. OLIPHANT.
Whiteladies. | The Primrose Path.
The Greatest Heiress in England.
  BY MRS. ROBERT O'REILLY.
Phœbe's Fortunes.
  BY OUIDA.
Held in Bondage. | Two Little Wooden
Strathmore. | Shoes.
Chandos. | Ariadne.
Under Two Flags. | Friendship.
Idalia. | Moths.
Cecil Castle- | Pipistrello.
  maine's Gage. | A Village Com-
Tricotrin | Puck. | mune.
Folle Farine. | Bimbi. | Wanda.
A Dog of Flanders. | Frescoes.
Pascarel. | In Maremma.
Signa. [ine. | Othmar.
Princess Naprax- | Wisdom, Wit, and
in a Winter City | Pathos.

CHEAP POPULAR NOVELS, *continued*—
  BY MARGARET AGNES PAUL.
Gentle and Simple.
  BY JAMES PAYN.
Lost Sir Massing- | Like Father, Like
  berd. | Son.
A Perfect Trea- | Marine Residence.
  sure. | Married Beneath
Bentinck's Tutor. | Him.
Murphy's Master. | Mirk Abbey. [Won
A County Family. | Not Wooed, but
At Her Mercy. | Less Black than
A Woman's Ven- | We're Painted.
  geance. | By Proxy.
Cecil's Tryst. | Under One Roof.
Clyffards of Clyffe | High Spirits.
The Family Scape- | Carlyon's Year.
  grace. | A Confidential
Foster Brothers. | Agent.
Found Dead. | Some Private
Best of Husbands. | Views.
Walter's Word. | From Exile.
Halves. | A Grape from a
Fallen Fortunes. | Thorn.
What He Cost Her | For Cash Only.
Humorous Stories | Kit: A Memory.
Gwendoline's Har- | The Canon's Ward
  vest. | Talk of the Town.
£200 Reward. | Holiday Tasks.
  BY C. L. PIRKIS.
Lady Lovelace.
  BY EDGAR A. POE.
The Mystery of Marie Roget.
  BY E. C. PRICE.
Valentina. | The Foreigners
Mrs. Lancaster's Rival.
Gerald.
  BY CHARLES READE.
It is Never Too Late to Mend.
Hard Cash. | Peg Woffington.
Christie Johnstone.
Griffith Gaunt.
Put Yourself in His Place.
The Double Marriage.
Love Me Little, Love Me Long.
Foul Play.
The Cloister and the Hearth.
The Course of True Love.
Autobiography of a Thief.
A Terrible Temptation.
The Wandering Heir.
A Simpleton. | A Woman-Hater.
Readiana. | The Jilt.
Singleheart and Doubleface.
Good Stories of Men and other
  Animals.
  BY MRS. J. H. RIDDELL.
Her Mother's Darling.
Prince of Wales's Garden Party.
Weird Stories. | Fairy Water.
The Uninhabited House.
The Mystery in Palace Gardens.
  BY F. W. ROBINSON.
Women are Strange.
The Hands of Justice.

CHEAP POPULAR NOVELS, *continued*—
BY JAMES RUNCIMAN.
Skippers and Shellbacks.
Grace Balmaign's Sweetheart.
Schools and Scholars.
BY W. CLARK RUSSELL.
Round the Galley Fire.
On the Fo'k'sle Head.
In the Middle Watch.
A Voyage to the Cape.
BY BAYLE ST. JOHN.
A Levantine Family.
BY GEORGE AUGUSTUS SALA.
Gaslight and Daylight.
BY JOHN SAUNDERS.
Bound to the Wheel.
One Against the World.
Guy Waterman. | Two Dreamers.
The Lion in the Path.
BY KATHARINE SAUNDERS.
Joan Merryweather.
Margaret and Elizabeth.
The High Mills.
Heart Salvage. | Sebastian.
BY GEORGE R. SIMS.
Rogues and Vagabonds.
The Ring o' Bells.
Mary Jane's Memoirs.
Mary Jane Married.
BY ARTHUR SKETCHLEY.
A Match in the Dark.
BY T. W. SPEIGHT.
The Mysteries of Heron Dyke.
The Golden Hoop.
BY R. A. STERNDALE.
The Afghan Knife.
BY R. LOUIS STEVENSON.
New Arabian Nights. | Prince Otto.
BY BERTHA THOMAS.
Cressida. | Proud Maisie.
The Violin-Player.
BY W. MOY THOMAS.
A Fight for Life.
BY WALTER THORNBURY.
Tales for the Marines.
Old Stories Re-told.
BY T. ADOLPHUS TROLLOPE.
Diamond Cut Diamond.
BY ANTHONY TROLLOPE.
The Way We Live Now.
The American Senator.
Frau Frohmann. | Marion Fay.
Kept in the Dark.
Mr. Scarborough's Family.
The Land-Leaguers.
The Golden Lion of Granpere.
John Caldigate.
By F. ELEANOR TROLLOPE.
Like Ships upon the Sea.
Anne Furness. | Mabel's Progress.
BY J. T. TROWBRIDGE.
Farnell's Folly.
BY IVAN TURGENIEFF, &c.
Stories from Foreign Novelists.
BY MARK TWAIN.
Tom Sawyer. | A Tramp Abroad.

CHEAP POPULAR NOVELS, *continued*—
MARK TWAIN, *continued*.
A Pleasure Trip on the Continent of Europe.
The Stolen White Elephant.
Huckleberry Finn
Life on the Mississippi.
The Prince and the Pauper.
BY C. C. FRASER-TYTLER.
Mistress Judith.
BY SARAH TYTLER.
What She Came Through.
The Bride's Pass.
Saint Mungo's City.
Beauty and the Beast.
Lady Bell. | Noblesse Oblige.
Citoyenne Jacqueline | Disappeared
BY J. S. WINTER.
Cavalry Life. | Regimental Legends.
BY H. F. WOOD.
The Passenger from Scotland Yard
BY LADY WOOD.
Sabina.
BY EDMUND YATES.
Castaway. | The Forlorn Hope.
Land at Last.
ANONYMOUS.
Paul Ferroll.
Why Paul Ferroll Killed his Wife.
POPULAR SHILLING BOOKS.
Jeff Briggs's Love Story. By BRET HARTE. [BRET HARTE.
The Twins of Table Mountain. By
A Day's Tour. By PERCY FITZGERALD.
Mrs. Gainsborough's Diamonds. By JULIAN HAWTHORNE.
A Dream and a Forgetting. By ditto.
A Romance of the Queen's Hounds. By CHARLES JAMES.
Kathleen Mavourneen. By Author of "That Lass o' Lowrie's."
Lindsay's Luck. By the Author of "That Lass o' Lowrie's."
Pretty Polly Pemberton. By the Author of "That Lass o' Lowrie's."
Trooping with Crows. By C. L. PIRKIS
The Professor's Wife. By L. GRAHAM.
A Double Bond. By LINDA VILLARI.
Esther's Glove. By R. E. FRANCILLON.
The Garden that Paid the Rent By TOM JERROLD.
Curly. By JOHN COLEMAN, Illustrated by J. C. DOLLMAN.
Beyond the Gates. By E. S. PHELPS.
Old Maid's Paradise. By E. S. PHELPS.
Burglars in Paradise. By E.S.PHELPS.
Jack the Fisherman. By E.S. PHELPS.
Doom: An Atlantic Episode. By JUSTIN H. MCCARTHY, M.P.
Our Sensation Novel. Edited by JUSTIN H MCCARTHY, M.P.
Bible Characters. By CHAS. READE.
The Dagonet Reciter. By G. R. SIMS.
Wife or No Wife? By T. W. SPEIGHT.
By Devious Ways. By T.W.SPEIGHT.
The Silverado Squatters. By R. LOUIS STEVENSON.

J. OGDEN AND CO, LIMITED, PRINTERS, GREAT SAFFRON HILL E.C.

www.ingramcontent.com/pod-product-compliance
Lightning Source LLC
Chambersburg PA
CBHW032042220426
43664CB00008B/825